International Humanitarian Law

The Laws of War

International Humanitarian Law

The Laws of War

Wing Commander (Retd)

Dr U C Jha

Vij Books India Pvt Ltd
New Delhi (India)

Published by

Vij Books India Pvt Ltd
(Publishers, Distributors & Importers)
2/19 (Second Floor), Ansari Road, Darya Ganj
New Delhi - 110002
Phones: 91-11-43596460, 91-11- 65449971
Fax: 91-11-47340674
e-mail : vijbooks@rediffmail.com

ISBN: 978-93-80177-75-5

In the memory of Satish

Contents

Foreword

It is a pleasure to write a foreword foWing Commander (Retired) Dr U C Jha's latest work entitled "International Humanitarian Law".

International Humanitarian Law (IHL, or the law of armed conflict) grew out of the battlefield, and its first explicit codification in a multilateral instrument followed from the devastating consequences of a battle in 1859 in northern Italy. Since then, a key component of those engaged in IHL training, and the legal debates relating to IHL, has included those with military experience. In this respect, Wing Commander (Retired) Dr UC Jha is very well placed to write such a book.

Dr UC Jha has lectured at numerous events held by the International Committee of the Red Cross (New Delhi Regional Delegation) in South Asia, including at its SouthAsia Teaching Sessions. For these presentations, he has specialized in the law relating to the methods and means of armed conflict. However, in the 18 chapters of this book, he provides a wide overview of the main areas of international humanitarian law (IHL), in textbook form.

This effort will no doubt be useful to those persons wishing to familiarize themselves with the most important core aspects of IHL, set out in Chapters 1 to 11. These include the protection of civilians, prisoners of war, and soldiers on the battlefield, as well as the methods and means of armed conflict. Chapters 12 to 18 describe the law related to the implementation of IHL, peacekeeping, and private military companies, as well as the role of the ICRC.

However, as with many areas of public international law, IHL is not static, and there have been numerous new developments in the past few years. These include new treaties (e.g., the 2008 Convention on Cluster Munitions), the development of customary law (the ICRC' s 2005 Study on Customary International Humanitarian Law and the appearance in 2010, online and for free, of its latest updates), as well as the interpretation of existing IHL (varied jurisprudence as well as the ICRC's 2009 Interpretive Guidance on the Notion of Direct Participation in Hostilities). It is anticipated that there will be further developments in the coming years. The President of the ICRC outlined, in August 2010, interest in work being undertaken towards greater protection for victims in non-international armed conflict. This is but one such likely development, while work on an arms trade treaty, and interpretation of the law regulating computer network attacks are others.

This book is also important as it is one of the first textbooks written on IHL from a South Asian perspective. As a result, it may very well prove useful in academic settings in the region.

In closing, I wish to commend Wing Commander (Retired) Dr UC Jha's efforts in writing this latest book on IHL.

Christopher Harland
ICRC Regional Legal Adviser for South Asia
New Delhi, India
March 2011

Preface

I have been associated with the training programmes in international humanitarian law at the Indian Society of International Law , New Delhi for almost a decade. As a student, I always felt the need for a textbook wherein the essentials of the 'laws of conflict' or 'humanitarian law' could be found. This prompted me to bring out this textbook on international humanitarian law (IHL).Though evidence of practices intended to alleviate the sufferings of war can be found in the writings of the ancient Indian and other civilizations, the modern codification of the customs and usages of war began with the Lieber Code (1863) during theAmerican Civil War. A year later, the concerted efforts of Henry Dunanat resulted in the adoption of the First Geneva Convention (1864), containing ten articles, as the first international treaty on humanitarian law . The laws of war or IHL have since grown manifold and can be found in customary as well as treaty laws. The purpose of IHL is to protect combatants and non-combatants from unnecessary sufferings and to safeguard the fundamental human rights of persons who are not or no longer taking part in the conflict.

Today, the non-international (internal) conflict in Libya is drawing international attention. Gross violations of the rules of IHL are taking place, with the pro-government forces using warplanes and artillery to attack protesting citizens. The strife is causing a humanitarian crisis; tens of thousands are fleeing the country and seeking asylum in the neighbouring states. The conflict has reminded the world of the solemn declaration made in 2005, that where the governments manifestly failed in their sovereign duty, the international community acting through the United Nations, would take "timely and decisive" action to honour the collective responsibility to protect (R2P) people against atrocity crimes. Libya today presents an occasion to redeem that pledge. There are reports that the President of Libya and others responsible for the suspected gross violations of humanitarian law would face a war crime trial at the International Criminal

Court, the Hague. In this book, I have tried to discuss all the issues relating to IHL in today's context.

The book contains 18 chapters. In **Chapter 1**, the historical evolution and the foundation of IHL have been discussed. **Chapter 2** describes the relationship between IHL and human rights law and the refugee law . In **Chapter 3,** the rules of IHL as applicable to air and maritime operations during an armed conflict are covered. International humanitarian law as applicable to non-international armed conflicts has been covered in **Chapter 4** of the book. **Chapter 5** offers an in-depth discussion on the means and methods prohibited in armed conflict, and the obligations relating to the development and use of new weapons.

In **Chapter 6**, protections enjoyed by prisoners of war have been covered, as is minimum protection of all prisoners. **Chapter 7** deals with the protection of civilians in occupied territory the precautions that should be taken in attack, and the concept of 'responsibility to protect'. In **Chapter 8**, challenges in the sphere of protection of women as combatants and in occupied territory have been discussed. **Chapter 9** offers an in-depth study of the problems associated with the protection of children in armed conflict. The current aspects of the protection of the environment in armed conflicts have been covered in **Chapter 10**. There are significant challenges to the protection of cultural property in international and non-international armed conflicts. In **Chapter 11**, the protection of cultural property and recent developments in the field has been covered.

In order to secure the guarantees provided by IHL treaties, it is essential that the states implement their provisions to the fullest possible extent. In **Chapter 12**, the implementation of IHL, the need for a national committee and the role of military commanders have been discussed. The use of UN peacekeepers is a relatively recent development. Initially there was some doubt about the applicability of IHL to UN forces. In **Chapter 13**, the law relating to the application of IHL to peacekeepers has been explained. The International Criminal Court (ICC) has a mandate to try individuals for the most serious crimes of concern to the international community . **Chapter 14** covers the role and functioning of the ICC. The responsibility of a military commander for the conduct of his subordinates in an armed conflict has been explained in **Chapter 15**. It is believed that the private military and security companies (PMSCs) constitute a new form of mercenarism. In **Chapter 16**, the issue of mercenaries, PMSCs and their accountability has been critically analysed.

The role, mission and activities of the International Committee of the Red Cross have been covered in **Chapter 17** of the book. This chapter also covers the three distinctive emblems and provisions relating to prevention and repression of their misuse. New developments in IHL are discussed in **Chapter 18**, the last chapter , which covers issues like cyber warfare, targeted killing, chemical incapacitation and a few weapon systems that fail to meet the principles of IHL.

The Regional Delegation of the International Committee of the Red Cross in New Delhi has supported me with advice and access to material from their library. In particular, I am thankful to Mr Christopher Harland, Regional Legal Adviser; Dr Burra Srinivas, Legal Adviser; and Ms K C Sowmya, Legal Officer, for their advice and help in bringing out this book. I also thank Prof Manoj Kumar Sinha (former Director, Indian Society of International Law) for his comments on a few chapters of the book.

I am obliged to Harvard University's Program on Humanitarian Policy and Conflict Research (HPCR) for allowing me to quote portions from their 2010 Manual on International Law Applicable to Air and Missile Warfare.

I express gratitude to my wife, Ratna, for all her support and to Ms Medha and Ms Chandana for editorial assistance. My son, Aditya, has contributed with his helpful comments on certain technical aspects in the book, for which I am grateful to him. Finally, I thank Vij Books India Pvt Ltd, New Delhi for their professional cooperation in bringing out this edition.

- Author

CHAPTER 1

International Humanitarian Law: Introduction

Introduction

War is as old as human civilization and the laws of war are probably as old as war itself. There was always a general understanding of the necessity of having some kind of regulations during wars.There was also a feeling that under certain circumstances, human beings, whether friends or foesdeserve some protection. In the wars fought around the world in ancient times, there was evidence of interesting customs and agreements with "humanitarian" elements. There were rules protecting certain categories of victims of armed conflicts, as well as regulations prohibiting the use of certain means and methods of warfare. These ancient customs might not have been adopted for a humanitarian purposebut with a purely tactical or economic objective; their effect was, however, humanitarian. For instance, the "prohibition to poison water bodies" was a customary practice and reaffirmed in modern treaties. Perhaps the main reason for the "prohibition to kill prisoners of war" was to guarantee the availability of future slaves, rather than to save the lives of former combatants. The existence of such customs can be found in cultures, regions and civilizations as diverse as Asia, Africa and Europe.

In Asia, the ancient scriptures are replete with detailed rules on waging a war, the area where a war will take place, methods of warfare, proportionality of the use of force, kinds of armed forces, weapons to be used, and so on. Weapons causing unnecessary suffering were prohibited and there were rules relating to the treatment of prisoners and civilians. Respect for human beings and considerations of humanity were the basis for these rules.

Sun Tzu, in *The Art of War*, the foremost classic of Chinese literature on military strategy, written around B.C. 500, spoke of some important requirements relating to humanity during combat: a commander must show intelligence, sincerity, humanity, courage and dignity; he may utilize captured enemy equipment but must respect prisoners of war; he should endeavour to win the victory without harming enemy military and civilian personnel and should avoid using needless violence; and he should not seek the total annihilation of an enemy The principle of civilian protection was also accepted in the Japanese and Chinese traditions. There are numerous references to the protection of civilians, and specifically women and children, in theAsian texts. Similarly, Islamic tradition favours respect for the principle of civilian protection.The Prophet showed his disapproval of the killing of the old and women and children.

Manu Smriti, is one of the oldest and probably the most important of the Smritis, contains the laws (conduct in life) that need to be followed in various orders of life and by persons of various tendencies (varnas[1]). Some examples of 'smritis' relating to the laws of war are follows.

> When he fights with his foes in battle, let him not strike with weapons concealed (in wood), nor with (such as are) barbed, poisoned, or the points of which are blazing with fire.
>
> Let him not strike one who (in flight) has climbed on an eminence, nor a eunuch, nor one who joins the palms of his hands (in supplication), nor one who (flees) with flying hair , nor one who sits down, nor one who says 'I am thine';

---

[1] The Code of Manu (*Manu Smriti*), which formed the basis for the laws, morals and customs of India and developed between B.C. 200 and 200 A.D., also referred to the protection of war victims. Smritis means "that which has to be remembered". Unlike the Vedas, which are considered of divine origin, the Smritis are of human compositions and guide individuals in their daily conduct according to time and place. They list the codes and rules governing the actions of the individual, the community, society and the nation. They are also called Dharma Sastras or laws of righteous conduct. Manu is considered a law giver in the Hindu tradition. *Manu Smriti* is one of the 18 Smrtis. The laws set forth by Manu, in *Manu Smriti*, although followed in some form even today, are not considered divine, and may be modified by the society to keep up with the times. Indeed, it has been speculated that in its current form, *Manu Smriti* represents laws that have been added or modified throughout history. <http://www.bharatadesam.com/spiritual/manu_smriti/manu_smriti_7.php>

> Nor one who sleeps, nor one who has lost his coat of mail, nor one who is naked, nor one who is disarmed, nor one who looks on without taking part in the fight, nor one who is fighting with another (foe);
>
> Nor one whose weapons are broken, nor one aflicted (with sorrow), nor one who has been grievously wounded, nor one who is in fear, nor one who has turned to flight; (but in all these cases let him) remember the duty (of honourable warriors).

In Europe, in 1590, the Free Netherlands adoptedArticles of War and in 1621, Sweden's Adolphus published his *Articles of Military Lawwes to Be Observed in the Warres*, which were to become the basis for England's later Articles of War. Those English Articles, in turn, became the basis for the United States' first Articles of War.[2]

Religious figures, powerful Kings, wise men and warlords from all continents have attempted to limit the consequences of war by making binding rules. In spite of their humanitarian importance, the ancient rules and customs suffered from serious drawbacks. First, their applicability was limited to specific regions; secondly they were very often limited to a specific war; and thirdly, their implementation was the sole responsibility of the belligerents. In the last 150 years or so, international rules have been made to limit the ef fects of war for humanitarian reasons. Usually called international humanitarian law (IHL), it is also known as the 'law of war' or the 'law of armed conflict'.

International Humanitarian Law

IHL is a branch of international law which limits the use of violence in armed conflicts. IHL achieves this by: (i) sparing those who do not or no longer directly participate in hostilities (for example civilians; injured, sick or wounded soldiers; or those who have surrendered or been taken prisoners of war; and (ii) limiting the violence only to weaken the military potential of the adversary—the amount necessary to achieve the aim of the conflict. IHL can be defined as the whole of the international conventions or customary rules which are specifically intended to regulate humanitarian

---

2 Solis Gary D . 2010. *The Law of Armed Conflict:International Humanitarian Law in W ar*, Cambridge University Press, p.7.

problems arising directly from both international or non-international armed conflicts, and which restrict the right of parties to the conflict to use means and methods of warfare of their choice and to protect people and objects affected by the conflict.[3] IHL aims to limit the ef fects of armed conflicts for humanitarian reasons. It protects persons who are no longer taking part in hostilities, and also defines the rights and obligations of the parties to a conflict in the conduct of hostilities.

An international armed conflict means fighting between the armed forces of at least two S tates. IHL is applicable in international armed conflicts. A non-international armed conflict (or internal armed conflict) means fighting on the territory of a State between the regular armed forces and identifiable armed groups, or between armed groups.To be considered a non-international (or internal) armed conflict, fighting must reach a certain level of intensity and extend over a certain period of time. The provisions of common Article[4] 3 of the Geneva Conventions and Additional Protocol II apply in situations of non-international armed conflict. Internal disturbances in a country, riots, struggles between factions or against the authorities are not considered non-international armed conflict. These situations are covered by the municipal law of the country.

IHL and International Law

IHL is part of the body of international law that regulates relations between states. It is dif ficult to answer as to when international law originated. However, if we consider international law as a set of substantive principles applying uniquely to 'states', then the seventeenth century could be

---

[3] IHL has been defined as: international rules, established by treaties and customs, which are specifically intended to solve humanitarian problems directly arising from international or non-international armed conflicts and which, for humanitarian reasons, limit the rights of the parties to a conflict to use the methods and means of warfare of their choice or protect persons and property that are, or may be, affected by conflict. Y Sandoz, *Commentary on the Additional Protocols of 8 June 1977 to the Geneva Conv entions of 12 August 1949* , Geneva: ICRC.

[4] Common Article is a critical term used in IHL. It refers to a certain number of articles that are identical in all four of the 1949 Geneva Conventions. Normally these relate to the scope of application and parties' obligations under the treaties. Some of the Common Articles are identically numbered (for example Article 3 in the four Geneva Conventions of 1949), while others are worded virtually the same way but numbered differently. For example, the article dealing with special agreements is Article 6 of the first three Conv entions, but Article 7 of the fourth Convention.

considered as the starting time. International law establishes four criteria that must be established for an entity to be regarded as a State: (i) a defined territory; (ii) a permanent population; (iii) a government; and (iv) the capacity to conduct international relations. Under international law, a State has sovereignty over its territory and exercises authority over its nationals. It has the status of a legal person, with the capacity to make contracts, enter into international agreements and become a member of international organizations. The State also has the capacity to join with other states in making international law . For states to co-exist in an international community, they are obliged to follows certain norms: to refrain from intervening in the af fairs of other states, to settle international disputes peacefully, to refrain from threat or the use of force, and to carry out treaty obligations in good faith.The chart on Page 6 shows the relationship between international law and IHL.

The Statute of the International Court of Justice, in Article 38, lists the main sources of international law as: international conventions,[5] international customs[6] and general principles of law[7] in accordance with which the Court decided disputes. It further states that judicial decisions

---

[5] The international conventions and treaties constitute a multilateral agreement that establishes international rules and norms for the conduct of states in their mutual relationship. Examples of such law-making are the 1949 Geneva Conventions on the Laws of War, the 1966 International Covenant on Civil and Political Rights, the 1982 UN Convention on the Law of the Sea, the 1991 Convention on Chemical Weapons, and the 2010 Convention for the Protection of All Persons from Enforced Disappearance.

[6] During the last two or three centuries, when international interactions were less complex, states adopted in their mutual relationship certain standard practices that evolved into obligatory rules. Some principles of international law are considered peremptory norms and cannot be derogated, even by treaty. Examples include prohibitions against slavery, genocide, and torture. Customary international law and treaty law are equal in stature, with the later in time controlling.

[7] The general principles of law recognized by civilized nations' are the third major source of international legal rules. General principles were historically important in the development of international law. Early general principles were often the only international laws and were based upon the theory that states were applying these principles in their domestic law and therefore were bound by them internationally. A number of 'general principles' have been recognized by the states in their dealings with one another. Some of them are: (i) a sovereign is subject to the law; (ii) the sovereign state is not above the rule of law, and political leaders of states are subject of only limited authority; and (iii) the right of self-defence by a state is limited. As international law has developed the use of general principles has declined because many general principles have become codified into treaties or recognized as custom. General principles are used as gap fillers only when authority cannot be found in treaties or in customary law. Examples of general principles include good faith and judicial impartiality.

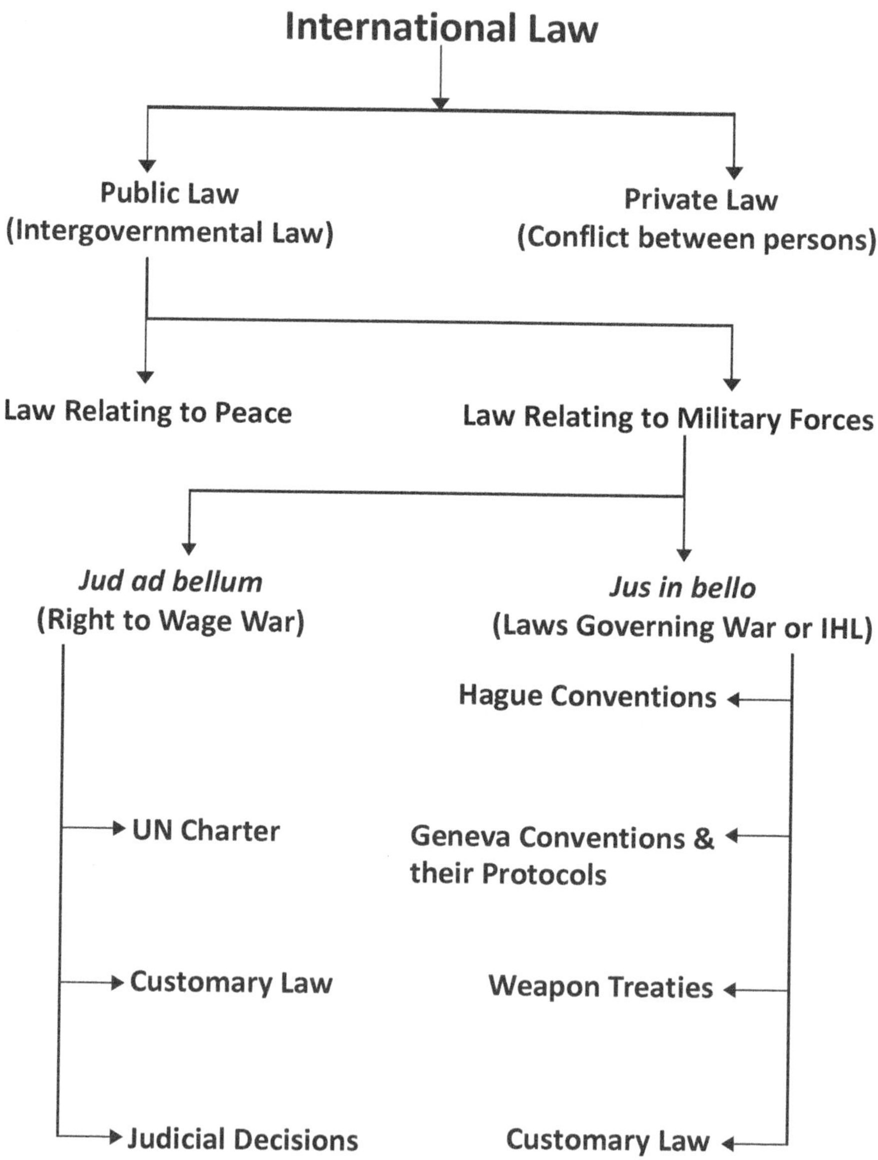

Chart 1: Relationship between International Law and IHL

and the teachings of the most highly qualified publicists of various nations are subsidiary means for the determination of the rules of law. International custom is further defined in Article 38 as "evidence of a general practice accepted as law". Though Article 38 of the Statute does not provide a hierarchy among the main sources of international law, there is a common belief that treaties are the most important sources of international law. Customary international law has historically preceded treaty law and has been a source of principles on which future treaties are based. For example, different traditions prohibit certain types of weapons, particularly poison, and this prohibition is now embodied in a number of important international treaties.

The Sources of IHL

A. Customary Law

Customary law consists of the rules which, as a result of state practice over a period of time, have become accepted as legally binding. The origin of IHL, in fact, lies in the customs and usages followed by armies to minimize the miseries of war from ancient times. Many of the rules of IHL are considered part of customary international law and, therefore, mandatory for all parties to an armed conflict. Customary IHL fills in certain gaps in the protection provided to victims of armed conflict by treaty law. These gaps result either from the lack of ratification of relevant treaties or from the lack of detailed rules on non-international armed conflicts in treaty law. The advantage of customary law is that it is not necessary for a State to formally accept a rule in order to be bound by it, as long as the overall State practice on which the rule is based is accepted as law. Although most of IHL has now been codified in treaties, important aspects of belligerent activity, especially in naval warfare, continue to be regulated by customary law.

The advantage of customary rules of IHL is that they bind all those who participate in armed conflict, whether they are parties to a specific treaty or not. Customary IHL restricts the ability of States to opt out of the rules and adds to their morally binding character as they are seen as being embedded and deeply rooted in community values. An excellent example of this process is the 'Martens Clause', which was drafted by Feodor Martens in the preamble to the Hague Convention of 1907.[8] In addition, customary law rules are not restricted in their field of application. Many of them apply to all forms of conflict, whether international or non-international. The customary law rules of IHL bind all belligerents on both sides of a conflict. They also fill the gaps that exist in the treaty rules applicable in non-international armed conflicts, including tar geting, proportionality, precautions in attack and the protection of civilians and civilian property.

Customary IHL continues to provide an important framework for the conduct of hostilities, including in recent armed conflicts in Iran, Afghanistan and Sri Lanka, and between Israel and Lebanon. In coalition warfare in Afghanistan, customary IHL represents the common rule applicable to all coalition partners. Joint operations must comply with the rules of customary IHL, although individual partners may still have wider obligations under the respective treaties they have ratifiedThe Rome Statute of the International Criminal Court is a good example of the crystallization of customary rules. Many of the components of crimes against humanity and war crimes were articulated for the first time in treaty form in the Rome Statute. The drafters of the S tatute referred to customary law in formulating these crimes.

Advantages of Customary Rules of IHL: Custom is the oldest and the original source of international law as well as of law in general. Customary rules have the advantage that they do not require any express act of ratification or further acceptance by States. The following are the advantages of customary rules.

- The customary rules of IHL bind all those who participate in armed conflict, whether they are parties to a specific treaty or not. They bind all belligerents on both sides of a conflict.
- Customary rules are not restricted in their field of application. Many of them apply to all forms of conflict, whether international or non-international.
- Customary rules fill the gaps that exist in the treaty rules applicable in non-international armed conflicts, including tar geting, proportionality and precautions in attack.

---

[8] For further details on 'Martens Clause' please refer to page 19 of the book.

- They also greatly strengthen the weaker areas of treaty law , such as the protection of civilians and civilian property in times of internal armed conflict.
- The customary rules of IHL are particularly important and relevant to regions prone to situations of armed violence and countries have a weak record of ratification of IHL treaties.

International law is continuously evolving. The existing treaties may not always accurately reflect the current status of the law. Because of the challenges associated with relying on treaties, customary law plays an important role. Customary norms develop through state practice and *opinio juris* (an opinion of the law). As this process is more flexible than that involved in treaty negotiation and ratification, it helps international law to keep pace with the dynamic and fast-paced world it regulates. Many of today's armed conflicts occur outside the framework of the Geneva Conventions and their Protocols. In such conflicts, customary IHL takes on added importance.

The ICRC Study: In December 1995, the ICRC was mandated to prepare a report on customary rules of IHL applicable in international and non-international armed conflicts. In 2005, after extensive research and widespread consultation between experts, the ICRC study on customary IHL was released. Volume 1 of the study dealing with Rules contains a comprehensive analysis of the customary rules of IHL applicable in international and non-international armed conflicts. The 161 rules have been catalogued in six parts: (i) Principle of distinction, (ii) specifically protected persons and objects, (iii) specific methods of warfare, (iv) weapons, (v) treatment of civilians and persons *hors de combat*,[9] and (vi) implementation. Of the 161 rules identified, 159 apply in international armed conflicts and 149 in non-international armed conflicts. The rules are accompanied by a commentary which explains why the rule in question was found to be customary. Volume 2 is in two parts and mentions relevant state practice, including legislation on each aspect of IHL.[10]

---

[9] *Hors de combat* is a French term, literally meaning "outside the fight". It is used in international law to refer to soldiers who are incapable of performing their military function being sick, wounded, detained, or otherwise disabled. Soldiers *hors de combat* are to be granted special protections under IHL.

[10] Henckaerts Jean-Marie, Study on customary international humanitarian law: A contribution to the understanding and respect for the rule of law in armed conflict, *International Review of the Red Cross*, Vol 87, No. 857, March 2005, p. 175-212.

There have been important judgments and opinions indicating that The Hague Regulations and Common Article 3 of the Geneva Conventions of 1949 are accepted as customary law and thus binding on all States. The International Court of Justice in the *Military and Paramilitary Activities in and against Nicaragua (Nicaragua v. United States) Case* (1984) referred to the rules in Common Article 3 as constituting 'a minimum yardstick' in international armed conflicts.

The International Criminal Tribunal for the former Yugoslavia (ICTY) operated on the basis of Article 3 of its Statute, which gave the Tribunal jurisdiction over 'violations of the laws of customs of war'. Any conviction based on Article 3 of the Statute requires proof that the crime in question is part of customary international law. For example, in *Prosecutor v. Hadzihasanovic*, the Appeals Chamber of the Tribunal concluded that the prohibition of wanton destruction of cities, plunder of public or private property, attacks against cultural property and attacks on civilian objects was a customary norm whose violations, including in non-international armed conflict, entails individual criminal responsibilities under customary international law. The Appeals Chamber cited practice recorded in Volume II of the ICRC study on customary IHL.[11]

The rules of customary IHL have also been referred to in national judicial proceedings. For example, the Israeli Supreme Court, in a judgment in December 2005, on the 'neighbour procedure' used by the Israel Defence Forces (IDF) to capture persons, referred to the ICRC's Rules of Customary IHL on the customary nature of the precautions to give effective, advance warning of attack (Rule 20) and to remove civilians from the vicinity of military objectives (Rule 24), as well as the prohibition of human shields (Rule 97). The Israeli Supreme Court, in another judgment in December 2006 on the policy of 'targeted killing', referred to the principles of distinction between civilians and combatants and between civilian objects and military objectives (Rules 1 and 7), the principle that civilians are protected against attack, unless and for such time they take a direct part in hostilities (Rule 6), the prohibition of indiscriminate attacks (Rule 11) and the prohibition on causing excessive incidental loss to civilian life, injuries

---

11 Prosecutor v. Hadzihasanovic and Kubura, IT-01-47-AR 73.3, March 11, 2005.

to civilians, and damage to civilian objects (Rule 14).[12]

The ICRC study points out that "the negotiation of the Rome Statute of the ICC was based on the premise that, to amount to a war crime to be included in the S tatute, the conduct had to amount to a violation of a customary rule of international law".

Enforcement of customary IHL: In principle, there is no difference in the enforcement of treaty law and customary international law, as both are sources of the same body of law . Military commanders have the responsibility to ensure that their troops respect the lawIn case of violation, IHL can be enforced through diplomatic means, including by international organizations, such as through measures adopted by the UN Security Council. Another means of the enforcement the law is its application by national and international courts and tribunals, for example the trial of an individual responsible for a violation.

B. International Treaties

International conventions[13] or treaties establishing rules expressly recognized by the contesting states are the main sources of law[14] Particularly since WWII, treaties have assumed a clear prominence as the primary source of law-making on the international plane. W ith the increased focus on

---

[12] Israel: *Adalah and others v. GOC Central Command, IDF*, June 23, 2005, HCJ 3799/02; and *The Public Committee against T orture in Isr ael and others v . The Go vernment of I srael*, December 13, 2006, HCJ 769/02.

[13] From the mid-19th century, the mult ilateral treaties on the IHL ha ve been designated as 'convention', 'declar ation', 'pr otocol', and 'statute' . Article 2 (1) (a) of the 1969 Vienna Convention on the Law of Treaties defines the term 'treaty' as 'an international agreement concluded between States in written form and go verned by international law , whether embodied in a single instrument or in two or more related instruments and whatev er its particular designation.' The term treaty is therefore a generic term for such arrangements irrespective of the varied nomenclature used. The term 'protocol' usually denotes a treaty amending or supplementing another treaty The examples are the 1954 First Hague Protocol or the 2005 Additional Protocol III to Geneva Conventions of 1949. The term 'statute' can denote a treaty (for example the 1988 Rome Statute of International Criminal Court), athough it has also been used to denote the constitutional document of a tribunal established by resolution of the UN Security Council.

[14] Even before the second half of the 19th century when the laws of war began to be codified in multilateral treaties, some principles relating to the conduct of armed hostities had been included in bilateral treaties. For example, the 1785 Teaty of Amity and Commerce between the United States and Prussia concluded with two articles making explicit and detailed

relations between States that comes with globalization, there has been greater pressure and demand to codify rules affecting States. This codification has been done mainly through treaties because they are a relatively simple, clear and quick way of crystallizing existing international rules and developing new ones. The Hague Peace Conferences of 1898 and 1907 are often cited not only as a watershed in the institutionalization of international co-operation, but also as the first major international 'law-making' conferences. The Rome Statute is regarded by some as the most important multilateral instrument negotiated in the last decade of the twentieth century The Rome Statute codifies international law regarding war crimes and other crimes against humanity.

The present-day rules of IHL are contained in a number of conventions dealing with matters ranging from the prohibition on the use of certain weapons which cause indiscriminate damage and cause unnecessary suffering, to those that deal with means and methods of warfare. Today there are nearly 50 international treaties directly related to IHL.

In addition to customary rules of IHL and international treaties; judicial decisions, legal philosophers and military manuals also serve as important sources of IHL. Each source of law plays its own critical role in advancing the objectives of the law. The treaty law, as compared to customary IHL, takes a backseat in today's conflicts for four main reasons: (i) ratification is required for treaties to apply and all treaties are not universally ratified; (ii) the characterization of an armed conflict is required prior to determining which treaty law applies, and this is not always easy; (iii) treaty law governing non-international armed conflicts is still rudimentary; and (iv) in coalition warfare, where the dif ferent coalition partners have not subscribed to the same treaties, only customary IHL provides a common set of rules that is applicable to all coalition partners.[15]

---

provisions for observance of certain basic rules if war wer to break out between two parties. These articles defined the immunit y of mer chants, women, children scholars and cultivators,and proper treatment to prisoners of w ar. Roberts Adam and Richard Guel ff. 2000. *Documents on the Laws of War*, Oxford: OUP, p.4.

[15] Henckaerts Jean-Marie. 2008. 'The Development of International Humani tarian Law and the Continued Reliance of Custom,' in Hensel Howard M (ed.). *The Legitimate Use of Miltary Force: Just War Tradition and the Customary Law of Armed Conflct*, USA: Ashgate Publshing Company, p. 118.

Development of IHL

A. Lieber Code

In 1862, the US President, Abraham Lincoln, asked Columbia University professor, Francis Lieber, to formulate rules of conduct in war for use by the Union army during theAmerican Civil war. Professor Lieber produced "Instructions for the Government of Armies of the United States in the Field", known as the Lieber Instructions or the Lieber CodeThe Code was promulgated as General Order No. 100 by President Lincoln in 1863. Though the Lieber Code was not a treaty , it represented a codification of the current usages and customs of war in North America and Europe. The Lieber Code strongly influenced the further codification of the laws and customs of war and the adoption of similar regulations by other States.

The Lieber Code was divided into ten sections relating to areas of conduct within conflict and contained a total of 157 articles:

Section I: Martial Law; Military jurisdiction; Military necessity ; Retaliation.

Section II: Public and private property of the enemy; Protection of persons, and especially of women, of religion, the arts and sciences; Punishment of crimes against the inhabitants of hostile countries.

Section III: Deserters - Prisoners of war; Hostages; Booty on the battlefield.

Section IV: Partisans; Armed enemies not belonging to the hostile army; Scouts-Armed prowlers; War-rebels.

Section V: Safe-conduct; Spies; War-traitors; Captured messengers; Abuse of the flag of truce.

Section VI: Exchange of prisoners; Flags of truce; Flags of protection.

Section VII: The Parole.

Section VIII: Armistice; Capitulation.

Section IX: Assassination.

Section X: Insurrection; Civil War; Rebellion.

The Lieber Code represented a codification of the international customary law of the time and would be heavily drawn upon as a basis for subsequent Hague and Geneva law. Parts of the Code have been expressly withdrawn as they are no longer considered legitimate methods of warfare, for example:

> **Article 17**: War is not carried on by arms alone. It is lawful to starve the hostile belligerent, armed or unarmed, so that it leads to the speedier subjection of the enemy.
>
> **Article 18**: When a commander of a besieged place expels the non-combatants, in order to lessen the number of those who consume his stock of provisions, it is lawful, though an extreme measure, to drive them back, so as to hasten on the surrender.
>
> **Article 19**: Commanders, whenever admissible, inform the enemy of their intention to bombard a place, so that the non-combatants, and especially the women and children, may be removed before the bombardment commences. But it is no infraction of the common law of war to omit thus to inform the enemy. Surprise may be a necessity.
>
> **Article 56**: A prisoner of war is subject to no punishment for being a public enemy, nor is any revenge wreaked upon him by the intentional infliction of any suffering, or disgrace, by cruel imprisonment, want of food, by mutilation, death, or any other barbarity.

The Lieber Code created a distinction between the conduct that was permitted toward combatants and non-combatants. Non-combatants were clearly articulated as being protected from the ravages of the conflict. The Lieber Code also established the conditions that were to be followed for the treatment of prisoners of war by the capturing force. It followed the principle that all soldiers were to be treated equally regardless of their social, ethnic or economic origins. The particular concern behind this principle was for the treatment that the black soldiers of the Union force might receive if captured by the Confederacy.

B. The Geneva and The Hague Laws

IHL has two branches: the Geneva laws and the Hague laws. The Geneva Laws have been designed to safeguard military personnel who are no longer taking part in the fighting and people not actively involved in hostilities, i.e. civilians. The Hague laws establish the rights and obligations of belligerents in the conduct of military operations, and limit the means of harming the enemy. The two branches of IHL draw their names from the cities where each was initially codified.With the adoption of theAdditional Protocols of 1977, which combine both branches, that distinction is now of merely historical and perceptive value.

C. The Geneva Convention of 1864

The beginning of modern IHL relates to the battle of Solferino in northern Italy between French, Italian, and Austrian forces in 1859. Henry Dunant, a businessman from Geneva, witnessed this carnage, in particular the miserable fate of the wounded left on the battlefield. He tried to alleviate the sufferings of the wounded and sick on the battlefield with the women of the surrounding villages. In 1862, Dunant published a short book, A Memory of Solferino, in which he evoked the horrors of the battle, but also tried to find remedies to the suf ferings he had witnessed. He invited the States "to formulate some international principle, sanctioned by a Convention inviolate in character" and give a legal protection to the military wounded in the field. Dunant' s proposal was successful and a small committee, the ancestor of the International Committee of the Red Cross, was founded in Geneva. Its main objective was to examine the feasibility of Dunant's proposals and to identify ways to formalize them. In 1863, the Geneva Committee persuaded the Swiss government to convene a diplomatic conference.

The conference met in Geneva inAugust 1864 and adopted the "Geneva Convention for theAmelioration of the Condition of theWounded in Armies in the Field". Thus, the modern IHL, consisting of 10 Articles, was born. The text of the 1864 Convention is as follows:

> **Article 1**: Ambulances and military hospitals shall be recognized as neutral, and as such, protected and respected by the belligerents as long as they accommodate wounded and sick. Neutrality shall end if the said ambulances or hospitals should be held by a military force.
>
> **Article 2**: Hospital and ambulance personnel, including the quarter - master's staff, the medical, administrative and transport services, and

the chaplains, shall have the benefit of the same neutrality when on duty, and while there remain any wounded to be brought in or assisted.

Article 3: The persons designated in the preceding Article may, even after enemy occupation, continue to dischar ge their functions in the hospital or ambulance with which they serve, or may withdraw to rejoin the units to which they belong.

When in these circumstances they cease from their functions, such persons shall be delivered to the enemy outposts by the occupying forces.

Article 4: The material of military hospitals being subject to the laws of war, the persons attached to such hospitals may take with them, on withdrawing, only the articles which are their own personal property. Ambulances, on the contrary, under similar circumstances, shall retain their equipment.

Article 5: Inhabitants of the country who bring help to the wounded shall be respected and shall remain free. Generals of the belligerent Powers shall make it their duty to notify the inhabitants of the appeal made to their humanity, and of the neutrality which humane conduct will confer.

The presence of any wounded combatant receiving shelter and care in a house shall ensure its protectionAn inhabitant who has given shelter to the wounded shall be exempted from billeting and from a portion of such war contributions as may be levied.

Article 6: Wounded or sick combatants, to whatever nation they may belong, shall be collected and cared for . Commanders-in-Chief may hand over immediately to the enemy outposts enemy combatants wounded during an engagement, when circumstances allow and subject to the agreement of both parties.

Those who, after their recovery, are recognized as being unfit for further service, shall be repatriated.The others may likewise be sent back, on condition that they shall not again, for the duration of hostilities, take up arms.Evacuation parties, and the personnel conducting them, shall be considered as being absolutely neutral.

Article 7: A distinctive and uniform flag shall be adopted for hospitals, ambulances and evacuation parties. It should in all circumstances be accompanied by the national flag.

An armlet may also be worn by personnel enjoying neutrality but its issue shall be left to the military authorities.

Both flag and armlet shall bear a red cross on a white ground.

Article 8: The implementing of the present Convention shall be arranged by the Commanders-in-Chief of the belligerent armies following the instructions of their respective Governments and in accordance with the general principles set forth in this Convention.

Article 9: The High Contracting Parties have agreed to communicate the present Convention with an invitation to accede thereto to Governments unable to appoint Plenipotentiaries to the International Conference at Geneva. The Protocol has accordingly been left open.

Article 10: The present Convention shall be ratified and the ratifications exchanged at Berne, within the next four months or sooner if possible.

D. The Hague Conventions

The Hague Conventions were international treaties negotiated at the First and Second Peace Conferences at The Hague, Netherlands in 1899 and 1907, respectively, and were, along with the Geneva Conventions, among the first formal statements of the laws of war and war crimes. The First Peace Conference was held from May 18 and signed on July 29, 1899, and entered into force on September 4, 1900. The Hague Convention of 1899 consisted of four main sections and three additional declarations (the final main section is for some reason identical to the first additional declaration):

I - Pacific Settlement of International Disputes

II - Laws and Customs of War on Land

III - Adaptation to Maritime Warfare of Principles of Geneva Convention of 1864

IV - Prohibiting Launching of Projectiles and Explosives from Balloons

Declaration I - On the Launching of Projectiles and Explosives from Balloons

Declaration II - On the Use of Projectiles the Object of Which is the Diffusion of Asphyxiating or Deleterious Gases

Declaration III - On the Use of BulletsWhich Expand or Flatten Easily in the Human Body

The main effect of the Convention was to ban the use of certain types of modern technology in war: bombing from the air, chemical warfare and hollow point bullets.

The Second Peace Conference was held from June 15 to October 18, 1907, to expand upon the original Hague Convention, modifying some parts and adding others. It had a greater focus on naval warfare. It was signed on October 18, 1907 and entered into force on January 26, 1910. It consisted of thirteen sections, of which twelve were ratified and entered into force:

I — The Pacific Settlement of International Disputes

II —The Limitation of Employment of Force for Recovery of Contract Debts

III — The Opening of Hostilities

IV — The Laws and Customs of War on Land

V —The Rights and Duties of Neutral Powers and Persons in Case of War on Land

VI — The Status of Enemy Merchant Ships at the Outbreak of Hostilities

VII — The Conversion of Merchant Ships into War-Ships

VIII — The Laying of Automatic Submarine Contact Mines

IX — Bombardment by Naval Forces in Time of War

X — Adaptation to Maritime W ar of the Principles of the Geneva Convention

XI — Certain Restrictions with Regard to the Exercise of the Right of Capture in Naval War

XII — The Creation of an International Prize Court [Not Ratified]

XIII - The Rights and Duties of Neutral Powers in Naval War

E. Martens Clause

The Martens Clause was based upon and took its name from a declaration read by Professor von Martens, the Russian delegate at the Hague Peace Conferences in 1899. The Martens Clause was originally devised to cope with a disagreement between the parties to the Conference regarding the status of resistance movements in occupied territory , i.e., the 'status of civilians who took up arms against an occupying force'. Lar ge military powers argued that they should be treated as *francs-tireurs* [16] and subject to execution, while smaller states contended that they should be treated as lawful combatants. Although the clause was originally formulated to resolve this particular dispute, it has subsequently reappeared in various but similar versions in later treaties regulating armed conflicts. The Martens Clause has formed a part of the laws of armed conflict since its first appearance in the preamble to the 1899 Hague Convention (II) with respect to the laws and customs of war on land. The Preamble to the 1899 Hague Convention II[17], states:

> "Until a more complete code of the laws of war is issued, the High Contracting Parties think it right to declare that in cases not included in the Regulations adopted by them, populations and belligerents remain under the protection and empire of the principles of international law, as they result from the usages established between civilized nations, from the laws of humanity and the requirements of the public conscience."

The Clause appears in a slightly modified form in the 1907 Hague Conventions:[18]

---

16 Literal meaning "free shooters": during the w ars of the French Revolution, a f ranc-tireur was a member of a corps of light infantry organized separately from the regular army.

17 The Hague Convention (II) with Respect to the Laws and Customs of War on Land and its annex: Regulations concerning the Laws and Customs of War on Land. The Hague, 29 July 1899.

18 The Hague Conv ention (IV) respecting the Laws and Customs of W ar on Land and its annex: Regulations concerning the Laws and Customs of W ar on Land. The Hague, 18 October 1907: Preamble paragraph 8.

> Until a more complete code of the laws of war has been issued, the High Contracting Parties deem it expedient to declare that, in cases not included in the Regulations adopted by them, the inhabitants and the belligerents remain under the protection and the rule of the principles of the law of nations, as they result from the usages established among civilized peoples, from the laws of humanity, and the dictates of the public conscience.

Today there is no formal agreement amongst humanitarian lawyers on the interpretation of the Martens Clause. It is subject to a variety of meanings: both narrow and expansive. In its restrictive sense, the Clause serves as a reminder that customary international law continues to apply after the adoption of a treaty norm.A wider interpretation is that, as few international treaties relating to the laws of armed conflict are ever complete, the Clause provides that something which is not explicitly prohibited by a treaty is not *ipso facto* permitted. The widest interpretation is that conduct in armed conflicts is not only judged according to treaties and custom but also to the principles of international law referred to by the Clause.

The Martens Clause is important because it stresses the importance of customary norms in the regulation of armed conflicts. In addition, it refers to "the principles of humanity" and "the dictates of the public conscience". It is important to understand the meaning of these terms. The expression "principles of humanity" is synonymous with "laws of humanity"— the earlier version of the Martens Clause (Preamble, 1899 Hague Convention II) refers to "laws of humanity"; the later version (Additional Protocol I of 1977) refers to "principles of humanity".Article 1, paragraph 2 of the 1977 Additional Protocol I states: "In cases not covered by this Protocol or by other international agreements, civilians and combatants remain under the protection and authority of the principles of international law derived from established custom, from the principles of humanity and from dictates of public conscience."The principles of humanity are interpreted as prohibiting means and methods of war which are not necessary for the attainment of a definite military advantage.

F. Modern IHL Treaties

Initiated in the form of 10 articles in the First Geneva Convention of 1864, contemporary humanitarian law has evolved in stages to meet the ever growing need for humanitarian aid resulting from developments in weaponry and new types of conflict. The following are the main IHL treaties in chronological order of adoption:

1864 Geneva Convention for the amelioration of the condition of the wounded in armies in the field.

1868 Declaration of S t. Petersburg (prohibiting the use of certain projectiles in wartime).

1899 The Hague Conventions respecting the laws and customs of war on land and the adaptation to maritime warfare of the principles of the 1864 Geneva Convention.

1906 Review and development of the 1864 Geneva Convention for the amelioration of the condition of the wounded in armies in the field.

1907 Review of The Hague Conventions of 1899 and adoption of new Conventions.

1925 Geneva Protocol for the prohibition of the use in war of asphyxiating, poisonous or other gases and of bacteriological methods of warfare.

1929 Two Geneva Conventions: 1. Review and development of the 1906 Geneva Convention, for the amelioration of the condition of the wounded in armies in the field; and 2. Geneva Convention relating to the Treatment of Prisoners of War (new).

1949 the four Geneva Conventions:[19]

I Amelioration of the condition of the wounded and sick in armed forces in the field

II Amelioration of the condition of wounded, sick and shipwrecked members of armed forces at sea

---

[19] In 1949 the former Geneva Conventions were revised: the Geneva Convention of 1929 for the Relief of the W ounded and Sick in Armies in the Field; the Xth Hague Conv ention of 1907 for the Adaptation to Maritime War of the Principles of the Geneva Convention; and 1929 Convention on the Treatment of Prisoners of war. Further, there was an urgent need for a Convention for the Protection of Civilans, the absence of which had, during the world conflict, led to grievous consequences. The main principles laid down in the 1864 Convention and maintained by the later Geneva Conventions are: (i) relief to the wounded without any distinction as to nationality; (ii) neutrality (inviolability) of medical personnel and medical establishments and units; and (iii) the distinctive sign of the Red Cross on a white ground.

III Treatment of prisoners of war

IV Protection of civilian persons in time of war.[20]

1954 The Hague Convention for the protection of cultural property in the event of armed conflict.

1972 Convention on the prohibition of the development, production and stockpiling of bacteriological (biological) and toxic weapons and on their destruction (BWC).

1976 UN Convention on the Prohibition of Military or Any Other Hostile use of Environmental Modification Techniques (ENMOD).

1977 Two Protocols additional to the four 1949 Geneva Conventions, which strengthen the protection of victims of international (Protocol I) and non-international (Protocol II) armed conflicts. [The Geneva Conventions of 1949 and their Additional Protocols of 1977 contain almost 600 articles and are the main instruments of IHL]

1980 Convention on prohibitions or restrictions on the use of certain conventional weapons which may be deemed to be excessively injurious or to have indiscriminate effects (CCW), which includes:

- Protocol I of 1980 on non-detectable fragments.
- Protocol II of 1980 on prohibitions or restrictions on the use of mines, booby traps and other devices.
- Protocol III of 1980 on prohibitions or restrictions on the use of incendiary weapons.
- Protocol IV of 1995 relating to blinding laser weapons.
- Revised Protocol of 1996 on prohibitions or restrictions on the use of mines, booby traps and other devices.
- Amendment of 2001 relating toArticle I of the CCWof 1980.

---

[20] The Second W orld War (1939-1945) saw civi lians and mi litary personnel kil led in equal numbers, as against a atio of 1:10 in the First World War. In 1949 the international communty responded to those tragic figures, and more particularly to the terrible effects the war had on civilians, by revising the Conventions then in force and adopting a new instrument: the Fourth Geneva Convention for the Protection of Civilians.

- Protocol V of 2003 on Explosive Remnants of War.

1993 Convention on the prohibition of the development, production, stockpiling and use of chemical weapons and on their destruction (CWC).

1997 Convention on the prohibition of the use, stockpiling, production and transfer of anti-personnel mines and on their destruction.

1998 Rome Statute of the International Criminal Court.

1999 Protocol to the 1954 Convention on Cultural Property.

2000 Optional Protocol to the Convention on the Rights of the Child (CRC) on the involvement of children in armed conflict.

2005 Rules of Customary International Humanitarian Law released by the ICRC.

2005 third ProtocolsAdditional to the four 1949 Geneva Conventions Relating to Adoption of Additional Protective Emblem.

2008 Convention on Prohibition of the Use, Development and Destruction of Cluster Munitions.

Jus ad bellum and *Jus in bello*

The Latin phrases*jus ad bellum*and*jus in bello*describe the law governing resort to force and the law governing the conduct of hostilities. These are two recognized branches of international law that relate to the military force. The first is the *jus ad bellum*, or "just war" also known as the law relating to the right to wage a war or the use of force. It is concerned with whether to resort to force is lawful or unlawful i.e., under what circumstances the use of military force is lawful. The second branch is the *jus in bello*, also known as the international humanitarian law or the law of armed conflict, which serves as guidelines for fighting once war has begunThese two branches of international law are conceptually distinct, but related. For example, the concept of 'necessity' and 'proportionality' are present both in the *jus ad bellum* and *jus in bello*.[21]

---

[21] The trial Chamber of the Special Court for SiearLeone (SCSL), on 9 October 2007 sentenced two leaders of the Civil Defence Forces (CDF), one of the parties to Siera Leone's civil war. The Chamber had convicted them of exeptionally brutal crimes like mutilation, amputation,

According to Walzer (2000), the moral reality of war is divided into two parts. War is always judged twice, first with reference to the reasons the States have for fighting, and second with reference to the means they adopt. The first kind of judgement is adjectival in character: we say that a particular war is just or unjust.The second is adverbial: we say that the war is being fought justly or unjustly....The two sorts of judgements are logically independent. It is perfectly possible for a just war to be fought unjustly and for an unjust war to be fought strictly in accordance with the rules. It is a crime to commit aggression, but aggressive war is a rule-governed activity It is right to resist aggression, but resistance is subject to moral (and legal) restraints. The dualism of *jus ad bellum* and *jus in bello* is at the heart of all that is most problematic in the moral reality of war.[22]

Jus ad bellum

Traditionally, States had full right to opt for war . The legal control on a State's right to resort to war is a new phenomenon. The concept of *jus ad bellum* can be traced back to the Roman era. The Romans believed they had to please the gods in order to wage war . According to Cicero, a war was not just unless the aggressor (i) made an official demand for satisfaction with a time allotted for a response; and (ii) issued a formal declaration of war. It was, therefore, an issue of morality and righteousness.

The principles central to *jus ad bellum* are right authority , right intention, reasonable hope, proportionality and last resort.[23] The principle of right authority suggests that a war is just only if waged by a legitimate

---

hacking civilians to death with machetes, and other sadistic killings. The defendants had urged that they had fought for a legitimate cause "to restore the democratically elected Government". The trail Chamber held that their sentences should therefore be mitigated significantly, though their conduct transgressed "acceptable limits", they served a cause that is just and defendable for "facilitating the restoration of democracy, peace and security in Sierra Leone". The SCSL Appeals Chamber disagreed and commented that trial chamber' adoption of just cause as a mitigating factor violated "the basic distinction and historical separation between *jus ad bellum* and *jus in bello*," which is characterized as "a bedrock principle" of the law of war.

22 Michael Walzer. 2000. *Just and Unjust Wars*, New York: Basic Books, p. 21-22.

23 Dan Smith (1998) has elaborated 'just war criteria by category': ***Jus ad bellum***: (1) Right authority: Only a legitimate authority has the right to declare a war. (2) Just cause: We are not only permitted but may be required to use lethal force if we have a just cause. (3) Right intention: In war, not only the cause and the goals must be just, but also our motive for responding to the cause and taking up the goals. (4) Last resort: We may resort to war only

authority. Such authority is rooted in the notion of state sovereignty and derived from popular consent. Even if their cause is just, individuals or groups whose authority is not sanctioned by society members cannot justifiably initiate war. According to the principle of right intention, the aim of war must not be to pursue narrowly defined interests, but rather to re-establish a just peace. This state of peace should be preferable to the conditions that would have prevailed had the war not occurred. Right intention is tied to *jus in bello*, and forbids acts of vengeance and indiscriminate violence. Just war must also have a reasonable chance of success, meaning there are good grounds for believing that the desired outcome can be achieved. The principle of proportionality stipulates that the violence used in the war must be proportional to the attack suffered. States are prohibited from using force not necessarily to attain the limited objective of addressing the injury suffered.

For example, if one nation invades and seizes the land of another nation, the second nation has just cause to launch a counterattack in order to retrieve its land. However, if the second nation invades the first, reclaims its territory and then also annexes the first nation, such military action is disproportional. In addition, the minimum amount of force necessary to achieve one's objective should be used. The principle of last resort stipulates that all non-violent options must be exhausted before the use of force is justified. A just war can only be waged once all other diplomatic avenues have been pursued. A good example of *jus ad bellum* was India's military action against Pakistan during the Kargil conflict in Jammu & Kashmir in 1999.[24]

---

if it is the last viable alternative. (5) Proportionality: We must be confident that resorting to war will do more good than harm.(6) Reasonable hope: We must have reasonable grounds for believing the cause can be achieved. (7) Relative justice: No state can act if it proposes absolute justice. (8) Open declaration: An explicit formal statement is required before resorting to force. ***Jus in bello***: (1) Discrimination: Non-combatants must be given immunity and protection. (2) Proportionality: Military actions must do more good than harm. Smith, Dan and Mona Fixdal, Humanitarian Intervention and Just war, *Mershon International Studies Review, Vol. 42, No. 2 (1998), p.* 283–312.

[24] During the winter season, due to extreme cold in the snow-capped mountainous areas of Kashmir, it was a common practice for both the Indian and Pakistan armies to abandon some forward posts on their respective sides of the Line of Control (LOC) and to reduce patrolling of areas that may be avenues of infiltration. When weather conditions became less severe, forward posts would be reoccupied and patrolling resumed. During January-February 1999, the Pakistan Army re-occupied the posts it had abandoned on its side of the LOC in the Kargil region, and also sent forces to occupy some posts on the Indian side of the LOC. Troops from the elite Special Service Group as well as four to seven battalions of the

The concept of *jus ad bellum* developed at the beginning of the twentieth century afterWorld War I. The international community attempted to prosecute individuals for crimes against peace. Articles 228-230 of the Treaty of V ersailles mention prosecution of German combatants for violations of the laws and customs of war. The Versailles Treaty formally arraigned Kaiser Wilhelm II, the German ruler who initiated World War I, for "a supreme of fence against international morality and the sanctity of treaties". Kaiser Wilhelm II, however, did not face trial because he fled to Holland, where the Dutch government refused extradition.The next attempt to limit the states' discretion in opting for war was made in 1919. Article 12 of the Covenant of the League of Nations provided:

> The Members of the League agree that, if there should arise between them any dispute likely to lead to a rupture they will submit the matter either to arbitration or judicial settlement or to enquiry by the Council, and they agree in no case to resort to war until three months after the award by the arbitrators or the judicial decision, or the report by the Council. In any case under this Article the award of the arbitrators or the judicial decision shall be made within a reasonable time, and the report of the Council shall be made within six months after the submission of the dispute.

In Paris in 1928, several nations signed the General Treaty for Renunciation of War as an Instrument of National Policy (Kellogg-Briand Pact). The Pact renounced war as a solution for international controversies and dictated that all disputes be settled by pacific means. It "established the illegality of war as an instrument of national policy". These attempts provided a backdrop to the post-1945 regime of the UN Charter. Article 2

Pakistan Light infantry (a paramil itary regiment not part of the regular P akistani army at that time) covertly and overtly set up bases on the vantage points of the Indian-contrdled region.

In the second week of Ma y 1999, the ambushing of an Indian patrol team b y Pakistani troops led to the exposure of the infil tration. The non-v oilent measures and diplomatic avenues for removal of Pakistan Army form Indian soil failed. Subsequently, in a four-months-long-operation, the Indian army was sucessful in recapturing its territory. The Indian Navy also prepared to blockade the Karachi Port of Pakistan to cut off supply routes. Following the outbreak of armed fighting, Pakistan sought the US's help, however, President Clinton refused to intervene until Pakistan had removed all forces from the Indian side of the LOC. Pakistan was criticized by other countries for instigating the war. The Government of India showed restraint and did not allow its mitary to cross the LOC, once miltary objective was achieved.

(4) of the Charter provides: "All States shall refrain from the threat or use of force against the territorial integrity or political independence of any State, or in any other manner inconsistent with the Purposes of the United Nations." Though Article 2 (4) prohibits against the use of military force, the UN Charter at two places provides exception to this. The UN Security Council may authorize the use of military force if it determines that there is in existence a threat to the peace, breach of the peace, or an act of aggression. The second exception is the use of forces in self-defence, which the UN Charter refers to as an 'inherent' right of individual or collective self-defence under Article 51. This permits NATO agreement which provides that for an attack on one state is an attack on all. It also allows for an individual State of superior military might to come to the aid of a weaker State under attack.

Jus in bello

Jus in bello, or laws governing the conduct of hostilities or IHL, serves as a guidelines for fighting well once war has begun. The belligerent armies are entitled to try to win, but there are restraints on the extent of harm, if any, that can be done to non-combatants and restraints on the means and methods of warfare. The idea underlying IHL finds resonance in the ancient notions of bravery and chivalry.[25] Today the most important IHL treaties are the four Geneva Conventions of 1949 and their three Additional Protocols of 1977 and 2005. In addition to the Geneva Conventions, there are about 40 IHL treaties on issues ranging from protection of cultural property to child soldiers and ban on or control of weapons in war. Customary international law also contains various provisions of IHL which have been recently compiled by the ICRC. The international human rights guarantee certain rights during international and non-international conflicts.

Jus in bello requires that the agents of war must be held responsible for their illegal actions. When soldiers attack non-combatants, pursue their enemy beyond what is reasonable, or violate other rules of fair conduct, they commit war crimes. *Jus in bello* provides that every individual, regardless of his rank or governmental status, is personally responsible for any war crime that he might commit. In certain circumstances, the military

---

[25] Chivalry means the duty to act honourably, even in war. The humane and noble ideals of chivalry included justice and loyalty, courage, honour and mercy, the obligations not to kill or otherwise take advantage of the vanquished enemy and to keep one's word.

or civilian superior could be held responsible for a crime committed by his subordinate.[26]

The 1977 Additional Protocol I, in its preamble, clarifies both aspects. First, while IHL applies to violations of *jus ad bellum*, it does not justify them: "The High Contracting Parties...expressing their conviction that nothing in this Protocol or in the Geneva Conventions of 12 August 1949 can be construed as legitimizing or authorizing any act of aggression or any other use of force inconsistently with the Charter of the United Nations". Second, IHL must be respected by all sides, independent of who is right or wrong under *jus in bello*: "Reaffirming further that the provisions of the Geneva Conventions of 12 August 1949 and of this Protocol must be fully applied in all circumstances to all persons who are protected by those instruments, without any adverse distinction based on the nature or origin of the armed conflict or on the causes espoused by or attributed to the Parties to the conflicts."[27] *Jus in bello* rules and principles apply equally to all combatants, whatever each belligerent' s avowed *ad bellum* rationale for resorting to force: self-defence, the restoration of democratic government, territorial conquest, or the destruction of a national, ethnic, racial, or religious group, as such.

Principles of IHL

The definition of IHL contained in this Chapter revolves around a few basic principles: (i) the distinction between civilians and combatants; (ii) the principle of proportionality (iii) the prohibition on inflicting unnecessary suffering; and (iv) the principle of military necessity.

A. Distinction

The principle of distinction is the cornerstone of IHL. It states that a

---

[26] The concept of *jus in bello* applies to international as well as non-international armed conflicts. The Appeals Chamber of the International Criminal Tribunal for the Former Yugoslavia (ICTY), in its judgment of 2 October 1995 in the *Tadiæ* case, expressly recognized that the concept of serious violations of the laws and customs of war applied to internal as well as international conflicts. The Statute of the International Criminal Court also allows the Court to impose penalties for war crimes committed during non-international armed confl icts as well as those committed during international armed conflicts.

[27] Sassoli Mar co. 2007.'*Ius ad bellum* and *Ius in Bell o*', in Schmi tt Michael N., and Jelena Pejic(ed.), *International Law and Armed Conflct: Exploring the Faultlines*, Boston: Martinus Nijhoff Publishers, p. 244.

distinction must always be made between combatants and civilians,[28] and between civilian objects and military objectives. [29] The principle of distinction prohibits all means and methods that cannot make a distinction between those who take part in hostilities, i.e., combatants, and those who do not and are therefore protected (Article 48, Additional Protocol I of 1977). The sick and wounded, medical personnel, civilians and prisoners of war (POWs) are called protected persons. However, there is one exception. Civilians directly participating in hostilities - either individually or as part of a group - become legitimate targets of attack, though only for the duration of their direct participation in hostilities.

The UN General Assembly Resolution 2444 (XXIII of 1968) states that "it is prohibited to launch attacks against the civilian population" and "that distinction must be made at all times between persons taking part in

---

[28] The term civilian means any person who is not a combatant or who does not belong to one of the categories of persons referred to in Article 4 A (1), (2), (3) and (6) of the Third Geneva Convention and in Article43 of AP I. In case of doubt whether a person is a civilian, that person shall be considered to be a civilian. Civilians enjoy the protection unless and for such time as they take a direct part in hostilities. Under the customary IHL, a combatant is anyone who is the member of the armed forces, and a civilian is anyone who is not a member of the armed forces. The civilian population comprises all persons who are civilians.

[29] The immunity from being object of attack extends to civilian objects. All objects that are not military objects are civilian ones. Military objectives are objects contributing to the enemy's war-fighting or war sustaining capability. Article 52 (2) of the Additional Protocol I of 1977 states that military objectives are limited to those objects which by their nature, location, purpose or use make an effective contribution to military action and whose total or partial destruction, capture or neutralization, offers a definite military of advantage. 'Nature' denotes intrinsic military significance, thereby including objects like ordnance factory, ammunition depots, tanks, combat aircraft, military headquarters or barracks. 'Location' refers to areas that have 'special importance to military operations'. The example could be mountain pass that can be blocked to foil the enemy's advance. Where reliable information indicates that the enemy intends to use an object militarily in the future, the object qualifies as a military objective through 'purpose'. Finally, 'use' means that the enemy is presently utilizing an object militarily. Any object or location may become a lawful military objective through use (or abuse) by a belligerent. In case of doubt whether an object which is normally dedicated to civilian purposes, such as a place of worshipa house or other dwelling or a school, is being used to make an effective contribution to military action, it shall be presumed not to be so used. The dual use facilities such as power stations, electrical grid, railway communication system, which serves both civilian and military need, would be a legitimate military target. However, if foodstuff and water necessary for the survival of civilian populations is also used to feed the military, they must not be destroyed. Also see: Michael N Schmitt, 'Fault Lines in the Law of Attack', p. 280. Available at:http://www.estig.ipbeja.pt/~ac_direito/FaultLinesintheLawofTargeting.pdf, accessed 22 March 2011.

the hostilities and members of the civilian population to the effect that the latter be spared as much as possible". The parties to conflict are obligated to separate their fighting forces and military objectives from the civilian population and civilian objects.The employment of human shields to protect military objectives or individual military units or personnel is a fundamental violation of the principle of distinction.

B. Proportionality

The concept of proportionality is described inArticle 22 of the Regulations to the 1907 Hague Convention IV which states that the right of belligerents to adopt means of injuring the enemy is not unlimited.The principle states that even if there is a clear military taget, it must not be attacked if the risk of civilians or civilian property being harmed is lar ger than the expected military advantage.A military target is an object that contributes effectively to the military operation.[30]

The principal purpose of proportionality is to weigh the anticipated gains of a military operation against reasonably foreseeable consequences to the civilian population.This principle is to be considered by a commander in determining whether, in engaging in an operation, his actions may be expected to cause incidental loss of civilian life, injury to civilians, or damage to civilian objects, which would be excessive in relation to the concrete and direct military advantage anticipated by those actions. Proportionality does not prohibit injuries to civilians that is incidental to lawful military operations.

Proportionality may be applied by decision-makers at the national, strategic, operational or tactical level. Article 57, paragraph 2 (a) (iii), of Additional Protocol I (AP I), which deals with precautions in attack, states: "Those who plan an attack shall....refrain from deciding to launch any attack which may be expected to cause incidental loss of civilian life, injury to civilians, damage to civilian objects, or a combination thereof, which would be excessive in relation to the concrete and direct military advantage

---

[30] The definition of a miltary target is clear in theory but sometimes harder to apply in practice, especially when it comes to double-use facilities. These may be used both by civilians and combatants. For example, a TV or a radio station can be a legitimate miltary target if used as a military command or communication centre, but if it is used for civilian purposes only it cannot be targeted.

anticipated."[31] Article 51.5 (b) of AP I accordingly states that "an attack which may be expected to cause incidental loss of civilian life, injury to civilians, damage to civilian objects, or a combination thereof, which would be excessive in relation to the concrete and direct military advantage anticipated" will be considered an indiscriminate attack. Article 57.2 (b), which relates to precautions in attack, states: "An attack shall be cancelled or suspended if it becomes apparent that the objective is not a military one or is subject to special protection or that the attack may be expected to cause incidental loss of civilian life, injury to civilians, damage to civilian objects, or a combination thereof, which would be excessive in relation to the concrete and direct military advantage anticipated."

The issue of collateral damage is related to the principle of proportionality. New technology and weapon systems attempt to minimize loss of life and damage but cannot eliminate collateral damagesThe injuries to civilians and damage to civilian property would not be unlawful if incidental to attack on military objectives or combatant personnel. The injury or damage must not be excessive in the light of the military advantage anticipated by the attack. Military commanders, therefore, have an obligation to minimize injury or damage. Though proportionality is not referred to in Additional Protocol II of 1977, it is inherent in the concept of humanity and cannot be ignored in internal armed conflicts.

C. Unnecessary Suffering or Superfluous Injuries

Several rules of IHL treaties contain the caveat that the right of a party to a conflict is not unlimited in terms of its selection and use of means or methods of war. The principle of avoiding the employment of arms, projectiles or material of a nature that causes unnecessary suf fering (also referred to as

---

[31] Article 23(g) of the Regulations Annex to Hague Convention IV of 1907 prohibits the destruction or seizure of enemy property "unless such destruction or seizue be imperatively demanded by the necessities of war," while Article 53of the fourth Geneva Convention of 1949, declares that: Any destruction by the Occupying Power of real or personal property belonging individually or collectively to private persons, or to the State, or to other public authorities, or to social or cooperative or ganizations, is prohibited, except where such destruction is rendered absolutely necessary by military operations. Article 147, of the fourth Geneva Convention makes extensive destruction or seizure of property a grave breach if it is "not justified by military necessity and carried out unlawfully and wantonly." Article 52 of Additional Protocol I prohibits attacks of objects other than military objectives.

superfluous injury) is codified in Article 23 (e) and (g) of the Regulations to the Hague Convention IV of 1907 , which especially forbids the employment of "arms, projectiles or material calculated to cause unnecessary suffering..." and the destruction or seizure of "the enemy' s property, unless such destruction or seizure be imperatively demanded by the necessities of war". Article 35 of AP I prohibits the employment of weapons, projectiles and material and methods of warfare of a nature to cause superfluous injury or unnecessary suffering. In determining whether a means or method of warfare causes unnecessary suffering, a balancing test is applied between lawful force dictated by military necessity to achieve a military objective and the injury or damage that may be considered superfluous to the achievement of the stated or intended objective.

The act of combatants killing or wounding enemy combatants in battle is a legitimate act under IHL if accomplished by lawful means or methods. The prohibition of unnecessary suffering does not limit the use of force on an opposing military force in order to subdue or destroy it. However , the use of certain means of warfare has been prohibited in an armed conflict, because they are regarded as causing unnecessary sufering. These include poison, chemical and biological weapons, munitions containing fragments not detectable by x-ray and blinding laser weapons. IHLprohibits the design or modification and employment of a weapon for the purpose of increasing or causing suffering beyond that required by military necessity Intentional attack on *hors de combat* (i.e., combatants who are no longer in the fight), unlawful destruction of civilian objects, and unlawful injury to civilians not taking a direct part in hostilities are also prohibited.

The terms 'unnecessary suffering' and 'superfluous injury' have not been defined anywhere and are regarded as synonymous. Each refers to damage to objects as well as injury to persons. Unnecessary suf fering is used in an objective rather than a subjective sense, that is, it is not measured in terms of the suffering of the victim but rather, by the suffering that can be caused by a particular weapon by virtue of its design or in the way of its employment. The common interpretation is that "international law only prohibits the use of weapons that increase suffering without really increasing military advantage". A weapon is proscribed only if it causes injury or suffering that can be avoided, given the military constraints of the situation. Under Article 3 (a) of the Statute of the International CriminalTribunal for the Former Yugoslavia (ICTY), the employment of weapons calculated to cause unnecessary suffering is regarded as a violation of the laws and customs of war, giving rise to individual criminal responsibility.[32]

Anti-personnel weapons are designed to kill or disable enemy combatants and are lawful, notwithstanding the death, pain and suffering they inflict. On the other hand, weapons that are designed to cause unnecessary suffering or superfluous injury are prohibited. Article 8 (2) (b) (xx) of the Rome Statute of the ICC states: ".....employing weapons, projectiles and material and methods of warfare which are of a nature to cause superfluous injury or unnecessary suffering or which are inherently indiscriminate in violation of the international law of the armed conflict" would be a war crime.

D. Military Necessity

The principle of military necessity authorizes the use of force required to accomplish the mission. It is related to two other principles: unnecessary suffering and proportionality. The term 'military necessity' has been mentioned in all four Geneva Conventions of 1949 and the two Additional Protocols of 1977. However, it has not been defined. No more force should be used to carry out a military operation than is necessary in the circumstances. Military necessity justifies the infliction of suffering upon an enemy combatant, and only that much sufering as is necessary to bring about the submission of the enemy.

The principle of military necessity is codified in Article 23, paragraph (g) of the Regulations to Hague Convention IV, which forbids a belligerent "to destroy or seize the enemy's property, unless such destruction or seizure is imperatively demanded by the necessities of war". Military necessity does not authorize actions specifically prohibited by IHL, such as wanton destruction of civilian property or bombardment of civilian localities. Therefore, military commanders and others responsible for making decisions

---

[32] Statute of the International Tribunal for the Prosecution of Persons responsible for Serious Violation of International Humanitarian Law Committed in the Territory of the Former Yugoslavia Since 1991 (ICTY), Report of the Secretary-General Pursuant to Paragraph 2 of Security Council Resolution 808 (1993), 32 *International Legal Materials (ILM)* 1159, 1192 (1993).

must make those decisions in a manner consistent with the spirit and intent of IHL. Where an express prohibition has been stated, neither military necessity, nor any other rationale of necessity may override that prohibition. The Rome S tatute of the ICC provides for prosecution of violations of military necessity: Articles 8 (2) (a) (iv) and 8 (2) (b) (xiii) state that intentionally launching an attack, knowing that it will cause excessive death or damage; and destroying or seizing enemy property would be a "war crime".

The term *Kriegsrason* (military necessity) appeared for the first time in late eighteenth-century German literature. It held that military necessity overrides everything. In order to win, it granted belligerents, even individual combatants, the right to do whatever was required in an armed conflict. However, the concept is obsolete today and military necessity cannot overrule IHL.

Basic Rules of IHL

The ICRC (1988) has provided seven basic rules containing the crux of IHL. These rules are based on the principle of distinction that civilians should never be specifically made a target and combatants have to abide certain limitations in choosing the means and methods of warfare.

1. Persons *hors de combat* (those out of combat, taken prisoner of war, or injured) and those who do not take a direct part in hostilities are entitled to respect for their lives and their moral and physical integrity. They shall in all circumstances be protected and treated humanely without any adverse distinction.

2. It is forbidden to kill or injure an enemy who surrenders or who is *hors de combat* .

3. The wounded and sick shall be collected and cared for by the party to the conflict which has them in its power Protection also covers medical personnel, establishments, transports and equipment.The emblem of the Red Cross or the Red Crescent is the sign of such protection and must be respected.

4. Captured combatants and civilians under the authority of an adverse party are entitled to respect for their lives, dignity, personal rights

and convictions. They shall be protected against all acts of violence and reprisals. They shall have the right to correspond with their families and to receive relief.

5. Everyone shall be entitled to benefit from fundamental judicial guarantees. No one shall be held responsible for an act he has not committed. No one shall be subjected to physical or mental torture, corporal punishment or cruel or degrading treatment.

6. Parties to a conflict and members of their armed forces do not have an unlimited choice of methods and means of warfare. It is prohibited to employ weapons or methods of warfare of a nature that causes unnecessary losses or excessive suffering.

7. Parties to a conflict shall at all times distinguish between the civilian population and combatants in order to spare civilian population and property. Neither the civilian population as such, nor civilian persons shall be the object of attackAttacks shall be directed solely against military objectives.

CHAPTER 2

IHL: Relation with Human Rights and Refugee Law

Introduction

IHL and international human rights law (IHRL) are traditionally two distinct branches of international law. The first regulates the conduct of Parties to an armed conflict and is based on the reciprocal expectations of two Parties at war and notions of chivalry and humanity . The second emerged in the post-World War II period in response to the atrocities committed by the German armed forces as well as the allied powers and deals with the subjective rights of the individual (or groups) against the State. Both the branches of international law are today largely codified. There is a general perception that human rights law is applied principally in times of peace and protects individuals from their own governments, while humanitarian law governs relations between States in times of war and protects individuals from enemy powers.The recent developments in international and national jurisprudence and practice have shown that these two bodies of law not only share common humanitarian goals, but overlap substantially in practice. In essence, both bodies of law are dedicated to the overarching goal of the protection of the individual, i.e., protection of the dignity and integrity of the individual, the protection of the right to life, prohibition of torture or cruel treatment, basic rights to a criminal justice process, prohibition of discrimination, protection of women and children, and right to food and health. Both IHRL and IHL are applicable in international armed conflicts and may both apply simultaneously.

International Human Rights Law (IHRL)

IHRL is composed of international and regional instruments[1] in the form of declarations, treaties, protocols and other instruments.These provide a legal framework for the worldwide protection and promotion of human rights. The foremost among these are the Universal Declaration of Human Rights, 1948 (UDHR), the International Covenant on Civil and Political Rights (ICCPR) and the International Covenant on Economic, Social and Cultural Rights (ICESCR). These three instruments are together known as the International Bill of Human Rights.

Other conventions relating to human rights are: the International Convention on the Elimination of All Forms of Racial Discrimination (CERD), the Convention on the Elimination of All Forms of Discrimination against Women (CEDAW), the Convention against Torture and Other Cruel, Inhuman or Degrading Treatment or Punishment (CAT), the Convention on the Rights of the Child (CRC) and its Protocol, the International Convention for the Protection of All Persons from Enforced Disappearance, and the Convention on the Rights of Persons with Disabilities (CRPD). While IHL and IHRL have developed separately, recent treaties include provisions from both the bodies of law. Some examples are the CRC and its Optional Protocol on the Participation of Children in Armed Conflict, the Convention for the Protection of All Persons from Enforced Disappearance and the Rome Statute of the International Criminal Court.

In addition, specific standards have been developed by the United Nations in various fields. Some of these standards are intended to protect all people from human rights abuses such as discrimination, genocide, torture and slavery, while others are meant to safeguard members of specific groups whose human rights are often violated, e.g., stateless persons, refugees, prisoners, workers, children and women.

Some international human rights instruments, like protection from torture, have become part of customary international law and are binding

---

[1] The main regional instruments are the European Convention for the Protection of Human Rights and Fundamental Freedoms (1950), the American Declaration of the Rights and Duties of Man (1948) and Convention on Human Rights (1969), and the African Charter on Human and Peoples' Rights (1981).

on all States, whether they have ratified the instruments or not. Others, such as ICCPR and ICESCR are binding on States Parties which have ratified the instruments. In order to monitor the implementation of the human rights treaties a monitoring body has been established under each treaty. For example, the Human Rights Committee was created to monitor the implementation of ICCPR, while the Committee against Torture was established to monitor the implementation of the Convention against Torture. The Human Rights Council was created by the UN General Assembly on 15 March 2006 with the main purpose of addressing situations of human rights violations, including gross and systematic violations. The Council in its resolution on, "Torture and other Cruel, Inhuman or Degrading Treatment or Punishment: the Role and Responsibility of Judges, Prosecutors and Lawyers (2010)", has urged the States to respect and ensure respect for the critical role that judges, prosecutors and lawyers play in the prevention of torture and other cruel, inhuman or degrading treatment or punishment, including with respect to arbitrary detention, due process safeguards and fair trial standards, and bringing perpetrators to justice.

In principle, IHRL applies at all times, i.e. both in peacetime and in situations of armed conflict. However, some IHRL treaties permit governments to derogate from certain rights in situations of public emergency threatening the life of the nation. Such derogations must, however, be proportional to the crisis at hand, must not be introduced on a discriminatory basis and must not contravene other rules of international law – including rules of IHL. Certain human rights are never derogable. Among these are the right to life, prohibition of torture or cruel, inhuman or degrading treatment or punishment, prohibition of slavery and servitude and prohibition of retroactive criminal laws.[2]

---

[2] The rights contained in IHRL instruments are not absolute, but are subject to reasonable restrictions in order to protect public safety. During an internal armed conflict, governments may restrict or suspend the exercise of many of the rights established under these IHRL instruments. The governments may temporarily suspend certain rights altogether in cases where a treaty contains a separate 'derogation clause'. For example, Article 4 (1) of the ICCPR provides: 'In time of public emergency which threatens the life of the nation and the existence of which is officially proclaimed, the States Parties to the present Covenant may take measures derogating from their obligations under the present Covenant to the extent strictly required by the exigencies of the situation, provided that such measures are not inconsistent with their other obligations under international law and do not involve discrimination solely on the ground of race, colour, sex, language, religion or social origin.'

International humanitarian Law (IHL)

IHL safeguards a set of rights from which States cannot derogate even in the extreme case of armed conflict. It has two main objectives: (i) To protect people who are not, or are no longer participating in the hostilities; and (ii) To limit the means and methods of warfare. The main instruments of IHL are the four Geneva Conventions of 1949 and their two Additional Protocols of 1977. Virtually every State is party to the Geneva Conventions of 1949 and the acceptance of the Additional Protocols is progressing towards becoming universal.

The first Geneva Convention relates to the protection of the wounded and the sick in the field; the second to the wounded and the sick at sea; the third to prisoners of war; and the fourth to civilians. With the exception of one article, viz Article 3 common to all four Conventions, the Geneva Conventions apply to international armed conflict. The Additional Protocol I applies to international armed conflicts, and Additional Protocol II applies to non-international armed conflicts, that is to all armed conflicts not covered by the Protocol I in the territory of a High Contracting Party between its armed forces and dissident armed forces or organized armed groups which exercise control over a part of its territory.

The common Article 3 (CA3) applies to armed conflicts that are not of an international character occurring in the territory of a High Contracting Party. It expressly prohibits at any time and in any place: (i) violence to life and person; (ii) taking of hostages; (iii) outrages upon personal dignity, in particular humiliating and degrading treatment; (iv) the passing of sentences and the carrying out of executions without previous judgement being pronounced by a regularly constituted court.

The provisions of the Geneva Conventions and the Additional Protocols I and II are very specific. The important rules of conduct, which apply to all armed conflicts under IHL are as follows.

However, most derogation clauses provide that certain rights including the right to life, the prohibitions against torture, slavery, and retroactive application of penal law, cannot be made the subject of derogation. Article 4(2) of the ICCPR provides that 'no derogation from articles 6, 7, 8 (paragraphs 1 and 2), 11, 15, 16 and 18 may be made under Article 4 (1). Certain IHRL treaties like the CERD, the CRC, or the Torture Convention do not permit derogations at all.

- People who are not, or are no longer , taking an active part in hostilities, such as the wounded and sick, prisoners and civilians, must be respected and protected in all circumstances.
- Non-combatants must be treated humanely; in particular, violence to their life and person is prohibited, as are all kinds of torture and cruel treatment, the taking of hostages, and the passing of sentences without a fair trial.
- Outrages upon personal dignity, such as humiliating and degrading treatment, rape, enforced prostitution or any form of indecent assault are prohibited.
- The armed forces must always distinguish between civilians and combatants, and between civilian objects and military objectives. Attacks on civilians and civilian objects are prohibited and all precautions must be taken to spare the civilian population.
- Attacks on or the destruction of objects indispensable to the survival of the civilian population (e.g. foodstufs, crops, livestock, drinking, water installations and irrigation works); and the use of starvation as a method of warfare are prohibited.
- The wounded and the sick must be collected and cared for and hospitals, ambulances, and medical and religious personnel must be respected and protected.
- The emblem of the Red Cross, Red Crescent and Red Crystal, [3] which symbolizes this protection, must be respected in all circumstances and any abuse or misuse thereof must be punished.
- Parties to a conflict must agree to relief operations of a humanitarian, impartial and non-discriminatory nature on behalf of the civilian population and aid agency personnel must be respected and protected.

IHL and IHRL: Commonalities

The development of the UDHR and the Geneva Conventions were not mutually inspired. Human rights were initially a matter of constitutional

[3] The third Protective emblem "Red Crystal" added by the Additional Protocol III of 2005.

law, an internal affair between a government and its citizens.After WW II, human rights became part of international law, starting with the adoption of the UDHR in 1948. IHL developed as the law of international armed conflict on the reciprocal expectations of two parties at war . Its main objective was to protect victims. With the adoption of the Fourth Geneva Convention of 1949, the provisions of IHL were amalgamated with IHRL, especially with regard to civilians in detention. The Common Article 3, applicable in situations of internal armed conflict, brought IHL closer to human rights law, because it is concerned with the treatment of a State's own nationals. Some rules of IHL and IHRL are similar, for example: (i) non-discrimination is one of the fundamental principles of international human rights law and also a key concept of the Geneva Conventions; (ii) IHL invokes the right to life as far as possible during hostilities and prohibits murder or arbitrary executions of persons in the power of an authority (although collateral damage is tolerated); and (iii) both IHL and IHRL prohibit torture in all circumstances.

Applicability of IHRL and IHL

1. **International Armed Conflict**: In such situations, the provisions of IHL become operative, particularly those contained in the four Geneva Conventions and Additional Protocol I (AP I). In addition, most human rights guarantees remain applicable, subject to certain derogations permitted to governments. Article 75 of the AP I has introduced certain fundamental guarantees and procedural requirements derived from human rights treaties into IHL.[4]

The International Court of Justice has emphasized in its Advisory Opinion on the *Construction of the Wall in the Occupied Palestinian Territory* and *DRC v. Uganda*, that human rights treaties together with humanitarian law continue to apply in wartime. [5] The UN Report on the situation of the detainees in Guantanamo emphasizes the

---

[4] The influence of IHRL on IHL can be seen in Article 75(4) of AP I, which was drafted on the basis of Article 14 of the ICCPR (the right to fair trial under IHRL). The right to a fair trial is derogable under IHRL, but its core values contained in Article 75 of AP I have been considered to be non-derogable during international armed conflict.

[5] *Legal Consequences of the Construction of a Wall in the Occupied Palestinian Territory*, Advisory Opinion of 9 July 2004;*Case Concerning the Armed Activities on the Territory of the Congo* (*Democratic Republic of the Congo v Uganda*), Judgment of 19 December 2005.

complementarity of human rights law and humanitarian law especially referring to the applicability of human rights in wartime.[6] In terms of the applicability of IHL, the International Criminal Tribunal for the Former Yugoslavia (ICTY) noted that "Once the existence of an armed conflict has been established, IHL, including the law on crimes against humanity, continues to apply beyond the cessation of hostilities." The ICTY held that IHRL and IHL are mutually complementary.[7]

2. **Internal Armed Conflict**: In an internal armed conflict, there are three main sources of IHL protection: (i) the Martens Clause; (ii) Common Article 3 of four Geneva Conventions of 1949; and (iii) Additional Protocol II of 1977 (AP II).

The Martens Clause, which has acquired customary status pursuant to a variety of judgments by international bodies, provides that the parties to any armed conflict must act "in accordance with the principles of the law of nations derived from the usages established among civilized peoples, from the laws of humanity and the dictates of public conscience". The Common Article 3 provides that parties to an armed conflict not of an international character (i.e., internal armed conflicts) must apply certain minimum standards to persons taking no active part in the hostilities. In particular, it establishes an affirmative obligation to collect and care for the wounded and sick, and expressly prohibits: (i) violence to life and person, in particular murder of all kinds, mutilation, cruel treatment and torture; (ii) taking of hostages; (iii) outrages upon personal dignity, in particular humiliating and degrading treatment; and (iv) the passing of sentences and the carrying out of executions without previous judgment pronounced by a regularly constituted court, affording all the judicial guarantees which are recognized as indispensable by civilized peoples.

The AP II improves upon the 'minimum' protections afforded by the Martens Clause and CA 3. Article 4(2) of the Protocol supplements the prohibitions contained in CA 3 by adding the prohibition of collective punishment, terrorism, slavery, pillage, and threats to carry

---

6 Situation of detainees at Guantanamo Bay, E/CN.4/2006/120.

7 ICTY *Prosecutor v. Kunarac and Others*, Case Nos. IT-96-23 & IT-96-23/1, Trial Chamber, (Feb. 22, 2001); confirmed by the Appeals Chamber judgment (June 12, 2000).

out these acts. It also provides special protections for children (Article 4(3)) and persons whose liberty has been restricted (Article 5)Article 6 sets out a rigorous set of standards regarding the prosecution and punishment of criminal offences related to a conflict. AP II prohibits attacks or violent threats against civilians (Article 13), starvation of civilians (Article 14), and forced displacements of civilians (Article 17). It also protects works containing dangerous forces (Article 15). There are a number of international human rights treaties like Convention against Torture, the CRC, the CEDA W, and the CERD which continue to af ford protection in the during internal armed conflicts.

In the *Tadic case*, the ICTY Appeals Chamber ruled that many principles and rules previously considered applicable only in international armed conflicts are now applicable in internal armed conflicts, and serious violations of IHL committed within the context of such internal conflicts constitute war crimes.[8] This blurring of the distinction between international and non-international armed conflicts points to a shift in focus from the state sovereignty to a human rights approach to international problems.

3. **Internal Tensions and Wars of National Liberation** : There are two other conflict situations: (i) internal tensions and disturbances, and (ii) wars of national liberation, in which IHRL or IHL could be applicable. The former refers to situations that fall short of armed conflict, but involve the use of force and other repressive measures by a government to maintain or restore public order or public safety . Only IHRL applies in such situations. The term 'war of national liberation' refers to armed conflicts in which "peoples are fighting against colonial domination and alien occupation and against racist regimes in the exercise of their right to self-determination".Generally the same provisions of IHL and IHRL that apply in the context of international armed conflict apply also in the context of wars of national liberation.

---

[8] *Prosecutor v. Tadic* (Case No. IT-94-1-AR72), The International Criminal Tribunal for Yugoslavia: The Decision of the Appeals Chamber on the Interlocutory Appeal on Jurisdiction in the *Tadic case*.

In an internal armed conflict, IHRL and IHL are not enough to ensure adequate protection to victims. There are two reasons for this. First, the IHRL and IHL norms applicable in internal armed conflicts generally apply only to State actors, and therefore have no application to individuals or non-state actors such as members of guerilla forces. Second, since the threshold for the application of Protocol II is quite high, it is dif ficult to apply the Protocol because as States refuse to accept that the Protocol applies to their situation. Thus Protocol II, which was established to supplement the rudimentary protections of CA 3, often proves an unreliable source of protection for victims of internal armed conflicts.

The Rome Statute seeks to overcome the shortcomings of IHRL and IHL by the establishment of the category of 'crimes against humanity'. The definition of this category of crimes is containedArticle 7 of the Rome Statute. Unlike the IHRL and IHL, the crimes against humanity apply to state and non-state actors alike. Thus, the protections provided by IHRL and IHL, when combined with the supplementary protections afforded by the category of crimes against humanity, appear to offer a substantial level of international legal protection for victims of internal armed conflicts.

Bothe (2004) is of the opinion that the regimes of IHL and IHRL overlap, but as they were not meant to do so originally , it is necessary to apply them concurrently and to reconcile them: ".... triggering events, opportunities and ideas are key factors in the development of international law. This fact accounts for the fragmentation of international law into a great number of issue-related treaty regimes established on particular occasions, addressing specific problems created by certain events. But as everything depends on everything, these regimes overlap. Then, it turns out that the rules are not necessarily consistent with each other , but that they can also reinforce each other. Thus, the question arises whether there is conflict and tension or synergy between various regimes."[9] The Report on Fragmentation of International Law, prepared by the ILC Study Group, treats the issue of fragmentation mainly as the issue of normative conflict. The Report explains, "On the one hand, fragmentation does create the danger of conflicting and incompatible rules, principles, rule-systems and institutional practices. On the other hand, it reflects the rapid expansion of

---

[9] Michael Bothe. 2004. 'The Historical Evolution of International Humanitarian Law, International Human Rights Law, Refugee Law and International Criminal Law', in H. Fischer and Ulrike Froissart (ed.), *Crisis Management and Humanitarian Protection*, Berlin: BWV.

international legal activity into various new fields and the diversification of its objects and techniques."[10]

The UN Human Rights Committee in its concluding observations on country reports in the cases of Congo, Belgium, Colombia, Sri Lanka, Israel, UK and USA has applied the rights contained in the ICCPR to both non-international and international armed conflicts.[11]

The International Court of Justice (ICJ), while delivering its advisory opinion in *Legality of the Thr eat or Use of Nuclear W eapons* in 1996 observed "that the protection of the International Covenant on Civil and Polit-ical Rights does not cease in times of war".[12]

The ICJ (2004) while reexamining the relationship between IHRL and IHL, in the context of the 'lawfulness of the con-struction of a wall in occupied Palestinian' opined that the protection of the Conventions on human rights did not cease in case of armed conflictAnd held further: "As regards the relationship between IHL and IHRL, there are thus three possible situations: some rights may be exclusively matters of IHL; others may be exclusively matters of IHRL; yet others may be matters of both these branches of international law."[13] In a dispute between Georgia and Russia, the ICJ in its order dated 15 October 2008, held that the International Convention on the Elimination of All Forms of Racial Discrimination (CERD) applied in any event during an armed conflict. It stated that the acts alleged by Geor gia appeared to be capable of contravening rights provided for by CERD even if certain of the alleged acts were covered by other rules of international law, including humanitarian law.[14]

---

[10] *Fragmentation of International Law: Difficulties Arising from the Diversification and Expansion of International Law*, Report of the Study Gr oup of the International Law Commission, Finalized by Martti Koskenniemi, A/CN.4/L.682, 13 April 2006.

[11] Democratic Republic of Congo, UN Doc. CCPR/C/COD/CO/3, 26 April 2006 ; Belgium, UN Doc. CCPR/CO/81/BEL, 12 A ugust 2004 ; Colombia, UN Doc. CCPR/CO/80/COL, 26 May 2004 ; Sri Lanka, UN Doc. CCPR/CO/79/LKA, 1 December 2003 ; Israel, UN Doc. CCPR/CO/78/ISR, 21 August 2003 ; United Kingdom, UN Doc. CCPR/C/GBR/CO/6, 30 July 2008 ; and United States of America, UN Doc. CCPR/C/USA/CO/3/Rev1, 18 December 2006.

[12] *Legality of the Threat or Use of Nuclear Weapons* [1996] ICJ Rep 226.

[13] *Legal Consequences of the Construction of a W all in the Occupied Palestinian Territory*, Advisory Opinion of 9 July 2004.

[14] *Application of the I nternational Con vention on the El imination of Al l Forms of R acial Discrimination*, Order, 15 Oct. 2008, at para. 112, available at: www.icj-cij.org/docket/files/140/14801.pdf. Assessed 23 January 2011.

IHL binds all actors to an armed conflict: in international conflicts it must be observed by the states involved, whereas in internal conflict it binds the government, as well the groups fighting against it or among themselves. IHL imposes obligations on individuals and also provides that persons may be held individually criminally responsible for grave breaches of the Geneva Conventions and of the Additional Protocol I, and for other serious violations of the laws and customs of war (war crimes).It establishes universal jurisdiction over persons suspected of having committed all such acts. With the entry into force of the International Criminal Court, individuals can be held accountable for war crimes committed in non-international armed conflict. While individuals do not have specific duties under IHRL treaties, IHRL does provide for individual criminal responsibility for violations that may constitute international crimes, such as genocide, crimes against humanity and torture. These crimes are also subject to universal jurisdiction. The International Criminal Court has jurisdiction over violations of both IHL and IHRL.

The human rights treaties and other documents, specifically of recent origin, have incorporated provisions from both human rights and IHL. Some examples are the Convention on the Rights of the Child of 1989 and its Optional Protocol of 2000 on the involvement of children in armed conflict; the Rome S tatute of the International Criminal Court, the 2006 Basic Principles and Guidelines on the Right to a Remedy and Reparation for Victims of Gross Violations of International Human Rights Law and Serious Violations of International; and the Convention for the Protection of All Persons from Enforced Disappearance. The provisions of the Common Article 3 support the growing acceptance that human beings are entitled to certain basic, fundamental rights even in times of internal armed conflict. By gaining acceptance first as customary law , then as a set of criminal prohibitions, Common Article 3 demonstrates the convergence of IHRL and IHL. The humanization of IHL and its penetration into non-national armed conflicts has also influenced other developments, such as expanding prohibitions and restrictions on the use of certain weapons, especially those that make it impossible to distinguish between civilians and combatants, such as anti-personnel mines, and chemical and biological weapons. It would be impossible to completely compartmentalize IHLand IHRL. While their origins and developments are quite distinct, recent international instruments and jurisprudent of ICJ and international tribunals have taken both into account. In times of armed conflict both bodies apply concurrently.

The Protection of Refugees and IDPs

Like IHL, international refugee law (IRL) originated out of the need to address the protection of persons in the hands of a State of which they are not nationals. IRL aims to protect and assist individuals crossing an international border because of persecution in their home countryThe 1951 Geneva Convention Relating to the Status of Refugees states that a person benefits from that status if he has a well-founded fear of being persecuted for reasons of race, religion, nationality membership of a particular social group or political opinion; is outside the country of his nationality; and is unable or, owing to such fear is unwilling to avail himself of the protection of that country; or who, not having a nationality and being outside the country of his former habitual residence as a result of such events, is unable or, owing to such fear, is unwilling to return to it".

IHL, as compared to IRL law has certain advantages in conflict situations. The four 1949 Geneva Conventions and their 1977 Additional Protocols, which constitute the core of IHL, have been ratified by a larger majority of the States as compared to the 1951 Refugee Convention and its 1967 Protocol. The fundamental rules of IHLare not only codified as treaty law but have also become customary law They apply in all circumstances, regardless of whether a Party to an armed conflict has formally accepted them or not. The rules of IHL govern not only the conduct of S tates, or those representing a State but also the conduct of individuals. Violation of these rules incurs individual criminal responsibility , during international armed conflicts as also internal armed conflicts. When refugees find themselves under the territorial control of a non-governmental entity in a situation of non-international (internal) armed conflict, they would be entitled to protection afforded by IHL.

In an armed conflict, refugees are under the dual protection of IRL and IHL, which may apply concurrently. IHL and refugee law, instead of applying concurrently, or even successively forming a sort of continuum in terms of protection. Both as civilians and as persons who do not enjoy the protection of their government, refugees are protected by IHL and by customary law, in international and non-international armed conflict. In other words, protection by IRL does not result in the abolition of the broader rights granted by IHL. For example, Article 5 of the Refugee Convention provides: "Nothing in this Convention shall be deemed to impair any rights and benefits granted by a Contracting State to refugees apart from this Convention."

While defining the term "refugee", the 1951 Conventions also provides 'exclusion clauses'. An individual cannot be considered a refugee if he has committed a crime against peace, a war crime, or a crime against humanity; as defined in the relevant international instruments; or if he has committed a serious common law crime outside the country of refuge prior to his admission to that country as a refugee; or if he has been guilty of acts contrary to the purposes and principles of the United Nations. However, even if IRL does not afford protection to such individuals, IHRL and IHL remain applicable and they are entitled to the 'fundamental guarantees' under Article 75 of the Additional Protocol I.

IHL (in non-international armed conflict) and IHRL are applicable to those fleeing from one location to another inside the borders of their own country, i.e., to internally displaced persons (IDPs). The UN Guiding Principles on Internal Displacement (1998) are not legally binding; but its provisions, for the most part, are derived by analogy from IHL, human rights law and refugee law. IHL prohibits hostage-taking (in both international and non-international armed conflicts), and applies directly to all parties to an armed conflict, not only to government armed forces or where the actions can be attributed to the government through a chain of command or control or a failure to act to prevent them. IHL provides certain standards for the minimum humane treatment of persons whose liberty has been restricted in both international and non-international armed conflicts.

ICRC and Protection of Refugees and IDPs

In 1946, one year after the end of theWW II, out of 1.7 million refugees in Europe, Africa and the Middle East, nearly 320,000 refugees were placed under the ICRC's responsibility. When the International Refugee Organization (IRO) was established in 1947, the activities of the ICRC gradually tapered off. The activities of the ICRC on behalf of IDPs are at the heart of its mandate. In all its work in connection with armed conflicts it has provided protection and assistance to the entire civilian population including women, children and the elderly Besides the extensive operations deployed by the ICRC in the 1980s and 1990s in Ethiopia, Sudan, Angola and Mozambique, particular mention must be made of the one it conducted in Rwanda in aid of one million civilians displaced by hostilities in 1993 and 1.2 million in 1994.The ICRC is currently working to help millions of IDPs in nearly fifty countries. [15] During the year 2009, ICRC activities to ensure economic security directly benefited households and communities in 37 countries. More than 4 million IDPs, returnees, residents and people deprived of their freedom received aid.

In Resolution XXI of the ICRC Movement adopted by the 24th International Conference of the Red Cross in Manila in 1981, it was emphasized that the primary responsibility for refugee protection and assistance lies with governments. Furthermore, in legal terms UNHCR has a primary role in providing international protection and material assistance. The subsidiary and complementary role of the Red Cross is clearly shown by this resolution. Point 1 of the Statement of Policy emphasizes that: "The Red Cross should at all times be ready to assist and to protect refugees, displaced persons and returnees, when such victims are considered as protected persons under the Fourth Geneva Convention of 1949, or when they are considered as refugees under Article 73 of the 1977 Protocol I additional to the Geneva Conventions of 1949, or in conformity with the Statutes of the International Red Cross, especially when they cannot, in fact, benefit from any other protection or assistance, as in some cases of IDPs."[16]

In Resolution 1 of the 27th International Conference, held in Geneva in 1999, a plan of action for the years 2000-2003 was adopted. The plan

---

[15] In 2009, the ICRC ran assistance programmes in 47 countries. The bulk of the work was carried out in Afghanistan, Chad, Cote d'Ivoire, the Democratic Republic of the Congo, Georgia, Iraq, Israel and the occupied Palestinian territory, Pakistan, the Philippines, the Russian Federation, Sri Lanka, Somalia, Sudan, Uganda and Zimbabwe. Annual Report 2009, Geneva: ICRC. Available at: http://www.icrc.org/eng/resources/annual-report/index.jsp.

[16] Article 73 of AP I dealing with refugees and stateless persons provides : "Persons who, before the beginning of hostilities, were considered as stateless persons or refugees under the relevant international instruments accepted by the Parties concerned or under the national legislation of the State of refuge or State of residence shall be protected persons within the meaning of Parts I and III of the Fourth Convention, in all circumstances and without any adverse distinction."

provides for measures to be taken by the National Societies, the International Federation and the ICRC, according to their respective mandates and in accordance with international humanitarian law to aid refugees and asylum-seekers in cooperation with UNHCR, as well as internally displaced persons.

The ICRC has been mandated by the States to protect and assist victims of international and non-international armed conflicts. Refugees as civilians are protected by IHL under the fourth Geneva Convention of 1949 and the Additional Protocols I and II. In such situations, people would be protected both by IRL and IHL, the two organizations would have a parallel responsibility. In cases where UNHCR is able to discharge its mandate, the ICRC may remain available for specific tasks. For instance, it may at any time offer the services of its Central Tracing Agency.

In its written form, IHLcame into being in the mid-nineteenth century while IRL is a creation of the twentieth century. Unlike IHL, refugee law was not designed for the special circumstances existing in times of war . IHL and IRL share the strengths and weaknesses of having a field-based protection and assistance agency . In certain situations, IHL provides protections that are either stronger than or complementary to those of IRL. During armed conflict, refugee law has certain weaknesses, which can be partly corrected by IHL as both the legal systems aim at granting international protection for the unprotected.

CHAPTER 3

Laws of Air and Naval Warfare

Introduction

The laws of air and naval warfare (maritime warfare) are not to be considered as a separate branch of IHL. They contain the rules of IHLas applicable to air and maritime operations during an armed conflict. The international law regarding armed conflicts at sea has evolved from state practices. The same is the case with the rules relating to air warfare.[1] The drafting of the 1923 Hague Rules was the first attempt to codify the law of armed conflict applicable in air warfare, but these rules were never adopted by any country.[2] Subsequent international agreements have, however , included specific references to certain aspects of aerial operations. The laws of air and naval warfare are largely derived from the general law of armed conflict which is to be found in treaty law and customary international law . The body of international agreements applicable to armed conflict may be conveniently divided into two groups: the Hague and Geneva laws. Hague law deals generally with the means and methods of armed conflict. It includes the

[1] Compared with ground and naval forces, the aircraft is a relatively new weapon. The Hague Peace Conference of 1899 adopted a declaration prohibiting any aerial bombardment for a period of five y ears. At the Second Confe rence in 1907, this pr ohibition had meanwhile become the object of lengthy debate and could not be effectively renewed. Instead, a few words were inserted into Article 25 of the Hague R egulations respecting the Laws and Customs of War on Land so that the same provision governing artillery bombardment and other attacks by land forces would also apply to aerial bombardment.

[2] In 1923, the Rules of Air Warfare were informally drafted at The Hague by a Commission of Jurists (established in 1922 by the Washington Conference on the Limitation of Armament). The Hague Rules, albeit not binding, have had considerable impact on the development of the customary law of armed conflict.

Hague Conventions of 1899 and 1907. Geneva law deals generally with reducing the suffering both of combatants and civilians caused as a result of armed conflict.[3]

Basic Principles

The basic principles of IHL applicable in air and naval warfare (as also in land warfare) are distinction, military necessity unnecessary suffering, and proportionality. The principle of distinction casts an obligation in air and naval warfare to distinguish between combatant forces and the civilian population or individual civilians not taking a direct part in the hostilities. Combatants must direct the application of force solely against other combatants. For further details about the principles of IHL, please refer to Chapter 1 of the book.

Air Warfare

Since WW II, no international treaty relating to air warfare has been drawn up. More recent international agreements focus on specific issues, such as a comprehensive ban on chemical weapons (the 1993 Chemical Weapons Convention), and bans and restrictions on some conventional weapons (the 1980 Conventional Weapons Convention and its protocols). The 1954 Cultural Property Convention and Article 49 (paragraph 3) of AP I makes Section I, Part IV of AP I applicable to air and sea warfare. Though AP I contains provisions governing air warfare, it has not yet assumed due significance owing to the hesitancy shown in ratifying it.

There are secondary sources which deal with the laws of air warfare.[4] These are based on customary international law and nations are bound to

---

[3] The Geneva Laws consists of (i) Geneva Convention I of 1949 (relating to the wounded and sick in the armed forces), (i) Geneva Convention II of 1949 (relating to wounded, sick, and shipwrecked armed forces at sea), (iii) Geneva Convention III of 1949 (relating to the treatment of prisoners of war), (iv) Geneva Convention IV of 1949 (relating to the protection of civilians), (v) 1977 Additional Protocol I to the Geneva Conventions (relating to the protection of victims of international armed conflicts), (vi) 1977 Additional Protocol II to the Geneva Conventions (relating to the protection of victims of non-international armed conflicts), and (vii) 2005 Additional Protocol III to the Geneva Conventions (relating to adoption of a distinctive emblem).

[4] Some of these sources are: (i) The UK's Manual of the Law of Armed Conflict (2004); (ii) Air Force Operations and the Law (2009), published by the US's Judge Advocate General (Air) School and a vailable at: ht tp://www.afjag.af.mil/library/; (iii) The HPCR Manual on International Law Applicable to Air and Missile Warfare (2010). The HPCR Manual provides

them. Evidence of custom may be found in draft international agreements, declarations of international organizations like the UN, judicial decisions of international tribunals such as the ICTYICTR and International Criminal Court, and other acts of States. In addition, general legal practices common to the major legal systems of the world and the opinions of leading jurists may constitute some evidence of customary law.

The principal international agreement on aviation, the Convention on International Civil Aviation (Chicago Convention), establishes two separate classes of aircraft: state and civil. S tate aircraft are defined as "aircraft used in military, customs and police services". [5] A civil aircraft may be attacked if it becomes a military objective. State aircraft used in customs or police services or other non-military roles are distinct from military aircraft. Accordingly, their markings should differ from those applied to military aircraft. Military aircraft engaged exclusively in specified medical functions are subject to a separate legal regime under the 1949 Geneva Conventions.[6] Aircraft operated by private security companies or other private contractors not meeting the requirement to qualify as military aircraft, are civilian aircraft. Once a former military aircraft is operated, or commanded, by private companies, it loses its status as a military aircraft and may no longer engage in attacks in international armed conflicts, though it may carry out security functions for the government, as assigned.[7]

Military Aircraft: Military aircraft must bear a distinctive external mark indicating nationality and military character.[8] The aircraft must be under command of a person duly commissioned or enlisted in military service

---

an updates statement of existing international law applicable to air and missile warfare. The Manual and its Commentary are the results of a sixyear-long endeavor led by the Program on Humanitarian Policy and Conflict Research at Harvard University (HPCR), during which it convened an international Group of Experts to reflect on existing rules of international law applicable to air and missile warfare.

[5] Article 3, Chicago Convention.

[6] GC I Article 36; GC II Article 39-40; GC III Article 22; and AP I Articles 24-31.

[7] Commentary (para 6) Article 17 (a); The HPCR Manual on International Law Applicable to Air and Missile Warfare (2010).

[8] Every military aircraft should bear the sovereign emblem of its state as its distinctive national mark. Distinctive markings assist in distinguishing friend from foe and serve to reduce the risk of misidentification of neutral or civil aircraft. The military aircraft must not bear markings of the enemy or markings of neutral aircraft while engaging in combat. However, aircraft

and be crewed by military personnel. State practice has not established a requirement for an exclusively military crew. The British Manual defines 'military aircraft' as an aircraft operated by commissioned units of the armed forces of a state, bearing the military marks of that state, commanded by a member of the armed forces, and manned by a crew subject to regular armed forces discipline. The US government publications define military aircraft as "all aircraft operated by commissioned units of the armed forces of a nation bearing the military marking of that nation, commanded by a member of the armed forces, and manned by a crew subject to regular armed forces discipline, as well as unmanned aerial vehicles". [9] Military aircraft can be used for bombing, interdiction, rescue, transportation and reconnaissance.

Extent of Airspace: There are different views on the precise vertical and horizontal extent of airspace. For practical purposes, it can be said that the upper limit to a state' s rights in airspace is above the highest altitude at which an aircraft can fly and below the lowest possible perigee of an earth satellite in orbit. Therefore, anything in orbit or beyond can be regarded as in outer space.[10] Belligerent military aircraft may not enter neutral airspace. In case they stray , the neutral S tate can use the means at its disposal to require the aircraft to land within its territory and shall intern the aircraft and its crew for the duration of the armed conflict. Should the aircraft fail to follow the instructions to land, it may be attacked.

Military Aircrew: Military aircrews are combatants and entitled to participate in hostilities. While civilians are not entitled to participate in

---

may be used fo r military purposes wi thout bearing mil itary markings. For example, a civil aircraft might be chartered to carry troops or suppl ies. Such an airc raft may be a v alid military target for the purposes of the law of armed conflict. There is no requirement that such an aircraft be marked as a military aircraft unless used to take a direct part in hostilities. Article 13, the 1923 Hague Rules of Aerial Warfare, Part II. Article 39, AP I prohibits the use at any time by any party to a conflict of the flags, military emblems, insignia, or uniforms of neutral or other states not party to the conflict. The use of flags, military emblems, insignia, or uniforms of an adverse party is prohibited 'while engaging in attacks or in order to shield, favour or impede military operations'.

[9] Article 14 of the 1923 Hague R ules of Aerial W arfare. Though these draft rules wer e not adopted by any nation; the practices of air forces ar e often consistent wi th certain rules contained therein. Article 4(A)(4) of GC III recognizes civilian as members of military aircraft crews.

[10] Para 12.13, The UK's Manual of the Law of Armed Conflict (2004).

hostilities, those accompanying the force on military aircraft are entitled to POW status. In case civilians participate directly in hostilities, they are not protected from prosecution under the domestic law of the enemy if captured. Both military aircrew and civilian crew on military aircraft are entitled to POW status on capture by the enemy. Military aircrews on the ground are required to distinguish themselves from the civilian population in the same manner as other combatants. The captain, crew and military passengers of military aircraft must wear a clearly recognizable uniform with badges of rank at all times.[11]

When an aircraft is disabled and the occupants escape by parachute, they shall not be attacked on their descent.[12] This protection is not afforded to paratroopers descending from an aircraft; [13] it is recognized that a paratrooper can form intent to surrender while in descent, but for practical purposes it is difficult to conceive how that intent would be communicated effectively to the enemy on the ground.While in descent, downed aircrews are *hors de combat.* A person descending from a disabled aircraft who takes part in hostilities (*e.g.*, fires a weapon at the enemy) or attempts to escape loses protection and may be attacked. The destruction or an attempt at destruction of the aircraft or any equipment or related document would constitute a hostile act.[14]

Downed aircrew on the ground is subject to immediate capture and retains combatant status. On reaching the ground in territory controlled by the adversary they should be given the opportunity to surrender before being made the object of attack. They may be attacked if they take part in hostilities, resist capture, undertake evasion or escape, or are behind their own lines. Their POW status and the protection begins with their surrender or capture. A 'downed' aircrew who evades capture in enemy-held territory is, until he surrenders, a lawful target for attack. If he is captured when not in uniform he runs the risk of being treated as a spy.

---

[11] Article 44, AP I.

[12] Article 42, AP I states that a person parachuting f rom an aircraft in distress shall not be made the object of atack during his descent. Upon eaching the gound in terrtory controlled by an adverse Party, he should be given an opportunity to surender before being made the object of attack, unless it is apparent that he is engaging in a hostile act

[13] Article 42, paragraph 3, AP I.

[14] Para 12.67.1, *The UK's Manual of the Law of Armed Conflict* (2004).

There is no specific law that prohibits the use of civilian clothing or enemy uniform by downed aircrew when seeking to evade capture in enemy territory. However, if downed aircrew engages in hostilities while dressed in civilian clothing they may violate the prohibition against perfidyIf they collect intelligence information while out of uniform, or give the appearance of having done so, they risk being treated as a spy under the domestic law of the enemy if captured.The lack of a military uniform or other distinctive symbol establishing combatant status *per se* does not deprive downed aircrew of their right to POW status on capture, but it will increase the possibility that such status may be denied. Military aircrew forced to land in neutral territory due to navigational failure, combat damage, mechanical failure or other emergencies are subject to internment by the neutral State for the duration of the conflict.

Attacks on Military Objectives on the Gr ound: The general principles of the law of armed conflict apply to air attack upon military objectives on the ground. Air attacks on military objectives have the same legal standard as other means and methods of warfareIn the conduct of air attacks against targets on land, the following rules are to be followed: (i) attacks are to be directed only against military objectives; (ii) the civilian population and individual civilians must not be attacked and must be protected against the dangers arising from military operations; (iii) civilian objects are to be protected; (iv) indiscriminate attacks are prohibited; (v) cultural objects are specially protected; (vi) air bombardment must not destroy or render useless objects indispensable to the survival of the civilian population; (vii) the natural environment is to be specially protected; (viii) works and installations containing dangerous forces are to be protected from attack; (ix) attacks on non-defended localities and zones under special protection are prohibited; (x) precautions must be taken in air bombardment to avoid civilian death or injury and damage to civilian objects; (xi) unless circumstances do not permit it, efective advance warning must be given of air bombardment that may affect the civilian population.[15]

Military aircraft and other aircraft that are military objectives may be attacked by any method, means, or weapon not otherwise prohibited, including ground-to-air and air-to-air missiles, and explosives or incendiary

---

[15] Para 12.26, *The UK's Manual of the Law of Armed Conflict.*

projectiles. It is prohibited "to make any military objective located within a concentration of civilians the object of attack by airdelivered incendiary weapons". It is also prohibited "to employ laser weapons specifically designed, as their sole combat function or as one of their combat functions, to cause permanent blindness to unenhanced vision".

Missile Warfare: Missiles or unmanned combat aerial vehicles (UCAVs), whether remotely piloted or acting autonomously, may engage in attacks as long as they qualify as military aircraftActs or threats of violence in the course of missile operations cannot be pursued for the sole or primary purpose of spreading terror among the civilian population. [16] Belligerents conducting missile operations must take all possible measures to search for and collect the wounded, sick and shipwrecked, ensure their adequate care, permit their removal, exchange and transport, and search for the dead.[17] Missile attacks must be conducted in accordance with those feasible precautions applicable in case of air attack and must avoid or minimize collateral damage.

Medical Aircraft: Medial aircraft are military or civilian aircraft, designed exclusively for medical transport on a permanent or ad hoc basis and subordinate to a competent authority of a party to conflict, and must have national emblem and the distinctive emblem on their wings and hulls. [18] Medical aircraft may not be the object of attack. Unless agreed otherwise, flights over enemy or enemy-occupied territory are prohibited. Medical aircraft flying over enemy territory or close to enemy lines can be given a summons to land by the enemy to under go an inspection. The purpose of the inspection is to verify that the aircraft is being used in compliance with the Geneva Conventions. The pilot must obey this summons as refusal allows the enemy to legally open fire on it. The aircraft with its occupants must be allowed to continue its flight after examination. In the event of alighting involuntarily on land or water in enemy territory, the wounded, sick and shipwrecked, as well as the crew of the aircraft, are to be treated as POWs.

The parties to the conflict are prohibited from using their medical

[16] Article 51 (2), AP I.

[17] Article 15, GC I.

[18] Article 39, GC II; and Articles 26 (para 1), and 29, AP I.

aircraft to attempt to acquire any military advantage over an adverse party The presence of medical aircraft shall not be used in an attempt to render military objectives immune from attack. Medical aircraft shall not carry any armament except small arms and ammunition taken from the wounded, sick and shipwrecked on board and not yet handed to the proper service, and such light individual weapons as may be necessary to enable the medical personnel on board to defend themselves and the wounded, sick and shipwrecked in their charge. [19]

Naval Warfare

Development of Law: Early maritime law was designed to ameliorate conflict at sea. Perhaps the first law directly af fecting sea power was the set of customary rules governing the law of "prize", i.e., the capture of vessels in wartime. In 1618, the Dutch jurist, Hugo Grotius, set forth the natural-law doctrine of "freedom of the seas", a concept that preserved access to the seas for all nations and thereby fuelled an explosion in international trade. By 1758, the Swiss lawyer Vattel had expounded two fundamental principles of the law of neutrality that had gained widespread acceptance: belligerents were obligated to respect the neutrality of S tates remaining neutral, and a neutral State had a duty to remain impartial.

In 1856, at the end of the Crimean War, the plenipotentiaries adopted the non-binding Declaration Respecting Maritime Law in conjunction with the Treaty of Peace. A proposal for an international prize court, reduced to writing in the Convention of an International Prize Court 1907 (Hague No. XII of 1907), it never entered into force because it did not secure any state ratification. In 1909, however, the Declaration of London Concerning the Laws of Naval War adopted the doctrine of ultimate destination, which permitted capture of absolute contraband whether its route to an ultimate destination in enemy territory was direct or indirect and circuitous, through neutral state waters or ports. It was observed by several nations during World War I, although the document never entered into legal force. The first Hague Peace Conference, which met in 1899, adopted the Convention for the Adaptation to Maritime Warfare of the Principles of the Geneva Convention of 1864 (Hague III). The 1868 Additional Articles Relating to the Condition ofWounded in War provided protections for certain categories

[19] Article 28, AP I.

of persons at sea.

The second Hague Peace Conference in 1907 adopted seven treaties relating to naval operations, which include the Convention (NoVI) Relating to the Status of Enemy Merchant Ships at the Outbreak of Hostilities; the Convention (No. VII) Relating to the Conversion of Merchant Ships into Warships; the Convention (No. VIII) Relative to the Laying of Automatic Submarine Contact Mines; the Convention (No. IX) Concerning Bombardment by Naval Forces in Time of War; the Convention (No. X) for the Adaptation to Maritime Warfare of the Principles of the Geneva Convention; the Convention (No. XI) on Restrictions with Regard to the Exercise of the Right of Capture in Naval War; and the Convention (No. XIII) Concerning the Rights and Duties of Neutral Powers in Case of Maritime War. This corpus of Hague law was complemented by the Helsinki Principles on the Law of Maritime Neutrality , which codified the rules applicable to the relations between parties to a conflict and provided that neutral States should be governed by the law of peace, not war.

Customary international law and the 1936 London Protocol prohibited the destruction of enemy merchant vessels unless the passengers and crew were first disembarked and their safety assured. This rule did not apply if the merchant vessel resisted the belligerent' s right of visit and search to determine the enemy character of the vessel. DuringWorld War II, however, both the Axis and theAllies disregarded this rule and intentionally targeted the merchant ships of the enemy.

Modern Laws: The modern law regulating naval and submarine warfare could be construed from three branches of international law: the law of sea, the law of neutrality and IHL.The Second Geneva Convention of 1949 has restated customary rules of IHL applicable to international armed conflict at sea. It does not govern the use of submarine warfare. The UN Convention on the Laws of Sea is the modern source of the law of the sea. It contains various provisions regarding the non-forcible uses of ocean space by warships. In addition, certain secondary sources provide further guidelines and insight into the application of IHL in naval and submarine warfare.[20]

---

[20] Some of these secondary sour ces are: (i) The F ederal Republic of Germany Ministry of Defence Manual, Humanitarian Law in Armed Conflict (1992), (ii) San Remo Manual on

Military Objectives: Similar to the laws of air warfare, those of naval warfare state that only military objectives may be attacked. Military objectives are combatants and those objects which, by their nature, location, purpose or use, effectively contribute to the enemy's war-fighting or war-sustaining capability and whose total or partial destruction or neutralization would constitute a definite military advantage. Naval surface warships may employ their conventional weapons systems to attack enemy surface, subsurface and air targets wherever located beyond neutral territory.

The targets for naval attack include enemy warships and military aircraft, naval and military auxiliaries, naval and military bases ashore, warship construction and repair facilities, military depots and warehouses, petroleum and oil storage areas, docks, port facilities, harbours, bridges, airfields, military vehicles, armor , artillery, ammunition stores, troop concentrations and embarkation points, communication systems and other objects used to conduct or support military operations. The naval targets also include geographic targets, such as a mountain pass, and facilities that provide administrative and personnel support for military and naval operations such as barracks, communications and command and control facilities, headquarters buildings, and training areas.[21]

The economic targets for naval attack include enemy lines of communication, rail yards, bridges, industrial installations producing war-fighting products, and power generation plants. Economic targets which effectively support and sustain the enemy's war-fighting capability may also be attacked. While targeting, all reasonable precautions must be taken to ensure that only military objectives are targeted so that civilians and civilian objects are spared as much as possible from the ravages of war .[22] The intentional destruction of food, crops, livestock, drinking water and other objects indispensable to the survival of the civilian population, for the specific purpose of denying the civilian population their use, is prohibited.

International Law Applcable to Armed Conflcts at Sea (1995), (ii) The US Navy Commanders Handbook on the Law of Naval Operations (1997) and Annotated Supplement to the Commander's Handbook (1997), (iv) Fleck Dieter (2008), *The Handbook of International Humanitarian Law*, Oxford University Press.

[21] Para 8.1.1, Annotated Supplement to the Commander's Handbook (1997).

[22] Article 52, paragraph 2, AP I.

A naval commander must ensure that methods or means of warfare are used with due regard to the protection and preservation of the natural environment. He has an obligation to avoid unnecessary damage to the environment. The destruction of the natural environment not necessitated by mission accomplishment and carried out wantonly is prohibited.[23] After each engagement, belligerents must, without delay, search for and collect the shipwrecked, wounded and sick, and recover the dead.[24] The crews of captured or destroyed enemy warships, military aircraft, and naval and military auxiliaries should be made POW.

Certain classes of enemy vessels and aircraft are exempt under the law of naval warfare from capture or destruction, provided they are innocently employed in their exempt category. These specially protected vessels and aircraft must not take part in the hostilities, must not hamper the movement of combatants, must submit to identification and inspection procedures, and may be ordered out of harm's way. These specifically exempt vessels and aircraft include: (i) vessels and aircraft designated for and engaged in the exchange of POWs; (ii) properly designated and marked

---

[23] Article 35 (paragraph 3), and 55 of AP I; The 1977 Convention on the Prohibition of Military or Any Other Hostile Use of Environmental Modification Techniques (ENMOD); The UN General Assembly Resolutions A/47/37 and A/49/50, adopted on 25 November 1992 and 9 December 1994, also call upon States to incorporate into their miltary manuals guidance on the international law applicable to protection of the environment in time of armed conflict. The ICRC compiled "Guidance for Military Manuals and Instructions on the Protection of the Environment in Times of Armed Conflict," which were annexed to UN document A/49/323 (1994). Pragraph 44 of the San Remo Manual provides: "Methods and means of warfare should be employed with due regard for the natural environment taking into account the relevant rules of international law Damage to or destruction of the natural environment not justified by military necessity and carried out wantonly is prohibited."

[24] Hague Convention (X) of 1907 for the Adaptation to Maritime Warfare of the Principles of the Geneva Convention requires belligerents to "take steps to look for the shipwrecked," after each engagement, "so far as military interests permit." This obligation is addressed more stringently in GC II (Geneva Convention of 1949 for the Amelioration of the Condition of Wounded, Sick and Shipwrecked Members of Armed Forces at Sea). Article 18 of GC II does not refers to military interests, and obligates Parties to act without delay: "After each engagement, Parties to the conflict shall, without delay, take all possible measures to search for and collect the shipwrecked, wounded and sick, to protect them against pillage and ill-treatment, to ensure their adequate care, and to search for the dead and prevent their being despoiled. Whenever circumstances permit, the Parties to the conflict shall conclude local arrangements for the removal of the wounded and sick by sea from a besieged or encircled area and for the passage of medical and religious personnel and equipment on their way to that area." Article 10, AP I enunciates a general obligation to respect and protect the shipwrecked.

hospital ships, medical transports and medical aircraft; (iii) vessels charged with religious, non-military scientific or philanthropic missions; (iv) vessels and aircraft guaranteed safe conduct by prior arrangement between the belligerents; and (v) small coastal (not deep-sea) fishing vessels and small boats engaged in local coastal trade. Civilian passenger vessels at sea and civil airliners in flight are subject to capture but are exempt from destruction. If an enemy vessel or aircraft assists the enemy's military effort in any manner, it may be captured or destroyed. Refusal to provide immediate identification upon demand is ordinarily sufficient legal justification for capture or destruction.

Ruses of war are permissible in naval warfare. Unlike land and air warfare, naval warfare permits the use of false flags or military emblems.[25] In view of the technological developments, the use of false flags has almost become a negligible issue. Before opening fire, however, the true flag shall always be displayed.[26]

Interdiction of Neutral Shipping: One of the principal objectives of naval warfare is to cripple the enemy's economy. In order to achieve this, the belligerent is required to interdict his opponent's sea-borne trade and that of others whose conveyance of material to the enemy enables the latter to continue the conflict. The 1909 London Declaration was never ratified, but its final draft contained rules which conformed to recognized contemporary international law principles. In war, the peacetime freedom of the seas is heavily circumscribed by the belligerents' necessities for the successful prosecution of their struggle. Neutral merchant ships could be stopped and searched outside neutral waters. The belligerents have a right of visit and search, and could capture a ship if it is carrying goods listed as contraband by the capturing State.[27]

---

[25] Article 39, paragraph 3, AP I.

[26] Fleck Dieter (ed.). 2008. *The Handbook of International Humanitarian Law*, Oxford: Oxford University Press, p. 494.

[27] Contraband consists of goods destined for the enemy of a belligerent and that may be susceptible to use in armed conflict. Traditionally, contraband has been divided into two categories: absolute and conditional. Absolute contraband consisted of goods for use in armed conflict, such as munitions, weapons, uniforms, and the like. Conditional contraband consisted of goods equally susceptible to either peaceful or warlike purposes, such as foodstuffs, construction materials, and fuel. Belligerents may declare contraband lists at the initiation of hostilities to notify neutral nations of the type of goods considered absolute or conditional contraband, as well as those not considered to be contraband. The precise

Certain goods are exempt from capture as contraband even though destined for enemy territory. Among these items are free goods such as: (i) articles intended exclusively for the treatment of wounded and sick members of the armed forces and for the prevention of disease; (ii) medical and hospital stores, religious objects, clothing, bedding and essential foodstuffs for the civilian population in general, and women and children in particular; (iii) items destined for POWs, including individual parcels and collective relief shipments containing food, clothing, medical supplies, religious objects, and educational, cultural and athletic articles; and (iv) goods otherwise specifically exempted from capture by international convention or by special arrangement between belligerents.

During the Arab-Israeli conflicts from 1949 to the late 1950s, Egyptian forces seized Israeli goods or Israel-bound goods in both Israeli ships and vessels of third parties. An Egyptian Prize Court established in Alexandria adjudicated on the seizures, drawing extensively on prize court decisions of the two world wars. During the Indo-Pakistan conflict of 1971, India seized three Pakistani merchant ships and also boarded and searched over 100 neutral vessels. India's naval superiority further enabled attacks to be carried out on neutral shipping in Pakistani ports and a blockade of eastern Pakistan was declared. The extent and effectiveness of this blockade was not clearly established since the conflict lasted only a fortnight. India established a prize court under its 1971 Naval and Aircraft Prize Act. In both conflicts, visit, search and other measures of economic warfare were exercised largely in accordance with traditional law practice.[28] During the Vietnam conflict, the Republic of Vietnam and its ally, the US, exercised the belligerent rights of visit, search and capture of neutral ships.

Neutral coastal fishing vessels, small local trading boats, hospital ships and vessels undertaking religious, scientific or philanthropic missions are exempted from either attack or capture. Neutral vessels put themselves in the same position as enemy merchant ships if they are being convoyed by enemy warships; taking part directly in hostilities; operating under the orders

---

nature of a beligerent's contraband list may vary according to the circumstances of the conflict. Also see: Robert W. Tucker, 'The Law of War and Neutrality at Sea', (1955) XLX, US Naval War College International Law Studies p.265.

28 Fenrick, W.J., 'Legal Aspects of Targeting in the Law of Naval Warfare', (1991) Vol. XXIX, *C.Y.I.L.*, p. 238.

or control of an onboard agent of the enemy government; operating in the exclusive employ of the enemy government; transporting enemy troops or transmitting intelligence to the enemy.

The modem laws of armed conflict at sea firstly require neutral merchant ships to submit to the belligerent right of visit and search during armed conflict outside neutral waters. Visit, search and seizure are rights exercisable only by belligerent war vessels (or helicopter). The belligerent must have reasonable grounds for suspecting that the neutral ship is subject to capture for the carriage of contraband, breach of blockade or other un-neutral service. The 'reasonable grounds' requirement is founded on the fact that if there are no such grounds for suspicion, the exercise of these rights would not be necessary and proportionate for the belligerent's self-defence.[29]

Submarine Warfare

Submarines could be used in three different purposes in modern warfare: reconnaissance, anti-ship operations and land attacks. In territorial sea, a submarine has the right of innocent passage, provided it navigates on surface and shows its true flag. The right of innocent passage also exists in archipelagic waters and adjacent territorial sea, and the submarine must navigate on the surface and fly its flag. If straits used for international navigation are overlapped by territorial seas, submarines may pass through the straits exercising the right of transit passage. In exclusive economic zones and the high seas, the submarine may operate submerged.

The fundamental principles of IHL that remain applicable in submarine warfare are as follows: (i) the right of the belligerent to adopt means of injuring the enemy is not unlimited; (ii) it is prohibited to launch an attack against the civilian population and civilian objects as such; and (ii) a distinction must be made between combatants and non-combatants, and non-combatants must be spared as much as possibleThese principles govern the targeting in submarine warfare.

Attack at Sea: IHL imposes essentially the same rules on submarines as those applying to surface warships. Submarines may employ their

---

[29] D.R. Humphrey, D.R., Belligerent Interdiction of Neutral Shipping in I nternational Armed Conflict, available at: <jcsl.oxfordjournals.org> accessed 07 February 2011.

conventional weapons systems to attack enemy surface, subsurface or airborne targets wherever located beyond neutral territory Enemy warships and military aircraft, including naval and military auxiliaries, may be attacked and destroyed without warning. The rules applicable to surface warships regarding enemy ships that have surrendered in good faith, or that have indicated clearly their intention to do so, apply to submarines as well. In 1982, the Argentine cruiser *General Belgrano* was sunk by the British Churchill-class submarine *HMS Conqueror*, as it was a legitimate military objective. Commanders must take all reasonable precautions to keep civilian casualties and damage to civilian property to the minimum. The submarine commander must also consider the likely environmental damage which will result from an attack on a legitimate military objective.

Interdiction of Enemy Merchant Shipping by Submarines : The rules of naval warfare pertaining to submarine operations against enemy merchant shipping are one of the least developed areas of the IHL. Although the submarine's effectiveness as a weapons system is dependent upon its capability to remain submer ged (and thereby undetected) and despite its vulnerability when surfaced, the London Protocol of 1936 makes no distinction between submarines and surface warships with respect to attacks upon enemy merchant shipping.The London Protocol specifies that except in case of persistent refusal to stop when ordered to do so, or in the event of active resistance to capture, a warship "whether surface vessel or submarine" may not destroy an enemy merchant vessel "without having first placed passengers, crew and ship' s papers in a place of safety". The London Protocol of 1936, coupled with the customary practice of belligerents during and following World War II, imposes upon submarines the responsibility to provide for the safety of passengers and crew , and the ship' s papers before destruction of an enemy merchant vessel unless:

- The enemy merchant vessel persistently refuses to stop when duly summoned to do so.
- It actively resists visit and search or capture.
- It is sailing under convoy of enemy warships or enemy military aircraft.
- It is armed.

- It is incorporated into, or is assisting in any way the enemy's military intelligence system.

- It is acting in any capacity as a naval or military auxiliary to an enemy's armed forces.

All ships, including submarines, must "take all possible measures" to search for and collect survivors after each engagement. If such humanitarian efforts would subject the submarine to undue additional hazard or prevent it from accomplishing its military mission, the location of possible survivors should be passed at the first opportunity to a surface ship, aircraft, or shore facility capable of rendering assistance. Firing upon shipwrecked survivors in the water is clearly a war crime. In the Lhdovery Castle Case (1921), a German tribunal tried and convicted the officers of a U-boat for, "contrary to international law", firing upon and killing survivors of an unlawfully torpedoed hospital ship during World War I. In the Peleus Case (1946), a British tribunal tried and convicted the commanding of ficer of a German submarine that during World War II had systematically fired upon the survivors of a torpedoed merchant vessel as they clung to wreckage and rafts.

Enemy Vessels and Aircraft Exempt from Submarine Interdiction: The specifically exempt vehicles include:

- Cartel vessels, i.e., those designated for and engaged in the exchange of POW.

- Properly designated and marked hospital ships, medical transports and medical aircraft.

- Vessels charged with religious, non-military scientific or philanthropic missions.

- Vessels guaranteed safe conduct by prior agreement between belligerents.

- Small coastal fishing vessels and small boats engaged in local costal trade.

- Civilian passenger vessels are exempt from destruction but are subject to capture.

Submarines and Neutral Merchant Ships: Flying a neutral flag does not establish neutral character of a merchant ship. Neutral merchant vessels are subject to visit and search, but may not be captured or destroyed by submarines. Any merchant ship owned or controlled by a belligerent possesses enemy character, regardless of whether it is operating under a neutral flag or bears neutral marking. Vessels acquiring enemy character may be treated by an opposing belligerent as if they are, in fact, enemy vessels, and may be attacked. Neutral vessels may acquire enemy character when engaging in either of the following acts: (i) taking a direct part in the hostilities on the side of the enemy, (ii) acting in any capacity as a naval or auxiliary to the enemy's armed forces, (iii) operating directly under enemy control or directions, and (iv) resisting an attempt to establish identity , including visit and search. The San Remo Manual states that merchant vessels flying the flag of a neutral State may not be attacked unless they:

- Are believed to be carrying contraband or breaching a blockade, and after warning intentionally refusing to stop, or intentionally resisting visit and search.
- Engage in belligerent acts on behalf of the enemy.
- Act as auxiliaries to the enemy's armed forces.
- Sail under convoy of enemy warship or military aircraft.
- Make an effective contribution to the enemy's military action.

Naval Bombardment of LandTargets: The Hague Convention IX (1907) Respecting Bombardment by Naval Forces in Time of War establishes the general rules of naval bombardment of land targets. These rules have been further developed by customary practice in World Wars I and II, Vietnam, the Falkland conflict and the Persian Gulf conflict. Underlying these rules are the broad principles of IHL that belligerents are forbidden to make non-combatants the tar get of direct attack, that superfluous injury and unnecessary suffering are to be avoided, and that wanton destruction of property is prohibited. To give ef fect to these concepts of humanitarian law, the following general rules governing bombardment must be observed.

- The wanton or deliberate destruction of areas of concentrated civilian habitation, including cities, towns and villages, is prohibited. A military objective within a city, town or village may, however, be bombarded if required for the submission of the enemy with the minimum expenditure of time, life and physical resources. However, incidental injury to civilians, or collateral damage to civilian objects must not be excessive in the light of the military advantage anticipated by the attack.

- Medical establishments and units (both mobile and fixed), medical vehicles, and medical equipment and stores may not be deliberately bombarded. Belligerents are required to ensure that such medical facilities are, as far as possible, situated in such a manner that attacks against military targets in the vicinity do not imperil their safetyA distinctive medical emblem, a Red Cross, Red Crescent or Red Crystal is to be clearly displayed on medical establishments and units in order to identify them as entitled to protected status. If medical facilities are used for military purposes inconsistent with their humanitarian mission, the facilities become subject to attack.
- Bombardment for the sole purpose of terrorizing the civilian population is prohibited.
- Belligerents are forbidden to bombard a city or town that is undefended and that is open to immediate entry by their own or allied forces.
- An agreed demilitarized zone is also exempt from bombardment.

Naval Blockade: Blockade is a belligerent operation to prevent vessels of all nations, enemy as well as neutral, from entering or exiting specified ports or coastal areas belonging to, occupied by, or under the control of an enemy nation. The traditional rules of blockade are customary in nature, having derived their definitive form through the practice of maritime powers during the nineteenth century. The rules reflect a balance between the right of a belligerent possessing effective command of the sea to close enemy ports and coastlines to international commerce, and the right of neutral nations to carry out neutral commerce with the least possible interference from belligerent forces. The blockade is a method of warfare to which the general principles of naval warfare apply.[30]

---

[30] Use of naval blockades has been common in international conflict. During the US Civil War, the Union forces blockaded southern ports to prevent the export of cotton to Britain and

A belligerent's purpose in establishing a blockade is to deny the enemy the use of enemy and neutral vessels to transport personnel and goods to or from enemy territory. While the belligerent's right of visit and search is designed to interdict the flow of contraband goods, the belligerent's right of blockade is intended to prevent vessels, regardless of their cargo, from crossing an established and publicized cordon separating the enemy from international waters.

In order to be valid under the traditional rules of international law, a blockade must conform to the following criteria:[31]

- A blockade must be established by the government of the belligerent nation. This is usually accomplished by a declaration of the belligerent government or by the commander of the blockading force acting on behalf of his government.
- The declaration should include, as a minimum, the date the blockade is to begin, its geographical limits, and the grace period granted to neutral vessels and aircraft to leave the area to be blockaded.
- It is customary for the belligerent nation establishing the blockade to notify all affected nations of its imposition.
- In order to be valid, a blockade must be effective. To be effective, it must be maintained by a surface, air or subsurface force or other mechanism that is sufficient to render ingress or egress of the blockaded area dangerous.
- A blockade must be applied impartially to the vessels and aircraft of all nations. Discrimination by the blockading belligerent in favour

---

other countries and to prevent the import of food and supplies. During the Cuban missile crisis, the US maintained a brief naval blockade of Cuba to prevent Russian freighters from bringing missile components to Cuba. In a recent incident of May 31, 2010, the Turkish ship Mavi Marmara attempted to breach the Israel naval blockade of the coast of Gaza. Six of the seven ships of the flotilla were intercepted and escorted to port without violent incident. The Mavi Marmara was boarded by Israel military personnel and a violent clash ensued between Israel military personnel and operatives of the IHH, a radical Islamic group aboard the ship, resulting in the death of eight IHH persons, one Turkish national, and several Israel military casualties. It is believed that the sponsors of the Mavi Marmara had two objectives: one, to deliver humanitarian aid to Gaza; and two, to provoke a confrontation with Israel in the hope that they would overreact.

[31] Articles 4, 8, 9 and 12, London Declaration 1909.

of or against the vessels and aircraft of particular nations, including those of its own or those of an allied nation, renders the blockade legally invalid.

- A blockade must not bar access to or departure from neutral ports and coasts. Neutral nations retain the right to engage in neutral commerce that does not involve trade or communications originating in or destined for the blockaded area.
- Although neutral warships and military aircraft enjoy no positive right of access to blockaded areas, the belligerent imposing the blockade may authorize their entry and exit. Such special authorization may be made subject to such conditions as the blockading force considers necessary and expedient.
- Neutral vessels in distress should be authorized entry into a blockaded area, and subsequently authorized to depart, under conditions prescribed by the oficer in command of the blockading force.
- Neutral vessels engaged in the carriage of relief supplies for the civilian population and the sick and wounded should be authorized to pass through the blockade cordon (Article 70, AP I).[32]

The passage of a vessel through a blockaded area or entrance into it, without special entry or exit authorization from the S tate imposing the blockade, is considered a breach of the blockade. If there are reasonable grounds to believe it has breached a naval blockade, the State imposing the blockade is authorized to capture the vessel, and if it resists capture and refuses to stop, after prior warning, it may be attacked.

Mines and Torpedoes: In naval warfare, mines may be used for legitimate military purposes including the denial of sea to the enemy . The parties to conflict must record the locations where they have laid mines. The laying of armed mines must be notified unless the mines can detonate only against vessels which are military objectives. It is forbidden to use free-floating mines unless: (i) they are directed against a military objective; and (ii) they become harmless within an hour after loss of control over them. After the

---

[32] Starvation of civilians as method of warfare is prohibited Article 49 and Article 54 of the AP I.

cessation of hostilities, parties to the conflict must take necessary action to remove or render harmless the mines they have laidThe mine laying states must pay due regard to the legitimate uses of the seas beyond territorial limits by, providing safe alternative routes for shipping of neutral states. Mining of neutral waters by a belligerent is prohibited.[33] It is prohibited to use torpedoes that do not sink or otherwise become harmless when they have completed their run.

Hospital Ships: Hospital ships, including military hospital ships and coastal rescue craft, while operating in compliance with Geneva Conventions, enjoy special protection and cannot be attacked, sunk or captured under any circumstances. However, in order to prevent a hospital ship from interfering with an enemy's military operations, the enemy may exercise control over it. This control includes searching the hospital ship, dictating its course, putting a commissioner on board, detaining it, or controlling its use of communications equipment.[34] The searching ensures that the hospital ship is operating in compliance with the Geneva Conventions. The enemy may dictate its course by refusing help, ordering it off or determining its direction and speed. The purpose of a commissioner on board is to ensure that the hospital ship follows the orders given it. The enemy may detain a hospital ship, but only under exceptional circumstances, and this detention may not exceed 7 days. Hospital ships are forbidden to possess or use secret codes in communication equipment.

A hospital ship, its crew and the medical personnel assigned to it are exempt from capture. These medical personnel are treated in a fundamentally different fashion than other medical personnel. The reason for this is that exempting a hospital ship from capture without exempting its crew and personnel would prevent it from carrying out its mission and would turn it into a mere derelict. The exemption from capture extends throughout the period of time the crew and personnel are assigned to the ship, whether or not they happen to be on board at the time they fall into enemy hands. Similarly, their immunity from capture may not be suspended even if there

---

33 Hague Convention VIII of 1907 Relative to the Laying of Automatic Submarine Contact Mines, Articles 1(1), (2), (3), and 5.

34 Articles 22-35, GC II (1949 Geneva Convention II for the Amelioration of the Condition of the Wounded, Sick, and Shipwrecked Members of Armed Forces at Sea); and Articles 22 and 23, AP I.

happens not to be any wounded or sick on board. Medical personnel captured while serving aboard warships or in situations other than serving aboard hospital ships can be retained by the enemy The wounded and sick aboard hospital ships or other ships become prisoners of war if captured, but the belligerent capturing them must be able to care for them before moving them.

Hospital ships may be as big or as small as a nation wishes to make them, although, for the comfort and safety of the patients on board, the GC II recommends that they be over 2,000 tons.[35] Ships may be built specifically as hospital ships, or merchant ships may be converted into hospital ships. However, once a merchant ship becomes a hospital ship, it must remain a hospital ship throughout the duration of the hostilitiesAdvance notification of 10 days is required before employment of a hospital ship.[36]

Article 43 of GC II lays down specifications on the marking of hospital ships and small crafts. All exterior surfaces of hospital ships should be white. One or more dark red crosses, as large as possible, are to be painted and displayed on each side of the hull and on the horizontal surfaces, so placed as to afford the greatest possible visibility from the sea and from the air. All hospital ships must hoist their national flag and further , if they belong to a neutral State, the flag of the Party to the conflict whose direction they have accepted. A white flag with a red cross should be flown at the mainmast as high as possible. Lifeboats of hospital ships, coastal lifeboats and small craft used by the medical service should be painted white with dark red crosses, prominently displayed. They must comply with the identification system prescribed for hospital ships. States must take adequate measures for the prevention and repression of any abuse of the distinctive signs.[37]

---

[35] This provision (Article 26) was included in GC II of 1949 because of UK' s announcement during World War II that it would refuse to recognize as protected any hospital ship of less than 3,000 tons. This announcement was in response to the large number of small rescue craft used by Germany to pick up downed pilots in the immediate vicinity of Britain's coastal defenses at a time when invasion by Germany was thought imminent.

[36] During World War I it had been the practice of Great Britain to move merchant ships in and out of medical service, prompting Germany to torpedo a number of them. Also, there were instances of hasty conversion of merchant ships into hospital ships to avoid capture, such as the German ship Rostock in the besieged port of Bordeaux in 1944. A rule requiring a 10-day advanced notification before employment of a hospital ship should prevent abuses of this sort.

[37] Articles 43-45, GC II.

If hospital ships are misused for military purposes or act in any other way contrary to their obligations, in particular by clearly resisting an order to stop, to turn away or follow a distinct code, they lose their protected status. The protection shall cease after due warning has been given.[38] The fact that the crews of ships or sick-bays are armed for the maintenance of order, for their own defence or that of the sick and wounded, would not deprive a hospital ship of protection.[39] If after due warning a hospital ship persists in breaking a condition of its exemption, it renders itself liable to capture or other necessary measures to enforce compliance.[40]

---

[38] Article 34, GC II.

[39] Article 35 (1), GC II.

[40] San Remo Manual, para 50.

CHAPTER 4

IHL in Internal Armed Conflicts

Introduction

The rules of IHL have evolved by balancing military necessity and concern for humanity. These rules seek to protect persons who are not, or are no longer, taking direct part in hostilities - such as civilians, prisoners of war and other detainees, and the injured and sick. They also restrict the means and methods of warfare to avoid unnecessary suf fering and destruction. IHL is applicable to any armed conflict, whether international or non-international and irrespective of the origin of the conflict. It also applies to situations of occupation arising from an armed conflict. Different legal regimes apply to international armed conflicts, which are between S tates, and non-international (or internal) armed conflicts, which take place within a State. States are obliged to comply with the rules of IHIto which they are bound by treaty or which form part of customary international law. These rules also apply to non-State actors.

International law applicable to non-international armed conflicts includes Article 3 common to the Geneva Conventions of 1949 as the basic principles of IHL; Additional Protocol II of 1977 and all other conventions applicable to non-international armed conflicts; the customary principles and rules of IHL on the conduct of hostilities and the protection of victims applicable to non-international armed conflicts; principles and rules of international law guaranteeing fundamental human rights; and the rules of international law applicable in internal armed conflicts relating to war crimes, crimes against humanity, genocide and other international crimes.

Article 3 Common to the Geneva Conventions of 1949

Martens clause, a provision contained in the Preamble of the Hague Convention of 1907 stipulate that in cases not included in the Regulations 'the inhabitants and the belligerents remain under the protection of the principles of the law of nations, as these result from the usages established among civilized peoples, from the laws of humanity and from the dictates of public conscience.' However, until the adoption of the 1949 Geneva Conventions, the IHL applied only to international armed conflicts. After that IHL became applicable in non-international armed conflicts by the adoption of Article 3 common to the 1949 Geneva Conventions, which introduced three major innovations into international law:

- The norms of international law became applicable to the relationship between a State and its own citizens/residents, a relationship which had up to then been regarded as a matter within the sovereign powers of the State, regulated only by its own domestic legal system.
- These norms became applicable not only to the armed forces of a States, but also to non-State actors, namely organized armed groups that did not belong to a State and were involved in an armed conflict with the S tate's armed forces or with other armed groups in its territory.
- A role for the International Committee of the Red Cross (ICRC) was introduced in non-international armed conflicts.

Article 3 common to the four Geneva Conventions of 1949 (CA 3) provides:

Conflicts not of an international character

In the case of armed conflict not of an international character occurring in the territory of one of the High Contracting Parties, each Party to the conflict shall be bound to apply , as a minimum, the following provisions:

(1) Persons taking no active part in the hostilities, including members of armed forces who have laid down their arms and those placed *hors de combat* by sickness, wounds, detention, or any other cause, shall in all circumstances be treated

humanely, without any adverse distinction founded on race, colour, religion or faith, sex, birth or wealth, or any other similar criteria.

To this end, the following acts are and shall remain prohibited at any time and in any place whatsoever with respect to the above-mentioned persons:

(a) violence to life and person, in particular murder of all kinds, mutilation, cruel treatment and torture;

(b) taking of hostages;

(c) outrages upon personal dignity , in particular humiliating and degrading treatment;

(d) the passing of sentences and the carrying out of executions without previous judgement pronounced by a regularly constituted court, af fording all the judicial guarantees which are recognized as indispensable by civilized peoples.

(2) The wounded and sick shall be collected and cared for . An impartial humanitarian body, such as the ICRC, may offer its services to the Parties to the conflict.

The Parties to the conflict should further endeavour to bring into force, by means of special agreements, all or part of the other provisions of the present Convention.

The application of the preceding provisions shall not af fect the legal status of the Parties to the conflict.

The CA 3 is an attempt to provide the minimum humanitarian protection to victims in an internal conflict and has therefore also been referred to as a 'Convention in miniature'. It is the only provision of the four Geneva Conventions that directly applies to internal armed conflicts. The text of the Article 3 states that it is applicable "in the case of armed conflict not of an international character occurring in the territory of one of the High Contracting Parties". The emphasis is on basic humane treatment and minimum procedural guarantees. The article imposes on the Parties to an internal conflict, certain legal obligations for the protection of those individuals who have not, or are no longer , actively participating in the hostilities. In contrast to human rights law , which generally restrains violations inflicted only by a government and its agents, the CA 3 expressly binds both government and opposing forces.

It forbids murder, mutilation, cruel treatment and torture, and other outrages upon personal dignity, and the passing of sentences and carrying out executions other than by duly constituted court observing internationally recognized norms of due process.The last paragraph of the CA3 states that the application of the preceding provisions shall not affect the legal status of the Parties to the conflict. This clause is essential because it leaves one in no doubt that the object of the article is purely humanitarian and that it is in no way concerned with the internal affairs of States.

In the *Tadic* jurisdiction decision, the International Criminal Tribunal for the Former Yugoslavia (ICTY) looked at the content of customary law applicable in internal armed conflict and held that the common Article 3 had become a part of customary law[1] In the *Akayesu* case, the International Criminal Tribunal for Rwanda (ICTR) held that the norms of the common Article 3 have acquired the status of customary law and that most S tates had by their domestic penal codes criminalized acts which committed during internal armed conflict, would constitute violations of the Article 3.[2]

Shortcomings of CA 3

The world has witnessed a number of internal conflicts world over since the adoption of the Geneva Conventions of 1949. However , the CA3 has hardly ever been applied in these non-international armed conflicts.When Algeria sought to attain political independence from France in 1954; Congo gained its independence from Belgium in 1960; or Bangladesh attained independence from Pakistan in 1971; the governments in power refused to accept that the situations were of international concern. The governments maintained that the affairs were essentially within the domestic jurisdiction. In certain internal conflicts, though the laws of war were observed to some extent, the CA 3 failed to alleviate the suffering caused by hostilities. In Yemen, for example, the ICRC was allowed to visit a few POW camps and

1 *The Prosecutor v. Tadic*, case No. IT-94-1-A, Appeals Chamber Judgment of 15 July 1999.

2 *The Prosecutor v. Jean-Paul Akayesu*, Case No. ICTR-96-4-T, Trial Chamber I, 30 May 1996.

arrange the exchange of prisoners. In Rwanda and Bosnia, there were widespread violations of the basic principles of IHL, although the parties to the conflicts had agreed to apply the CA 3. Gross violations of the CA 3 have occurred during the recent conflict in Sri Lanka and there have been very little concern even for civilians.

The major drawback in the implementation of the CA3 has been that the term 'non-international armed conflict' has not been defined. Another reason as to why it has not been applied by governments is that it imposes a few essential obligations which a government must respect on a regular basis under its own civil or penal laws while dealing with common criminals. There is also no modality to ensure that the dissident groups also observe the fundamental guarantee contained in it. In situations where governments have used armed police rather than the armed forces to counter insurgency, they have legitimately declined to implement the provisions of the CA 3 on the grounds that the situation did not warrant it. In practice, low intensity conflicts are not considered armed conflicts. An armed conflict between two or more insurgent fractions could be regulated by the CA 3, but then again the issue of the absence of a monitoring body makes the provision ineffective.

The CA 3 fails to include rules that govern the means and methods of warfare, and therefore does not explicitly protect the civilian population from attacks or the efects of such attacks. Moreover, none of the provisions of the CA3 mention the words 'civilian'or 'combatants'. However, the CA 3 does explicitly prohibit 'violence to life and person' of 'persons taking no active part in the hostilities'.

There is no internationally administered supervisory body for the implementation of the CA3. The only provision made in this regard is that an impartial humanitarian body, such as the ICRC may offer its services to the Parties to a conflict.Though a State may or may not accept this offer, in practice any offer made by the ICRC is generally not rejected. However , the State party accepting the offer, usually defines the limits of service in such a way as to preserve the appearance of compliance while enjoying the putative benefits of violence.

The CA 3 says that its application shall not af fect the legal status of the Parties to the conflict. However , any declaration made by a S tate to accept its application in the case of an armed rebellion targeted against it would tantamount to recognizing the armed rebellion or conferring upon it a belligerent status which would entail the application of the law of armed conflict to that situation.The decision of a State in such a situation is based less on the reasons of humanitarian consideration than on political concern.

Additional Protocol II of 1977

In 1977, there was a major revision of the Geneva Conventions and two Additional Protocols (AP I and II) to the Geneva Conventions of 1949 were adopted. The first dealt with international armed conflict, whereas the second concerned with protection of victims of non-international armed conflicts.

The Martens Clause included in the Preamble of theAP II holds cases that are not protected under the Protocol, would still be subject to the principles of humanity and the dictates of public conscience.The principle of humanity complements and limits the doctrine of military necessity by proscribing direct attacks against the civilian population and the use of violent acts which result in unnecessary suffering. The AP II refers to the principle of humanity as contained the customary law principle of civilian immunity and the principle of distinction in United Nations Resolution 2444, to internal armed conflicts.[3]

Articles 1 and 2 of theAP II contain the scope of its applicationArticle 2 provides that all persons affected by an armed conflict are to receive protection under the Protocol, without any adverse distinction based on race, colour, sex, language, religion or belief, political opinion, national or social origin, wealth or other status.

While the CA 3 does not define the term 'non-international armed conflict', Article 1 of the AP II defines it as "armed conflicts which are not

[3] Resolution 2444 (XXIII) of the UN General Assembly, 19 December 1968. Respect for Human Rights in Armed Conflicts. ItAffirms' resolution XXVIII of the XXth International Conference of the Red Cross held at Vienna in 1965, which laid down, "the following principles for observance by all governmental and other authorties responsible for action in armed conflicts: (a) That the right of the parties to a conflict to adopt means of injuring the enemy is not unlimited; (b) That it is prohibited to launch attacks against the civilian populations as such; and (c) That distinction must be made at all times between persons taking part in the hostilities and members of the civilian population to the effect that the latter be spared as much as possible". These fundamental humanitarian law principles apply in both international and internal conflicts.

covered by Article 1 of the Additional Protocol I (international armed conflicts) and which take place in the territory of a High Contracting Party between its armed forces and dissident armed forces or other or ganized armed groups which, under responsible command, exercise such control over a part of its territory as to enable them to carry out sustained and concerted military operations and to implement this Protocol." Thus, according to the AP II the terms applies only to the most intense and lage-scale conflicts. The requirements of control over a part of the territory of the State, and the ability to carry out sustained and concerted military operations, make the AP II armed conflicts similar in many respects to international armed conflicts.

Article 3 of the AP II provides that the Protocol cannot be invoked to affect a State's sovereignty, its responsibility to maintain or re-establish law and order or its defence of national unity and territorial integrity . It further provides that the Protocol cannot justify any intervention, either direct or indirect, in a conflict or in the internal or external affairs of the State.

Article 4 on fundamental guarantees relates to civilians who either do not take part in the hostilities or who have ceased to take part in hostilities. It specifically prohibits the "order of no quarter". It also prohibits the following acts "at any time and in any place":

- violence to the life, health and physical or mental well-being of persons, in particular murder as well as cruel treatment such as torture, mutilation or any form of corporal punishment;
- collective punishments;
- taking of hostages;
- acts of terrorism;
- outrages upon personal dignity , in particular humiliating and degrading treatment, rape, enforced prostitution and any form or indecent assault;
- slavery and the slave trade in all their forms;
- pillage;

- threats to commit any of the foregoing acts.

Article 4 (3) provides detailed protection to children and, in particular guarantees the right to education, including religious and moral education; and the reunion of families temporarily separated. It provides that children who have not attained the age of fifteen years shall neither be recruited in the armed forces or groups nor be allowed to take part in hostilities. In case children below the age of fifteen years take a direct part in hostilities, they shall be provided special protection. Children temporarily removed from the areas of hostility to safer locations must be accompanied by persons responsible for their safety and well-being.

Article 5 of the Protocol deals with persons whose liberty has been restricted for reasons related to the armed conflict. It covers essential aspects of treatment which must be observed as a minimum in all cases (medical treatment, food, water, freedom of religion, etc.), and also other important issues like accommodation, communication, and medical experimentation. Article 5 does not have any provision relating to visit by impartial bodies to places of detention, whereasArticle 126 of the third Geneva Convention refers to such visits. Thus the Protocol allows a detaining power to ensure a complete cloak of secrecy around the treatment meted out to detainees.

Article 6 of the Protocol applies to the prosecution and punishment of perpetrators of criminal of fences related to armed conflicts. It states that no sentence shall be passed and no penalty shall be executed on a person found guilty of an offence except pursuant to a conviction pronounced by a court offering the essential guarantees of independence and impartialityIn particular, these guarantees require that an accused must be informed about the details of the offence alleged against him and he must be af forded all the necessary rights and means of defence during the trial. These rights are based on Article 14 of the ICCPR relating to the right to a fair trialArticle 6 also requires that the death penalty not be pronounced on persons who were under the age of 18 years at the time of the ofence and not be carried out on pregnant women or mothers of young children. At the end of hostilities, an endeavour must be made by the authorities in power to grant amnesty to persons who have participated in the armed conflict, or those deprived of their liberty for reasons related to the armed conflict.

The Protocol also provides rules for the treatment of the wounded, sick and shipwrecked (Articles 7 and 8), and the protection of medical and religious personnel, and medical units and transports (Articles 9 to 11). Article 12 provides for the display and respect of the distinctive emblem of the Red Cross. The provisions for the protection of the civilian population and cultural property are contained in Articles 13 to 18. Article 13 which relates to civilian immunity does not define the terms 'individual civilians' and 'civilian population'. The Protocol covers not only the peaceable population, but also civilians who participate or have participated in hostilities without a combatant status. While taking a direct or active role in hostilities, these individuals forfeit their immunity from direct attack, but retain their status as civilians. Unlike combatants, once their participation ceases, these civilians may no longer be attacked, although they may be subject to trial and punishment by the adverse party for having assumed the role of a combatant. The provisions relating to dissemination, ratification, signature, accession, denunciation and registration are contained in the last part (Articles 19 to 28) of the Protocol.

Unlike the Geneva Conventions of 1949, the AP II has not been universally accepted and ratified. As on 31 December 2010, the Geneva Conventions of 1949, had been ratified by 190 countries, whereas the AP II had been ratified by only 165 countries. The countries which had not signed and ratified the AP II included the USA, India, Iraq, Iran, Myanmar, Pakistan, Afghanistan, Israel, and Sri Lanka.

Even countries that have ratified the Protocol have violated its provisions. For instance, Rwanda acceded to the AP II in 1984, however, breaches of the AP II were committed systematically in the country's internal conflict since the 1990s. Civilians and the wounded were attacked and murdered, as were medical staff and relief workers. In the conflict in Bosnia-Herzegovina, all parties flouted the norms of IHL and engaged in widespread rape, torture, murder and ethnic cleansing. The disproportionate and indiscriminate use of force by the Russian military in Chechnya and the attacks against civilians were against the principles of IHL. The internal armed conflicts in El Salvador and the Philippines are among the few where both the government forces and the insurgents accepted the application of the AP II.

Customary Rules of IHL

The recent study on customary IHL published by the ICRC in 2005, demonstrates that that customary international law regulates non-international armed conflict in more details than does treaty law. Out of a total of 161 rules of IHL listed in the study, 147 relate to non-international armed conflicts. The most significant contribution of customary IHLto the regulations of internal armed conflict is that it goes beyond the provisions of the AP II. There are a substantial number of customary rules that are more detailed than those contained in the AP II.

Few examples of customary rules of IHL which have corresponding provisions in the AP II are: the prohibition of attacks on civilians; the obligation to respect and protect medical and religious personnel, medical units and transports; the obligation to protect medical duties; the prohibition of starvation; the prohibition of attacks on objects indispensable to the survival of the civilian population; the obligation to respect the fundamental guarantees of civilians and persons*hors de combat*, the obligation to search for and respect and protect the wounded, sick and shipwrecked; the obligation to search for and protect the dead; the obligation to protect persons deprived of their liberty; the prohibition of forced movement of civilians; and the specific protections afforded to women and children.

The general principles prohibiting the use of weapons that cause superfluous injury or unnecessary suf fering and weapons that are indiscriminate are included in the rules of customary IHL. The prohibited weapons include: poison or poisoned weapons; biological weapons; chemical weapons; expanding and exploding bullets, weapons the primary effect of which is to injure by fragments which are not detectable by X-rays in the human body; booby-traps which attached to or associated with objects and laser weapons that are specifically designed to cause permanent blindness. In addition, the use of riot-control agent and herbicides as a method of warfare is prohibited under the rules of customary IHL.[4]

---

[4] For more detai ls on the ICRC study see: Henckaerts Jean-Marie, Study on customary international humanitarian law: A contribution to the understanding and respect for the rule of law in armed confl ict, *International Review of the R ed Cross*, Vol. 87, No. 857, March 2005, p. 175-212.

Other relevant IHL Treaties

The 1980 Convention on Prohibition or Restrictions on the Use of Certain Conventional Weapons (CCW) which may be deemed to be excessively injurious or to have indiscriminate efects applies only to international armed conflicts. However, during the second review conference of the CCW, on 21 December 2001, an amendment to Article 1 was adopted. It states that the 1980 Convention and its annexed protocols "shall also apply to situations referred to in Article 3 common to the 1949 Geneva Conventions". This amendment entered into force as of 31 December 2010, and 72 States are party to it. The Protocols I (prohibition of the use of non-detectable fragments) and III (prohibition on the use of incendiary weapons) are therefore applicable in internal armed conflicts, if the State has ratified the amendment to Article 1 of the 1980 Convention. The Protocol II to the CCW, relating to prohibitions or restrictions on the use of mines, booby-traps and other devices imposes a strict regime of restrictions on the use of landmines in internal armed conflicts.

The 1993 ChemicalWeapons Convention prohibits all use of chemical weapons in warfare under any circumstances. It could be interpreted as including internal armed conflicts. The 1997 UN Convention on the Prohibition of the Use, Stockpiling, Production and Transfer of Anti-Personnel Mines and on Their Destruction prohibits State parties to this convention from using anti-personnel mines under any circumstancesThis treaty calls for a complete ban on the use of anti-personnel mines in all kinds of armed conflicts. The 2008 Convention on Cluster Munitions has come into force since 01 August 2010. Under Article 1 of the Convention, the State Parties are obliged not to use cluster munitions under any circumstances.

The first Review Conference of the Rome Statute of the International Criminal Court, convened in Kampala from 31 May 2010 to 1 June 2010, adopted a resolution amending the Rome Statute to bring under the jurisdiction of the Court the war crimes of (i) employing poison or poisoned weapons, (ii) employing asphyxiating, poisonous or other gases, and all analogous liquids, materials and devices, and (iii) employing bullets which expand or flatten easily in the human body , when committed in non-international armed conflicts.

Despite the vague nature of its contents, the common Article 3 represents one of the most important developments in the history of IHL. Its adoption was the first decisive step in the evolution of modern IHL. It recognized a universal standard applicable to situations of non-international armed conflict and provided minimum protection to the civilians. From the early 1950s to the middle of the 1970s, internal armed conflicts increased both in frequency and intensity. In order to enhance legal protection to civilians and combatants in internal armed conflicts, the Additional Protocol II to the Geneva Conventions was adopted in 1977. It supplements the common Article 3. There have been very few instances where the provisions of the AP II have been respected by armed groups. The main problem lies not in the content of the rules, but rather in their enforcementThe Security Council has called for parties to internal armed conflicts to respect the principles of IHL and has condemned certain acts that have been qualified as serious violations of IHL: (i) the indiscriminate attack against civilian population, (ii) mass forcible expulsion and deportation of civilians (iii) practice of ethnic cleansing, (iv) rape and detention of women, (v) attack on non-military objectives, and (vi) attack on safe areas and undefended localities. The creation of international criminal tribunals by the Security Council, and the International Criminal Court has demonstrated that the administration of justice in internal armed conflicts is possible.

CHAPTER 5

Prohibited Means and Methods in Warfare

Introduction

The St Petersburg Declaration of 1868 declared that "the only legitimate object which States should endeavour to accomplish during war is to weaken the military forces of the enemy ." It continued, "This object would be exceeded by the employment of arms which uselessly aggravate the sufferings of disabled men, or render their death inevitable" and that the use of such arms would "be contrary to the laws of humanity".A little more than 100 years later , the Additional Protocol I (AP I) to the Geneva Conventions of 1949 attempted to restrain the acts of Parties to a conflict. The Basic Rules contained in Article 35 of the AP I provide: (i) In any armed conflict, the right of the Parties to the conflict to choose methods or means of warfare is not unlimited; and (ii) It is prohibited to employ weapons, projectiles and material and methods of warfare of a nature to cause superfluous injury or unnecessary suffering. In this context, 'means' of warfare refer to the weapons of war, while 'methods' refer to the tactics and strategy applied in military operations to weaken the adversary . The treaties placing limits on methods and means of war are the Hague Convention of 1907, the 1977 Additional Protocols to the Geneva Conventions and a number of international agreements relating to specific weapons. Certain principles of IHL also place a limit on the employment of means and methods of warfare.

Principles Governing Means and Methods of Warfare

The principle of distinction prohibits all means and methods that cannot make a distinction between those who take part in hostilities i.e., combatants, and those who do not and are therefore protected (AP I, Article 48). IHL prohibits the use of an indiscriminate weapon that cannot be directed at a military target. An indiscriminate weapon is one that cannot be controlled, through design or function. Some examples of indiscriminate weapons could be anti-personnel mines, cluster munitions, drifting armed contact mines, biological weapons and long-range unguided missiles. However, a weapon is not unlawful simply because its use may cause incidental civilian casualties or collateral damage. A precision-guided munition (PGM) which can be directed at a military objective, but which may also miss its tar get because of a failure in its guidance system, is not an indiscriminate weapon because of this potential for failure. On the other hand, uncontrolled balloon-borne bombs, like those used during World War II, lack the capability of direction and are, therefore, unlawful. Where a conventional weapon is able to be directed at a target with sufficient accuracy, there is no additional obligation to use a precision-guided weapon. Free-fall or 'dumb' weapons are lawful provided that the overriding IHL principles of necessity, proportionality, unnecessary suf fering and other applicable rules are not violated.

The principle of proportionality (Article 22, 1907 Hague Regulations IV) states that even if there is a clear military target, it must not be attacked if the risk of civilians or civilian property being harmed is lar ger than the expected military advantage. A military target is an object that contributes effectively to a military operation. The definition of a military target is clear in theory but sometimes harder to apply in practice, especially when it comes to double-use facilities that may be used both by civilians and combatants. For example, a railway-track can be a legitimate military target if used for transporting military goods but if it is used for civilian purposes only it cannot be targeted.

IHL prohibits the use of weapons that increase suffering without really increasing military advantage. Anti-personnel weapons are designed to kill or disable enemy combatants, and are lawful, notwithstanding the death, pain and suffering they inflict. On the other hand, weapons that are designed to cause unnecessary suf fering or superfluous injury, for example, laser weapons designed to cause permanent blindness, poisoned projectiles and soft-nosed lead bullets (dum-dum bullets) are prohibited. Similarly, the use of projectiles and bullets manufactured from materials that are undetectable by x-rays, such as glass or clear plastic, is prohibited since they unnecessarily inhibit the treatment of wounds. [1]

The principle of military necessity is related to two other principles: unnecessary suffering and proportionality. Military necessity justifies the infliction of only that much suffering upon an enemy combatant which is necessary to bring about the submission of the enemyThe Rome Statute of the ICC provides for the prosecution of violations of military necessity: Articles 8 (2) (a) (iv) and 8 (2) (b) (xiii) state that intentionally launching an attack knowing it will cause excessive death or damage; and destroying or seizing enemy property would be a war crime.

In addition to these principles, chivalry has long been associated with the conduct of soldiers in warfare. It demands a certain amount of fairness during combat, and a degree of mutual respect and trust between opposing forces. It denounces and forbids dishonourable means, expedients, or conduct that would constitute a breach of trustAn example of dishonourable conduct is perfidy, i.e., committing a hostile act under the cover of a legal protection. Pretending to be a civilian, incapacitated by wounds, or otherwise pretending to have a protected status is also a form of perfidy. For further details on these principles, please refer to Chapter 1 of the book.

Prohibited Weapons in Warfare

Weapons which cause unnecessary suf fering or superfluous injury are proscribed by the Regulations annexed to the Hague Convention of 1907 and by the Additional Protocol I of 1977. The 1907 Convention draws particular attention to the employment of poison and poisoned weapons. There are other conventions and laws in which attempts have been made by the international community to control the use of particular weaponsA list of these treaties is placed at the end of this chapter . The following weapons causing superfluous injuries or unnecessary suffering have been

---

[1] Under Article 3 (a) of the Statute of the International Criminal T ribunal for the F ormer Yugoslavia (ICTY), the employment of weapons calculated to cause unnecessary suffering is regarded as a violation of the laws and customs of war giving rise to individual criminal responsibility. Article 8 (2) (b) (xx) of the R ome Statute of the ICC states: ".....employing weapons, projectiles and material and methods of warfare which are of a nature to cause superfluous injury or unnecessary sufering or which ae inherently indiscriminate in violation of the international law of the armed conflict," would be a war crime.

prohibited. The prohibition is applicable in international armed conflicts and limited to only those S tates which are party to these treaties or conventions. Some of the provisions of these treaties are universally applicable because they are considered customary international law.

1. **Poison or Poisonous Weapons.** Article 23 (a) of the Hague Regulations of 1899/1907 prohibits the employment of poison or poisonous weapons. The use of poison and poisonous weapons was prohibited by many ancient cultures because it was thought to be cowardly and unworthy of a warrior . The modern prohibition law is founded on the fact that as a weapon, poison is inherently indiscriminate and may cause superfluous injury or unnecessary suffering. The use of poison referred to in the document relates mainly to the poisoning of drinking water or foodstuff likely to be used by enemy forces, while poisoned weapons include poisoned arrows or spears. Article 8 (2) (b) (xvii) of the Rome Statute calls "employing poison or poisoned weapons" a war crime.

2. **Incendiary and Explosive Bullets.**An incendiary bullet is intended to cause harm through a burn injury, while an exploding bullet is intended to cause harm through an explosive ef fect. The use of incendiary or exploding bullets weighing less than 400g is prohibited by the S t Petersburg Declaration of 1868. The use of exploding rounds in an anti-aircraft or anti-vehicle role is not prohibited, although in combat such rounds may incidentally hit personnel as well as the intended target.

3. **Expanding Bullets.** An expanding bullet expands or flattens easily in the human body, e.g., a bullet which has a hard envelope that does not entirely cover the core, or one that has incisions.The use of expanding dum-dum bullets in international armed conflict is prohibited by the 1899 Hague Declaration (IV , 3) Concerning Expanding Bullets. The unlawfulness of expanding bullets is one of the most well-known provisions of modern IHLThe prohibition does not apply to domestic policing, in which soft-nosed bullets may be used because of their ability to remove a threat immediately and with the least risk of incidental injury to others.

4. **Poisonous Gases**. Following the extensive use of chemical

weapons, such as chlorine and mustard gas, during the First Wrld War, the international community agreed to strengthen the existing legislation on these weapons so as to prevent their future use. This led Member States of the League of Nations to sign the Protocol for the prohibition of the use in war of asphyxiating, poisonous or other gases and of bacteriological methods of warfare on 17 June 1925. This treaty, which is usually referred to as the Geneva Protocol of 1925, entered into force on 8 February 1928. The Protocol prohibits "the use in war of asphyxiating, poisonous or other gases and of all analogous liquids, materials or devices" and also "extends this prohibition to the use of bacteriological methods of warfare".

5. **Mines**

A. **Anti-personnel Mines.** An 'anti-personnel mine' is a munition designed to be placed under , on or near the ground or other surface area and to be exploded by the presence of or proximity or contact with a person and that will incapacitate, injure or kill one or more persons. The 1997 Anti-Personnel Mine Ban Convention (APMBC) prohibits the production, stockpiling, transfer and use of all anti-personnel mines. Although it has many of the characteristics of a disarmament treatyits purpose is humanitarian. Countries like the USA, India, China and Pakistan have not signed theAPMBC. However, there is every reason to believe that the prohibition of anti-personnel mines will gradually become a part of customary international law.

The 1980 Convention on Certain Conventional Weapons (CCW) has two protocols regulating all landmines, booby-traps and other devices. Protocol II of the CCW treats landmines at par with booby-traps in so far as prohibitions and restrictions are concerned. Article 5 places limitations on the employment of remotely delivered mines, especially by requiring the use of an effective self-neutralization mechanism to render such mines harmless once they stop serving military purposes.

In 1996, the Protocol II was amended to prohibit the use of certain types of landmines equipped with (i) a mechanism designed to detonate the munition in response to the operation of commonly available mine detectors; or with (ii) an anti-handling device capable of functioning after the mine has been deactivated. The amended text forbids the use of non-detectable anti-personnel mines and stipulates that such mines must either be equipped with a self-deactivating device or be placed in an area marked, fenced and monitored by military personnel.

B. **Booby-traps.** A 'booby-trap' is a device which is created or adapted so as to kill or injure. It functions when a person disturbs or approaches an apparently harmless object or performs an apparently safe act. Article 6 of the Protocol II of the 1980 Convention prohibits the use of booby-traps in the following circumstances:

   a. In the form of an apparently harmless portable object which is specifically designed and constructed to contain explosive material and to detonate when it is disturbed or approached;

   b. In any way attached to or associated with internationally recognized protective emblems, sick, wounded or dead persons; burial or cremation sites; medical facilities, equipments, supplies or transportation; childrens toys and other portable objects specifically designed for the feeding, health, hygiene, clothing or education of children; food or drinks; kitchen utensils or appliances, except in military locations; object of a religious nature; historic monuments, works of art or places of worship; animals and their carcasses;

   c. Designed to cause superfluous injury or unnecessary suffering.

C. **Anti-Vehicle Landmines.** An anti-vehicle mine is any munition placed under, on or near the ground and designed to be detonated or exploded by the presence of or proximity or contact with a vehicle. Anti-vehicle landmines are largely synonymous with anti-armour mines or anti tank mines, which are anti-vehicle mines of sufficient power to destroy armoured vehicles. Such weapons are also referred to as 'mines other than anti-personnel mines' (MOTAPM). Anti-vehicle landmines may be deployed only against or to protect military objectives and feasible precautions must be taken to protect civilians from their effects. It is prohibited to use anti-vehicle mines:

a. against the civilian population or individual civilians;

b. that use a method of delivery which cannot be directed at a specific military objective;

c. by placement which is not on or directed against a military objective;

d. that can be expected to cause incidental loss of civilian life, injury or damage which would be excessive in relation to the military advantage anticipated;

e. that are designed to cause unnecessary suffering;

f. that use fragments to wound which cannot be detected in the body by X-rays;

g. that detonate in the presence of a mine detector;

h. that use an anti-handling device which is capable of functioning after the mine is deactivated.

D. **Naval Mines.** Modern naval mines are technologically advanced and are controlled, meaning that they have no destructive capability until activated by some form of arming order. They can be supervised and hence, the principle of distinction has no bearing on them. Sophisticated naval mines, that are designed to seek out and destroy submarines, obviously do not pose any risk to surface ships. Some naval mines are even fitted with sensors activated by particular types of surface warships. However, not every naval mine in use at present is so sophisticated. Naval mines not equipped with a high-technology target selection device or free-floating mines can indiscriminately endanger ships, including neutral vessels, merchant ships and passenger liners. These mines can also affect neutral territory if they get swept away by currents.

6. **Torpedoes.** A torpedo, having run its course, may lie in water like a free-floating mine and cause danger to a neutral target. Article 1 (3) of The Hague Convention (VIII) prohibits the use of torpedoes which do not become harmless once they have missed their mark.

7. **Explosive Remnants of War.** The problem of explosive remnants of war (ERW) has become more and more alarming in recent years. The rapidly expanding use of mass-produced cluster munitions, quality-control problems in the highly competitive international arms market and budgetary pressures in the defence industry have increased the likelihood of malfunctioning munitions posing a threat to the civilian population and military personnel long after a conflict has ended. In the 1991 Gulf War and the 2000 Kosovo conflict, ERW killed and injured more military personnel after the end of the conflict than during the conflict. ER W not only endanger the life of the civilian population, but also impede post-conflict reconstruction efforts, including the repatriation of displaced civilians.

   The CCW Protocol V was adopted in November 2003 to address the serious post-conflict humanitarian impact of ERW. The Protocol has been designed to eradicate the deadly threat that ERW pose to the civilian population and to humanitarian personnel working in post-conflict settings. It entered into force on 12 November 2006.

8. **Blinding Laser Weapons.** A blinding laser weapon is a weapon which is designed, as its sole combat function or as one of its combat functions, to cause permanent blindness to unenhanced vision. In 1996, a Protocol on Binding Laser Weapons (Protocol IV) was added to the 1980 Convention. Article 1 of the Protocol bans the use and transfer of laser weapons "as their sole combat function is to cause permanent blindness". The prohibition is inapplicable if the blinding effect is temporary or an incidental or collateral efect of the (military) employment of laser systems. Thus, lasers can be used for range-finding and target designation.

9. **Non-detectable Fragments.** Under Protocol I of the 1980 CCW, "it is prohibited to use any weapon, the primary effect of which is to injure by fragments which in the human body escape detection by X-rays". The rationale is that since such fragments cannot be detected by X-rays, they render medical treatment almost impossible and thereby , cause unnecessary suf fering. Metal fragments produced by ordinary hand grenades are not afected by the protocol, which is applicable only to materials that cannot be detected by X-rays, such as plastic or glass.

10. **Environment Altering Weapons.** The Convention on the Prohibition of Military orAny Other Hostile Use of Environmental Modification Techniques (ENMOD), 1976 prohibits the military use of climate modification techniques that are intended or could be expected to cause "widespread, long-lasting, or severe" destruction or damage to the enemy environment. For more details on the subject, please refer to Chapter 10 of the book.

11. **Incendiary Weapons.** The CCW invokes certain rules which restrict the use of incendiary weapons. An incendiary weapon is any weapon or munition which is primarily designed to set fire to objects or to cause burn injuries to persons through the action of heat and flame. Some examples are flame throwers, shells, rockets, bombs and other containers of incendiary substancesWeapons such as illuminants, tracers, smoke or signalling systems, and munitions designed to combine blast or fragmentation efects with incendiary effects are not regarded as incendiary weapons.

    Under Article 2 (1) of Protocol III of the CCW, it is prohibited in all circumstances to make the civilian population/ objects the targets of attack by incendiary weapons. Article 2 (2) forbids belligerent States from making military objects/positions located within a concentration of civilians the tar get of attack by air -delivered incendiary weapons. Article 2 (3) proscribes such attack when the incendiary weapon is not airdelivered. Protocol III does not protect combatants from incendiary weapons (napalm) when they are away from the civilian population.

    The specific rules regarding the use of incendiary weapons under the CCW are: (a) It is prohibited in all circumstances to attack the civilian population, individual citizens or civilian objects with air delivered incendiary weapons; (b) It is prohibited in all circumstances to make any military objective located within a concentration of civilians the object of attack by air -delivered incendiary weapons; (c) It is prohibited to make any military objective located within a concentration of civilians the object of attack by other than airdelivered incendiary weapons, except where the military objective is clearly separated from the civilians and all feasible precautions are taken to minimize incidental loss of civilian life and damage to civilian objects; and (d) It is prohibited to make forests or other kinds of plant cover the object of attack by incendiary weapons except when such elements are used to cover, conceal or camouflage combatants or other military objectives, or they are themselves military objectives.

12. **Cluster Munitions.** A cluster bomb consists of two primary elements: a container or dispenser; and sub-munitions, called bomblets. They may be deployed from aircraft or ground-launchers, by rocket or artillery shell. There are four main categories of sub-munition: (i) anti-personnel; (ii) anti-tank; (iii) combined ef fects munition (an anti-tank bomblet with incendiary capacity); and (iv) landmines. A cluster bomb may contain as many as 250–450 sub-munitions. Cluster bombs are capable of turning huge areas of territory into killing fields to achieve primary military objectives. They may cause immediate fatalities or injuries and undermine the strategic objectives of enemy forces.

Since cluster bombs release many small munitions over a wide area, they pose risks to civilians both during attacks and afterwards. The failure rate of sub-munitions could be between 10 and 30 per cent. During attacks, the weapons are prone to indiscriminate effects, especially in populated areas.

The 2008 Convention on Cluster Munitions prohibits all use, stockpiling, production and transfer of cluster munitions. It concerns assistance to victims, clearance of contaminated areas and destruction of stockpiles.Article 5 of the Convention provides that the state parties, in accordance with applicable international humanitarian and human rights law, shall adequately provide age- and gender-sensitive assistance, including medical care, rehabilitation and psychological support, to the victims. The Convention has come into force since August 1, 2010.

13. **Riot Control Agents.** Riot control agents are those liquids, gases and similar substances that are widely used by civil law enforcement agencies. Riot control agents, in all but the most unusual circumstances, cause transient effects that disappear within minutes of exposure. Tear gas is one example of a riot control agent. The use of such agents as a method of warfare is prohibited by the 1992 Chemical Weapons Convention. Situations in which the use of riot control agents may be considered are: (i) to control rioting prisoners of war (POWs); (ii) in rescue missions involving downed aircrew or escaped POWs; (iii) to protect supply depots, military convoys and other rear echelon areas from civil disturbances and terrorist activities; and (iv) during civil disturbance where the military is providing aid to the civil power.

Weapons of Mass Destruction

1. **Biological Weapons.** Biological warfare is the intentional use of microorganisms and toxins, generally of microbial, plant or animal origin, to produce disease and death in humans, livestock and crops. The international community adopted the Convention on the Prohibition of the Development, Production and S tockpiling of Bacteriological (Biological) and Toxin Weapons and on their Destruction on 10April 1972 (BWC).The treaty entered into force on 26 March 1975. The BWC is designed to complement the prohibition of the use of biological weapons embodied in the 1925 Geneva Protocol.

   The State Parties to BWC are prohibited from developing, producing, stockpiling, acquiring or retaining (i) microbial, biological agents, or toxins that have no justification for prophylactic, protective or other peaceful purposes; and (ii) weapons, equipment or means of delivery designed to use such agents or toxins for hostile purposes or in armed conflict. The State

Parties are under an obligation to destroy, or to divert to peaceful purposes, all agents, toxins, weapons, equipment and means of delivery, which are in their possession or under jurisdiction or control. The States are not to transfer; assist; encourage; or induce any State, or international organizations to manufacture or acquire any of the biological agents, toxins or weapons or means of delivery which can be used for hostile purposes. The BWC has been in force since 1975, but has no enforcement mechanism.

2. **Chemical Weapons.** Chemical weapons are intended to kill, seriously injure or incapacitate living systems. Choking agents such as phosgene cause death; blood agents such as cyanide-based compounds are more lethal than choking agents; and nerve agents such as *sarin* and *tabun* are still more lethal than blood agents. The use of chemicals (for example, poisoned arrows) as tools of war is almost as old as humanity. The Convention on the Prohibition of the Development, Production, Stockpiling and use of Chemical Weapons and on their Destruction was opened for signature on 13 January 1993, and entered into force on 29 April 1997 (CWC). The CWC prohibits the development, production, acquisition, stockpiling, retention, transfer and use of chemical weapons. It also forbids State parties to assist, encourage or induce anyone to be involved in such outlawed activities. Like the BWC, the CWC uses a general-purpose criterion to define its scope so that State parties have the right to conduct activities involving toxic chemicals for purposes not prohibited under the CWC. Similarly, the provisions of the CWC must also be implemented in such a way as to avoid hampering the economic and technological development of the State parties.

   The CWC stipulates that the state parties must totally destroy their existing stockpiles of chemical weapons and the related production facilities located on their territory or under their jurisdiction, or control within 10 or, under certain conditions, 15 years after the CWC's entry into force.This destruction process must be completed in such a way as to ensure the safety of the population and the protection of the environment. Finally, the CWC establishes an international system for verifying compliance.This relies on several types of verification techniques and methods that allow for the protection of national security. This verification machinery, which includes declarations by the S tate parties, routine inspections as well as means (such as challenge inspections) to investigate allegations of violations of the treaty , is operated by the Organization for the Prohibition of Chemical Weapons (OPCW). The main element of the system is factual information obtained through verification procedures in accordance with the Convention that are independently conducted by the OPCW Technical Secretariat, the sufficiency of such information being essential for successful operation.

3. **Nuclear Weapons.** A nuclear weapon is defined inArticle 5 of the Treaty of Tlatelolco as "any device which is capable of releasing nuclear energy in an uncontrolled manner and which has a group of characteristics that are appropriate for use with warlike purposes". Nuclear weapons are characterized in particular by their destructive power, the suffering caused by their use, the difficulty in bringing aid to victims, the risk of escalation and proliferation, and the dangers which such weapons pose to the environment, future generations and the survival of humanity.

   Nuclear weapons, unlike chemical or biological weapons, are not subject to any general treaty banning their use. However, they are within the ambit of the limitations on international armed conflicts. There are a number of treaties prohibiting the deployment of nuclear weapons in designated areas, such as Antarctica, outer space and the seabed; their testing, and even their possession by certain countries; establishing nuclear -free zones; and creating non-proliferation obligations. The UN has, in various resolutions, encouraged the creation of nuclear-free zones, which have become a part and parcel of the nuclear non-proliferation regime. The proposal for the establishment of a nuclearfree zone in SouthAsia has been rejected by India because it feels that the matter requires a global rather than regional approach.

   A number of authors argue that the existing conventions, such as the St Petersburg Declaration, 1968,The Hague Rules of 1907, the

Geneva Gas Protocol, 1925, the Genocide Convention, 1948, the Geneva Conventions of 1949 and the Additional Protocols of 1977, make the use of nuclear weapons an infringement of international law. The position of the ICRC on nuclear weapons (2002) is as follows:

- The principles and rules of international humanitarian law and in particular the principles of distinction and proportionality and the prohibition on causing superfluous injury or unnecessary suffering, apply to the use of nuclear weapons.
- In view of the unique characteristics of nuclear weapons, the States must ensure that these weapons are not used, irrespective of whether they consider them to be lawful or not.
- Nuclear weapons are characterized in particular by their destructive power, the unspeakable suffering caused by their use, the fact that it is extremely difficult to bring aid to victims, the fact that it is impossible to control their ef fects in space and time, the risk of escalation and proliferation which any use of nuclear weapons necessarily involves, and the dangers which such weapons entail for the environment, future generations and the survival of humanity.
- The States must take every appropriate measure to limit the risk of the proliferation of nuclear weapons and achieve a complete prohibition on nuclear weapons as well as the elimination of such weapons.

It can be argued that in a few situations, nuclear weapons can be used in conformity with the parameters of humanitarian law: (1) a strike upon troops and armour in an isolated desert region with a low-yield air-burst in conditions of no wind; and (2) detonation of 'clean' nuclear weapons against an enemy fleet in the middle of the ocean. In neither of these exceptional situations should the employment of nuclear weapons give rise to significant collateral damage to civilians. But these are hypothetical situations. Members of the nuclear club are aware of the colossal ramifications of a decision to unleash nuclear weapons in warfare. For further details on nuclear weapons, please refer to Chapter 18 of the book.

Prohibited Methods in Warfare

Article 22 of the Hague Regulations provides that the right of belligerents to adopt means of injuring the enemy is not unlimited. This statement is further strengthened by Article 35 (1) of the AP I, which states that the right of parties to an armed conflict to choose methods of combat is not unlimited. The following prohibitions apply to land, sea or air warfare and regardless of whether the conflict is of an international character or not.

Order of No Quarter

An order of 'no quarter' means that a force does not intend that any prisoners be taken, even amongst those persons who surrender or who are rendered *hors de combat* by being wounded, sick or shipwrecked. The Hague Regulations Article 23(d); AP I Article 40; AP II Article 4(1); and Rome Statute Art 8(2)(b)(xii) and 8(2)(e)(x) prohibit an order of 'no quarter'. It is prohibited to (i) declare or order that no quarter will be given; (ii) threaten an adverse party that such an order will be given; or (iii) conduct hostilities on the basis that no prisoners will be taken or that there will be no survivors. If prisoners are taken during the course of special operations in circumstances where it is impractical to detain or confine those persons, they must be released. It is not permissible to deny quarter in special operations. A person directly involved in hostilities who, at his discretion, surrenders to the armed forces of a State, must be taken prisoner, respected and protected.

Treachery and Perfidy

It is prohibited to kill, injure or capture a member of the opposing force by 'treachery' or 'perfidy'. Treachery or perfidy refers to an act intended to kill, injure or capture members of the opposing force by leading members of the opposing force to believe that they (i) are entitled to certain protections under IHL when those protections will not, in fact, be granted; or (ii) must afford the protections of IHL to a person who is not, in fact, entitled to them, and who intends to use that protection in order to carry out acts harmful to the opposing force. (Hague Regulations, Article 23 (b) and AP I, Articles 37 (1)).

In particular, it is prohibited to kill, injure or capture a member of the opposing force by feigning (i) an intent to negotiate under a flag of truce; (ii) incapacitation through wounds, sickness, or shipwreck; (iii) civilian or non-combatant status; and/or (iv) protected status by use of signs, emblems or uniforms of the United Nations or of neutral or other S tates which are not parties to the conflict; or (v) protected status of a humanitarian mission or vessel.

Improper Use of Enemy Uniforms

Closely linked with perfidy is the prohibition against using the flags, military uniform, emblems or insignia of the enemy during attacks or to shield, protect or impede military operations. (Hague Regulations, Art 23(f) and AP I Art 39(1) & (2)). For the same reason, the uniforms, etc., of neutral States or those not involved in the conflict must not be used. Enemy uniforms can be used for training purposes and POWs may use enemy uniforms to help them escape.

Ruses of War: Ruses of war may be employed in an armed conflict. A 'ruse of war' is a trick played upon the opposing force to confuse or mislead them provided that (i) the trick is not intended to lead the opposing force to believe that a protection under LOAC is being relied upon (API, Article 37 (2)); and (ii) the trick is not treacherous, such as the use of the uniforms of the enemy.

Examples of ruses of war include constructing dummy positions or tank formations, supplying disinformation as to the time or place of an attack, making use of the enemy's passwords, codes or radio frequencies to find out details of their plans, providing disinformation, leading the enemy to believe that one' s own forces are either stronger or weaker than they actually are, or laying dummy minefields.

Pillage

'Pillage', 'plunder' and 'looting' are all types of theft conducted for private gain, exploiting the circumstances of armed conflict. In particular , it is prohibited to pillage (i) towns and other places of habitation, (ii) occupied territory, (iii) the civilian population, (iv) cultural property, and (v) POWs, retained personnel, detainees, the wounded, sick and shipwrecked.[2]

While in earlier times pillage was considered a legitimate reward for the efforts of soldiering, it is now universally prohibited. It is an exhibition of undisciplined soldiers and of poor military commanders who take advantage of the chaos of battle and use their power over defenceless combatants or civilians for personal gain. S tealing is an of fence under national laws and it remains an ofence in operations. Taking of non-military items such as jewellery, household-goods, etc., is forbidden, whereas and the taking of military equipment such as weapons and ammunition, vehicles, electronic equipments, etc., is permitted. It is known as war booty and can be properly collected, accounted and used against the enemy . Where militarily useful equipment (e.g. vehicles) belongs to civilians, it may be taken but must be returned and compensation provided at the end of hostilities.

Starving of Civilians

It is prohibited to starve civilians as a method of warfare. It is also prohibited to direct attacks against, destroy, remove or render useless objects vital to their survival, such as foodstuf fs, agricultural areas for the production of food, crops, livestock, drinking water installations and supplies for irrigation works.[3] This prohibition does not apply to objects that are being used solely by the armed forces or in direct support of military action. However, if the attacks would adversely affect the civilian population, i.e., leave it with inadequate food or water, cause starvation or force it to move, then they are prohibited.

---

[2] IHL prohibits pillage of (i) towns and other places of habitation (Hague Regulations, Articles 28 and 47; R ome Statute, Article 8 (2) (b) (xvi) and 8(2)(e)(v); (ii) occupied territory (Hague Regulations, Art 47 and Geneva Convention IV, Art 33); (iii) the civilian population (Geneva Convention IV, Art 33 and AP II, Art 4(2)(g)); (iv) cultural property (Hague Cultural Property Convention 1954, Art 4); (v) POWs, retained personnel, detainees, the wounded, sick and shipwrecked (Geneva Convention I, Article 15; Geneva Convention II, Article 18 and Geneva Convention IV, Article 16).

[3] Under Article 54, Addi tional Protocol I; Article 14 , Additional Protocol II; and the R ome Statute Article 8(2)(b)(xxv) it is prohibited to (i) attack, destroy, remove or render useless objects indispensable to the survival of the civilian population, e.g., food, crops, livestock, drinking water, irrigation, etc., with the intention of causing starv ation of civilians; or (ii) impede relief supplies provided for under the Geneva Convention.

Human Shields

Human shielding involves the use of persons protected by IHL, such as POWs or civilians, to deter attacks on combatants and military objectives. Article 51 (7) of theAP I provides the specific proscription: "The presence or movement of the civilian population or individual civilians shall not be used to render certain points or areas immune from military operations, in particular in attempts to shield military objectives from attacks or to shield, favour or impede military operations. The Parties to the conflict shall not direct the movement of the civilian population or individual civilians in order to attempt to shield military objectives from attacks or to shield military operations."

Article 51(7) is a corollary toArticle 48, the general rule of distinction between combatants and military objectives on the one hand and civilians and civilian objects on the other, as well as Article 51(1), which provides that "the civilian population and individuals civilians shall enjoy general protection against dangers arising from military operations". Article 58 of AP I complements the prohibition on using civilian shields by imposing an affirmative obligation on Parties to "endeavour to remove the civilian population, individual civilians and civilian objects under their control from the vicinity of military objectives".The article further provides that parties must avoid "locating military objectives within or near densely populated areas".

Taking of Hostages

A 'hostage' is a person taken into custody from the civilian population or from amongst other persons entitled to special protection under IHL (persons in detention or *hors de combat*) to force the opposing power, or any other government or authority to take a particular course of action.The taking of hostages, which is closely related to 'human shield', is prohibited.[4]

Reprisal

It is prohibited to conduct reprisals against persons and objects protected by IHL. A 'reprisal' is an action taken by a party to a conflict, which would

---

[4] Articles 34 and 147, GC IV; Article 3 common to four Geneva Conventions; Article 75 (2(c), AP I, Article 4(2)(c), AP II; and Art 8(2)(a)(viii), Rome Statute.

otherwise be unlawful for the purpose of forcing another party to the conflict to comply with IHL. Reprisals have historically been regarded as the ultimate method of forcing an opposing force to comply with IHL. However , the consequences of reprisal and counter-reprisal can lead to a vicious cycle of atrocities in which the innocent are punished. It is unlawful to carry out reprisals against persons and objects which are protected under IHL.

Reprisals are prohibited in all circumstances against prisoners of war; the wounded, sick and shipwrecked; medical and religious personnel; civilians; civilian objects; protected buildings, equipment and vessels; cultural property; objects indispensable to the survival of the population; works containing dangerous forces; and the natural environment.[5]

The scope of reprisals is severely limited by the lawReprisals may be ordered in limited circumstances only as the last resort to make an opponent comply or fall in line with the law; or the most serious and blatant abuses of the law by the enemy . A reprisal can be ordered only at the highest political and military level - it is not the tool of a junior commander . Reprisals, in these circumstances must be proportionate to the breach committed by the adversary and it must cease when the opponent stops the violation.[6]

Torture

Torture and inhumane or degrading treatment or punishment is universally prohibited under the IHL and international human rights laws. Rape and sexual assault are forms of torture. Torturing captured soldiers or civilians to obtain information, to punish, or to humiliate them is absolutely prohibited. It is a war crime in both international and non-international armed conflicts. States are required to bring offenders to justice.[7] The prohibition applies to all levels of conflict: international, non-international,

---

[5] Article 14, GC I; Article 16, GC II; Article 13, GC III; Article 33, GC IV; Articles 20, 51 (6), 52 (1), 53 (c), 54 (4), 55 (2) and 56, AP I; Article 4(4), the Cultural Property Convention, 1954.

[6] Para 16.16, *The British Manual of the Law of the Armed Conflict* 2004. Oxford: OUP, p. 420-421.

[7] Article 17, GC III; Article 32, GC IV; and Article 8, Rome Statute. In the case of *Prosecutor v Delalic (Celebici Case)* (1996) 38 ILM 57, the International Criminal Tribunal for the Former Yugoslavia (ICTY) held that rape was capable of amounting to torture under international humanitarian law.

UN missions and situations of internal violence and disturbances (internal security operations). The argument of military necessity can never be used to justify torture.

Wanton Destruction of Enemy Property

Wanton destruction is the destruction of property which is not justified by military necessity. The related issue is unlawful appropriation of enemy property which is not justified by military necessity . In particular , it is prohibited to carry out wanton destruction and unlawful appropriation of the following:

a. Property belonging to the wounded, sick or shipwrecked, medical or religious personnel;

b. Property belonging to detainees, internees, PW or retained personnel;

c. Housing or other buildings, or personal property belonging to private persons in occupied territory;

d. Property belonging to the S tate or public authorities in occupied territory;

e. Property belonging to social or cooperative organisations in occupied territory; or

f. Property belonging to aliens in the territory of a party to the conflict.

It is prohibited to destroy or seize property belonging to the adverse Party except where demanded by military necessity. It is a grave breach to cause extensive destruction and appropriation of property not justified by military necessity and carried out unlawfully and wantonly .[8] Property of the opposing party may only be seized when required by military necessity Where private property is seized a receipt must be given and the owner must be given fair compensation.

---

[8] Article 22 (g), the Hague Regulations; Article 50, GC I, Article 51, GC II; Article 130, GC III, Article 53 and 147, GC IV; and Article 8(2) (a) (iv), the Rome Statute.

Protection of Works and Installations Containing Dangerous Forces

Works or installations containing dangerous forces, namely dams, dykes and nuclear electrical generating stations, shall not be made the object of attack, even where these objects are military objectives, if such attack may cause the release of dangerous forces and consequent severe losses among the civilian population (Article 56,AP I). Other military objectives located at or in the vicinity of these works or installations shall also not be made the object of attack if such attack may cause the release of dangerous forces from the works or installations and consequent severe losses among the civilian population. The Parties to a conflict, under Article 56 (5) of AP I, are under an obligation to avoid locating military objectives in the vicinity of dams, dykes and nuclear electrical generating stations. However, military installations positioned for the sole purpose of defending the protected works or installations from attack are permissible and should not be made the object of attack, provided that they are not used in hostilities except for defensive actions.

Attack of Persons *Hors de combat*

It is prohibited to attack a person who is *hors de combat* (out of combat). A person is *hors de combat* if he:

a. has been captured and detained by the opposing force (POW);

b. clearly expresses an intention to surrender;

c. has been rendered unconscious or is incapacitated by wounds or sickness and is therefore incapable of defending himself or herself;

d. is shipwrecked; or

e. is a member of the crew or a passenger of an aircraft in distress parachuting to the ground.

A person is *hors de combat* if incapable of continuing combat operations or has removed himself from combat through surrender. The expression does not extend to combatants of the opposing force who are running away or who are unable to defend themselves because they have been caught by surprise. It is only by surrender that an enemy combatant can deliberately remove himself or herself from being a lawful target. The protection is applicable topersons hors decombat only for such time as the person does not commit any hostile act; or escapes or resist capture.

Aircrew and passengers who are forced to bail out of their aircraft are *hors de combat* and must not be attacked during their descent. Aircrew who parachute to safety or crash-land their aircraft must be given the opportunity to surrender. However they may be attacked if they carry out any hostile act. Such acts may include attempting to destroy their aircraft or equipment or to send radio messages (Article 42 (2) (3),AP I). Airborne troops and paratroopers, on the other hand, are combatants and can be the object of attack at all times until they are rendered *hors de combat*.

Indiscriminate Attack

Indiscriminate attacks are prohibited. Indiscriminate attacks are attacks of a nature to strike military objectives and civilians and civilian objects alike (Article 51 (4), AP I). In particular it is prohibited to make attacks which: (i) are not directed at a specific military objective; or (ii) employ a means or method of warfare which cannot be directed at a specific military objective; or (iii) employ a method or means of combat the ef fects of which cannot be limited.An attack which violates the rule of proportionality would be an indiscriminate attack. An attack can be indiscriminate even if no civilians are killed or injured by it, but a grave breach would only occur if the civilian population or civilian objects are knowingly affected (Article 85 (3)(b), AP I). Acts or threats of violence, the primary purpose of which is to spread terror among civilian population are also prohibited (Article 51 (2), AP I).

Precautions in Attack

Attack means any act of violence against the opposing force, and includes offensive and defensive operations. There is a general obligation on the Parties to a conflict to take care in the conduct of military operations to spare civilians and their property and to direct their operations only against military objectives. In military parlance, the term 'conduct of military operations' has a wider meaning than 'attacks' and would include the movement or deployment of armed forces. In the conduct of military operations, precautions must be taken to spare the civilian population, civilians and civilian objects.The military commanders who plan or decide upon an attack must do everything feasible to verify that the objectives to be attacked are military objectives and are not (i) civilians or civilian objects; and (ii) subject to special protection.The commander must take all feasible precautions in the choice of means and methods of attack with a view to avoiding, and in any event to minimizing, incidental loss of civilian life, injury to civilians and damage to civilian objects. The commander must refrain from deciding to launch any attack which may be expected to cause incidental loss of civilian life, injury to civilians, damage to civilian objects, or a combination of these effects, which would be excessive in relation to the concrete and direct military advantage.[9]

An attack must be cancelled or suspended if it becomes apparent that the (i) objective is not a military one; (ii) objective is subject to special protection; or (iii) attack may be expected to cause incidental loss of civilian life, injury to civilians, damage to civilian objects, or a combination of these effects, which would be excessive in relation to the concrete and direct military advantage.Where there is a choice between diferent military objectives which, if attacked, will produce the same military advantage, the one which is expected to result in the least incidental damage, should be chosen.[10]

Precautions Against the Effects of Attack

In order to avoid loss of civilian life and property , the Parties to conflict must remove civilians and civilian objects under their control from the vicinity of military objectives.They must avoid locating military objectives within or near densely populated areas.They should also take the necessary precautions to protect civilians and civilian objects under their control against the dangers resulting from military operations. Consideration should be given to declaring certain areas as undefended or setting up demilitarized or safety zones.The attack or bombardment, by whatever means, of towns, villages, or buildings which are undefended is prohibited under Article 25 of the Hague Regulations. Under Article 59.1 of the AP I, it is prohibited for the Parties to a conflict to attack, by any means whatsoevenon-defended localities.

[9] Article 57. 2 (a), AP I.

[10] Articles 48, 49(1), 51 (1), 57.2 (b), AP I.

Legal Review of New Weapons, Means and Methods

For a State that is party to the Additional Protocol I, determining the legality of new weapons is a treaty obligation pursuant to Article 36 of the Protocol. It states:

> In the study, development, acquisition or adoption of a new weapon, means or method of warfare, a High Contracting Party is under an obligation to determine whether its employment would, in some or all circumstances, be prohibited by this Protocol or by any other rule of international law applicable to the High Contracting Party.

The aim of Article 36 is to prevent the use of weapons that would violate international law in all circumstances and to impose restrictions on the use of weapons that would violate international law in some circumstances, by determining their lawfulness before they are developed, acquired or otherwise incorporated into a State's arsenal.[11] A State party to the AP I is required by Article 36 to carry out legal reviews of weapons it is developing or acquiring. Article 36 requires each State to determine whether the employment of 'a weapon, means or method of warfare' that it studies, develops, acquires or adopts would, 'in some or all circumstances', be prohibited by international law applicable to the state.

Scope of Article 36

Article 36 of the AP I refers to weapons, means or methods of warfare. The material scope of the legal review under Article 36 is, therefore, very broad. It would cover:

- weapons of all types, be they anti-personnel or anti-material, "lethal", "non-lethal" or "less lethal", and weapons systems;
- the ways in which these weapons are to be used pursuant to military doctrine, tactics, rules of engagement, operating procedures and counter-measures;

[11] *A Guide to the Legal Review of New Weapons, Means and Methods of Warfare: Measures to Implement Article 36 of Addtional Protocol I of 1977.* 2006. Geneva: ICRC, p. 4. In 2006, in order to assist States, the ICRC prepared the Guide in consultation with military and international law experts from ten countries. Available at: http://www.icrc.org/eng/assets/files/other/icrc_002_0902.pdf, accessed 15 Mar 2011.

- all weapons to be acquired, be they procured further to research and development on the basis of military specifications, or purchased "off-the-shelf";
- a weapon which the state intends to acquire for the first time, without its necessarily being "new" in a technical sense;
- an existing weapon which is modified in a way that alters its function, or a weapon which has already passed a legal review but is subsequently modified; and
- an existing weapon where a state has joined a new international treaty which may affect the legality of the weapon.[12]

When in doubt as to whether the device or system proposed for study development or acquisition is a "weapon", legal advice should be sought from the weapons review authority. Article 36 is complemented by Article 82 of Additional Protocol I of 1977, which requires that legal advisers be available at all times to advise military commanders on IHL and "on the appropriate instruction to be given to the armed forces on this subject". Both provisions establish a framework for ensuring that armed forces will be capable of conducting hostilities in strict accordance with IHL, through legal reviews of planned means and methods of warfare.

In order to ensure that the new weapon adheres to international humanitarian law, a few states have constituted expert committee to determine: (i) the purpose of the new weapon; (ii) the factors which favour the introduction of the new weapons; (iii) the damage mechanism of the new weapon (blast, fragmentation, etc.); (iv) whether the new weapon is specifically designed to cause injury to personnel; (v) the human injuries that the new weapon is capable of inflicting; (vi) what other weapons, if any, would be capable of fulfilling the same purpose as the new weapon; (vii) whether the new weapon has been adopted by the armed forces of other states or by other agencies in the country or overseas and, if so, by which one; and (viii) whether evaluation data concerning the new weapons is available from the armed forces of other States or from other agencies.

---

[12] *A Guide to the Legal Review of New Weapons, Means and Methods of Warfare: Measures to Implement Article 36 of Additional Protocol I of 1977.* 2006. Geneva: ICRC, p. 9-10.

In assessing the legality of a particular weapon, the reviewing authority must examine not only the weapons design and characteristics (the 'means' of warfare), but also how it is to be used (the "method" of warfare), bearing in mind that the weapon' s effects will result from a combination of its design and the manner in which it is to be used. However , other S tates, whether or not they are party to the AP I, must assess the lawfulness of their new weapons in order to ensure that they are able to comply with their international legal obligations during armed conflicts and other situations of violence. Having a 'national mechanism' to review the legality of new weapons is especially relevant in view of emer ging new weapons technologies, such as directed ener gy, incapacitants, behaviour change agents, acoustics and nanotechnology.

The ICRC has called on States to establish mechanisms and procedures to determine the conformity of weapons with international lawIn particular, the 28th Conference declared: "In light of the rapid development of weapons technology and in order to protect civilians from the indiscriminate efects of weapons and combatants from unnecessary suf fering and prohibited weapons, all new weapons, means and methods of warfare should be subject to rigorous and multidisciplinary review ." However, very few States not party to Additional Protocol I have adopted formal weapons review procedures.

The obligation to review the legality of new weapons implies at least two things. First, a State should have in place some form of permanent procedure to that effect, in other words, a standing mechanism that can be automatically activated at any time that a state is developing or acquiring a new weapon. Second, such a procedure should be made mandatoryby law or by administrative directive, for the authority responsible for developing or acquiring new weapons.

List of Weapon Ban/Prohibition Treaties

TREATY Short Name	TREATY Full Name	Date of Signing	Regulation/ Ban	No. of State Parties
Certain Explosive Projectiles	Declaration Renouncing the Use, in Time of war, of Certain Explosive Projectiles. St Petersburg.	1868	Ban	20
1899 Hague Balloon Declaration	Declaration (IV, 1) to Prohibit for the Term of Five Years, the Launching of Projectiles and Explosives from Balloons, and Other methods of Similar Nature, The Hague	1899	Ban	24
Hague Gas Declaration	Declaration (IV, 2) Concerning Asphyxiating Gases, The Hague	1899	Ban	31
Hague Dum-dum Bullet Declaration	Declaration (IV, 3) Concerning Expanding Bullets, The Hague	1899	Ban	31
1907 Hague Balloon Declaration	Declaration (XIV) Prohibiting the Discharge of Projectiles and Explosives from Balloons, The Hague	1907	Ban	20
1907 Hague Sea Mines Convention	Convention (VIII) Relative to the Laying of Automatic Submarines Contact Mines, The Hague	1907	Regulation	27
Gas Convention	Treaty Relating to the Use of Submarines and Noxious Gases in Warfare, Washington	1922	Regulation and Ban	10
1925 Geneva Protocol	Protocol for the Prohibition of the Use of Asphyxiating, Poisonous or Other gases, and Bacteriological Methods of Warfare, Geneva	1925	Ban	135

Biological Weapons Convention	Convention on the Prohibition of the Development, Production and Stockpiling of Bacteriological (Biological) and Toxin Weapons and Their Destruction, London.	1972	Ban	163
ENMOD	UN Convention on the Prohibition of Military or Any Other Hostile use of Environmental Modification Techniques.	1976	Ban	73
Convention on Conventio-nal Weapons (CCW)	Convention on the Prohibition or Restrictions on the Use of Certain Conventional Weapons Which may be Deemed to be Excessively Injurious or to Have Indiscriminate Effects, Geneva	1980	Ban and Regulation	109
CCW Protocol I	Protocol I on Non-Detectable Fragments, Geneva	1980	Ban	107
CCW Protocol II on Anti-Personnel Landmines	Protocol II on Prohibition or Restrictions on the Use of Mines, Booby-traps and Other Devices, Geneva	1980	Regulation	92
CCW Protocol III on Incendiary Weapons	Protocol III on Prohibition or Restriction on the Use of Incendiary Weapons, Geneva	1980	Regulatio-ns	102
Chemical Weapons Convention	Convention on the Prohibition of the Development, Production, Stockpiling and Use of Chemical Weapons and on Their Destruction, Paris	1993	Ban	188
CCW Pro IV on Blinding Laser Weapons	Protocol IV on Blinding Laser Weapons, Geneva	1995	Ban	93

CCW Amended Protocol II	CCW Amended Protocol on Prohibition or Restrictions on the Use of Mines, Booby-traps and Other Devices, Geneva	1996	Regulation	92
Mine ban Treaty	Convention on the Prohibition of the Use, Stockpiling, Production and Transfer of Anti-Personnel Mines and Their Destruction, Ottawa	1997	Ban	156
CCW Protocol V on ERW	Protocol V on Explosive Remnants of War, Geneva.	2003	Regulation	59
Conv on Cluster Munitions	Convention on Prohibition of the use, Development and Destruction of Cluster Munitions. (1 August 2010).	2008	Ban	31

CHAPTER 6

Protection of Prisoners of War

Introduction

The humane treatment of prisoners of war (POWs) is one of the main characteristics of 'civilized war '. The principles of international law on the treatment of POWs, which have evolved gradually since the 18th century, are based on the principle that war captivity is neither revenge nor punishment, but solely protective custody, the only purpose of which is to prevent prisoners from further participation in the warThis is in accordance with the view held by all armies that it is contrary to military tradition to kill or injure helpless people. [1] International humanitarian law relating to treatment of POWs is contained in the third Geneva Convention Relative to the Treatment of Prisoners of War, 1949 (GC III). In addition, Articles 43 to 47 of theAdditional Protocol I of 1977 deal with the combatants and POWs and the issue of spies and mercenaries.

The Geneva Convention III, applies to all armed conflicts between the parties to the convention, whether war has been declared or not, and even if one of the parties refuses to recognize a state of war It also applies to all parties and to the territory under the occupation of the of a partyeven if the occupation is not resisted.The Parties undertake to respect and ensure respect for the convention in all circumstances, including those in which

---

The 'Bushi-Do', the medieval code of honour of the warrior caste of Japan, included the rule that humanity must be exe rcised even in batt le and towa rds prisoners of w ar. In the seventeenth century the military tactician Sorai wrote that whoever kills a prisoner of war shall be guilty of manslaughter, whether that prisoner has surrendered or fought 'to the last arrow'. Fleck Dieter (ed.). 2008. *The Handbook of International Humanitarian Law*, Oxford: Oxford University Press, p. 18.

one or more of the participants are not parties to the GC III. A party may withdraw from the GC III, but such denunciation of the treaty , if made during a conflict in which the party is involved, cannot take ef fect until peace has been restored and after operations connected with the release and repatriation of the persons protected by the convention have been concluded. The denunciation has ef fect only in respect of the party that denounces.

The GC III covers members of the armed forces and certain categories of other personnel who fall into the hands of the enemy i.e., POWs. It contains 143 Articles divided into VI parts, and also has V annexures.

Part I	General Provisions: Articles 1-11
Part II	General Protection of POW: Articles 12-16
Part III	Captivity: Articles 17-108
Part IV	Termination of Captivity: Articles 109-121
Part V	Information Bureaux & Relief Societies:Articles 122-125
Part VI	Execution of the Convention: Articles 126-143

Wounded and sick combatants who are captured are prisoners of war but are evacuated initially through medical channel. Until fully recovered they have the additional protection of the first Geneva Convention (GC I).

Who is a Prisoner of War?

The following categories of personnel become POWs under Article 4A of the GC III, when they fall into the power of enemy:

(1) Members of the armed forces of a party to the conflict, as well as members of militias or volunteer corps forming part of such armed forces

(2) Members of other militias and members of other volunteer corps, including those of organized resistance movements, belonging to a party to the conflict and operating in or outside their own territory even if this territory is occupied, provided that such militias or volunteer corps, including such organized resistance movements, fulfil the following conditions:

(a) that of being commanded by a person responsible for his subordinates

(b) that of having a fixed distinctive sign recognizable at a distance

(c) that of carrying arms openly

(d) that of conducting their operations in accordance with the laws and customs of war

(3) Members of regular armed forces who profess allegiance to a government or an authority not recognized by the detaining power

(4) Persons who accompany the armed forces without actually being members thereof, such as civilian members of military aircraft crews, war correspondents, supply contractors, members of labour units or of services responsible for the welfare of the armed forces, provided that they have received authorization, from the armed forces which they accompany , who shall provide them for that purpose with an identity card similar to the annexed model

(5) Members of crews, including masters, pilots and apprentices, of the merchant marine and the crews of civil aircraft of the parties to the conflict, who do not benefit by more favourable treatment under any other provisions of international law

(6) Inhabitants of a non-occupied territory, who on the approach of the enemy spontaneously take up arms to resist the invading forces, without having had time to form themselves into regular armed units, provided they carry arms openly and respect the laws and customs of war.

Under Article 4B of GC III, the following categories of personnel shall also be treated POWs:

(1) Persons belonging, or having belonged, to the armed forces of the occupied country, if the occupying power considers it necessary by reason of such allegiance to intern them

(2) Persons belonging to one of the categories enumerated in Article 4, who have been received by neutral or non-belligerent powers on their territory and whom these powers are required to intern under international law.

Medical personnel and chaplains while retained by the detaining power to assist POWs, are not considered as POWs. They are entitled, however, to receive as a minimum the benefits and protection of the GC III, and shall also be granted all facilities necessary to provide for the medical care of, and religious ministration to POWs (Article 33, GC III).

Protection: General Provisions

Prisoners of war are in the hands of the enemy power , but not of the individuals or military units who have captured them. Irrespective of the individual responsibilities that may exist, the detaining power is responsible for the treatment given to such prisoners. Prisoners of war may only be transferred by the detaining power to a power which is a party to the Convention and after satisfying itself of the willingness and ability of such transferee power to apply the GC III. When POWs are transferred under such circumstances, responsibility for the application of the Convention rests on the power accepting them while they are in its custody.

Prisoners of war must at all times be humanely treated.Any unlawful act or omission by the detaining power causing death or seriously endangering the health of a POW in its custody is prohibited, and will be regarded as a serious breach of the Convention. In particular, no POW may be subjected to physical mutilation or to medical or scientific experiments of any kind which are not justified by the medical, dental or hospital treatment of the prisoner concerned and carried out in his interest. They must at all times be protected, particularly against acts of violence or intimidation and against insults and public curiosity. Measures of reprisal against POWs are prohibited.

Prisoners of war are entitled to respect for their persons and their honour. Taking into consideration the provisions of the GC III, relating to rank and sex, and subject to any privileged treatment which may be accorded to them by reason of their state of health, age or professional qualifications, all prisoners of war are to be treated alike, without any adverse distinction based on race, nationality , religious belief or political opinion. Women prisoners are to be treated with the regard due to their sex. The power detaining POWs is bound to provide free of charge for their maintenance and for the medical attention required by their state of health. Prisoners, under no circumstances can renounce in part or in entirety the rights secured to them by the GC III.

Questioning of prisoners

Article 17 of the GC III, is the key provision relating to the questioning of POWs. Every POW, when questioned, is bound to give his surname, first name and rank, date of birth, and armyregimental, personal or serial number or equivalent information. If he wilfully infringes this rule, he may render himself liable to a restriction of the privileges accorded to his rank or status. No physical or mental torture, nor any other form of coercion, is to be inflicted on POWs to secure from them information of any kind whatever Prisoners of war who refuse to answer may not be threatened, insulted, or exposed to unpleasant or disadvantageous treatment of any kind. Prisoners, who owing to their physical or mental condition are unable to state their identity, are to be handed over to the medical service. By virtue of Article 17.3 of GC III, each party to a conflict is required to furnish the persons under its jurisdiction who are liable to become POWs with an identity card containing at least the bearer's surname, first name, rank, army regimental, personal or serial number and date of birth, or failing this, equivalent information. Further information may be added to the card at each party's discretion.

POW status does not prevent a prisoner from being tried for crimes committed before capture. A POW could therefore be questioned on his involvement in alleged war crimes, crimes against humanity and genocide.

Evacuation

Prisoners of war must be evacuated, as soon as possible after their capture, to camps situated far enough from the combat zone for them to be out of danger. Only those who, owing to wounds or sickness, would run greater risks by being evacuated than by remaining where they are, may be temporarily kept back in a danger zone. They should not be unnecessarily exposed to danger while awaiting evacuation from a fighting zone.

The evacuation of POWs must be efected humanely and in conditions similar to those for the forces of the detaining power in their changes of station. The detaining power must supply POWs sufficient food, drinking water, necessary clothing and medical attention; and must ensure their safety during evacuation. If POWs must pass through transit camps during evacuation, their stay in such camps must be brief.

Internment

The detaining power may intern POWs and impose on them the obligation of not leaving, beyond certain limits, the camp where they are interned, or if the said camp is fenced in, of not going outside its perimeterPrisoners of war may not be held in close confinement except where necessary to safeguard their health. They may be partially or wholly released on parole or promise, however, they cannot be compelled to accept liberty on parole or promise. Upon the outbreak of hostilities, each party to the conflict is to notify the adverse party of the laws and regulations allowing or forbidding its own nationals to accept liberty on parole or promise.

Quarters, Food and Clothing

Prisoners of war must be quartered under conditions as favourable as those for the forces of the detaining power who are billeted in the same area, making allowance for the habits and customs of the prisoners, and in no case prejudicial to their health.The premises provided for the use of POWs must be protected from dampness and adequately heated and lighted, in particular, between dusk and lights outAll precautions must be taken against the danger of fire. Separate dormitories must be provided for women POWs in mixed camps.

The daily food rations must be suficient in quantity, quality and variety to keep POWs in good health and to prevent loss of weight or the development of nutritional deficiencies. Suficient drinking water must be supplied to POWs and they should be associated with the preparation of their meals and may be employed in the kitchensAdequate premises should be provided for messing. Collective disciplinary measures af fecting food are prohibited.

Clothing, underwear and footwear must be supplied to POWs in sufficient quantities by the detaining power , making allowance for the climate of the region where they are detained.The regular replacement and repair of the clothing articles must be ensured. In addition, POWs who work must be provided appropriate clothing, wherever the nature of the work demands.

All camps must have canteens where POWs may procure foodstuf f, soap, tobacco and articles of daily use. The tariff must never exceed local market prices. The profits made by canteens must be used for the benefit of the prisoners, and a representative of the prisoners must be associated with the management of the canteen and its funds.

Hygiene and Medical Attention

The detaining power is bound to take all sanitary measures necessary to ensure the cleanliness and hygiene of camps and to prevent epidemics. Prisoners must have for their use, day and night, conveniences which conform to the rules of hygiene and are maintained in a constant state of cleanliness. In camps in which women prisoners of war are accommodated, separate conveniences are to be provided for them. Prisoners must be provided with sufficient water and soap for their personal toilet and for washing their personal laundry.

Every camp must have an adequate infirmary where prisoners may have the required attention and appropriate diet. Prisoners suffering from serious disease, or whose condition necessitates special treatment, a surgical operation or hospital care, must be admitted to any military or civilian medical unit where such treatment can be given. Special facilities should be afforded for the disabled, in particular to the blind. Prisoners must not be prevented from presenting themselves to the medical authorities for examination. The detaining authorities must, upon request, issue to every prisoner who has undergone treatment, an official certificate indicating the nature of his illness or injury and the duration and kind of treatment received. A duplicate of this certificate should be forwarded to the Central Prisoners of War Agency.

Prisoners must have opportunities for taking physical exercise, including sports and games, and for being out of doors. Sufficient open spaces must be provided for this purpose in all camps. Regular medical inspections of prisoners must be held at least once a month, during which the weight of each prisoner must be checked and recorded. Also, the general state of health, nutrition and cleanliness of prisoners must be examined to detect contagious diseases, especially tuberculosis, malaria and venereal disease.

The medical personnel and chaplains retained by the detaining power with a view to assisting prisoners shall not be considered POWs. They must receive, as a minimum, the benefits and protection due to them under the GC III, and must be granted all facilities necessary to provide medical care, and religious ministration to POWs.

The fitness of prisoners must be periodically (at least once a month) verified by medical examination, with particular regard to the nature of the work which prisoners are required to do. If any prisoner considers himself incapable of working, he must be permitted to appear before the medical authorities. Medial authorities may recommend that prisoners who are unfit for work, be exempted. Prisoners have the right to make requests regarding their conditions of captivity to the military authorities in whose power they are. Their representatives may send periodic reports on the situation in the camps and the needs of the prisoners to the representatives of the protecting powers.

Discipline

Every POW camp must be put under the immediate authority of a responsible commissioned officer (camp commander) belonging to the regular armed forces of the detaining power. This officer must have a copy of the GC III and ensure that its provisions are known to the camp staf f and the guard. He must be personally responsible for the application of the Convention.

Prisoners of war must salute the camp commander. Officer prisoners are bound to salute the camp commander regardless of his rank, and officers of higher rank. The wearing of badges of rank and nationality as well as of decorations, must be permitted. The GC III and its annexes, regulations, orders, notices and publications relating to the conduct of POWs must be displayed in the camp, in the prisoners' language, at places where all may read them.

The use of weapons against POWs, especially against those escaping or attempting to escape, constitutes an extreme measure, and must always be preceded by warning.

Relations with the Exterior

As soon as prisoners of war have fallen into its power, the detaining power must inform the powers to which they belong, of their capture through the protecting power. Immediately upon capture, or not more than one week after arrival at a camp, every POW must be enabled to write to his family and to the Central Prisoners ofWar Agency (Article 123, GC III) about his capture, address and state of health. Prisoners must be allowed to send and receive letters and cards, which may be subject to necessary censorship. They must also be allowed to receive, by post or by any other means, individual parcels or collective shipments containing, foodstuff, clothing, medical supplies and articles of a religious, educational or recreational character, including books, devotional articles, scientific equipment, examination papers, musical instruments, sports outfits and materials allowing them to pursue their studies or their cultural activities.

Penal and Disciplinary Sanctions

A POW is subject to the laws and regulations of the armed forces of the detaining power. That power shall be justified in taking judicial or disciplinary measures in respect of any ofence committed by a POWagainst such laws or regulations. However, no proceedings or punishments contrary to the Chapter III of the GC III are permitted. In deciding whether proceedings concerning an alleged ofence shall be judicial or disciplinary the detaining power must ensure that the competent authorities exercise the greatest leniency and adopt, wherever possible, disciplinary rather than judicial measures.

A POW must be tried only by a military court, unless the existing laws of the detaining power expressly permit civil courts to try a member of the armed forces of the detaining power in respect of the alleged of fence committed by the POW. A prisoner must never be tried by a court which does not follow the essential guarantees of independence and impartiality and does not afford the accused the rights of defence provided in Article 105 of the GC III. A prisoner must not be punished more than once for the same act or on the same charge. Collective punishment for individual acts, corporal punishment, imprisonment in premises without daylight and, in general, any form of torture or cruelty, are forbidden. A prisoner must not be deprived of his rank by the detaining power, or prevented from wearing his badges.

Officers, non-commissioned of ficers and men who are POWs undergoing a disciplinary or judicial punishment, must not be subjected to more severe treatment than that applied in respect of the same punishment to members of the armed forces of the detaining power of equivalent rank. A woman POW must not be sentenced to a punishment more severe or treated more severely than a woman member of the armed forces of the detaining power dealt with for a similar ofence. Disciplinary punishments must not be inhuman, brutal or dangerous to the health of prisoners.

Escape

According to Article 91, GC III, the escape of a POW shall be deemed to have succeeded when: (i) he has joined the armed forces of the power on which he depends, or those of an allied power; (ii) he has left the territory under the control of the detaining power , or of an ally of the said power; (iii) he has joined a ship flying the flag of the power on which he depends, or of an allied power, in the territorial waters of the detaining power , the said ship not being under the control of the last named power Prisoners of war who have made good their escape and who are recaptured, are not be liable to any punishment in respect of their previous escape. A prisoner who has made an unsuccessful attempt to escape is liable only to a disciplinary punishment, even if it is a repeated of fence. The record of disciplinary punishments must be maintained by the camp commander , which must be open to inspection by representatives of the protecting power

Article 75 of the Additional Protocol I contains additional protection to prisoners captured during armed conflicts. Whatever their status, such prisoners are entitled to humane treatment. It is generally accepted that Article 75 reflects customary international law . The use of torture and inhuman or degrading treatment is prohibited. The authorities are entitled to question a prisoner but there is no obligation on the prisoner to answer the questions. Coercing a prisoner to confess is unlawful. Article 75(4) is particularly significant. It provides: "No sentence may be passed and no penalty may be executed on a person found guilty of a penal offence relating to the armed conflict except pursuant to a conviction pronounced by an impartial and regularly constituted court respecting the generally recognized principles of regular judicial procedure."

Judicial Proceedings

A POW must not be tried or sentenced for an act which is not forbidden by the law of the detaining power or by international law in force at the time the said act was committed. No moral or physical coercion may be exerted on a prisoner to induce him to plead guilty of the act of which he is accused. He may not be convicted without having had an opportunity to present his defence and the assistance of a qualified counsel.

Prisoners of war and the protecting powers must be informed of the offences which are punishable by the death sentence under the laws of the detaining power. Other offences shall not thereafter be made punishable by the death penalty without the concurrence of the power on which the prisoners of war depend. If the death penalty is pronounced on a POW the sentence must not be executed before the expiration of a period of at least six months from the date when the protecting power receives, at an indicated address, the detailed communication provided for in Article 107of the GC III.

The prisoner is entitled to assistance by one of his prisoner comrades, to defence by a qualified advocate or counsel of his own choice, to the calling of witnesses and, if necessary, to the services of an interpreter. He must be advised of these rights by the detaining power before the trial. Failing a choice by the prisoner, the protecting power must provide an advocate or counsel for his defence at the trial.The prisoner must have the right to appeal against a sentence, in the same manner as do the members of the armed forces of the detaining power. He must be informed of his right to appeal and of the time limit within which he may do so.

Release and Repatriation

Prisoners of war who are seriously wounded and sick may be accommodated in neutral countries. Each of the parties to the conflict may, in addition, conclude agreements with a view to the direct repatriation or internment in a neutral country of able-bodied prisoners who have undergone a long period of captivity. No prisoner on whom a disciplinary punishment has been imposed and who is eligible for repatriation or for accommodation in a neutral country, may be kept back on the plea that he has not undergone his punishment. Prisoners must be released and repatriated without delay after the cessation of active hostilities. [2] There is one exception to immediate

[2] After the 1971 Indo-Pak war, the Indian government initially refused to repatriate more than 85,000 Pakistani held as POWs, on the grounds that a renewal of hostil ities could not be excluded. Repatriation started late 1973, almost two years after the cessation of hostities.

repatriation. In case a POW is convicted or prosecuted for criminal offence, he may be detained until the end of legal proceedings and if necessary , until he has completed his sentence.

The repatriation of POWs against their will has been a contentious issue. The UK follows a policy that POWs should not be repatriated against their will. However, an attempt to insert such a provision into the GC III failed as it was felt that the proposal might give rise to the exercise of undue influence on the part of the detaining power.

Death

The GC III specifies the conditions of burial or cremation, appropriate to ensure respect for the dead and to safeguard the interests of their families and stipulates that death certificate must be forwarded as rapidly as possible to the POW Information Bureaux. In case of death from suspicious causes, an enquiry is opened in order to determine responsibility particularly with a view to possible compensation for beneficiaries. Prisoners of war are entitled to make wills.

Information Bureaux and Central Tracing Agency

A Central Prisoners of War Agency (now known as the Central Tracing Agency) must be created in a neutral country. The International Committee of the Red Cross (ICRC) may propose to the powers concerned the organization and location of such an Agency. To facilitate the work of the national Bureaux and the Central Tracing Agency, States must grant them free postage and exemptions/reduced rates for telegraphic charges. The parties to a conflict must grant the ICRC all facilities within their power to enable it to carry out the humanitarian functions assigned to it by the GC III and the AP I to assure protection and assistance to the victims of conflict.

Customary International Humanitarian Law

The long-standing rule of customary international humanitarian law states that upon capture, combatants are entitled to POW status. They may neither be tried for their participation in the hostilities nor for acts that do not violate international humanitarian law (IHL). Rule 106 to 108 of the customary IHL are as follows:

Rule 106: Combatants must distinguish themselves from the civilian population while they are engaged in an attack or in a military operation preparatory to an attack. If they fail to do so, they do not have the right to prisoner-of-war status.

Rule 107: Combatants who are captured while engaged in espionage do not have the right to prisoner -of-war status. They may not be convicted or sentenced without previous trial.

Rule 108: Mercenaries, as defined in Additional Protocol I, do not have the right to combatant or prisoner -of-war status. They may not be convicted or sentenced without previous trial.

Additional Protocol I

The Additional Protocol I (AP I) formalizes a number of provisions of customary IHL. These provisions broaden the definition of lawful combatants. Article 44 ofAP I defines POWstatus in the following manner:

Combatants and Prisoners of War

1. Any combatant, as defined in Article 43, who falls into the power of an adverse party shall be a POW.
2. While all combatants are obliged to comply with the rules of international law applicable in armed conflict, violations of these rules shall not deprive a combatant of his right to be a combatant or, if he falls into the power of an adverse party of his right to be a prisoner of war, except as provided in paragraphs 3 and 4.
3. In order to promote the protection of the civilian population from the effects of hostilities, combatants are obliged to distinguish themselves from the civilian population while they are engaged in an attack or in a military operation preparatory to an attack. Recognizing, however, that there are situations in armed conflicts where, owing to the nature of the hostilities an armed combatant cannot so distinguish himself, he shall retain his status as a combatant, provided that, in such situations, he carries his arms openly:

   (a) during each military engagement, and

   (b) during such time as he is visible to the adversary while he is engaged in a military deployment preceding the launching of an attack in which he is to participate.

Acts which comply with the requirements of this paragraph shall not be considered as perfidious within the meaning of Article 37, paragraph 1 (c).

4. A combatant who falls into the power of an adverse party while failing to meet the requirements set forth in the second sentence of paragraph 3 shall forfeit his right to be a prisoner of war , but he shall, nevertheless, be given protections equivalent in all respects to those accorded to prisoners of war by the GC III and by this Protocol. This protection includes protections equivalent to those accorded to prisoners of war by the GC III in the case where such a person is tried and punished for any offences he has committed.

5. Any combatant who falls into the power of an adversparty while not engaged in an attack or in a military operation preparatory to an attack shall not forfeit his rights to be a combatant and a prisoner of war by virtue of his prior activities.

6. This Article is without prejudice to the right of any person to be a prisoner of war pursuant to Article 4 of the GC III.

7. This Article is not intended to change the generally accepted practice of states with respect to the wearing of the uniform by combatants assigned to the regular , uniformed armed units of a party to the conflict.

8. In addition to the categories of persons mentioned inArticle 13 of the GC I and II, all members of the armed forces of a party to the conflict, as defined in Article 43 of this Protocol, shall be entitled to protection under those Conventions if they are wounded or sick or, in the case of the GC II, shipwrecked at sea or in other waters.

Article 44.3 has modified the traditional requirement of the GC III that lawful combatants should wear a distinctive sign or emblem recognizable from a distance and that they must carry their arms openly . Article 45 of the AP I provides the following protection to persons who have taken part in the hostilities:

Protection of persons who have taken part in hostilities

1. A person who takes part in hostilities and falls into the power of an adverse party shall be presumed to be a POW, and therefore shall be protected by the GC III, if he claims the status ofPOW, or if he appears to be entitled to such status, or if the party on which he depends claims such status on his behalf by notification to the detaining power or to the protecting powerShould any doubt arise as to whether any such person is entitled to the status of POW, he shall continue to have such status and, therefore, to be protected by the GC III and this Protocol until such time as his status has been determined by a competent tribunal.

2. If a person who has fallen into the power of an adverse party is not held as a POW and is to be tried by that party for an offence arising out of the hostilities, he shall have the right to assert his entitlement to POW status before a judicial tribunal and to have that question adjudicated. Whenever possible under the applicable procedure, this adjudication shall occur before the trial for the of fence. The representatives of the protecting power shall be entitled to attend the proceedings in which that question is adjudicated, unless, exceptionally, the proceedings are held in camera in the interest of State security. In such a case the detaining power shall advise the protecting power accordingly.

3. Any person who has taken part in hostilities, who is not entitled to POW status and who does not benefit from more favourable treatment in accordance with the GC IV shall have the right at all times to the protection of Article 75 of this Protocol. In occupied territory, any such person, unless he is held as a spy, shall also be entitled, notwithstanding Article 5 of the GC IV , to his rights of communication under that Convention.

Under Articles 46 and 47 ofAP I, spies and mercenaries are not lawful combatants, and therefore not entitled to POWstatus. However, they retain their right to humanitarian protection under Article 75 of AP I.

ICRC and Prisoners of War

The First World War led to a considerable expansion of the ICRC's activities. During the 1914-18 war the ICRC monitored compliance with the 1906 Geneva Convention and the 1907 Hague Convention for the Adaptation to Maritime Warfare of the Principles of the Geneva Convention (a revised version of the Geneva Convention of 22 August 1864). In October 1914, after the opening of the war in which many prisoners were taken, the ICRC opened its International Agency in Geneva. During the conflict it listed almost five million POWs, visited many of them and enabled families to send relief parcels. The Agency, during the war, made out more than 4.8 million index cards and dispatched over 1.8 million parcels and consignments of collective relief. Throughout the conflict, the ICRC was to protest against the inhumane treatment to which both combatants and civilians were subjected. In particular, it led a vigorous campaign against the use of chemical weapons. On 31 December 1919, after the peace treaties had been signed, the ICRC closed the Agency down. In the period between the two World Wars it was replaced by a special department at the ICRC which was responsible for handling individual inquiries, making representations concerning missing persons and providing former prisoners with certificates enabling them to claim benefits.

The specific rules protecting POWs were for the first time provided in the 1929 Geneva Convention. However, during the World War II, a large number of POWs received inhuman and degrading treatment and deaths at the hands of Nazi and Soviet forces. The POWs were subjected to mass murder, execution, starvation and exposure. Casualty figures of captured POWs varied considerably and sometimes went as high as 95 per cent. The provisions relating to protection of POWs were thereafter refined in the third Geneva Convention of 1949, following the lessons of World War II, as well as in Additional Protocol I of 1977.

The GC IV of 1949 and Additional Protocol I of 1977 also provide extensive protection for civilian internees during international armed conflicts. If justified by imperative reasons of security a party to the conflict may subject civilians to assigned residence or to internment. Internment of civilians as a security measure is justified, but cannot be used as a form of punishment. This means that each interned person must be released as soon as the reasons which necessitated his internment no longer exist. Rules governing the treatment and conditions of detention of civilian internees under IHL are similar to those applicable to POWs. In non-international armed conflicts, Article 3 common to the 1949 Geneva Conventions and Additional Protocol II provide that persons deprived of liberty for reasons related to the conflict must also be treated humanely in all circumstances. In particular, they are protected against murder , torture, as well as cruel, humiliating or degrading treatment. Those detained for participation in hostilities are not immune from criminal prosecution under the applicable domestic law for having done so.

Mandate to ICRC

The ICRC is mandated by the international community, under the Geneva Conventions, to visit POWs and civilian internees to verify whether they are being treated according to relevant international standards. In addition, it seeks to visit those held in situations of internal violence. ICRC'detention visits aim to ensure respect for the life and dignity of the detainees and to prevent torture, ill-treatment or abuse.

The objective of the ICRC' s activities for people deprived of their freedom is purely humanitarian, to ensure that their physical and mental integrity is fully respected and that their conditions of detention are in line with internationally recognized standards or IHL.The ICRC also strives to prevent forced disappearances or extrajudicial executions, ill-treatment and failure to respect fundamental judicial guarantees, and, whenever necessary takes action to improve conditions of detention.This involves in particular:

- Negotiating with the authorities to obtain access to people deprived of their freedom wherever they may be held;
- Visiting all detainees, assessing their conditions of detention and identifying any shortcomings and humanitarian needs;
- Monitoring individual detainees for specific protection, medical or other purposes;
- Maintaining family links such as facilitating family visits;
- Providing material and medical relief supplies to detainees or engaging in cooperation on specific projects with the detaining authorities.

Visits to places of detention are carried out by the ICRC under strict conditions: (i) delegates must be provided with full and unimpeded access to all detainees falling within the ICRC's mandate and to all places where they are held; (ii) delegates must be able to hold private interviews with the detainees of their choice; (iii) delegates must be able to repeat their visits; (iv) detainees falling within the ICRC' s mandate must be notified individually to the ICRC, and the ICRC must be able to draw up lists of their names; and (v) at the end of each visit, the delegates hold a final talk with the detaining authorities to inform them about the ICRC' s findings and recommendations. .

ICRC visits are a means of collecting first-hand information about the treatment and living conditions of detainees.Trained ICRC staff visit places of detention, talk with the authorities concerned, hold private interviews with detainees/internees and prepare an overall analysis of their findings. ICRC findings, assessments and related recommendations are discussed confidentially with the authorities at the appropriate levels.

Health during Detention

The ICRC is concerned with the welfare of persons detained in connection with armed conflicts or internal disturbances that require intervention by a neutral organization. Its objective is to ensure acceptable conditions of detention and safeguard the physical and mental welfare of prisoners. It monitors their situation in detention and, where appropriate, prior to detention through direct visits to the victims and dialogue with their captors.

The ICRC emphasizes the responsibility of the detaining authority to respect and protect detainees. It draws attention to any breaches of international law and standards and recommends remedial action. In emergency situations where the basic needs of detainees cannot be met by authorities, it can provide temporary assistance in the form of water and food supplies or basic medical items.

ICRC doctors, nurses and delegates who visit places of detention to evaluate factors bearing on the health of the detainees need to have experience in prison and public health issues, knowledge of environmental hygiene, epidemiology, nutritional needs, and of the inter -relationship between nutrition, sanitation, health care, violence and overcrowding.Their aim is to advise on improvements to the overall functioning of prison health systems, rather than individual diagnosis and treatment. When torture and other forms of ill-treatment are evident, ICRC physicians document individual situations to strengthen the case for formal intervention by the organization. This documentation is not in itself part of any judicial investigation, but aims to trigger such action by the relevant authority.

Violation of International Norms

The ICRC is mandated by the High Contracting Parties to the Geneva Conventions to monitor the full application of and respect for the GC III and IV regarding the treatment of persons deprived of their liberty . The ICRC reminds the High Contracting Parties concerned, maintaining confidentiality, of their humanitarian obligations under the four Geneva Conventions, Additional Protocol I, the customary law and universally acknowledged principles of humanity. The ICRC team had visited places of detention in Iraq in 2003. In its "Report on the Treatment by the Coalition Forces of Prisoners of War and other protected persons in Iraq", the ICRC has drawn the attention of the Coalition Forces (CF) to a number of serious violations of IHL. [3] These violations were documented and sometimes observed while visiting POWs, civilian internees and other protected persons by the Geneva Conventions in Iraq between March and November 2003. During its visits to places of internment of the CF , the ICRC collected allegations during private interviews with persons deprived of their liberty relating to the treatment by the CF of protected persons during their capture, arrest, transfer, internment and interrogation. The main violations, which are described in the ICRC report and presented confidentially to the CF , include:

- Brutality against protected persons upon capture and initial custody sometimes causing death or serious injury.
- Absence of notification of arrest of persons deprived of their liberty to their families causing distress among persons deprived of their

[3] The Wall Street Journal of 7 May 2007 had published extensive excerpts from a confidential document entitled "REPORT OF THE INTERNA TIONAL COMMITTEE OF THE RED CROS S (ICRC) ON THE TREA TMENT BY THE COALITION FORCES OF PRISONERS OF W AR AND OTHER PROTECTED PERSONS BY THE GENEVA CONVENTIONS IN IRAQ DURING ARREST, INTERNMENT AND INTERROGATION" of January 2004.

liberty and their families.

- Physical or psychological coercion during interrogation to secure information.
- Prolonged solitary confinement in cells devoid of daylight.
- Excessive and disproportionate use of force against persons deprived of their liberty resulting in death or injury during their period of internment.

In additions there were serious problems of conduct by the CF affecting persons deprived of their libertyThese included (i) seizure and confiscation of private belongings of persons deprived of their liberty; (ii) exposure of persons deprived of their liberty to dangerous tasks; and (iii) holding persons deprived of their liberty in dangerous places where they are not protected from shelling. Consequently the ICRC asked the authorities of the CF in Iraq:

- To respect at all times the human dignity , physical integrity and cultural sensitivity of the persons deprived of their liberty held under their control.
- To set up a system of notifications of arrest to ensure quick and accurate transmission of information to the families of persons deprived of their liberty.
- To prevent all forms of ill-treatment, moral or physical coercion of persons deprived of their liberty in relation to interrogation.
- To set up an internment regime which ensures the respect of the psychological integrity and human dignity of the persons deprived of their liberty.
- To ensure that all persons deprived of their liberty are allowed sufficient time every day outside in the sunlight, and that are allowed to moved and exercise in the outside yard.
- To define and apply regulations and sanctions compatible with IHL to ensure that persons deprived of their liberty are fully informed upon arrival of such regulations and sanctions.

- To thoroughly investigate violations of IHL in order to determine responsibilities and prosecute those found responsible for violations.
- To ensure that battle group units arresting individuals and staff in charge of internment facilities receive adequate training enabling them to operate in a proper manner and fulfill their responsibilities as arresting authority without resorting to ill-treatment or making excessive use of force.

CHAPTER 7

Protection of Civilians in Armed Conflict

Introduction

The past century has seen an increase in the proportion of non-combatant deaths in conflict. During the First World War, an estimated 5 per cent of casualties were civilians. In the Second World War, the figure was 50 per cent. Today, 80–90 per cent of war casualties are civilians, the majority of them women and children. A large number of non-combatants die from the indirect effects of conflict—from disease, famine and lack of services. Nearly 600,000 civilians in 27 African countries have been massacred in the past two decades.[1] In Afghanistan, in the first six months of the year 2010, civilian casualties, including deaths and injuries, increased by 31 per cent over the same period in 2009.[2] The 2004 Report of the UN Secretary-

---

1 Williams Paul D., Enhancing Civilian Protection in Peace Operations: Insights from Africa, September 2010, Africa Center for Strategic Studies Research Paper No. 1, Washington DC: National Defence University Press.

2 The United Nations Assistance Mission in Afghanistan: 'Mid Year Report on Protection of Civilians in Armed Conflict 2010'. In Afghanistan, where the ongoing conflict is non-international, the civilian casualties could be divided into two: directly resulting from armed conflict and others not directly related to conflict– including those arising from military operations conducted by pro-government forces (Afghan Government Forces and/or International Military Forces) such as force protection incidents; air raids, search and arrest operations, counter insurgency operations. It also includes casuaties arising from the activties of anti-government elements (AGEs), such as targeted killings, IEDs or direct engagement with pro-government forces, etc. Other casuaties resulting indirectly from the conflict include those caused by explosive remnants of war, deaths in prison, deaths fom probable underlying medical conditions that occurred during military operations, or where access to medical care was denied or was not forthcoming. It also includes deaths arising from incidents where responsibility cannot be determined with any degree of certainty, such as deaths or injuries arising from cross-fire. The 'Report' available at: http://unama.unmissions.org/Portals/UNAMA/Publication/August102010_MID-YEAR%20REPORT%202010_Protection%20of%20Civilians%20in%20Armed%20Conflict.pdf

General on the protection of civilians in armed conflict states: "In Iraq the increasingly serious threats to security and continued fighting have resulted in disproportionate and avoidable civilian deaths and injuries, and detainees have been subjected to torture and other serious violations of human rights and IHL".[3] Torture, sexual violence, exploitation, forced recruitment into fighting forces and other forms of abuse frequently accompany conflict, and are now more commonly documented as a feature of warfare.There is stark and disturbing evidence that civilians continue to bear the brunt of armed conflicts today. Compliance by all parties to conflict with IHL, human rights, refugee and criminal law is critical in all of these situations, whether they are situations of armed conflict, occupation or transition.

Who are civilians?

In abstract terms, civilians can be broadly defined as non-combatants. In a conventional international armed conflict involving two or more states, it may not be difficult to distinguish a combatant from a non-combatant. The problem is that in present-day situations of non-international armed conflicts, distinguishing civilians from combatants is becoming more and more difficult. Article 50 (1) of the Additional Protocol I of 1977 (AP I) defines civilians as persons who do not belong to one of the categories referred to in Article 4 of the Third Geneva Convention as well as in Article 43 of the Protocol. Article 4 (A) (1), (2), (3) and (6) of the third Geneva Convention lists the following persons as combatants:

- Members of the armed forces of a Party to the conflict, as well as members of militias or volunteer corps forming part of such armed forces
- Members of other militias and members of other volunteer corps, including those of organized resistance movements, belonging to a Party to the conflict and operating in or outside their own territory even if this territory is occupied, provided that such militias or volunteer corps, including such organized resistance movements, fulfil the following conditions of (i) being commanded by a person responsible for his subordinates; (ii) of having a fixed distinctive sign recognizable at a distance; (iii) of carrying arms openly; and

[3] S/2004/431, 28 May 2004.

(iv) of conducting their operations in accordance with the laws and customs of war.

- Members of regular armed forces who profess allegiance to a government or an authority not recognized by the detaining power
- Inhabitants of a non-occupied territory , who on the approach of the enemy spontaneously take up arms to resist the invading forces, without having had time to form themselves into regular armed units, provided they carry arms openly and respect the laws and customs of war

Article 43 of the AP I likewise states that the armed forces of a Party to a conflict consist of all organized armed forces, groups and units which are under a command responsible to that Party for the conduct of its subordinates. The Article further states that members of the armed forces of a Party to a conflict (other than medical personnel and chaplains covered by Article 33 of GC III) are combatants. Combatants have the right to participate directly in hostilities. Therefore, all persons who are neither members of the armed forces nor directly take part in the hostilities are civilians. In order to promote the protection of the civilian population from the effects of hostilities, combatants are obliged to distinguish themselves from the civilian population while they are engaged in an attack or in a military operation preparatory to an attack.

Protection of Civilians: Legal Framework

The First Geneva Convention of 1864 provided only for the protection of combatants, as at that time it was considered that civilians would remain outside the war zone. The Regulations concerning the Laws and Customs of War on Land, annexed to the Fourth Hague Convention of 1907, also did not make any provision for civilians, except where there was occupation of territory by enemy armed forces. It contained a few rules (Articles 42 to 56), assuming the necessary measures to be taken by the occupants to ensure public order and safety. Pillage was forbidden and no general penalty could be inflicted upon the population on account of the acts of individuals. Certain efforts were made by the ICRC during the 1930s to prepare a draft convention for the protection of civilians, but the convention was postponed on account of war. When the Second World War broke out, civilians were not provided with ef fective protection under any convention or treaty . However, an undertaking was obtained by the ICRC from the belligerent States that the essential provisions of the POW convention would be extended to interned civilians who were in enemy territory at the outbreak of hostilities. As a result, about 160,000 civilians enjoyed the same legal status and the same safeguards as POWs for the duration of the hostilities.

At the end of the Second World War, in the light of the experience gained, it was felt that the Geneva Conventions needed revisionThe Fourth Geneva Convention exclusively meant for the protection of civilians was signed on August 12, 1949 along with the other three Conventions. This 'civilian' Convention does not invalidate the Regulations Concerning the Laws and Customs ofWar on Land and is not a substitute for that agreement. It is supplementary to Sections II and III of the said Regulations. The common Article 3 of the four Geneva Conventions of 1949 commits parties in non-international conflicts to respect the human rights of all those placed *hors de combat* (out of action/combat), and the Fourth Geneva Convention on the Protection of Civilians (GC IV) of fers legal protection to civilians in occupied territories. The Additional Protocol I of 1977 extends the protection afforded to non-combatants by stipulating that armed attacks be strictly limited to military objectives (Article 52, Protocol I)The protection of civilians in armed conflicts is covered under the following headings.

General Principles

The 1968 Declaration of St Petersburg states that in any armed conflict, the right of the Parties to a conflict to choose the methods and means of warfare is not unlimited. Article 51 (1) of the AP I provides that the civilian population and individual civilians shall enjoy protection against dangers arising from military operations.Article 48 of theAP I affords fundamental protection to the civilian population. It states that the Parties to a conflict shall at all times distinguish between the civilian population and combatants and between civilian objects and military objectives and accordingly shall direct their operations only against military objectives.

Indiscriminate attacks are prohibited. Indiscriminate attacks are those (i) which are not directed at a specific military objective; (ii) which employ a method or means of combat which cannot be directed at a specific military objective; or (iii) which employ a method or means of combat the ef fects of which cannot be limited. Similarly attacks against the civilian population or civilians by way of reprisals are prohibited.[4] Acts or threats of violence the primary purpose of which is to spread terror among the civilian population are prohibited.[5]

Protection of Civilian Objects

A 'civilian object' may not be made the object of attack or reprisal. A 'civilian object' is any object which does not by virtue of its nature, location or use make an effective contribution to military action and whose neutralization would not afford a definite military advantage. In case of doubt whether an object which is normally dedicated to civilian purposes, such as a place of worship, a house or other dwelling or a school, is being used to make an effective contribution to military action, it shall be presumed not to be so used.[6] Article 53 of the AP I provides protection to cultural objects and of places of worship in an international armed conflict.[7]

Article 54, of the AP I dealing with the protection of objects indispensable to the survival of the civilian population provides that starvation of civilians as a method of warfare is prohibited. It further prohibits attack, destruction, or rendering useless objects indispensable to the survival of the civilian population, such as foodstuffs, agricultural areas for the production of foodstuffs, livestock, drinking water installations and supplies and irrigation works. The belligerents are also to take care to protect the natural environment against widespread, long-term and severe damage. Attacks against the natural environment or foodstuffs, crops, livestock, drinking water installations etc., by way of reprisals are prohibited.

Works or installations containing dangerous forces, namely dams,

---

[4] Article 51 (4) (5) and (6) AP I. Article 51 (5) AP I also provides: Among others, the following types of attacks are to be considered as indiscriminate: (a) An attack by bombardment by any methods or means which treats as a single military objective a number of clearly separated and distinct military objectives located in a city, town, village or other area containing a similar concentration of civilians or civilian objects; and (b) An attack which may be expected to cause incidental loss of civilian life, injury to civilians, damage to civilian objects, or a combination thereof, which would be excessive in relation to the concrete and direct military advantage anticipated.

[5] Article 51 (2) AP I.

[6] Article 52 AP I.

[7] For details see Chapter 11 of the book.

dykes and nuclear electrical generating stations, must not be made the object of attack, even where these objects are military objectives, if such attack may cause the release of dangerous forces and consequent severe losses among the civilian population. Other military objectives located at or in the vicinity of these works or installations must also not be made the objects of attack if such attack may cause the release of dangerous forces from the works or installations and consequent severe losses among the civilian population.

The special protection against attacking dams, dykes or nuclear electrical generating stations will not be applicable if they are contributing significant and direct support of military operations and if such an attack is the only feasible way to terminate such support. The Parties to a conflict must therefore avoid locating any military objectives in the vicinity of works or installations containing dangerous forces. The Parties to a conflict may have additional agreements among themselves to provide additional protection for objects containing dangerous forces and may mark them with a special sign consisting of a group of three bright orange circles placed on the same axis.[8]

General Protection against the Effects of War

Protected Persons: Article 4 of the GC IV defines two categories of 'protected persons' who benefit from the Convention: (i) enemy nationals within the national territory of each of the parties to the conflict and (ii) the whole population of occupied territories (excluding nationals of the occupying power). Article 13 goes beyond the limits set by Article 4 and covers the population as a whole, i.e., not only 'protected persons', but also those who cannot avail themselves of this protection and, in particular those who are nationals of the parties to a conflict, or of the occupying Power by whom they are held. Article 73 of the AP I brings refugees and stateless persons within the ambit of protected persons.

Part II of the GC IV (Articles 13 to 26) concerns the general protection of populations against certain consequences of war . It provides for the establishment of hospitals and safety zones and localities in own territory or occupied areas (Article 14) and neutralized zones (Article 15) for the

---

[8] Article 56, AP I.

protection of civilian hospitals (Article 18), for measures relating to child welfare (Article 24) and for the exchange of family news (Article 25). It also provides for general protection and respect of the wounded and sick, and for the search for the killed and wounded, and their evacuation (Article 16 and 17).

Protected persons cannot renounce the rights provided to them by the GC IV nor can their rights be taken away by any special agreements. The rights contained in the GC IV or AP I can be denied to a protected person suspected of or engaged in activities hostile to the security of the S tate. This would apply, for example, to rights of communication in the case of suspected spies. However, such persons must be treated humanely and not be deprived of the rights of fair and regular trial prescribed by the Convention and Article 75 of the AP I.

Treatment of Protected Persons

Part III of the GC IV (Articles 27 – 141) defines the status and treatment of protected persons and is divided into five sections. It distinguishes between foreign nationals on the territory of a Party to a conflict and the population of occupied territory. Section I contains provisions common to the above two categories of persons. Section II relates to aliens in the territory of a party to a conflict, while Section III contains prescriptions for occupied territories. Section IV deals with internment and is divided into 12 Chapters. Section V is devoted to information bureaux and the central agency.

All person protected under the GC IV are entitled to humane treatment, being protected from violence, insult and public curiosity, and respect for their person, honour , family rights, religion and customs. No adverse distinction may be drawn amongst them on the basis of age, sex, health, race, religion or politics. The treatment of protected persons is the responsibility of the party in whose power they are, irrespective of any responsibility which may be attached to its agents (Articles 27-29). These rights are based on the obligation laid down in the 1929 Geneva Convention on POWs. The right of respect for the person must be understood in its widest sense. It covers all the rights of the individual, that is, the rights and qualities which are inseparable from the human being by the very fact of his existence and his mental and physical powers. It includes, in particular the right to physical, moral and intellectual integrity—an essential attribute of the human person.

Article 31 prohibits physical or moral coercion against protected persons, in particular, to obtain information from them or from third parties. Protected persons are also immune from all measures which would cause physical suffering or extermination, including murder, torture, corporal punishments, mutilation and medical or scientific experimentation. Protected persons must also not be subjected to collective punishmentActs of terrorism, pillage, reprisals or hostage-taking are prohibited against them (Articles 32-34).

For special protection of women and children please refer to Chapters 8 and 9 of the book.

Protection of Foreigners

Articles 35 to 46 of the GC IV deal exclusively with the protection of aliens in the territory of a party to a conflict. Protected persons, who desire to leave the territory at the outset of, or during a conflict, must be allowed to do so, unless their departure is contrary to the national interests of the State. Their application for departure must be decided in accordance with the procedure laid down and on priority . If any such person is refused permission to leave the territory , he should be allowed to appeal to an appropriate judicial or administrative board. Protected persons are not be transferred to a Power which is not a Party to the Convention and under no circumstances to a country where he may have reason to fear persecution for his political opinions or religious beliefs.

Protection in Occupied Territories

Section III of the GC IV comprises Articles 47 to 78 and deals with the treatment which the inhabitants of an occupied territory must receive from the occupying Power. A territory is considered occupied when it is actually placed under the authority of a hostile army. The occupation extends only to the territory where such authority has been established and can be exercised.[9] Article 1 of the AP I extends this to include people fighting against colonial domination and alien occupation.

---

[9] Article 42, Hague Land Warfare Regulations annexed to 1907 Hague Convention IV.

Safeguards: During the Second World War whole populations were excluded from the application of the laws governing occupation and were thus denied the safeguards provided by those laws and left at the mercy of the occupying power. In order to avoid a repetition of this state of affairs, Article 47 of the GC IV provides that an occupying Power must not abrogate the benefits of applicable protection under the Convention for the sake occupation administration. UnderArticle 48, protected persons who are not nationals of the Power whose territory is occupied have the right to leave the territory . Article 49 prohibits the deportation of the inhabitants (protected persons) of an occupied country. As an exception, the occupying Power is authorized to evacuate an occupied territory wholly or partly if the security of the population or imperative military reasons so demand. An occupying Power is prohibited to deport or transfer parts of its own civilian population into occupied territory.

Protection and Care of Children: The obligation of the occupying Power to facilitate the proper working of institutions for children is very general in scope. Article 50 of the GC IV provides that proper care be taken of children in occupied territory. The occupying Power must, with the co-operation of the national and local authorities ensure the proper working of children's institutions and facilitate their identification and registration. The provision applies to a wide variety of institutions and establishments of a social, educational or medical character and may include child welfare centres and orphanages.

Protection of Workers: Article 51 contains a rule of cardinal importance to the population of an occupied territory. The occupying power is forbidden to force protected persons to serve in its armed or auxiliary forces. The prohibition is absolute and no derogation from it is permitted. Its object is to protect the inhabitants of the occupied territory from actions of fensive to their patriotic feelings or from attempts to undermine their allegiance to their own countryProtected person above 18 years of age can be employed on works which are necessary either for the needs of the occupation army or relate to public utility service. Workers must be paid a fair wage and the work should be proportionate to their physical and intellectual capacities.

Prohibition on Destruction of Pr operty: Article 53 prohibits the destruction of all property (real or personal), whether it is the private property of protected persons (owned individually or collectively), State property of public authorities (districts, municipalities, provinces, etc.) or of cooperative organizations. The prohibition of destruction of property in occupied territory is subject to an important reservation. It does not apply in cases where such destruction is rendered absolutely necessary by military operations.

Food and Medical Supplies : The occupying Power has the duty to ensure the food, medical supplies and articles necessary to support the life of the population. The occupying Power may not requisition food stuf fs, articles or medical supplies available in the occupied territory, except for use by the occupation forces and administration personnel, after taking into account the requirements of the civilian population. They also have a duty to ensure and maintain medical establishments and services, and public health and hygiene in the occupied territory, with the help and cooperation of national and local authorities (Articles 55 and 56).

Requisition of Hospital : The occupying Power may requisition civilian hospitals on temporary basis only in cases of ugent necessity for the care of military wounded and sick, and then on condition that suitable arrangements are made in due time for the care and treatment of patients and for the needs of the civilian population. The material and stores of civilian hospitals cannot be requisitioned so long as they are necessary for the needs of the civilian population (Article 57).

Relief: In all cases where occupied territory is inadequately supplied the occupying Power is bound to accept relief supplies destined for the population. Relief schemes may be undertaken either by States or by an impartial humanitarian or ganization such as the ICRC. The principle of free passage applies to relief consignments for the population of an occupied territory. The State granting free passage to consignments can check them in order to satisfy itself that they do in fact consist of relief supplies and do not contain weapons, munitions, military equipment or other articles or supplies used for military purposes. The occupying Power is not to divert relief consignments, except in cases of urgent necessity, in the interests of the population of the occupied territory and with the consent of the protecting Power (Articles 59-62).

Law and Order : The occupying Power is responsible for the maintenance of law and order during continuance of occupation. The penal laws of an occupied territory remain in force, subject to such changes as the occupying power may make in the interest of its own security or for the better application of the GC IV or AP I. The penal provisions enacted by the occupying Power shall not come into force before they have been published and brought to the knowledge of the inhabitants in their own language.The effect of these penal provisions should not be retroactive.The administration of justice should remain in the hands of established officials in occupied territory who were in place prior to the commencement of occupation. In case judges or other public officials refuse to perform their duties, no coercion may be applied to them. (Articles 54, 64 and 65).

In case of a breach of the penal provisions promulgated by an occupying Power, Article 66 recognizes the right of the Power to try the offender before its own military court. Such courts must be properly constituted, non-political and situated in occupied territory . The military courts should apply only those provisions of law which were applicable prior to the offence and which are in accordance with the general principles of law that the penalty shall be proportionate to the offence. The court should also take into consideration the fact that the accused is not a national of the occupying PowerThe court of appeal should preferably sit in the occupied country (Articles 66 and 67).

Treatment of Detainees : A sentence may be pronounced by the competent courts of the occupying Power only after a regular trialAn accused must have the right to present evidence and produce witnesses. They should be assisted by a qualified advocate or counsel of their own choice, who must be allowed to visit them freely and be provided with the necessary facilities for preparing the defence. Protected persons who are convicted and sentenced to custodial penalties must serve their sentence within the occupied territoryPrisoners are entitled to adequate medical and spiritual help and to receive relief parcels.

Protected persons who have been accused of an offence or convicted by the courts in an occupied territory shall be handed over at the close of occupation, with the relevant records, to the authorities of the liberated territory. Protected persons who are detained shall have the right to be visited by delegates of the protecting Power and of the ICRC (Articles 69-78).

Death Penalty: Non-serious offences should be punishable by simple imprisonment or internment, while those which have serious consequences for the occupying Power may be punished by penalties of much greater severity, even the death penalty. The death penalty may only be imposed for three types of offence—espionage, serious sabotage against military installations, and intentional homicide, provided that the death penalty was provided for similar cases under the law in force before the occupation began. The death penalty may not be pronounced against a protected person below 18 years. An individual awarded the death sentence shall have the right of petition for pardon or reprieve. No death sentence shall be carried out before the expiration of a period of at least six months from the date of receipt by the protecting Power of the notification of the final judgment confirming such death sentence, or of an order denying pardon or reprieve (Article 68).

Treatment of Internees

Enemy civilians in the territory of a State Party to an armed conflict and protected persons in occupied territory may be interned. The internees retain their full civil capacity. The parties to a conflict who intern protected persons shall be bound to provide free of charge for their maintenance, and provide them the required medical needs. As far as possible, internees are to be accommodated according to their nationality, language and customs. During internment, members of the same family, and in particular parents and children, should be lodged together in the same place of internment. Internees whose children are left without parental care as a consequence of internment may request that they be interned with them. The following measures are required to be ensured for the interned.

Place of Internment: Prisons or penal establishments should not be used as places of internment. P laces of internment should not be exposed to the dangers of war . In order to protect internees against bombing, the detaining Power is to inform the geographical location of places of internment to other States engaged in conflict.Any building accommodating internees must be safe,hygienic and adequately heated and lighted. Internees may be provided with canteens where other suitable facilities are not available. Places of internment that areexposed to air raids must have adequate shelters to ensure the necessary protection. Due precautions against the danger of fire must be taken. Internees should be allowed to visit their homes in ur gent cases, particularly in the case of death or of serious illness of relatives.

Food and Clothing: Sufficient quantity of rations and drinking water should be provided to keep internees in a good state of health. Expectant and nursing mothers and children under 15 years of age should be given additional food, in proportion to their physiological needs. Internees should be given all facilities to provide themselves with the necessary clothing and footwear.

The deaths of an internee should be certified by a doctor, and a death certificate should be made out, showing the cause of death and the conditions under which it occurred. The detaining authorities must ensure that internees who die are honourably buried according to the rites of the religion to which they belonged and that their graves are respected, properly maintained and marked in such a way that they can always be recognized. Internees must be released by the detaining Power as soon as the reasons for their internment have ceased. Upon the close of hostilities, internees must be released as soon as possible and returned to their last place of residence or repatriated (Article 79-135).

Precautions in Attack and against Effects of Attack

In order to ensure that civilians and civilian objects are spared, certain obligations have been placed on persons who plan or decide upon an attack. These persons are to take the following precautions while conducting a military operation:

(a) Doing everything feasible to verify that the objectives to be attacked are neither civilians nor civilian objects and are not subject to special protection;

(b) Choosing means and methods of attack with a view to avoiding or minimizing incidental loss of civilian life, injury to civilians and damage to civilian objects; and

(c) Refraining from launching an attack which may be expected to cause incidental loss of civilian life, injury to civilians, damage to civilian objects, which would be excessive in relation to the concrete and direct military advantage anticipated.

An attack must be cancelled or suspended if it becomes apparent that the objective is not a military one or is subject to special protection or is expected to be in breach of the principle of proportionality. An effective advance warning must be given of attacks which may affect the civilian population, unless circumstances do not permit this. When there is a choice between several military objectives for obtaining a similar military advantage, the objective which may be expected to cause the least danger to civilian lives and to civilian objects should be selected (Article 57, AP I).

In order to minimize collateral damage to civilians, the Parties to a conflict should take the following measures:

(a) Remove the civilian population, individual civilians and civilian objects under their control from the vicinity of military objectives;

(b) Avoid locating military objectives within or near densely populated areas; and

(c) Take necessary precautions to protect the civilian population, individual civilians and civilian objects under their control against the dangers resulting from military operations (Article 58, AP I).

Civil Defence

The aim of civil defence is to protect the civilian population from the effects of hostilities. Civil defence is not a part of a countrys' war effort and belongs to the civilian sphere. Civil defence units must not perform military duties.

The task of civil defence units is warning, rescue and maintenance, fire protection, medical services, emergency assistance and maintaining order. Civil defence organizations, their personnel, buildings and vehicles as well as shelters provided for the civilian population are specially respected and protected. Medical personnel of civil defence organizations have a special status; they are protected members of civilian medical services. Members of the armed forces permanently assigned to a civil defence organization to perform civil defence work occupy a position different from that of civilian personnel. Such military personnel must be employed exclusively for civil defence and must not have a combat task. Civil defence organizations may be permitted to continue their humanitarian tasks in occupied territories. Abuse of the civil defence sign is forbidden and is punishable by the relevant Party to the conflict.[10]

Protection of Journalists

The term 'journalists' is not defined but is understood according to the ordinary meaning of the term. It should mean correspondents, reporters, photographers, and their technical film, radio and television assistants who are ordinarily engaged in any of these activities as their principal occupation.[11]

Accredited war correspondents: In international armed conflicts, war correspondents enjoy a special status under IHL. The general principle is that they are civilians (non-combatants), but with a special entitlement to POW status upon capture by a belligerent force. Article 13 of the Second Hague Convention with Respect to the Laws and Customs ofWar on Land and its annexed Regulations, refers to 'newspaper correspondents and reporters' as 'individuals who follow an army without directly belonging to it' and who are entitled to POW status 'provided they can produce a certificate from the military authorities of the army they were

---

10 Article 63, GC IV, Articles 61-67, AP I.

11 Article 79 of the AP I "purports to protect journalists engaged on dangerous missions from the harmful effects of armed conflict." Although it does not define the term 'journalists,' it is interpreted broadly and includes "any correspondent, reporter, photographer, and their technical film, radio and television assistants who are ordinarily engaged in any of these activities as their principal occupation". However, it does not include uniformed members assigned to Armed Forces Radio and Television Service. A separate, but related category of media representatives includes war correspondents and freelance journalists.

accompanying'. This approach is embodied in Article 4(A)(4) of the GC III, which specifies that POWs include the following who have fallen into the power of the enemy: "Persons who accompany the armed forces without actually being members thereof, such as...war correspondents..., provided that they have received authorization from the armed forces which they accompany, who shall provide them for that purpose with an identity card...". The possession of an identity card is not an indispensable condition of the right to be treated as a POW , but is evidence that the person has received the required authorization. In case of any doubt, whether a war correspondent is entitled to POW status, Art 5(2) of the GC III provides that such persons shall enjoy the protection of the present convention until such time as their status has been determined by a competent tribunal.

Civilian Journalist: A journalist, when operating independently, will not be entitled to POW status upon capture by the armed forces. He will, however, be treated as a 'protected person' under Article 4 of the GC IV.

Where journalists (including war correspondents) are situated near or among armed forces or other military objectives which are legitimate military targets liable to attack, their incidental or collateral killing in the course of such attacks will not be unlawful, assuming the attacking forces otherwise comply with the principles of IHL. Article 75 of the AP I, establishes minimum guarantees of humane and non-discriminatory treatment of all persons in the power of a Party to a conflict, including absolute prohibitions on personal violence, murder , torture, corporal punishment, mutilation, outrages on personal dignity , hostage taking, collective punishment, or threats to commit any of these acts. In addition, there are specific guarantees in detention and for a fair criminal trial before an impartial and regularly constituted court, respecting the generally recognized principles of regular judicial procedure.Those arrested, detained or interned in relation to a conflict remain protected until they are released, even after the end of the conflict.

For States which are parties to the AP I, the additional obligations as contained in Article 79 for the protection of journalists are as follows. Journalists engaged in dangerous professional missions in areas of armed conflict must be considered as civilians within the meaning of Article 50 (1). They shall be protected under the GC IV and AP I, provided they take no adverse action af fecting their status as civilians. They may obtain an identity card attesting their status as a journalist (Annex II to AP I). The card may be issued by the government of the State of which the journalist is a national or in whose territory he resides or is located.

Article 79 stipulates that journalists engaged in dangerous professional missions in areas of armed conflict are civilians within the meaning of Article 50 (1) and thereby benefit from all the protection conferred by IHL on civilians. Journalists are thus protected against the effects of hostilities and against arbitrary conduct on the part of a Party to a conflict if they are captured or arrested by it. The identity card issued to them does not create a special status; it simply attests to the bearer 's status as a journalist. In addition, although journalists are formally protected only in the context of international armed conflicts (Protocol I), they also benefit from the protection granted to civilians in non-international armed conflicts. The protection is lost only if they take 'action adversely affecting their status as civilians'.

The protection of journalists in non-international armed conflict is less developed. There is no international legal status of POW available in non-international armed conflicts and there is no provision for war correspondents or journalists. They would be entitled to humane and non-discriminatory treatment under the common Article 3.

United Nation Security Council' s Resolution: The Security Council Resolution 1738 (2006) specifically addresses the protection of journalists and condemns all attacks against journalists, media professionals and associated personnel in armed conflicts, and calls on all parties to end such practices. It reiterates that journalists are protected as civilians under IHL, unless they take action adversely affecting their status as civilians. It also states that media equipment and installations are civilian objects protected from attack, unless they are military objectives. It condemns media incitement of violence against civilians (such as genocide, crimes against humanity and serious violations of humanitarian law) and calls for the perpetrators to be brought to justice. It then calls on all parties to conflicts to comply with their obligations towards civilians (including journalists) and to prevent violations of humanitarian law , including through prosecutions.

Embedded Journalists

Embedded journalism took birth during the 1990-91 Gulf W ar. It was the first war in which war correspondents could instantaneously broadcast their stories to the world. However, due to operational secrecy, censorship limited the reporting ef fectiveness of war correspondents. During the Kosovo Conflict (1998–1999), the US/NA TO military leaders recognized that combat journalists could be used as 'force multipliers' on the battlefield, developing public opinion and enhancing military morale. At the outset of the Iraq War, the US Department of Defence (DoD) encouraged the military to deploy reporters to embed with the troops. It is estimated that over 300 journalists participated in the DoD initiated training before joining as embedded journalists. They were taught combat skills, for example, providing immediate medical attention to wounded US soldiers until medical personnel arrived, operating on military helicopters, detecting land mines, surviving a chemical weapons attack, and conducting land navigation.

Embedded journalism has been widely heralded as the future of combat reporting. The induction of embedded journalists in armed conflicts has raised an interesting question; Do embedded journalists strip war correspondents of their historical protection under IHL and make them lawful tar gets? There is a possibility that unlike war correspondents, embedded journalists could perform activities outside the scope of their 'professional mission' permitted by Article 79 of the AP I. These activities may involve engaging in information warfare in support of their armed forces. In view of Article 51(3) of the AP I, journalists who perform activities that are in direct support of combat operations can be viewed as taking "a direct part in hostilities".

If embedded journalists wear military uniforms on the battlefield or rely upon military transportation, they would be considered as combatants. By their willingness to maintain close proximity to military operations and expose themselves to the same dangers as front-line battle units, embedded journalists lose their status as civilians Article 51(3) provides that civilians who take direct part in hostilities will lose their protective status and immunity, "for such time as they take direct part in hostilities", and become legitimate military targets.

Responsibility to Protect (R2P)

The protection of civilians in armed conflict refers to the measures that can be taken to protect the safety , dignity, and integrity of all human beings under IHL, refugee law, and human rights law. Under these legal regimes, States bear the primary responsibility to respect, protect and meet the needs of civilians in times of armed conflict. Organized armed groups also have clear obligations toward civilians under IHL.[12] Humanitarian organizations, such as the ICRC, the UNHCR, the UNICEF, as well as the Office for the Coordination of Humanitarian Affairs (OCHA), and humanitarian NGOs, have a subsidiary role to press parties to an armed conflict to uphold their protection responsibilities and alleviate suffering where the parties to the conflict fail to do so.

The International Commission on Intervention and State Sovereignty (ICISS) in 2001 brought out the concept of the 'R2P' stating that: "sovereign states have a responsibility to protect their own citizens from avoidable catastrophe – from mass murder and rape, from starvation –but that when they are unwilling or unable to do so, that responsibility must be borne by the broader community of states.[13] The ICISS, from this proposition derived two basic principles which underpin the responsibility to protect, namely that a primary responsibility to protect people lies with the state and a secondary or surrogate responsibility to protect falls to the international community when the state is unable or unwilling to halt or avert a population suffering serious harm, whether resulting from internal war , insurgency, repression or state failure.

The responsibility to protect is a norm which seeks to ensure that the

---

12 In non-international armed conflicts, the non-State armed groups often try to overcome their military inferiority by employing strategies that flagrantly violate international law. These range from deliberate attacks against civilians, including sexual violence, to attacks on civilian objects such as schools, to abduction, forced recruitment and using civilians to shield military objectives. The risks for civilians are further increased as militarily superior parties, in fighting an enemy that is often difficult to identify, respond with means and methods of warfare that may violate the principles of distinction and proportionality, giving rise to further civilian casualties.

13 The International Commission on Intervention and State Sovereignty (ICISS) was established in 2000 to 'promote a comprehensive debate on the relationship between intervention and sovereignty, with a view to fostering global political consensus on how to move from polemics towards action within the international system'. The Report titled "The Responsibility to Protect" is available at: http://www.iciss.ca/pdf/Commission-Report.pdf.

international community never again fails to act in the face of genocide and other mass atrocity crimes. The international community has the responsibility to use appropriate "diplomatic, humanitarian and other peaceful means" to help protect populations from serious crimes, if the State manifestly fails to protect its population. In October 2005, world leaders unanimously adopted the 'Responsibility to Protect (R2P)' principle in the UN World Summit Outcome Document. Subsequently, the Security Council reaffirmed the principle in Resolution 1674 of 2000.The principles of the R2P state that the international community has a responsibility to protect civilians when the sovereign State in question is unwilling or unable to do so.

The R2P rests on three pillars: (i) each State is to use appropriate and necessary means to protect its own population from genocide, war crimes, ethnic cleansing, and crimes against humanity, and from their incitement; (ii) the international community should assist and encourage the S tate to exercise this responsibility; and (iii) if the S tate in question fails to act appropriately, the international community should respond through the UN in a timely and decisive manner to protect the population from the four crimes mentioned.

The ICISS report sees the Security Council as the most appropriate body to deal with military intervention for human protection purposes, particularly because under the UN Charter, it has the legal capacity to take such action (Chapter VII, Article 42). Since 1999, the UN Security Council has authorized over a dozen peacekeeping missions with an explicit mandate to protect civilians. Such missions require a rapid response from a group of well-trained, suitably-equipped military , police and civilian experts, willing to not only establish a secure environment within which peace can be built, but also mandated and resourced to protect civilians in armed conflict. The UN peace operations have expanded to include civilian experts, such as human rights monitors, refugee and child protection experts, rule of law experts to rebuild justice systems, and civilian police to monitor and train local police services.As far as the protection of civilians is concerned, peace operations can be categorized into two distinct types: firstly the civilian protection as an important, but not primary mission objective through the execution of a set of tasks within a multidimensional peace operation; and secondly, protecting civilians as the primary objective, where missions are mandated to use all the necessary means to prevent or halt genocide, ethnic cleansing or systematic and widespread abuses. Whilst the former embodies the full gamut of R2P principles from prevention to rebuilding, the latter fits firmly into the Responsibility to React component.

The Relationship between Protection of Civilians (POC) and R2P. The protection of civilians (POC) agenda and R2P share the same foundation: the protection of individuals.They share the same legal underpinning, both requiring States to uphold specific obligations that they have under IHL, refugee law, and human rights law. The States have primary responsibility to protect its citizens and persons within its jurisdiction from genocide, war crimes, ethnic cleansing and crimes against humanity . The R2P has advanced the 'normative framework' of the POC. Both the broader POC agenda as well as R2P specify a role for the Security Council to adopt measures to protect individuals from suffering, although neither agenda is limited to action by the Council but involves a wide range of players: the organized armed groups, governments, UN institutions, NGOs and other non-State actors.

The R2P is not synonymous with the POC in armed conflict though it shares many features with the latter. The R2P is only a part of the broader agenda of protecting populations during armed conflict, as it is specifically concerned with the protection of people from genocide, war crimes, ethnic cleansing, and crimes against humanity - some of the gravest violations of IHL and human rights. The rights and needs of populations caught up in armed conflict stipulated by the protection of civilians extend well beyond protection from mass atrocities. On the other hand, though the R2P may be limited in terms of the crimes it protects against, this responsibility is not limited to mass atrocities that occur in times of armed conflict.The R2P is concerned with preventing and halting mass atrocity crimes regardless of whether they take place in the context of armed conflict.

Accordinto Stephen (2010), the concept of R2P does not ensure that the international community is equipped with the capacity to act when it is warranted. Without meaningful reform of the UN and associated organizations, the R2P will remain still born.[14]

---

[14] The author has examined eight recent crises in Burma, Darfur, Zimbabwe, the Democratic Republic of Congo, Sri Lanka, Gaza, Geor gia and Somalia. Marks Stephen and Nicholas Cooper, The Responsibility to Protect: Watershed or Old Wine in a New Bottle, Vol. 2, *Jindal Global Law Review*, No. 1, September 2010, p. 130-131.

The Role of the UN

The Security Council's conceptualization of the protection of civilians has varied over time. It has used the term 'protection of civilians' in relation to protection norms set out in the Geneva Conventions of 1949 andAdditional Protocols of 1977.Alternatively, it has used the term in a much more narrow sense, to describe the mandated role of peacekeepers 'to provide physical protection' through their use of 'military capability in the field either to deter attacks on civilians or , sometimes, to use force to defend civilians from attack'.[15]

Quite often, the armed forces of the member of the UN peacekeeping mission do not have a clear concept of or doctrinal guidance on what it means to 'protect civilians' in the context of peacekeeping operations. Such a conceptual gap may led to operational gaps in the field that can impede the implementation of the mandate of protection of civilians when contingents are unfamiliar with or ill-prepared for the demanding nature of such missions. The lack of a meaningful definition for peacekeeping missions, and for the uniformed component of UN operations has only heightened confusion and crosstalk.[16]

The Security Council has, on many occasions, ur ged the Parties to armed conflicts to uphold their obligations under IHL, human rights laws and refugee law. Ithas adopted four resolutions specifically addressing the protection of civilians (1265, 1296, 1674, and 1738). In addition, Resolutions on women (1325), children (1612), the protection of humanitarian workers (1502), conflict prevention (1625) and sexual exploitation (1820) include elements of civilian protection in conflict situations. Numerous country-specific resolutions of the Security Council also include measures aimed

---

[15] For the ICRC, protection aims to ensur e that authori ties and other actorsrespect their obligations and the rights of individuals in order to peserve the lives, security, physical and moral integrity and dignity of those aff ected by armed conflicts and other situations of violence. Protection includes (i) efforts that prevent or stop actual or potential violations of IHL and other laws that protect human beings, and (ii) activities that seek to reinforce the security of individuals and reduce the threats they face and their exposure to risks, arising from armed conflict and other situations of violence.Enhancing Protection: For Civilians in Armed Conflict and Other Situations of Violence. 2008. Geneva: International Comnttee of the Red Cross, p. 9.

[16] Holt Victoria and Taylor Glyn. 2009. Protecting Civilans in the Context of UN Peacekeeping Operations: Successes, Setbacks and Remaining Challenges, New York: United Nations.

to protect civilians. The Council has also imposed sanctions on those violating IHL. In extreme cases, it has authorized action to hold individuals accountable for serious violations of IHL. For example, it has established the International Tribunal for the former Yugoslavia and the International Criminal Tribunal for Rwanda, as well as referred the situation in Darfur to the ICC.

The Security Council uses its power under Chapter VII to impose arms embargoes or authorizes UN peace operations, regional organizations or groups of memberS tates to use military force for the protection of civilians. Since 1999, at least 10 UN-authorized peace operations have been mandated to provide physical protection to civilians under the imminent threat of violence. In resolution 1894 (2009), the Security Council requested that peacekeeping missions with the mandate of protecting civilian, conducted pre-deployment training and senior leadership training on the protection of civilians. The Council further requested troop- and police-contributing countries to ensure appropriate training of their personnel participating in peacekeeping missions in order to increase awareness and responsiveness to protection concerns.[17]

The President of the Security Council has condemned all violations of international law, including IHL, human rights law and refugee law , committed against civilians in situations of armed conflict. In an aide memoire on the protection of civilians in armed conflict, annexed to his statement, he has called for strict compliance of IHL by Parties to armed conflicts, including the prohibitions against following:[18]

- Directing attacks against the civilian population or against individual civilians not taking direct part in hostilities;
- Directing attacks against civilian objects;

---

[17] There are five "core challenges" for the UN in protection of civlians during conflict: (1) The Security Council must strengthen complance with international law by parties to a conflict; (2) The UN needs more consistent engagement with non-state armed groups in order to ensure compliance; (3) Peacekeeping missions must discharge their protection mandates more effectively; (4) Humanitarian actors must have better and safer access to civilians in need; and (5) The UN must enhance accountability for individuals who violate humanitarian laws. The United National Peace Operations: Year in Review 2009, p. 26.

[18] S/PRST/2009/1, 14 January 2009.

- Launching an attack that is indiscriminate, i.e., of a nature to strike military objectives and civilians or civilian objects without distinction;
- Launching an attack which may be expected to cause incidental loss of life or injury to civilians or damage to civilian objects or a combination thereof which would be excessive in relation to the concrete and direct military advantage anticipated;
- Directing attacks against personnel, installations, material, units or vehicles involved in a humanitarian assistance or UN peacekeeping mission, as long as they are entitled to the protection given to civilians or civilian objects under IHL;
- Utilizing the presence of a civilian or other protected person to render certain points, areas or military forces immune from military operations;
- Rape and other forms of sexual violence;
- Directing attacks against buildings dedicated to religion, education, art, science or charitable purposes, historic monuments, hospitals and places where the sick and wounded are collected, provided they are not military objectives;
- Directing attacks against buildings, material, medical units and transport, and personnel using the distinctive emblems of the Geneva Conventions in conformity with international law;
- Destroying or seizing the property of the adversary unless required by military necessity;
- Using starvation of civilians as a method of warfare by depriving them of objects indispensable to their survival, including willfully impeding relief supplies as provided for under applicable international humanitarian law.

The protection of civilians in armed conflict is becoming increasingly complex. IHL demands of belligerents that they respect the principles of distinction (between combatants and non-combatants), proportionality (of violence used) and precaution (against disproportionate effects of military attacks on non-combatants) in using violent means in situations of conflict. The most important of these, certainly in relation to civilian protection, is that of distinction, which underpins the Geneva Conventions and their Additional Protocols. This requires combatants to distinguish between those actively engaged in hostilities, on the one hand, and civilians and others (including the sick, wounded and prisoners of war) on the other . It also demands that combatants distinguish between civilian objects and military objectives.The concept of 'civilian protection' includes the full range of activities that countries, the armed forces and individuals can pursue to advance the legal and physical protection of civilians. Challenges of ensuring physical protection and the concept of R2P require that protection demands the coordination of multiple actors with varying roles and responsibilities. In spite of conceptual and practical developments, the protection of civilians in armed conflict remains a contested issue and is viewed through different lenses.

CHAPTER 8

Protection of Special Groups: Women

Introduction

Recent conflicts have highlighted the systematic and specific tar geting of women by both S tate and non-S tate actors. In the conflicts in Bosnia, Rwanda, Sierra Leone, Liberia, DRC and Darfur rape, sexual assault, forced prostitution, sexual slavery, forced pregnancy and other forms of sexual violence have been used as a method of warfare. Systematic sexual violence carried out by fighting forces may be for the explicit purpose of destabilizing populations and destroying bonds within communities and families. In these instances, rape is often a public act, aimed to maximize humiliation and shame. Sexual violence can also serve to quell resistance by instilling fear in local communities or in opposing armed groups. In such cases, women's' bodies are used as an envelope to send messages to the perceived enemy.

In conflicts defined by racial, tribal, religious and other divisions, sexual violence may be used to advance the goal of ethnic cleansing. Public rapes in Bosnia, for example, were used to instigate the flight or expulsion of entire Muslim communities. Forced impregnations, mutilation of genitals and intentional HIV transmission have also been perpetrated with the aim of ethnic cleansing. Women in Rwanda were taunted by their genocidal rapists, who threatened to infect them with HIVIn Bosnia, Muslim women impregnated by Serbs were reportedly held captive until late term to prevent them from aborting. Women, and more often young girls are abducted for the purpose of supplying combatants with sexual services. In many cases, their victimization is termed 'military duty'. A woman who has suffered sexual violence is often ostracized by her family due to the perception that the she has brought dishonour upon them. Children born of sexual violence may need particular protection and assistance, as they share the stigma of the rape.[1]

An estimated 40 per cent of child soldiers around the world are girls, the majority of whom are forcibly or coercively conscripted. Their responsibilities may range from working as porter to active combat, with the additional expectation that they will provide sexual services to their superiors or fellow combatants. Even those women and girls who voluntarily join fighting forces are unlikely to anticipate the extent to which they will suffer sexual exploitation.

In case of forced displacement or during flight, women and girls are at high risk of sexual violence—committed by bandits, insur gency groups, and military and border guards. Women who are forced to flee without male relatives or community members are more vulnerable to abuseWithout money or other resources, displaced women and girls may be compelled to submit to sex in return for safe passage, food, shelter, and so on. They may also be the target of traffickers. The absence of border controls and normal policing make conflict-affected countries prime routes for traffickers.

Protection for women

The provisions of IHL which offer protection to women are generic, as contained in Article 12 of the First and Second Geneva Conventions which

---

[1] The sexual abuse of women in the context of armed conflict has a long history. It has been estimated that during the World War II, approximately 1.9 million women in Eastern Germany were sexually abused by Russian soldiers. In 1937, during the Japanese occupation, 20,000 women were sexually abused or killed in Nanjing alone. An estimated 200,000 Korean and women of other nationals living in Japanese territory were forced into brothels as 'comfort women' for Japanese troops between 1931 and 1945. At the end of war majority were killed by the Japanese or by allied bombing; the survivors were abandoned, and often repudiated by their own families. During 1970-71 in East Pakistan (now Bangladesh), there were nearing 400,000 cases of sexual violence against women committed by Pakistan Army. More recently in the conflicts in the former Yugoslavia and Rwanda, a large number of women were victims of mass rape and sexual violence. Tutsi women in the 1994 genocide in Rwanda, and Muslim, Serb, Croat and ethnic Albanian women in the former Yugoslavia were tortured because they were women of a particular ethnic, national or religious group. They were used as a means of warfare to terrorize and humiliate the civilian population. Rape and other forms of sexual violence against girls and women by rebel forces have been systematic and widespread during the internal armed conflict in Sierra Leone. Women have been subjected to ill-treatment by all participants in armed conflicts by friendly and enemy forces; by civilan and military personnel, including United Nations peacekeeping forces, who were tasked to protect women.

provide that "women shall be treated with all the regard due to their sex"; or more specific, as stated in the Third Convention which stipulates that there should be separate shelters and sanitary facilities for female prisoners of war (POWs). Women are placed at particular risk of sexual and physical abuse when male staff is employed in inappropriate capacities in women's prisons, or when they are imprisoned with men. The Third Convention therefore provides that women POWs must be under the immediate supervision of women if confined. The aim of these specific provisions is also to provide additional protection for women with regard to their particular medical and physiological needs, and may not be related to their child-bearing role or for considerations of privacyFor example, the Fourth Geneva Convention provides that expectant mothers are to be the object of particular protection and respect. In situations of occupation it requires expectant and nursing mothers to be given additional food in proportion to their physiological needs and expressly includes expectant mothers among the persons for whose benefit belligerents may establish hospital and safety zones. The protection of women is covered under the following categories:

(a) Combatants

(b) POWs

(c) In occupied territories (under the Fourth Geneva Convention and AP I)

(d) In non-international armed conflicts

A. Protection of Women Combatants

IHL have had the same legal protection for women as for men. During an international armed conflict, wounded and sick combatants are protected under the First and Second Geneva Conventions, [2] which provide that wounded and sick members of the armed forces, whether in land warfare or at sea, shall be respected and protected in all circumstances. They shall

---

2 Women have taken part in both the World Wars as combatants, and as compared to WWI, their involvement in WW II was more active. Howeve r, though mil itary opportunities for women have expanded in the past 20 years, even militaries with the highest participation of women among their ranks, e.g., the USA and the UK count only up to 15 per cent female military personnel. Gener ally, the participation of women has been confined to combat support, administration, logistics, nursing and medical positions. Participation of women in hostilities remains exceptional.

be treated humanely and cared for by the Parties to the conflict in whose power they may be without any adverse distinction founded on the basis of sex, race, nationality , religion, or political opinion. In particular , any violence to their persons, murder or exterminated and torture or biological experimentation is strictly prohibited. The provisions also state that the women shall be treated with all consideration due to their sex. (Articles 12, GC I and II).Though "consideration due to their sex" is not legally defined, it covers certain concepts such as physiological specificity , honour and modesty, and pregnancy and childbirth.

B. Protection of Women Prisoners of War

Historically, there have been very few instances of women combatants being taken as POWs. Nonetheless women who take part in hostilities and fall into the powers of the enemy are protected by theThird Geneva Convention. Women who take part in *levae en masse* [3] are protected by IHL and are entitled to POW status. Women falling into any other category underArticle 4 of the Third Geneva Convention and are entitled to POW status, once they are in the power of the enemy. These are: (i) members of militias, (ii) members of volunteer corps, and (iii) members of or ganized resistance movements belonging to a Party to the conflict and operating in or outside their own territory, provided: they are commanded by a person responsible for his subordinates; have a fixed distinctive sign recognizable at a distance; carry arms openly; and conduct their operations in accordance with the laws and customs of war.

In addition women (civilian) crews of military aircraft, war correspondents, supply contractors, members of labour units or of services responsible for the welfare of the armed forces are entitled to POW status and protection provided they have received authorization from the armed forces which they accompany and have an identity card.Women members of crews, including masters, pilots and apprentices of the merchant marine and the crews of civil aircraft of the Parties to the conflict, who do not benefit by more favourable treatment under any other provisions of international law, are likewise entitled to protection as POWs under the Third Geneva Convention.

[3] The inhabtants of a non-occupied terrtory spontaneously taking up arms at the approach of the enemy, without having had time to oganize themselves, provided they carry their arms openly and respect the laws and customs of war.

Article 4B of the third Geneva Convention provides that the following shall also be treated as POWs under the Convention: (i) persons belonging, or having belonged, to the armed forces of the occupied country , if the occupying Power considers it necessary by reason of such allegiance to intern them; (ii) persons belonging to one of the categories mentioned in Article 4, who have been received by neutral or non-belligerent Powers on their territory and whom these Powers are required to intern under international law.

Additionally, women members of the medical and religious wings of the armed forces, who fall under the other categories of persons not considered POWs, are entitled to receive POWs treatment (Articles 4B and 33 Third Convention, Article 44 (4) AP I). The difference between being entitled to POW status and POW treatment is that while entitlement to POW treatment ensures that persons deprived of their liberty are accorded the full range of safeguards and not just minimum guarantees laid down in Article 75 of the AP I, they may be prosecuted for having participated in the hostilities.

General Protection: Article 12 to 15 of the Third Geneva Convention, provide general protection to POWs. They provide that POWs are entitled, in all circumstances, to respect for their persons and their honour . They must at all times be treated humanely. Women POWs must be treated with all the regard due to their sex and shall in all cases benefit by treatment as favourable as that granted to men (Article 14). It is forbidden to subject POWs to torture, physical mutilation or to medical or scientific experiments which are not justified by their medical treatment and which are not in their interest. POWs must at all times be protected against acts of violence or intimidation and against insults and public curiosity. It is specified that POWs shall not be unnecessarily exposed to danger while awaiting their evacuation from a fighting zone. The detaining Power is bound to provide free of charge for their maintenance and medical attention.

Special Protection: The Third Geneva Convention (GC III) also makes provisions for privileged treatment based on the considerations of 'rank, sex, state of health, age or professional qualifications' of women POWs. The special protections afforded to women POWs under the GC III are:

- **Quartering**: In camps where women and men POW are

accommodated, separate dormitories and toilets shall be provided for women (Article 25, para 4). Male POWs shall not have access to women prisoners.

- **Hygiene**: In a POW camp where women POWs are accommodated, separate toilets shall be provided for them (Article 29).
- **Medical Attention**: POWs....whose condition necessitates special treatment, a sur gical operation or hospital care (for example a pregnant women), must be admitted to a military or civilian medical unit where such treatment can be given, even if their repatriation is contemplated in the near future (Article 30, para 2).
- **Labour**: Women POWs may be put to labour if they are physically fit, taking into account their age, sex, rank, physical aptitude, with a view to maintaining them in a good state of physical and mental health (Article 49).
- **Discipline**: Women POWs shall not be awarded or sentenced to a punishment more serious/severe, than women members of the detaining power dealt with for a similar ofence (Article 88, para 2 and 3).
- **Execution of Punishment**: Women POWs undergoing disciplinary punishment shall be confined in separate quarters from male POWs and shall be under the immediate supervision of women (Article 97, para 4).
- **Camp**: Women POW undergoing sentence shall be confined in a separate quarter than male POW and shall be under the immediate supervision of women (Article 108, para 2).

C. Protection in Occupied Territories

In the event of declared war or any other armed conflict which may arise between two or more States, the civilian population including women get protection under the provisions of the Fourth Geneva Convention of 1949 (GC IV) andAdditional Protocol I of 1977 (API). The protection under the Convention applies to all cases of partial or total occupation of the territory of a High Contracting Party , even if the said occupation meets with no armed resistance. Parties to a conflict may establish safety or neutralized zones in an attempt to shield the civilian population, including in particular the wounded, sick, aged, children, expectant mothers and mothers of children under seven from the effects of war (Articles 14 and 15, GC IV).

Article 27 of the Fourth Convention provides that protected persons are entitled, in all circumstances, to respect for their persons, their honour, their family rights, their religious convictions and practices, and their manners and customs. They shall at all times be humanely treated, and shall be protected especially against all acts of violence or threats thereof and against insults and public curiosity. Article further states that women shall be especially protected against any attack on their honour, in particular against rape, enforced prostitution, or any form of indecent assault. Articles 33 and 34 of the GC IV prohibits acts of reprisal against protected persons, pillage, collective penalties, taking of hostages and all measures of intimidation or terrorism. Article 76 of the API, provides that in an international armed conflict women shall be the object of special respect and shall be protected in particular against rape, forced prostitution and any other form of indecent assault.

Article 35 of the GC IV, dealing with aliens in the territory of a Party to a conflict, states that all protected persons who may desire to leave the territory at the outset of, or during a conflict, shall be entitled to leave, unless their departure is contrary to the national interests of the State. Amongst the non-repatriated persons, children under fifteen years, pregnant women and mothers of children under seven years shall be accorded preferential treatment.

In occupied territories, protected persons accused of offences shall be detained, and if convicted they shall serve their sentences therein. Women shall be confined in separate quarters and shall be under the direct supervision of women (Article 76, GC IV). In case women are interned, Article 85 provides: "Whenever it is necessary, as an exceptional and temporary measure, to accommodate women internees who are not members of a family unit in the same place of internment as men, the provision of separate sleeping quarters and sanitary conveniences for the use of such women internees shall be obligatory." Pregnant women and mothers having dependent infants who are arrested, detained or interned for reasons related to the armed conflict, shall have their cases considered with the utmost priority (Article 76, para 2, AP I). Article 124 of the Fourth Convention further provides that the women internees under going disciplinary punishment shall be confined in separate quarters from male internees and shall be under the immediate supervision of women. As regard, the death penalty, Article 76 of theAP I, provides that the Parties to the conflict shall endeavour to avoid the pronouncement of the death penalty on pregnant women or mothers having dependent infants for an offence related to the armed conflict. The death penalty for such offences shall not be executed on such women.

In situations other than occupation, where the civilian population of a Party to a conflict is not adequately provided with supplies, humanitarian and impartial relief actions must be undertaken, and priority must be given to children, expectant mothers, maternity cases and nursing mothers (Paragraph 1, Article 70, AP I).

The Parties to the conflict must endeavour during the course of hostilities, to conclude agreements for the release, the repatriation, the return to places of residence or the accommodation in a neutral country of certain classes of internees, in particular children, pregnant women and mothers with infants and young children, the wounded and sick, and internees who have been detained for a long time (Article 132, GC IV).

Finally, a woman who has taken part in the hostilities but has not been granted the status of POW must in principle benefit from the provisions of the fourth Convention unless she is detained as a spy or saboteur (Article 5, fourth Geneva Convention). In the latter cases, such persons must nevertheless be treated humanely and must benefit from the fundamental guarantees provided in Article 75, of the AP I.[4]

D. Protection in Non-international Armed Conflicts

Women do not get any specific treatment in non-international armed conflicts. Article 3 common to the four Geneva Conventions lays down the minimum standard to be respected by both sides in a non-international armed conflict. It provides that persons taking no active part in the hostilities,

[4] Article 75, paagraph 5, specfically provides that the women whose iberty has been estricted for reasons related to the armed conflict shall be held in quarters separ ated from men's quarters. They shall be under the immediate supervision of women. Nevertheless, in cases where families are detained or interned, they shal, whenever possible, be held in the same place and accommodated as family units.

including members of armed forces who have laid down their arms and those placed *hors de combat* by sickness, wounds, detention, or any other cause, shall in all circumstances be treated humanely, without any adverse distinction founded on race, colour, religion or faith, sex, birth or wealth, or any other similar criteria. To this end, the following acts are prohibited at any time and in any place whatsoever with respect to the above-mentioned persons: (i) violence to life and person, in particular , murder of all kinds, mutilation, cruel treatment and torture; (ii) taking of hostages; (iii) outrages upon personal dignity, in particular, humiliating and degrading treatment; (iv) the passing of sentences and the carrying out of executions without previous judgment pronounced by a regularly constituted court af fording all the judicial guarantees which are recognized as indispensable by civilized peoples.

Another important additional protection is provided by theAdditional Protocol II (AP II), Article 4 of which repeats the fundamental guarantees contained in Article 75 of the AP I, i.e., prohibition of "outrages against personal dignity, in particular humiliating and degrading treatment, rape, enforced prostitution and any form of indecent assault". In addition, the prohibition of sexual violence is implicit in the provisions of IHL, which prohibit violence to life, including cruel treatment and torture and outrages upon personal dignity, and which are applicable in both international and non-international armed conflicts.

In non-international armed conflicts the concept of "prisoner of war" is not applicable. Women who participate in hostilities may be prosecuted for mere participation. However, participants in hostilities who have fallen into the power of the enemy are protected by IHL and are entitled to the fundamental guarantees that must be ensured to all persons (AP II, Article 4). Women are entitled to certain basic protection under domestic laws. These include: (i) detained or interned women must be held separately from men and placed under the immediate supervision of women; (ii) interned women may be searched only by female guards; (iii) interned expectant and nursing mothers must be given additional food in proportion to their physiological needs; (iv) interned maternity cases must be admitted to institutions where they can receive adequate treatment; and (v) due account must be taken of physical capabilities in awarding disciplinary punishments to detained and interned women and in the utilization of their labour. As regards the death penalty , the A P II specifies that "the death penalty shall not be carried out on pregnant women or mothers of young children" (Article 6, para 4).

Under Article 3 common to the Geneva Conventions, an impartial body, such as the ICRC, may ofer its services to the Parties to the conflict. Although the express terms of the provision are limited, it is aimed at providing food, water and medical necessities. The customary rules of humanitarian law provide that women and children must be adequately supplied with food and have the right to individual and collective relief. Most of the customary provisions are aimed at ensuring that specific categories of women – principally pregnant or breast-feeding women – as well as children are provided with sufficient nourishment. With regard to the issue of health care, the commonArticle 3(2) of the Geneva Conventions provides that the wounded and sick shall be collected and cared for . The AP II provides that the wounded and sick must be respected, protected and treated humanely and must receive the medical care and attention required by their condition. Article 18 of the AP II regulates relief actions in non-international conflicts. It does not expressly mention clothing. Howeverin cold climates, warm clothing may be considered an "essential supply" for the survival of the civilian population, including women, within this provision.

Sexual Exploitation of Women by UN Peacekeepers

During armed conflicts and displacement, women and girls may face sexual violence and exploitation at the hands of, or with the complicity of, their supposed protectors – peacekeepers and aid workers. Cases of sexual assault by peacekeepers have shocked the international community . In certain cases, women were coerced to enter into sexual relationships in exchange for food and shelter. The UN has responded to exploitation of women by peacekeepers through gender training, gender mainstreaming and codes of conduct that apply to all categories of UN personnel (civilian, civilian police, military observers and military members of national contingents)The Code of Personal Conduct for Blue Helmetsincludes: 'Do not indulge in immoral acts of sexual, physical or psychological abuse or exploitation of the local population or United Nations staf f, especially women and children.' Recently, the UN Department of Peacekeeping Operations (UNDPKO) has taken stringent measures in this regard.The UN Security Council Resolution 1325, adopted in 2000, recognized the important role of women in the prevention and resolution of conflicts and in peace building. The Security Council has urged the UN to expand the role and contribution of women in all its field operations, in particular , peace operations. Within a gender mainstreaming framework, the UN has achieved significant progress in increasing women's involvement as peacekeepers over the last ten years.

Protection under International Tribunals

Post World War II, the International Military Tribunal for the Far East included rape as a violation of war in theTokyo Charter. This was perhaps the first time that protection against gender -based violence found a place in the statute of an international criminal tribunal. The inclusion of rape as a war crime served as the foundation for the wide acknowledgment of gender-based crimes and crimes specifically targeting women in an armed conflict. The ad hoc International Criminal Tribunals for the former Yugoslavia and Rwanda (ICTY and ICTR) were further developments in this field. The Statute of the ICTR includes "outrages against personal dignity and in particular, rape, enforced prostitution and any form of indecent assault" as violations of commonArticle 3 and of theAP II over which the Tribunal has jurisdiction.The jurisprudence of the ICTYhas also recognized that rape or other acts of sexual violence may be subsumed under torture or outrages upon personal dignity , in particular humiliating and degrading treatment, committed in armed conflicts – international or non-international – which are violations of the laws and customs of war (i.e.Article 3 common to the Geneva Conventions), over which theTribunal has jurisdiction. The ICTY and ICTR have treated rape and other forms of sexual violence as war crimes, crimes against humanity and acts of genocide. The fact that rape and other forms of sexual violence in armed conflicts have been prosecuted as war crimes is a major step forward.

The judgments of the ICTY and ICTR have expanded the scope of the definitions of sexual violence and rape in an armed conflict. For example the *Akayesu* judgment of the ICTR deemed rape to be a crime against humanity, and recognized it as a 'form of aggression'The judgment affirmed that rape could be classified as an act of genocide, where it constitutes an 'act committed with the intent to destroy in whole or part a national, ethnical, racial or religious group'. The ICTR statute [Article 2(2)(d)] refers to the deliberate 'imposition of measures intended to prevent births within the group', and considers rape to be a weapon of warThe judgment states: "In patriarchal societies, where membership of a group is determined by the identity of the father, an example of a measure intended to prevent births within a group is the case where, during rape, a woman of the said group is deliberately impregnated by a man of another group with the intent to have her give birth to a child who will consequently not belong to its mother 's group."[5] The ICTY in the *Kunarac* judgment adopted a similar stance towards rape. In this case, sexual enslavement was classified as a crime against humanity or a war crime under Article 27 of the Fourth Geneva Convention.[6]

Protection under the Rome Statute

The Rome Statute grants the International Criminal Court (ICC) jurisdiction over four major areas of crimes: genocide, war crimes, crimes against humanity, and aggression and protects women from gender-based violence. The ICC Prosecutor can choose to prosecute gender -based crimes under either crimes against humanity or war crimes. Under Article 7, which specifically addresses crimes against humanity an accused can be prosecuted for "rape, sexual slavery enforced prostitution, forced pregnancy enforced sterilization, or any other form of sexual violence of comparable gravity" if it is committed as part of a widespread or systematic attack against a

[5] *Prosecutor v. Akayesu,* ICTR-96-4, 13 February 1996, amended ICTR-96-4-I, 17 June 1997. The original Akayesu indictment did not include any charges for crimes of sexual violence despite overwhelming evidence of mass rapes at Taba commune. A lack of political will among some high-ranking Tribunal officials as well as deficient investigative methodologies employed by some of the investigative and prosecutorial staff of the ICTR accounted for this omission. The indictment was amended after numerous Tutsi women testified and spoke out publicly about sexual violence in Taba commune. In June 1997, the *Akayesu* indictment was amended to reflect the pivotal role that sexual violence played in the genocide of Tutsis in Taba commune.

[6] In June 1996, the ICTY issued an indictment against eight Bosnian Serbs for a range of sexual offences committed against women in Foca. The ICTY noted that the indictment was of major legal significance because it was "the first time that sexual assaults had been diligently investigated for the purpose of prosecution under the rubric of torture and enslavement as crimes against humanity". Kunarac was charged with command responsibility for the acts of sexual violence committed by his subordinates. Many of the victims were children; one girl was 12 and one 15 at the time they were raped and serially sexually abused at Foca. Many of the women were serially raped over long periods of time and suffered permanent gynecological damage.

civilian population. Additionally, Article 7 includes gender-based persecution as a crime against humanity .[7] Under the Rome Statute, rape, sexual slavery, enforced prostitution, forced pregnancy , enforced sterilization and any other form of sexual violence constitute grave breaches of the Geneva Conventions, and are war crimes when committed in international or non-international armed conflict (Article 8 (2) (b) (xxii) and 8 (2) (e) (vi) of the Rome S tatute). The ICC may prosecute crimes under Article 7 regardless of whether they occurred during an armed conflict; however, it may prosecute crimes underArticle 8 only if the crimes occurred during an armed conflict.

Is IHL Discriminatory in Protecting Women?

In recent armed conflicts, particularly non-international conflicts, women have suffered many consequences, including physical and sexual violence[8]. Summary executions, including beheadings, floggings, amputations, arbitrary arrests, restrictions on freedom of movement and violations of women's rights have been reported. Women's access to basic social and humanitarian services such as education, and healthcare has been drastically limited. The cessation of hostilities does not guarantee an end to the perpetration of sexual violence. On the contrary, evidence shows that even after a conflict has ended, high levels of sexual and gender-based violence tend to persist, creating long-term threats to the security , health and livelihoods, and their ability to participate in reconstruction and peace-building efforts. The regime of IHL has been criticized for being discriminatory in relation to women and its inadequacy in protecting women in armed conflicts. It has also been stated IHL does not address the issue of compensation for individuals affected by armed conflict.

However, this may not be entirely true. States have the duty to respect and ensure respect for IHL, including the rules protecting women, and, should violations occur, to bring the perpetrators to justice. Women who

---

[7] Rome Statute Article 7 (1) (h) provides that persecution on the basis of gender - as well as on political, racial, national, ethnic, cultural, religious or other grounds - may constitute a crime against humanity.

[8] The Middle East, the Palestinian, Cyprus, Western Sahara, Timor-Leste, Liberia, Somalia, Bosnia and Herzegovina, Georgia, Burundi, Afghanistan, Sierra Leone, the Great Lakes region, the Democratic Republic of the Congo, the Central African Republic, Eritrea and Ethiopia, Guinea-Bissau, Cote d'Ivoire, Iraq, Chad, the Sudan, the Central African Republic and Myanmar.

are not, or are no longer, taking part in hostilities are protected against the effects of fighting and also against abusive treatment by the parties to hostilities. Women are entitled to humane treatment, respect for their life and physical integrity, and to live free from torture, ill-treatment, acts of violence and harassment. In addition to this general protection, women are afforded special protection.

The absence of an eficient judiciary and security institutions to ensure accountability, prevent violence and combat impunity remain the main challenges in post-conflict situations. Threats of violence and abuse often remain long after an armed conflict ceases, intimidating women and preventing them from engaging fully in rebuilding the society for a peaceful future. The formal justice system often provides no recourse and may be inaccessible for many women. In many instances, the families of victims of sexual violence withdraw complaints and opt for extrajudicial settlement.

The Role of the United Nations

The Security Council resolution 1325, adopted in October 2000, was the first to focus specifically on women's experience of armed conflict.[9] It aimed to empower women at all levels of decision-making in conflict prevention, conflict resolution and peace-building, in addition to reducing gender-based violence. It referred to the existing obligations under the Geneva Conventions of 1949 and the Additional Protocols of 1977; the Refugee Convention of 1951 and the Protocol of 1967; the Convention on the Elimination of All Forms of Discrimination against Women (CEDAW) and the Optional Protocol of 1999; the Convention on the Rights of the Child 1989 and the two Optional Protocols of 2000; and relevant provisions of the ICC Statute. Clause 10 of the Resolution relating to gender-specific

[9] On 31 October 2000, the Security Council adoptedresolution 1325 (2000), drawing attention to the disproportionate and unique impact of armed conflict on women and girls and their exclusion from conflict prevention, peacekeeping, conflict resolution and peace-building. The resolution highlighted the fact that an understanding of the impact of armed conflict on women and girls and effective institutional arrangements to guarantee their protection and full participation in peace processes would contribute significantly to the promotion and maintenance of international peace and security. The adoption of the resolution was the culmination of years of concerted appeals and efforts, especially by civil society and women's organizations, to draw attention to and seek action to reverse the egregious and inhumane treatment of women and girls, the denial of their human rights and their exclusion from decision-making in situations of armed conflict.

protective measures, called on all parties to armed conflict to take special measures to protect women and girls from gender -based violence, particularly rape and other forms of sexual abuse, in situations of armed conflict. Clause 11 reinforced the recognition of sexual violence and rape as crimes against humanity and war crimes. It also supported protection measures under the Geneva Conventions.

Some recent developments in public international law, including the adoption of Security Council Resolution 1820 focused on women, peace and security, have sought to increase the visibility of gender in situations of armed conflict. The framework of Resolution 1820 takes the understanding of sexual violence in armed conflict beyond the limited remit of gender-based provisions under the Geneva Conventions. For example, Clause 1 not only recognizes the systematic use of sexual violence against civilian populations, but also elaborates how this can 'significantly exacerbate situations of armed conflict' and stresses the importance of prevention. Clause 3 sets out a range of measures to enhance the protection of civilians, with particular reference to women and girls. These measures include military training on the prohibition of all forms of sexual violence, and disciplinary action against those security forces who commit acts of rape or sexual violence. The evacuation of women and children under imminent threat of sexual violence to safety is also stipulated, which demonstrates a shift towards preventative rather than reactionary measures.

The ICRC and Protection of Women

The ICRC is an independent humanitarian organization which endeavors to bring protection and assistance to victims of armed conflict: both international and non-international. Being neutral, the ICRC remains detached from all political issues related to conflict and endeavors to promote dialogue in situations of internal violence, with a view to finding solutions for matters of humanitarian concern. In situations of armed conflict, the ICRC remains particularly concerned about the protection of women from the effects of hostilities, and especially against acts of violence. It tries to prevent such violations by making appropriate representations to parties to armed conflicts—both States and armed opposition groups, urging them to comply with the rules of IHL and to respect and protect persons not taking an active part in the hostilities. It also visits POWs and persons detained in relation to conflicts and political violence throughout the world.

The ICRC carries out its mandate throughout the world through its protection activities, its relief and medical assistance programs, its efforts to re-establish family links, and its dissemination activities. It has provided financial assistance to families of detainees to facilitate family visits and also assisted the families with administrative procedures. The ICRC in its dissemination sessions with the armed forces promotes awareness and implementation of IHL, including protective measures for women. It also supports psychological rehabilitation programmes for women and children who have been victims of violence, including rape. In Sri Lanka and Afghanistan, the ICRC has developed some small-scale programmes to provide assistance and a potential source of income to women. For women under detention, the ICRC tries to ensure:

- that women are protected from inhuman or degrading treatment;
- that appropriate detention conditions for women and specific conditions for mothers with children are met;
- that women are detained in separate quarters from male detainees;
- that women are guarded by female staff;
- the presence of female prison staff who are appropriately trained to deal with female detainees;
- that women prisoners have the opportunity to maintain contact with their families, and where possible, may receive family visits;
- that judicial guarantees are fully respected.

The law provides adequate protection to women in situations of both international and non-international armed conflict. Even though the written rules of IHL governing non-international armed conflict are limited, there is an important body of customary law which extends protection to women in such situations. While the protection of women in armed conflict s is adequately addressed, the challenge lies in ensuring respect for and implementation of the existing rules.The provisions related to the protection of women must be disseminated to as wide an audience as possible and enforced during situations of armed conflict. The prohibitions of sexual violence must be included in the military codes and training manuals. There must be a system for monitoring violations of IHL involving women. Efforts should be made to disseminate the rules concerning the protection of women among the parties to an armed conflict and the UN peacekeeping forces. In the context of increasing violence against women in armed conflicts, the Special Rapporteur on Violence Against Women, has recommended that the existing humanitarian legal standards should be evaluated and practices revised to incorporate developing norms on violence against women during armed conflict.[10]

[10] R. Coomaraswamy, Report of the Special Rapporteur on violence against women, its causes and consequences. UN Doc. E/CN.4/1998/54. Also see 2009 Report: "15 years of the United Nations Special Rapporteur on Violence Against Women, Its Causes and Consequences". The Report states: "Although sexual brutality, enslavement, forced prostitution and forced pregnancy have marked armed conflicts across the globe, these crimes have long remained invisible in international criminal and humanitarian law. Viewed as an unfortunate outcome of war, rather than crimes, they have been popularly explained in terms of aberrant behaviour by men under harsh conditions of war and separation from their families and communities." Available at: http://www2.ohchr.org/english/issues/women/rapporteur/docs/15YearReviewofVAWMandate.pdf

CHAPTER 9

Protection of Children

Introduction

The United Nations Children' s Fund (UNICEF) website on 'children in armed conflicts' reports that more than two million children have died as a direct result of armed conflict over the last decade. More than three times that number, have been permanently disabled or seriously injured. More than 1 million have been orphaned or separated from their families. Between 8,000 and 10,000 children are killed or maimed by landmines every year.[1] Children also routinely experience emotionally and psychologically painful events such as the violent death of a parent or close relative; witnessing loved ones being tortured; exposure to combat, shelling and other life-threatening situations; acts of abuse such as being abducted, arrested, held in detention, raped, tortured; disruption of school routine and community life; destitution and an uncertain future. Children of all ages are also strongly affected by the stress experienced by their adult caregivers.

An estimated 300,000 child soldiers - boys and girls under the age of 18 - are involved in more than 30 conflicts worldwide. Child soldiers are used as combatants, messengers, porters, cooks and to provide sexual services. Some are forcibly recruited or abducted, others are driven to join by poverty, abuse and discrimination, or to seek revenge for violence enacted against themselves and their families.

Armed conflicts affect children in the following ways:

- Attacks on their lives and also such attacks against their caregivers;
- Separation from their parents or other caregivers;

[1] http://www.unicef.org/protection/index_armedconflict.html.

- Sexual violence and/or attacks on their dignity and physical integrity (they are at greater risk when separated from their families);
- Association with armed forces/armed groups (recruitment, weapon bearer, live combat, physical and/or sexual exploitation, abuse);
- The lack of health services or of food and basic commodities, inadequate shelter, and the exposure to mines and explosive remnants of war;
- Attacks on educational structures and staf, which interrupt learning and causes psychological trauma and the loss of 'safe areas';
- Having to assume responsibility for their families, including being forced into prostitution for socio-economic reasons.

Legal Protection

Legal protection for children during armed conflicts is contained in two bodies of international law — international humanitarian law (IHL) and international human rights law (IHRL). Protection for children in wartime is enshrined in IHL, which is binding on both States and non-governmental armed groups. The prohibition on intentionally directing attacks against civilians in the armed conflicts, is one of the cornerstones of IHL and applies to children just as it does to other civilians. This prohibition derives from one of the key principle of IHL that a distinction is made between legitimate and illegitimate military targets. IHL includes the Geneva Conventions of 1949, their twoAdditional Protocols of 1977 andAdditional Protocol III of 2005 - provides general protection for all persons affected by armed conflicts and also contains provisions specifically related to children. The Geneva Convention IV is mainly concerned with the treatment of civilians who are in the hands of an opposing party or who are victims of war. In its general protection measures for civilians, it incorporates 17 articles (Articles 14, 17, 23 to 27, 40, 50, 51, 68, 76, 81, 82, 84, 89 and 132) of specific concern to children, affording general protection to them as civilians and special protection for children living in both occupied and non-occupied territories.

Human rights law – the Convention on the Rights of the Child (CRC), 1989 and its Optional Protocol on the Involvement of Children in Armed Conflict, 2000 – also specifically takes into account the need to protect children against the effects of armed conflict. The Optional Protocol to the CRC sets the age limit for compulsory recruitment and direct participation in hostilities at 18, and requires States parties to raise the minimum age for voluntary recruitment to at least 16. It prohibits insur gent armed groups "under any circumstances" from recruiting persons under 18 years or using them in hostilities.

The Rome Statute of the ICC provides a mechanism of accountability for war crimes, crimes against humanity and genocide, including crimes specific to children. For example, the S tatute classifies conscription, enlistment or use in hostilities of children below the age of 15 in both international and internal armed conflicts as a war crime. The CRC and the Rome Statute, have strengthened the international framework for the protection of children in situations of armed conflict.

Protection under International Humanitarian Law

A. The Geneva Conventions of 1949

IHL protects children in three ways: (i) it recognizes the need to provide children with special protection because of their age, which is a norm of customary international law; (ii) it questions the use of children in military operations; and (iii) it takes into account children' s immaturity if they commit offences during armed conflicts. It distinguishes between combatants and noncombatants. Article 1 common to the Geneva Conventions affords children, as members of the civilian population, protection against inhumane treatment and directed attacks during armed conflicts, whether international or non-international. The common Article 3 of the four Geneva Conventions protects persons "taking no active part in hostilities." However, children used as soldiers are not protected under either Article 1 or Article 3 common to the Geneva Conventions.

The Third Geneva Convention dealing with the care and protection of prisoners of war (POW) provides that POWs must be treated alike by the detaining power, subject to any privileged treatment which may be accorded to them by reason of their age, among other criteria (Article 16). The detaining power may utilize the labour of POWs who are physically fit, taking into account their age, among other criteria (Article 49).There is no age limit for entitlement of POWstatus under theThird Geneva Convention;

however, age may be a factor justifying privileged treatment.

The **Fourth Geneva Convention** contains a number of provisions which afford protection to children. The provisions could be divided into three categories:

1. General Protection Against Certain Consequences of war

- **Hospitals and Safety Zones:** In times of peace, the State Parties and, after the outbreak of hostilities, the belligerents, need to establish hospital and safety zones and localities with a view to protecting from the effects of war, wounded, sick and aged persons, children under 15, expectant mothers and mothers of children under seven (Article 14).

- **General Protection**: Expectant mothers must be the object of particular protection and respect (Article 16). Civilian hospitals organized to give care to maternity cases, in particular, may in no circumstances be the object of attack (Article 18).

- **Evacuation**: The parties to a conflict must endeavour to conclude local agreements for the removal from besieged or encircled areas, of wounded, sick, infirm, and aged persons, children and maternity cases, and for the passage of medical personnel and medical equipment on their way to such areas (Article 17).

- **Land, Sea and Air transport:** Convoys on land or sea conveying maternity cases, in particular, must be respected and protected in the same manner as the hospitals provided for in Article 18. Aircraft exclusively employed for the removal of maternity cases, may not be attacked, and must be respected while flying on routes specifically agreed upon between all the parties to the conflict concerned (Articles 21 and 22).

- **Consignment of medical supplies, food and clothing:** The State Parties must permit the free passage of all consignments of essential foodstuffs, clothing and medicines intended for children under 15, expectant mothers or maternity cases. The State Parties may, however, stipulate conditions to prevent the consignments from being diverted from their destination or a definite advantage from accruing to the military efforts or economy of the enemy through the substitution of those consignments (Article 23).

- **Child welfare:** The parties to a conflict must take the necessary measures to ensure that children under 15, who are orphaned or are separated from their families as a result of the war, are not left to their own resources, and that their maintenance, the exercise of their religion and their education are facilitated in all circumstances. Their education must, as far as possible, be entrusted to persons of a similar cultural tradition.The parties to the conflict must facilitate the reception of such children in a neutral country for the duration of the conflict. They must, furthermore, endeavour to arrange for all children under 12 to be identified by the wearing of identity discs, or by some other means (Article 24).

- **Family news:** All persons in the territory of a party to the conflict, or in a territory occupied by it, must be enabled to give news of a strictly personal nature to members of their families, wherever they may be, and to receive news from them.The parties to the conflict concerned may request the assistance of the CentralAgency (Article 25).

- **Dispersed families:** Each party to a conflict must facilitate enquiries made by members of families dispersed owing to the war, with the object of renewing contact with one another and of meeting, if possible. It must encourage, in particular, the work of organizations engaged in this task (Article 26).

2. Treatment of Protected Persons

- **Treatment:** Protected persons are entitled, in all circumstances, to respect for their persons, their honour , and their family rights (Article 27).

- **Non-repatriated persons:** Aliens in the territory of a party to a conflict who have not been repatriated enjoy the minimum protection afforded by the Convention. Children under 15 years, pregnant women and mothers of children under seven years must benefit by any preferential treatment to the same extent as the nationals of the State concerned (Article 38).

- **Deportations, transfers, evacuations:** When undertaking transfers or evacuations (which are authorized only if the security of the population or imperative military reasons so demand), the occupying power must ensure that members of a family are not separated (Article 49).

- **Care and education of Children:** The occupying Power must facilitate the proper working of all institutions devoted to the care and education of children. It must take all necessary steps to facilitate the identification of children and the registration of their parentage. It may not, in any circumstances, change their personal status or enrol them in formations or organizations under its authority. The occupying power must make arrangements for the maintenance and education, if possible by persons of their own nationality, language and religion, of children who are orphaned or separated from their parents as a result of the war.

  The occupying Power must not hinder the application of any preferential measures which may have been adopted prior to the occupation in favour of children under 15 years, expectant mothers, and mothers of children under seven years (in regard to food, medical care and protection against the effects of war) (Article 50).

- **Enlistment, labour:** The occupying Power may not compel protected persons to work unless they are over 18 years of age, and then only under specific conditions (Article 51).

- **Death penalty:** The occupying power may only apply the death penalty in specific cases. In any case, the death penalty may not be pronounced against a protected person who was under 18 years of age at the time of the offence (Article 68).

- **Treatment of detainees:** In the treatment of protected persons who are accused or have been convicted of offences, proper regard must be paid to the special treatment due to minors (Article 76). This provision also applies to detainees who are in the national territory of the detaining Power (Article 126).

3. Treatment of Internees

- **Maintenance:** The detaining power must provide for the support of those dependent on internees, if such dependants are without adequate means of support or are unable to earn a living (Article 81).
- **Grouping of internees:** Members of the same family , and in particular parents and children, must be lodged together in the same place of internment, except when separation of a temporary nature is necessitated for reasons of employment or health or for the application of disciplinary sanctions.Wherever possible, they must be given separate accommodation from other internees, together with facilities for leading a proper family life. Internees may request that their children who are left at liberty without parental care be interned with them (Article 82).
- **Accommodation, hygiene, food and healthcare:** Internees must have suitable bedding and sufficient blankets, account being taken of their age, among other criteria. Expectant and nursing mothers and children under 15 years of age must be given additional food, in proportion to their physiological needs. Maternity cases must be admitted to any institution where adequate treatment can be given and must receive care not inferior to that provided for the general population (Articles 85, 89 and 91).
- **Recreation, study, sports and games:** The education of children and young people must be ensured; they must be allowed to attend schools either within the place of internment or outside. Special playgrounds must be reserved for children and young people so that they can engage in physical exercise, sports and outdoor games (Article 89).
- **Disciplinary punishments:** The disciplinary punishments applicable to internees must take into account their age, among other criteria (Article 119).
- **Transfers of internees:** Maternity cases must not be transferred if the journey would be seriously detrimental to their health, unless their safety imperatively so demands (Article 127).

- **Release, repatriation and accommodation in neutral countries during hostilities or occupation:** The parties to a conflict must endeavour, during the course of hostilities, to conclude agreements for the release, repatriation, return to places of residence or the accommodation in a neutral country of certain classes of internees, in particular children, pregnant women and mothers with infants and young children (Article 132).

- **Official Information Bureaux and Central Agency:** Each of the parties to the conflict must establish an official Information Bureau responsible for receiving and forwarding information in respect of the protected persons who are in its power. One of the tasks of the Bureau is to notify the families of these persons and to identify children who are orphaned or have been separated from their families (Articles 136 to 140).

B. Additional Protocol I

Article 77 of the Additional Protocol I (API) of 1977 provides that children shall be the object of special respect and shall be protected against any form of indecent assault. The parties to the conflict must provide them with the care and aid they require, whether because of their age or for any other reason. Article 8 of the Protocol defines the terms "wounded and sick" to cover expectant mothers, maternity cases and new-born babies. The provisions of the AP I relating to the protection of children are as follows.

- **General protection of civilian objects:** Civilian objects must not be the object of attack or of reprisals. In the event of doubt, schools are presumed to be civilian objects (Article 52).

- **Relief actions:** In distributing humanitarian aid to the civilian population, priority must be given to children, expectant mothers, maternity cases and nursing mothers, among others (Article 70).

- **Reunion of dispersed families:** The States party to the Protocol and the parties to the conflict must facilitate in every possible way the reunification of families dispersed as a result of armed conflicts. They must encourage the work of the humanitarian organizations engaged in this task (Article 74).

- **Fundamental guarantees:** In cases where families are detained or interned, they must, whenever possible, be held in the same place and accommodated as family units (Article 75).

- **Protection of women:** The cases of pregnant women and mothers having dependent infants who are arrested, detained or interned for reasons related to the armed conflict must be considered with the utmost priority.

- **Protection of childr en:** The Parties to a conflict must take all feasible measures to ensure that children who have not attained the age of 15 years do not take a direct part in hostilities and, in particular, they must refrain from recruiting them into their armed forces. In recruiting among those persons who have attained the age of 15 years but who have not attained the age of 18 years, the parties to the conflict must endeavour to give priority to those who are oldest.

  If, in exceptional cases, children who have not attained the age of 15 years take a direct part in hostilities and fall into the power of an adverse party, they continue to benefit from the special protection accorded by this Article, whether or not they are prisoners of war.

  If arrested, detained or interned for reasons related to the armed conflict, children must be held in quarters separate from the quarters of adults, except where families are accommodated as family units. The death penalty for an ofence related to the armed conflict must not be executed on persons who had not attained the age of 18 years at the time the offence was committed (Article 77).

- **Evacuation of childr en:** No Party to a conflict may arrange for the evacuation of children, other than its own nationals, to a foreign country except in the case of a temporary evacuation which has become necessary for compelling reasons of the health or safety of the children. In this case, the written consent of the parents or legal guardians is required. The education of each evacuated child must be provided with the greatest possible continuity (Article 78).

C. Additional Protocol II

The Additional Protocol II makes specific provisions for protection of children in non-international armed conflicts. Article 4, dealing with 'Fundamental guarantees' provides that children must be provided with the care and aid they require, and in particular:

(a) they must receive an education, including religious and moral education;

(b) all appropriate steps must be taken to facilitate the reunification of families temporarily separated;

(c) children who have not attained the age of 15 years must neither be recruited into the armed forces or groups nor allowed to take part in hostilities;

(d) the special protection provided by thisArticle to children who have not attained the age of 15 years remains applicable to them even if they take a direct part in hostilities;

(e) measures must be taken, if necessary, and whenever possible with the consent of their parents or persons who are responsible for their care, to remove children temporarily from the area in which hostilities are taking place to a safer area within the country.

Article 6, entitled 'Penal prosecutions', states that persons prosecuted for a criminal of fence related to the armed conflict enjoy at least the minimum protection. In particular, the death penalty must not be pronounced on persons who were under the age of 18 years at the time of the offence, and must not be carried out on pregnant women or mothers of young children.

The Geneva Conventions and the AP I list a number of violations committed in international conflicts that are considered to be "grave breaches" of IHL. These include willful killing, torture or inhuman treatment, willfully causing great suf fering or serious injury , unlawful deportation, and making civilians and non-defended localities the object of attack. States are obliged to bring to justice any person, who is alleged to have committed grave breaches of the Geneva Conventions. While the list of grave breaches does not include any of the child-specific provisions of the Geneva Conventions, atrocities committed against children are covered by the general categories of grave breaches.

D. Rome Statute

The Rome Statute of the ICC defines war crimes as either grave breaches of the 1949 Geneva Conventions or other serious violations of the laws and customs applicable in armed conflicts. In the context of non-international conflicts, the ICC Statute defines war crimes as serious violations of common Article 3 to the Geneva Conventions or serious violations of customary law applicable in non-international conflicts. The Statute lists a number of acts that constitute these crimes:

- **Genocide:** Genocide means, inter alia, forcibly transferring children of a national, ethnic, racial or religious group to another group with intent to destroy, in whole or in part, that group as such (Article 6).
- **Crimes against Humanity—trafficking of children:** For the purpose of the Rome Statute, 'crime against humanity' includes 'enslavement' when committed as part of a widespread or systematic attack directed against any civilian population, with knowledge of the attack. Enslavement means the exercise of any or all of the powers attaching to the right of ownership over a person and includes the exercise of such power in the course of trafficking in persons, in particular women and children (Articles 7 (1) (c) and 7 (2) (c)).
- **Crimes against Humanity—sexual violence:** For the purpose of the Rome Statute, 'crime against humanity' means: rape, sexual slavery, enforced prostitution, forced pregnancy, enforced sterilization, or any other form of sexual violence of comparable gravity; when committed as part of a widespread or systematic attack directed against any civilian population, with knowledge of the attack (Article 7 (1) (g)).
- **War crimes:** Recruiting children under the age of fifteen, or using them as active participants in hostilities, is also considered a war crime under Article 8 of the Rome Statute.

E. Convention on the Rights of the Child

The 1989 Convention on the Rights of the Child (CRC) is one of the most important steps that the United Nations has taken to address the needs of children throughout the world. Article 1 of the Convention defines a child as a human being below the age of 18 years unless, under the law applicable to the child, majority is attained earlier. The four general principles of the CRC—non-discrimination (Article 2), best interest of the child (Article 3), the right to life, survival and development (Article 6) and the right of children to have their view heard and given due weight in all decisions af fecting them (Article 12) — These principles should be taken into account in implementing all the provisions of the CRC.All the provisions of the CRC are applicable to children during all levels of conflict and there is no provision that allows derogation in times of national emergencies.

Through the CRC, S tates Parties have recognized the right of those under the age of 18 to "the enjoyment of the highest attainable standard of health". The Convention requires States Parties to take appropriate measures to "ensure the provision of necessary medical assistance and health care" and to combat disease and malnutrition (Article 24)Article 38 specifically addresses the issue of protecting children in conflicts and applies to both international and non-international armed conflicts. It provides that the States Parties must respect rules of IHLapplicable to them in armed conflicts which are relevant to the child. The States Parties must take all feasible measures to ensure that persons who have not attained the age of 15 years do not take a direct part in hostilities. They must refrain from recruiting any person who has not attained the age of 15 years into their armed forces. In recruiting persons who have attained the age of 15 years but who have not attained the age of 18 years, S tates Parties must endeavour to give priority to those who are oldest. In accordance with their obligations under humanitarian law to protect the civilian population in armed conflicts, States Parties must take all feasible measures to ensure the protection and care of children who are affected by an armed conflict.

Article 39 of the CRC establishes that "S tates Parties shall take all appropriate measures to promote physical and psychological recovery and social reintegration of a child victim of: any form of neglect, exploitation, or abuse; torture or any other form of cruel, inhuman or degrading treatment or punishment; or armed conflicts. Such recovery and reintegration shall take place in an environment which fosters the health, self-respect and dignity of the child. The Optional Protocol on the involvement of children in armed conflict includes a similar provision for children who have been unlawfully recruited or used in hostilities.

Optional Protocol to CRC, 2000: In order to enhance further the protection of children during war, the international community agreed in January 2000, to adopt an Optional Protocol (OP) to the CRC. Article 1 of the Protocol relating to the direct participation in hostilities provides that States Parties must take all feasible measures to ensure that members of their armed forces who have not attained the age of 18 years do not take a direct part in hostilities. However, the OP does not prevent voluntary recruitment of children under 18 years of age. Under the OP, States are only obliged to raise their age of voluntary recruitment above the age of 15 [the standard in the CRC, Article 38 (3)] and put in place appropriate safeguards to ensure that recruitment is voluntary and the proof of age is verified.

As of 23 March 2011, the number of ratifications of the Optional Protocol to the Convention on the Rights of the Child on the involvement of children in armed conflict has increased to 139 countries.Upon ratification of or accession to the Protocol, States Parties must deposit a binding declaration that sets forth the minimum age at which they will permit voluntary recruitment into their national armed forces. If the age of voluntary recruitment is below 18 years, States Parties must maintain safeguards to ensure that: (i) such recruitment is genuinely voluntary; (ii) such recruitment is done with the informed consent of the persons' parents or legal guardians; (iii) such persons are fully informed of the duties involved in such military service; and (iv) such persons provide reliable proof of age prior to acceptance into the national military service. The requirement to raise the minimum age for voluntary recruitment does not apply to military academies. Article 4(1) prohibits armed groups opposing a government from recruiting children under 18, a stronger provision than that applied to States. Under Article 6, the States Parties need to take all feasible measures to ensure that children recruited or used in hostilities contrary to the Protocol are demobilized and must, when necessary, accord to these persons all appropriate assistance for their physical and psychological recovery and their social reintegration. Under the OP, States are also required to report regularly to the Committee on the Rights of the Child on measures taken to implement the Protocol.

Child Soldiers[2]

The recruitment of children into armed conflict has claimed the lives of more than two million children and left more than six million children maimed or permanently disabled. Currently , over 300,000 children are serving in 50 countries in every region of the world.[3] Children have served in government forces, paramilitaries or in opposition forces in Columbia, Mexico, Peru, Turkey, Yugoslavia, Algeria, Angola, Burundi, Chad, Democratic Republic of Congo, Eritrea, Ethiopia, Myanmar , Pakistan, Rwanda, Sierra Leone, Somalia, Sudan, Uganda, Afghanistan, Iran, Iraq, Israel and the Occupied Territories, Lebanon, India, Indonesia, Myanmar, Nepal, Pakistan, Philippines, Solomon Islands, Papua New Guinea, Sri Lanka, East Timor, Tajikistan, and Uzbekistan.[4] The practice of child soldiers is highly prevalent in Asia and Myanmar alone has more than 75,000 child soldiers, with some as young as eleven.[5]

---

[2] For the purposes of disarmament, demobilization and reintegration programmes, UNICEF defines a 'child soldier' as any child – boy or girl – under 18 years of age, who is part of any kind of regular or irregular armed force or armed group in any capacity, including, but not limited to: cooks, porters, messengers, and anyone accompanying such groups other than family members. It includes girls and boys recruited for forced sexual purposes and/or forced marriage. The definition, therefore, does not only refer to a child who is carrying, or has carried, weapons.

[3] Since 1989, the ban on the recruitment of children has been considered in a number of instruments that prohibit the recruitment and use of children under 18. For example, in 1990, the African Charter on the Rights and Welfare of the Child obliged States Parties to refrain from any recruitment of children and ensure that no person under 18 years takes a direct part in hostilities. ILO Convention 182 on the Worst Forms of Child Labour qualifies the forced or compulsory recruitment of children and their direct participation in armed conflicts as one of the "worst forms of child labour" , and defines children as "all persons under the age of 18".

[4] Human Rights Watch: Children's Rights, Where Child Soldiers Are Being Used, available at http:www.hrw.org/campaigns/crp/where.htm.

[5] Singer P.W. 2005. *Children at War*, Pantheon Books, p. 27.

[6] The UN Security Council Resolution 1379 called on the Secretary General to produce "a list of parties to armed conflict that recruit or use children in violation of the international obligations applicable to them. In response to this, the third report of the Secretary General on Children in Armed Conflict [S/2002/1299 of 26 November 2002] contained a list of 23 parties including both the governments and insurgents in five conflict situations – Afghanistan, Burundi, the democratic Republic of Congo, Liberia and Somalia – that recruit and use children.

The UN Secretary-General' s report[6] highlights that children are recruited by government, paramilitary and rebel forces under the threat of violence or death in the belief that they can be easily manipulated and intimidated by their commanders.The breakdown of societies during conflict often leaves children separated from their families and many children are driven to join armed groups as a means of survival. Others may join to seek revenge or refuge from poverty or abuse. When conflict situations de-escalate and end, many children are left physically disabled and/or psychologically traumatized. Having been exposed to a prolonged militarized way of life, denied education and stigmatized by members of their former communities, many struggle to adapt to a peaceful society . These children are often drawn to violence and crime for survival and are especially vulnerable to re-recruitment.

Child Soldier and Prisoner of War: Children between the ages of 15 and 18, enrolled in the armed forces or taking part in a mass uprising of the population (*levee en masse*), have a combatant status and are entitled to prisoner of war (POW) status, if captured. Children under 15, who are recruited (in violation ofArticle 77, paragraph 2 ofAP I) or are enrolled as volunteers in the armed forces, also have combatant status and will, if captured, have POW status. There is no age limit for entitlement of POW status. However, age may be a factor justifying privileged treatment. A child combatant under 15 years of age, who is captured, cannot be sentenced for having borne arms. Since the prohibition contained in Article 77, paragraph 2 of Protocol I is addressed to the Parties to the conflict and not to the children, the participation of children in hostilities does not constitute a breach of the law by them.The State Party to the conflict which recruited the children would be accountable for a breach of IHL. Penal proceedings can be initiated for serious violations of IHL committed by children, in particular war crimes. Children who participate in hostilities, but are not combatants within the meaning of IHL, remain subject to the domestic legislations of the countries of which they are nationals.

In non-international armed conflicts, no one is entitled to the status of combatant, thus there are no POWs. A child combatant captured during a non-international armed conflict is protected by Article 3 common to all four Geneva Conventions, which is applicable to all persons who are taking part in hostilities or have ceased to do so.A child combatant may be punished under domestic legislation for taking part in hostilities. In addition, children are protected by Article 4 (paragraph 3) of the AP II, which contains detailed provisions on the care and assistance which should be given to them.

UN Security Council Resolutions

The Security Council has expressed deep concern over the violation of the provisions of applicable international law relating to the rights and protection of children in armed conflicts.[7] It has condemned the recruitment and use of children by parties to armed conflicts as well as their re-recruitment, abduction, killing and maiming; rape and other sexual violence perpetrated on children; attacks against schools or hospitals; and all other violations of international law committed against children in situations of armed conflict. The Security Council in its resolutions[8] on 'Children and Armed Conflicts' has urged the Secretary-General to take the necessary steps to improve the monitoring and reporting mechanism, to allow for prompt advocacy and effective response to all violations and abuses committed against children. In resolution 1314, the Security Council noted that the deliberate targeting of civilian populations or other protected persons, including children, and the committing of systematic, flagrant and widespread violations of IHL and human rights law, including that relating to children, in situations of armed conflict may constitute a threat to international peace and security.

---

[7] The UN Security Council has identified the six grave violations against children during armed conflict: (i) killing or maiming, (ii) recruitment or use of child soldiers, (iii) rape and other forms of sexual violence, (iv) abduction, (v) attacks against schools or hospitals, and (vi) denial of humanitarian access. Each of the six violations during armed conflict may constitute: grave breach of the Geneva Conventions and the other laws of war; violation of customary norms of international law; a contravention of the Convention on the Rights of the Child and other international and regional human rights treaties; or war-crime and crime against humanity under the Rome Statute.

[8] Since 1999, the United Nations Security Council has adopted several resolutions on children and armed conflict, calling on States to respect the rights of children and ensure their protection; condemning the use of child soldiers; and highlighting the importance of special measures to prevent sexual violence against children. Security Council Resolutions 1261 (1999) S/RES/1261 (1999), 1314 (2000) S/RES/1314 (2000), 1379 (2001) S/RES/1379 (2001), 1460 (2003) S/RES/1460 (2003), 1539 (2004) S/RES/1539 (2003), 1612 (2005) S/RES/1612 (2005), and 1882 (2009) S/RES/1882 (2009). The Security Council has adopted other resolutions on the protection of civilians in general which have significance for children in armed conflicts: see resolutions 1265 of 17 September 1999 and 1296 of 19 April 2000.

In pursuance to the Security Council Resolution 1612 (2005), the Secretary General has submitted reports to the Security Council on children in armed conflict in Uganda,[9] Chad,[10] Congo,[11] Central African Republic,[12] Sudan,[13] Myanmar,[14] Colombia,[15] Burundi,[16] Sri Lanka,[17] the Philippines,[18] and Nepal.[19] A few highlights of these reports are as follows.

- The average age of recruitment of child soldiers in Colombia decreased from 13.8 years in 2002 to 12.8 years in 2006.
- In the CentralAfrican Republic, children were consistently recruited and used by non-State armed groups, including Government-backed self-defence militias. Children were the primary victims of the conflict, often recruited forcibly, displaced or abducted, raped and subjected to grave sexual violence by all parties to the conflict throughout the territory.
- In Congo, children were abducted for recruitment, sexual exploitation and forced labour by armed groups. They were subjected to cruel, degrading and inhumane treatment while in detention. Incidents of killing and maiming of children, abductions, and grave sexual violence were regularly reported from Congo.
- In Nepal, threats, coercion and economic necessity were factors that contributed to children's involvement with the armed groups. Certain armed groups provided economic incentives to the children's families for their initial involvement and the children were paid on a case-by-case basis according to the nature of their

---

9 S/2008/409, 23 June 2008 and S/2009/462, 15 September 2009.

10 S/2008/532, 7 August 2008.

11 S/2008/693, 10 November 2008.

12 S/2009/66, 3 February 2009.

13 S/2009/84, 10 February 2009.

14 S/2009/278, 1 June 2009.

15 S/2009/434, 28 August 2009.

16 S/2009/450, 10 September 2009.

17 S/2009/325, 25 June 2009.

18 S/2010/36, 21 January 2010.

19 S/2010/183, 13 April 2010.

involvement. They were put at risk in participating in protests, demonstrations, extortions and violent activities such as clashes with other youth groups and security forces.

- In Sudan, children were recruited and used by all Parties to the conflict. The State and non-State parties were responsible for grave violations against children, such as killing and maiming, abductions, rape and other grave sexual violence, attacks on schools and hospitals and denial of access to humanitarian services. Rape and sexual violence were systematic and widespread and children and women in an around refugee camps and internally displaced persons' settlements were especially vulnerable.

- In many of the countries the near total impunity with which grave crimes are perpetrated against children is disturbing and poses a serious challenge to the protection of children. The factors which lead to this impunity include the lack of political will, weak legal and judicial infrastructures. In some cases deliberate obstruction of the course of justice and failure to focus on command responsibility were reported.

In Resolution 1882 (2009), the Security Council stressed on the primary role of national Governments in providing protection and relief to all children affected by armed conflicts. It condemned all violations of applicable international law involving the recruitment and use of children by parties to armed conflict as well as their re-recruitment, killing and maiming, rape and other sexual violence, abductions, attacks against schools or hospitals and denial of humanitarian access by parties to armed conflict and all other violations of international law committed against children in situations of armed conflict.

In pursuance to paragraph 19 of the Security Council resolution 1882, the Secretary General submitted a report in April 2010.[20] The third part (section IV) of the report focuses on information on grave violations committed against children, in particular recruitment and use of children, killing and maiming of children, rape and other sexual violence against

---

[20] A/64/742–S/2010/181 of 13 April 2010.

children, abductions of children, attacks on schools and hospitals, and the denial of humanitarian access to children by parties to armed conflict in contravention to applicable international law.[21] The report states that in the year 2009 a number of important legislation by different States were adopted or existing laws modified to prevent, prohibit and criminalize child recruitment and other grave violations against children, in line with State obligations under international law. A few highlights of the report are as follows:

- The USA's Child Soldier Prevention Act of 23 June 2009 restricts the provision of extending military training, finance and other defence-related assistance to countries identified as recruiting or using child soldiers in government armed forces or Government-supported paramilitary organizations or militias, in violation of international law.
- On 10 January 2009, the Government of the Democratic Republic of Congo promulgated a new law on child protection, replacing the decree of 6 December 1950 on juvenile delinquency. Under the law, for the first time, the recruitment and use of children under 18 years of age by armed forces, the police and armed groups are prohibited and can result in a prison term of 10 to 20 years. The law also sets the age of legal majority at 18 years and calls for the creation of special tribunals and police units for the protection of children.
- On 9 April 2009, the President of the Government of South Sudan inaugurated the Child Act of South Sudan, the first-ever law in the country recognizing children's rights. The act criminalizes the recruitment and use of child soldiers, as well as torture and cruel

---

21 Applicable international law relating to the rights and protection of children in armed conflict includes, in particular, the Geneva Conventions of 1949 and obligations applicable under the Additional Protocols thereto of 1977, the Convention on the Rights of the Child of 1989, the Optional Protocol thereto of 25 May 2000, and the amended Protocol II and Protocol V to the Convention on Prohibitions or Restriction on the Use of Certain Conventional Weapons Which May Be Deemed to Be Excessively Injurious or to Have Indiscriminate Effects, International Labour Organization Convention No. 182 concerning the Prohibition and Immediate Action for the Elimination of the Worst Forms of Child Labour, the 1997 Convention on the Prohibition of the Use, Stockpiling, Production and Transfer of Anti-personnel Mines and on Their Destruction, and the Convention on Cluster Munitions.

treatment of children.

- The Federal Child Act passed by the Sudan National Assembly on 29 December 2009 brings Sudan' s legislation in line with international standards, including the Convention on the Rights of the Child and its two Optional Protocols. The Act prohibits the recruitment of children into armed forces or groups, ensures demobilization, and support for the reintegration and rehabilitation of child soldiers and victims of conflict, and abolishes the death penalty for any person under 18 years of age.
- In Burundi, the revised penal code adopted by the National Assembly on 22 April 2009 now prohibits the enlistment of children into the national defence forces, laying down that 18 years is the minimum age for conscription. It raises the age of criminal responsibility to 15 years, and provides alternatives to imprisonment and strengthens sentences against perpetrators of violance against children, in particular sexual violence.

Deployment of Child Protection Advisers

Recognizing the critical role of United Nations peacekeeping missions in protecting children in all phases of peacekeeping operations, the Security Council, in resolutions 1314 (2000), 1379 (2001), 1460 (2003) and 1539 (2004), endorsed the Special Representative's proposal for the deployment of child protection advisers to support the peacekeeping leadership in mainstreaming child protection in all aspects of peacekeeping operations. The child protection adviser initiative represents a practical step taken by the Security Council with regard to children affected by armed conflict and is an example of effective collaboration among relevant entities within the United Nations system to mainstream child protection in the context of peacekeeping and, ultimately, to improve the situation of children. The Office of the Special Representative, the Department of Peacekeeping Operations and UNICEF are working together to facilitate the implementation of the Security Council' s call for the inclusion of child protection advisers in peacekeeping operations.

Child protection advisers are central to the implementation of the UN Secretary-General's zero-tolerance policy on sexual abuse and exploitation, including through participation in conduct review mechanisms at the mission level. The child protection adviser acts as a point of contact between the mission and various in-situ actors working on childrens' issues, in particular the United Nations country team, the national government, NGOs and the diplomatic/donor community. Overall guidance for the work of child protection advisers is provided by the generic terms of reference for child protection advisers, developed jointly by the Of fice of the Special Representative, UNICEF and the Department of Peacekeeping Operations. Guided by these generic terms of reference, child protection advisers develop more specific work-plans, which reflecting the key issues in the specific context of a country.

ICRC and Protection of Children

The ICRC has been active in promoting the legal protection of children. In 1939, the ICRC and the International Union for Child Welfare prepared a draft convention for the protection of the child. In accordance with its tradition as a humanitarian or ganization, the ICRC is actively associated with the protection of children in the following ways.

- Prevention of Recruitment: The ICRC actively promotes the principle of non-recruitment and nonparticipation in armed conflict of persons under the age of 18 years. It reminds States and armed groups of their obligations under international law , and works to introduce those principles into the domestic legal systems.
- Care of the Wounded and Sick: When wounded, children benefit from the ICRC's activities on behalf of combatant*hors de combat.* In collaboration with national societies and in consultation or collaboration with the International Federation, the ICRC may involve itself in efforts to meet the psychological and physical needs of children who have participated in armed conflict and to ease their reintegration into the mainstream.
- Children under Detention: As part of its humanitarian mandate, the ICRC visits more than half a million detainees in over 70 countries every year. It identifies and registers detained children and may request armed forces or armed groups to release individual children. The organization works to monitor and improve the

conditions of detention, through regular confidential dialogue with the authorities in charge.

The ICRC enables detained boys and girls and the children of detainees to maintain regular contact with their families. It facilitates family visits and telephone conversations, and puts its family message services at the disposal of detainees. Its delegates monitor the material conditions of detention and ensure individual follow-up of detainees. The ICRC strives to ensure that detainees are provided with their basic needs: adequate food, water, clothing, medical care (including immunization), education, access to recreational activities, and baby items.

As part of its ef forts to improve the sanitary conditions in which detainees live, the ICRC often carries out maintenance, renovation or construction work in places of detention. It also attempts to persuade the authorities to provide access to legal assistance and speedy judicial procedures for detained children. It works with national authorities to improve legislation concerning detained children.

- Protection of Child Victims: The ICRC has adopted a comprehensive approach that includes both preventive action and assistance for victims. In its IHL training programmes for armed forces and armed groups, the ICRC emphasizes the prohibition of sexual violence and advocates its inclusion in military law or internal regulations. It provides volunteers at the community level with psychosocial training to enable them to counsel victims and to mediate between victims and their families.
- Protection from Mines: The ICRC is actively involved in the development, promotion and implementation of norms of IHL that prevent and address the human suffering caused by mines, cluster munitions and other Explosive Remnants of War (ERW), such as the Convention on the Prohibition of Anti-Personnel Mines, the Convention on Cluster Munitions and the Protocol on ER W. The ICRC takes action, in conjunction with national authorities, to reduce the effects of weapon contamination and provides support to national societies to develop their capacities. It carries out risk-education activities with the intention of bringing about long-term changes in behaviour and ensuring that communities have a central

role in determining clearance priorities.

- Rehabilitation: The ICRC assists in the provision of emer gency care for the war-wounded and aids hospitals and medical structures in many mine/ERW-affected countries. It operates and supports physical rehabilitation facilities for weapon victims and other physically disabled people in conflict-affected countries to help them regain mobility and economic independence. It may also help in the social reintegration of the disabled and in enabling them to play a productive role in society.

During armed conflicts, the vulnerability of children is very high. They are regularly recruited into armed forces or armed groups to take on a range of role, including fighting, acting as spies or messengers, cooks and porters, sexual slaves, human mine detectors, forced labourers, and even suicide bombers. This involvement may be forced or voluntary. Children may be coerced by threat or violence or be tempted by the power and status that accrue to weapon bearers. Avenging the death of a relative may be a motive as may be the desire to such relief from hunger and destitution. Armed conflicts expose children to a number of extreme risks, such as death, physical injury, psychological damage and sexual abuse. The psychological and social aspects of child development and the overall well-being of children in conflict situations are compromised. Return to civilian life can pose many challenges for both children and communities. In addition to meeting the basic needs of children, such as food and shelter, it is essential to consider the emotional and developmental needs of children. IHL and human rights law afford suitable protection to children against the effects of armed conflicts. The challenge today is to ensure their implementation on the ground.

CHAPTER 10

Protection of the Environment

Introduction

Throughout human history, the environment has been one of war 's many victims. Thucydides records the Greek tactic of scorching the earth during the Peloponnesian Wars. The Romans salted the soils of Carthage after winning the Punic Wars. The Dutch breached their dykes in 1792 to prevent a French invasion. In World War I, the British set afire Romanian oilfields to prevent the Central Powers from capturing them; in World War II, Germany and the Soviet Union engaged in 'scorched-earth' tactics; and in the Korean War, the United States bombed North Korean dams. During the Vietnam War, the US destroyed nearly 20% ofVietnam's forests, including 54% of its mangrove forests, through chemical defoliants, bulldozers and bombings. The US sprayed twelve million gallons of highly toxic chemical agents over more than six million acres of crops and trees in an effort to preclude the growth of groundcover and endeavoured to influence weather patterns for military advantage by engaging in cloud seeding. Towards the end of the First Gulf War, Iraq burned hundreds of oil wells and dumped massive amounts of oil into the Persian Gulf. The US and its allies dropped more than 47,500 cluster bombs, containing 13,167,500 bomblets, while NATO forces destroyed major oil refineries, and pharmaceutical and petrochemical plants in Kosovo.

More recently (between 27 December 2008 and 18 January 2009), Israeli forces conducting a combined military operation bombarded the Gaza Strip by land, sea and air , causing serious environmental damage. The ongoing conflicts in Afghanistan and Iraq too, have had serious repercussions on the nations' environment. More than two decades of war have played havoc with the physical environment and caused great damage to the natural resources, besides causing the loss of more than two million lives and crippling an additional half a million people.

Military Activities and the Environment

Military activities have a significant impact on the environment. Both nuclear and conventional weapons pose a serious threat to environment, not only when they are used but also during testing, development, production and maintenance. Lar ge quantities of hazardous and toxic substances, including nuclear wastes are produced, which cause a lage-scale depletion and degradation of natural resources.

Today, the world' s eight nuclear weapon states have nearly 36,000 nuclear bombs[1], containing 5,000 megatons of destructive ener gy—more than sufficient to destroy the world. The dimension of the destructive power of nuclear weapons is dificult to comprehend.A single large nuclear weapon could release explosive power comparable to all the energy released from the conventional weapons used in all past wars. Nuclear weapons have the potential to destroy the entire ecosystem of the planet.Those already in the world's arsenals have the potential of destroying life on the planet several times over.

During the Gulf War, the US and British forces introduced armour - piercing ammunition made of depleted uranium (DU), a radioactive and toxic waste. By the end of the war , more than 290,000 kg of DU contaminated the soil on the battlefields of Saudi Arabia, Kuwait, and southern Iraq. DU is not only chemically toxic like other heavy metals such as lead, but also an alpha particle emitter with a radioactive half-life of 4.5 billion years. DU weapons contaminate impact areas with extremely fine radioactive and toxic dust. In addition, DU fragments and intact DU penetrators also pose a hazard. DU is acknowledged to cause kidney damage, cancers of the lung and bone, non-malignant respiratory disease, skin disorders, neurocognitive disorders, chromosomal damage and birth defects.

---

[1] Nuclear-Weapon States: China, Fr ance, Russia, United Kingdom, United States. Each of these five states originally declared its nuclear-weapons program and was recognized under the 1968 Nuclear Non-Proliferation Treaty (NPT) as a nuclear weapon state because it had tested a nuclear weapon prior to January 1, 1967.Estimated total nuclear warhead stockpiles: United States, 12,070; Russia, 22,500; United Kingdom, 260; Fr ance, 450; China, 400. Non-NPT Nuclear-Weapons States: India, Israel, Pakistan.

DU contamination is unlikely to be cleaned up by the victor or the vanquished because of the great cost and the prospect of further environmental damage.

Cleaning up of DU contaminations involves removing the top layer of soil which could be potentially devastating for an environment, especially in the case of arable land or wetlands. Besides, the cost of such an operation could be astronomical. For example, the cost of cleaning up 290,000 kg of depleted uranium over thousands of hectares in SaudiArabia, Kuwait, and Iraq would be tens of billions of US dollars.

Landmines and unexploded military ordnance (UXO) also pose serious threat to the environment and to the process of sustainable development, affecting not only the present but also future generations. They prejudice economic development by disrupting the biosphere's life support systems and diminishing the capacity of the environment to supply natural resources. Mines deny access to natural resources, promote the rapid and unsustainable exploitation of marginal and ecologically fragile environments, deplete biological diversity by destroying flora and fauna, contaminate the surrounding soil and water with highly toxic substances, and destroy the ecosystem itself by disrupting soil and water processes.They kill livestock as well as wildlife. In Libya, between 1940 and 1980, mines and other UXO killed more than 125,000 camels, sheep, goats, and cattle. In Afghanistan, about 264,000 goats and sheep were killed at a value of about $31.6 million. Gazelles have disappeared from parts of Libya that were mined during World War II. Brown bears are regular victims of mines in Croatia, while barking deer, clouded leopards, snow leopards, and Royal Bengal tigers have been killed by landmines in India.

The increase in the intensity of environmental damage resulting from wars has been parallel to the technological 'advancement' in warfare. The use of more advanced arms and ammunition means greater damage to the environment. Currently, there are some 40 armed conflicts going on in the world involving tens of millions of people. Many of these are taking place in locations that are critical to maintenance of biodiversitysuch as,Africa, South Asia and Latin America. Being populated and economically less developed, these regions are already sufering severe environmental stresses.

Classification of Environmental Damage

A simple non-scientific and non-legal classification of environmental damage due to war is provided by Lanier-Graham (1993): (1) intentional direct destruction of the environment during war; (2) incidental direct destruction; and (3) indirect or induced destruction as a medium- or long-term consequence of war, but still attributable to war.[2] Intentional direct destruction refers to deliberate attacks on cultivated and uncultivated lands and resources, where the objective is environmental destruction for its own sake. The burning of oil wells during the Persian Gulf War is an example of this. An example of incidental direct destruction is soil disturbance caused by the movement of battle tanks from one location to another, where environmental damage is collateral, but not the primary objective of the action undertaken. Finally, indirect or induced destruction may occur when the migration of populations on account of war causes undue environmental stresses.

Protection of the Environment under IHL

The existing rules of IHL for the protection of the environment aim not to prevent damage altogether, but rather, to limit it to a level deemed tolerable. Unfortunately, there is reason to fear that the use of particularly devastating means of warfare (the effects of which are still unknown) could wreak such large-scale destruction as to render illusory the protection afforded to civilians under IHL. Indeed, severe environmental damage could seriously hamper or even prevent the implementation of the provisions to protect the victims of armed conflict. Two treaties under IHL have provisions relating to the protection of the environment.

1. The Convention on the Prohibition of Military or Any Other Hostile Use of Environmental Modification Techniques (ENMOD), 1976

The ENMOD was a response to the severe damage suffered by Vietnam's environment as a result of the use of chemicals and defoliants by the US.[3] It was intended to prohibit the military use of climate

[2] Lanier-Graham, Susan D. 1993. *The Ecology of War: Environmental Impacts of Weaponry and Warfare*. New York: Walker and Company.

[3] The UN general Assembly adopted Resolution 31/72 on December 10, 1976, which later became the ENMOD Convention.

modification techniques that are intended to or could be expected to cause 'widespread', 'long-lasting', *or* 'severe' destruction or damage to the enemy environment. These three terms are defined as follows.

Widespread: Encompassing an area on the scale of several hundred square kilometres;

Long-lasting: Lasting for a period of months, or approximately a season;

Severe: Involving serious or significant disruption or harm to human life, natural and economic resources, or other assets.

The ENMOD represents the foundation document regulating the 'active' use of the environment in warfare. It binds the State parties to take measures to prohibit and prevent any activity in violation of the provisions of the Convention anywhere under its jurisdiction and control. While the ENMOD does not pre-empt the customary principle of military necessity, it does try to balance environmental damage with military necessity by providing an upper limit the acceptable level of environmental damage. It prohibits "military or any other hostile use of environmental modification techniques having widespread, long-lasting, or severe effects as the means of destruction, damage, or injury to any other State Party".

2. Protocol I of 1977Additional to the Geneva Conventions of 1949

Articles 35 and 55 of Protocol I specifically address the protection of the environment during periods of armed conflict. Article 35 begins by restating two principles developed in St Petersburg and The Hague. First, the right to choose means of warfare "is not unlimited", and second, that it is prohibited to employ "methods of warfare of a nature to cause superfluous injury or unnecessary suf fering". Article 35(3) further strengthens the protection of the environment by stating that "it is prohibited to employ methods of warfare which are intended, or may be expected, to cause widespread, long-term, and severe damage to the natural environment". By placing subparagraph 3 in theArticle dealing with the well-established 'Basic Rule', the Protocol raises the restraint on wartime damage of the environment to a new level. In addition, Article 36 obligates parties to ensure that any new means or method of warfare comply with the existing international law.

Article 35(1) mentions the protection of the environment as a basic rule, while Article 55 is entirely devoted to the environment and thus represents the only truly environmental provision in Protocol IArticle 55 states:

> Care shall be taken in warfare to protect the natural environment against widespread, long-term, and severe damage. This protection includes a prohibition of the use of methods or means of warfare which are intended or may be expected to cause such damage to the natural environment and thereby prejudice the health or survival of the population.

The highest threshold of environmental damage within can be derived from the second sentence of Article 55, prohibiting the causation of environmental damage where that damage has the potential for consequent human injury. The prohibition appears only to apply where environmental damage would have the potential to cause consequent harm to humans.

Prior to Protocol I and the ENMOD, the international community had paid little attention to the consequences of war on the environment, as illustrated by the fact that the four Geneva Conventions following the Second World War failed to mention the environment. Media coverage during the Vietnam War, coupled with an increasing worldwide awareness of the environment, led to the adoption of Protocol I and the ENMOD.

As opposed to the cumulative threshold of harm contained in Protocol I (widespread, long-term, *and* severe damage), the three criteria in the ENMOD are disjunctive: only one needs to be fulfilled to constitute a breach of the Convention. The aim of the ENMOD is to prohibit all military manipulations of the natural environment, which is reflected in the relatively low requirement for the breach of the Convention.

The two treaties prohibit dif ferent types of environmental damage. While Protocol I prohibits recourse to environmental warfare, i.e., the use of methods of warfare likely to upset the vital balance of nature, the ENMOD prohibits what is known as 'geophysical warfare', or the deliberate manipulation of natural processes that may trigger natural phenomenon such as hurricanes, tidal waves, earthquakes, and rain or snow.

Despite growing international concern about the effect of war on the environment, neither of these agreements has been universally adopted. There is also a danger that the discrepancies in these laws might hamper their effective implementation in the future.

3. Protection of the environment in non-international armed conflict

Despite the obvious threat posed by situations of non-international armed conflict, none of the rules of IHL applicable to such situations provide specifically for the protection of the environment, however , certain provisions do cater for environmental protection. For example, common Article 3 to the four Geneva Conventions prohibits certain instances of environmental warfare, for example, poison gas, landmines, and scorched earth practices, which may cause 'violence to life and person.'

Additional Protocol II also lacks specific environmental protections. However, Articles 14, 15, and 17 ofAP II afford indirect protection to the environment. Article 14 states that starvation of civilians as a method of combat is prohibited. It is therefore prohibited to attack, destroy, remove or render useless, for that purpose, objects indispensable to the survival of the civilian population, such as foodstuffs, agricultural areas for the production of foodstuf fs, crops, livestock, drinking water installations and supplies and irrigation works. Article 15 on the protection of works and installations containing dangerous forces, states that "works or installations containing dangerous forces, namely dams, dykes and nuclear electrical generating stations, shall not be made the object of attack, even where these objects are military objectives, if such attack may cause the release of dangerous forces and consequent severe losses among the civilian population." Prohibitions against the forced movement of civilians are covered in Article 17.

4. Customary Rules of IHL

The fundamental principles of customary international law applicable to the protection of the environment are those of humanity , discrimination, proportionality, and military necessity. The principle of humanity, also known as the 'principle of unnecessary suffering and destruction', proscribes the use of means of warfare which cause unnecessary suffering not justified by legitimate military objectives. The principle of discrimination provides that the means and methods of warfare must distinguish between military and civilian targets.The principle of proportionality is a fact-specific concept requiring that the force employed by the attacker not be disproportionate to the military advantage sought. The principle of military necessity (or military advantage) states that a combatant may use only the level of force "required for the partial or complete submission of the enemy" that incurs the least "loss of time, life, and physical resources" in the attainment of a legitimate military objective. While at first glance, it might appear that the military necessity exception trumps all restrictions on the conduct of war , it is still subject to the limits of humanity , discrimination and proportionality.

The Rules 43 to 45 of the ICRC study on customary IHL deal with the protection of the environment during the conflict. [4] The general principles on the conduct of hostilities, contained in Rule 43, apply to the natural environment. It states: (a) no part of the natural environment may be attacked, unless it is a military objective, (b) destruction of any part of the natural environment is prohibited, unless required by imperative military necessity, and (c) launching an attack against a military objective which may be expected to cause incidental damage to the environment which would be excessive in relation to the concrete and direct military advantage anticipated is prohibited. Rule 44 states that the methods and means of warfare must be employed with due regard to the protection and preservation of the natural environment. In the conduct of military operations, all feasible precautions must be

---

[4] Jean-Marie Henckaerts and Louise Doswald-Beck. 2005. *Customary International Humanitarian Law,* International Committee of the Red Cross and Cambridge University Press, Cambridge, 2005, Vol. I, p. 143-158.

taken to avoid, and in any event to minimize, incidental damage to the environment. Lack of scientific certainty as to the ef fects on the environment of certain military operations does not absolve a party to the conflict from taking such precautions. The last part of Rule 44 constitutes an application of the precautionary principle, well-established in international environmental law , to the duty to take precaution in armed conflict. Finally, Rule 45 provides that the use of methods or means of warfare that is intended, or may be expected, to cause widespread, long-term and severe damage to the natural environment is prohibited. Destruction of the natural environment may not be used as a weapon.These customary rules are a simplified version of the provisions ofAdditional Protocol I and of ENMOD, and did not constitute any significant progress for better protection of the environment during armed conflict.

5. Indirect Protection under IHL

The IHL places limits on the conduct of combatants engaged in armed conflicts. It attempts to balance human values and military needs, such as the need of the military in fighting a war weighed against the protection of civilians. In the course of providing protection for people, a number of provisions do expressly address the protection of the environment. The rules of IHL that can be considered to indirectly protect the environment during armed conflict can be clustered into five categories: (i) rules limiting or prohibiting certain weapons and methods of warfare such as the ChemicalWeapons Convention, 1993 (CWC), and the Hague Convention IV of 1907 regulating the means and methods of warfare; (ii) clauses protecting civilian objects and properties; (iii) clauses protecting cultural heritage sites; (iv) rules concerning installations containing dangerous forces; and (v) limitations on certain specifically defined areas.The CWC specifically prohibits the disposing of chemical weapons by "dumping in any body of water, land burial and open pit burning", thereby ensuring that the human and environmental costs of disposal are minimal.

The 1981 Convention on Prohibitions or Restrictions on the Use of Certain Conventional Weapons which may be Deemed to be Excessively Injurious or to have Indiscriminate Ef fects (CCW) also provides protection to the environment. The CCW and its additional protocols restrict the use of inhumane weapons. Protocol III, which concerns prohibitions and restrictions on the use of incendiary weapons, is a case in pointArticle 2 contains a specifically applicable provision: "It is prohibited to make forests or other kinds of plant cover the object of attack by incendiary weapons except when such natural elements are used to cover, conceal or camouflage combatants or other military objectives or are themselves military objectives."

6. Rome Statute of the International Criminal Court (ICC)

The most recent work in the field has been the adoption of the Rome Statue of the International Criminal Court, granting the Court jurisdiction over certain acts causing environmental damage. ByArticle 8.2 (b)(iv), the following acts committed during international armed conflict constitute war crimes:

> Intentionally launching an attack in the knowledge that such an attack will cause incidental loss of life or injury to civilians or damage to civilian objects or widespread, long-term and severe damage to the natural environment which would be clearly excessive in relation to the concrete and direct military advantage anticipated.

This provision is interesting for a number of reasons. There are two significant modifications as regard the protection of environment in an armed conflict. First, the Rome Statute requires both intention and knowledge of the outcome rather than either intention or expectation as set forth in theAdditional Protocol I of 1977. Second, for the act to qualify as a war crime, the damage to the natural environment must be clearly excessive in relation to the military advantage anticipated.

Criminal responsibility will therefore extend to only those who order operations with the knowledge that widespread, long-term, and severe damage will occur . However, pursuant to Article 28 of the Rome Statute, a commander or superior who "knew , or owing to the circumstances, should have known" that those under his or her command and/or control were committing environmental crimes and "failed to take all necessary and reasonable measures within his or her power to prevent or repress their commission" is subject to prosecution. Indeed, commanders or superiors will be criminally responsible even if they merely fail to "submit the matter to the competent authorities for investigation and prosecution".

7. The San Remo Manual

The San Remo Manual on International Law Applicable to Armed Conflict at Sea (1994) states that 'methods and means of warfare should be employed with due regard for the natural environment'.The HPCR Manual on International Law Applicable to Air and Missile Warfare (2009) formulates rules along the same lines, stating that the 'destruction of the natural environment carried out wantonly is prohibited'. It also urges that 'when planning and conducting air and missile operations, due regard ought to be given to the natural environment (Rules 88 and 89)'.[5]

International Environmental Law

The 1972 Stockholm Declaration focuses exclusively on nuclear weapons. Principle 26 provides: "Man and his environment must be spared the effects of nuclear weapons and all other means of mass destruction. States must strive to reach prompt agreement, in the relevant international organs, on the elimination and complete destruction of such weapons."The 1982 World Charter for Nature adopts a more general approach, stating that "nature shall be secured against degradation caused by warfare or other hostile activities", and declaring that "military activities damaging to nature shall be avoided".

The 1992 Earth Summit in Rio de Janeiro was for a UN conference that was unprecedented in terms of both size and scopeThe Rio Declaration gets closer to the point, but is still ambiguous about environmental damage due to armed conflict. Although not legally binding, the wording of Rio Principle 24 requires States to respect those rules of international law which provide protection for the environment in times of armed conflict. It states, "Warfare is inherently destructive of sustainable development. States shall therefore respect international law providing protection for the environment

---

[5] Harvard University, Program on Humanitarian Policy and Conflict Research (HPCR), Manual on International Law Applicable to Air and Missile Warfare, Bern, 2009, Rules 88 and 89.

in times of armed conflict and cooperate in its further development, as necessary." Agenda 21, a comprehensive programme for global action in all areas of sustainable development adopted at Rio, makes progress in the direction of protecting the environment in times of armed conflict. Para 39.6 (a) of Agenda 21 states: "Measures in accordance with international law should be considered to address, in times of armed conflict, large-scale destruction of the environment that cannot be justified under international law. The General Assembly and the Sixth Committee are the appropriate fora to deal with this subject. The specific competence and role of the International Committee of the Red Cross should be taken into account." These two provisions testify to a heightened awareness of the risk which a conflict entails for the environment.

The international environmental treaties, including those on civil liability for damage, are silent on the issue of their applicability following the outbreak of military conflict. The UN Convention on the Law of the Sea (UNCLOS), 1982, requires states party 'to protect and preserve the marine environment', as well as 'to take measures to prevent, reduce, and control marine pollution'. Most of the environmental treaties have provisions excluding their applicability when damage occurs as a result of armed conflict. For example, the Convention on Biological Diversity (1992), the UN Convention to Combat Desertification (1994), and the Convention on the Conservation of Migratory Species of Wild Animals (1979) contain no reference to their applicability during armed conflict.

Concern for the environment also emeged at the national level.A few countries made provisions for the protection and preservation of the environment in their constitutions, and also adopted a lar ge number of legislative measures for the protection of the environment as such, or of its various components (such as water, air and forests).

Human Rights Law

Human rights law may provide additional guidance on the conduct of the states affecting the environment and natural resources during armed conflict. Both treaty law and customary international law contain rules that ensure that the basic social and political rights of individuals are respected, including several that have been linked to environmental protection. However, it is dif ficult to determine whether and to what extent human rights law is applicable for the protection of environment during an armed conflict.

The ICRC Guidelines

As a consequence of the Gulf war , the UN General Assembly urged the States to take all measures to ensure compliance with existing international law applicable in times of armed conflict.The General Assembly also called on the International Committee of the Red Cross (ICRC) to report on activities undertaken with regard to the protection of the environment in times of armed conflict.[6] In 1994, the ICRC drew up guidelines for military manuals and for instructions to the armed forces on the protection of the environment during armed conflicts.[7] The guidelines state that care should be taken to protect and preserve the natural environment during a war . They prohibit military or any other hostile use of environmental modification techniques having widespread, long-lasting or severe effects as the means of destruction, damage or injury to any other State party. They also prohibit attacks against the natural environment by way of reprisals. Under the guidelines, the States are urged to enter into further agreements providing additional protection to the natural environment in times of armed conflict. The guidelines provide that States must take all measures required by international law to avoid:

1. making forests or other kinds of plant cover the object of attack by incendiary weapons except when such natural elements are used to cover, conceal or camouflage combatants or other military objectives, or are themselves military objectives;
2. attacks on objects indispensable to the survival of the civilian population, such as foodstuffs, agricultural areas or drinking water installations, if carried out for the purpose of denying such objects to the civilian population;
3. attacks on works or installations containing dangerous forces,

---

6 Protection of Environment in Times of Armed Conflict, UN Doc. A/Res/47/37 , February 9, 1992.

7 International Committee of the Red Cross (ICRC), Guidelines for Military Manuals and Instructions on the Protection of the Environment in Times of Armed Conflict, Geneva, 1994.

namely dams, dykes and nuclear electrical generating stations, even where they are military objectives, if such attack may cause the release of dangerous forces and consequent severe losses among the civilian population and as long as such works or installations are entitled to special protection under Protocol I additional to the Geneva Conventions;

4. attacks on historic monuments, works of art or places of worship which constitute the cultural or spiritual heritage of peoples.

Liability for Environmental Damage

The existing international legal framework contains many provisions that either directly or indirectly protect the environment or govern the use of natural resources during armed conflict. In practice, however , these provisions have not always been effectively implemented or enforced. So far no individual has been held responsible for environmental harm caused during armed conflict. There were a few cases in World War II relating to serious environmental damage. German General Lothar Rendulic was charged before the International Military Tribunal at Nuremberg in pursuit of his scorched earth tactics. It was alleged that the German troops burnt and destroyed villages and surrounding facilities in the Norwegian province of Finmark when retreating from an advancing Russian army . Rendulic was acquitted of the chage of wanton destruction, as theTribunal accepted that he genuinely perceived the destruction to be militarily justified at the time.

Except Iraq, which was held accountable for damages caused during the 1990-1991 Gulf W ar, no other S tate has been held accountable for environmental damage during armed conflict and the environment continues to be the silent victim of armed conflicts worldwide.The acts of the United Nations Security Council during the 1991 Gulf W ar have created a legal precedent for future armed conflicts. In April 1991, the Security Council passed Resolution 687, holding Iraq liable under international law for "any direct loss, or damage, including environmental damage and the depletion of natural resources".

Given the lack of prosecutions, a question arises whether the lack of prosecutions for environmental damage constitutes an enforcement issue rather than a deficiency in the existing legal system. The ICRC in relation to the suggested creation of a fifth Geneva Convention for the protection of the environment, has been of the view that existing law is sufficient to protect the environment and that the issue is rather the enforcement of the law. There are indeed a number of provisions of IHL which prohibit or limit the opportunity for environmental destruction. For example, in making military targeting decisions, commanders are required to pay attention to the environment, and reprisals against the environment are prohibited. Intentionally attacking the environment violates the principle of distinction.

UNEP Report

The United Nations Environment Programme (UNEP) seeks to minimize environmental threats to human well-being. Through its Disasters and Conflicts Programme, it conducts field-based environmental assessments and strengthens national environmental management capacity in countries affected by conflicts and disasters. The UNEP, in its report "Protecting the Environment During Armed Conflict: An Inventory and Analysis of International Law" (2009), has made certain recommendations to strengthen international law for the protection of the environment.

One of the main recommendations made is that the International Law Commission (ILC), as the leading UN body with expertise in international law, should study the existing international law for protecting the environment during armed conflict and recommend how it can be clarified, codified and expanded. The UN General Assembly may request the ILC to conduct an examination of the law including: (i) making an inventory of the legal provisions and identifying the gaps and barriers to enforcement; (ii) exploring the options for clarifying and codifying this body of law; (iii) refining the definition of key terms such as 'widespread', 'long-term', and 'severe'; (iv) considering the applicability of multilateral environmental agreements during armed conflicts as part of its ongoing analysis of the 'effect of armed conflicts on treaties'; (v) extending the scope of the protection of the environment and natural resources in the context of non-international armed conflict; and (vi) considering how the standards, practice and case law of international environment law could be used to help clarify ambiguities in international humanitarian law.

In order to ensure that environmental violations committed during warfare are prosecuted, the provisions of international law that protect the environment in times of conflict should be fully reflected at the national level. States should incorporate the ICRC Guidelines on the Protection of the Environment during Armed Conflict (1994) in national legislation and military manuals, and sensitize their armed forces to environmental protection. The International Law Commission (ILC), as a UN bodyshould examine the effectiveness of the legal framework related to environmental protection, identify the gaps and barriers in the enforcement of the relevant laws and explore the possibilities of clarifying and codifying this body of law. A new legal instrument should be developed to grant place-based protection for critical natural resources and areas of ecological importance during international and non-international armed conflicts. These could include protection of watersheds, groundwater aquifers, agricultural and grazing lands, parks, national forests, and the habitats of endangered species. At the outset of any conflict, critical natural resources and areas of ecological importance should be delineated and designated as 'demilitarized zones', and parties to the conflict should be prohibited from conducting military operations within the boundaries of such zones.

CHAPTER 11

Protection of Cultural Property

Introduction

In the beginning of the last decade, the American forces in Iraq stood idle as looters ransacked government buildings, stores, churches and private homes, stealing anything they could carry and defacing symbols of the defunct Saddam Hussein regime. The looting of the museum and several other important cultural sites in Iraq has raised the important issue that the American military failed to provide adequate security to the cultural property of the Iraqi people. The United States has joined numerous international treaties that provide protection for cultural property, including the Hague Convention of 1907, the Roerich Pact, the fourth Geneva Convention of 1949, the UNESCO Convention of 1970, the World Heritage Convention and the UNIDROIT Convention. In addition to these obligations, the United Nations is also bound by the international customary rules of IHL. The response of the international community to the events in Iraq has also underlined a growing global consensus that cultural property is entitled to protection as a matter of international human rights.

Three sets of treaties form the framework for the protection of cultural heritage in time of war and its aftermathThese are (i) the Hague Convention of 1907, the fourth Geneva Convention of 1949, and theAdditional Protocols I and II to the Geneva Conventions; (ii) the Hague Convention of 1954 and its two protocols; and (iii) the rules of customary IHL, the ICTY and the 1998 Rome Statute of the International Criminal Court. Besides, the Lieber Code of 1863 has historical value and the Washington Treaty, 1929 is a Pan-American agreement for the protection of cultural property. Together, they address to four threats to cultural heritage: deliberate attack, incidental damage, pillage and outright theft.

The Lieber Code

The Lieber Code of 1863 defined cultural property as a form of "private property" subject to higher standards of protection and preservation than public or government property. Although the Code permitted the destruction and appropriation of property on the principle of military necessity , it provided strong protections for cultural property . The Code held that classical works of art, libraries, scientific collections as well as hospitals must be secured against all avoidable injury, even when they are contained in fortified places which are besieged or bombarded. The Code also provided that it is the duty of military commanders to "acknowledge and protect" cultural objects and sites in occupied territories.

The Hague Convention of 1907

The international protection of cultural property within the laws of armed conflict could be traced to the provisions of the Hague Convention IV of 1907 Respecting the Laws and Customs of War on Land. The Preamble to the Convention, containing the Martens Clause, provides: "Until a more complete code of the laws of war has been issued, the High Contracting Parties deem it expedient to declare that, in cases not included in the Regulations adopted by them, the inhabitants and the belligerents remain under the protection and the rule of the principles of the law of nations, as they result from the usages established among civilized peoples, from the laws of humanity, and the dictates of the public conscience."

The most important provision under the Hague Conventions in relation to cultural property is the Annexed Regulations. It contains a number of provisions relating to civilian private property such as Article 23(g), which provides that it is prohibited "to destroy or seize the enemy's property, unless such destruction or seizure be imperatively demanded by the necessities of war". Article 25 explicitly forbids attacks on undefended towns, buildings or dwellings. The Regulations further contain two articles specifically designed to provide protection for cultural property. Article 27 provides:

> In sieges and bombardments all necessary steps must be taken to spare, as far as possible, buildings dedicated to religion, art, science, or charitable purposes, historic monuments, hospitals,

> and places where the sick and wounded are collected, provided they are not being used at the time for military purposes. It is the duty of the besieged to indicate the presence of such buildings or places by distinctive and visible signs, which shall be notified to the enemy beforehand.

Like Article 23, the protection provided is not, from the terms of Article 27, absolute, being subject to the overriding exemption of military necessity contained in the Article in the form of the phrase "as far as possible". The protection provided by the Article 27 is narrow, applicable only in cases of siege or bombardment, and only if the besieged have notified the enemy of the existence of such cultural property beforehand and have then indicated the presence of this property with "distinctive and visible signs".

Article 56 of the Regulations concerns cultural property in occupied territory, and declares that the property of municipalities, that of institutions dedicated to religion, charity and education, the arts and sciences, even when State property, shall be treated as private property. All seizure of, destruction or willful damage done to institutions of this character, historic monuments, works of art and science, is forbidden, and should be made the subject of legal proceedings.

Article 5 of the Hague Convention (IX) of 1907 concerning Bombardment by Naval Forces in Time of War asserts that: "In bombardments by naval forces all the necessary measures must be taken by the commander to spare as far as possible sacred edifices, buildings used for artistic, scientific, or charitable purposes, historic monuments, hospitals, and places where the sick or wounded are collected, on the understanding that they are not used at the same time for military purposes". Also: "It is the duty of the inhabitants to indicate such monuments, edifices, or places by visible signs, which shall consist of large, stiff rectangular panels divided diagonally into two coloured triangular portions, the upper portion black, the lower portion white." As in Article 27 of the Regulations of the Fourth Convention of The Hague of 1907, the protection is not absolute, as it is limited by the consideration of military necessity. This protection is also limited geographically to the immediate area of combat.

However, during World War I the destruction of French and Belgian churches, cathedrals, museums and libraries revealed the ineffectiveness of the Hague Convention of 1907. The German forces removed valuable cultural objects and both sides targeted culturally protected sites.

The Washington Treaty, 1929

The Washington Treaty on the Protection of Artistic and Scientific Institutions and Monuments (The Roerich Pact, 1929) was developed on the initiative of Professor Nicholas Roerich. The United States and twenty other countries entered into a pan-American agreement, commonly referred to as the Roerich Pact, for the protection of cultural property. It came into force in 1935 and is the first treaty dedicated exclusively to the protection of cultural property. The language of the Roerich Pact mirrors the language of the Hague Convention of 1907, but the protections afforded to cultural property are broader. The Treaty provides historic, artistic, scientific and educational sites neutral status in times of war It holds that parties have an obligation to "respect and protect" these sites and also provides for the exchange of lists of institutions and monuments "for which the parties desire protection". This treaty remains the sole regional international instrument designed to protect cultural property during wartime.

The regime protecting cultural property during wartime was widely ignored during the Second World War. The Hague Convention of 1907 went largely unobserved as the Nazis engaged in lar ge-scale looting and cultural plunder, and bothAxis andAllied powers abandoned the principles of military necessity and razed thousands of important cultural sites in Europe.

The fourth Geneva Convention, 1949

In response to the vast losses in cultural property during World War II, in 1949 the international community adopted the fourth Geneva Convention with the hope that the Convention would clarify the responsibilities and duties of armed forces and governments during armed conflictsArticle 53 of the Convention forbids "extensive destruction and appropriation of property, not justified by military necessity and carried out unlawfully and wantonly", but these protections are no broader than those afforded by the 1907 Hague Convention. However , the Geneva Convention requires the contracting parties to disseminate the contents amongst the members of the armed forces.

The 1954 Hague Convention

The 1954 Hague Convention for the Protection of Cultural Property in the Event of Armed Conflict is the first international attempt to enunciate a comprehensive regime to protect cultural property during armed conflicts. The preamble of the Convention af firms that cultural properties have suffered grave damage during recent armed conflicts and that the technological development would further increase the danger for cultural property in war. It also confirms that damage to cultural property belonging to any people whatsoever , means damage to the cultural heritage of all mankind, which justifies its special protection by IHL.

The Convention emphasizes that the duty to protect cultural property is the joint obligation of both attackers and defenders. Defending parties must mark buildings and cultural sites with an internationally recognized shield and those who fail to safeguard their cultural property may lose protection under the Convention. Unlike prior treaties, attackers have an obligation under the 1954 Convention not only to respect and preserve cultural property, but also to take affirmative steps to prevent the theft of property in occupied territories.

The Convention provides a precise definition of objects falling under its protection. Article 1 of the Convention states that the term "cultural property", irrespective of origin or ownership, shall cover the following:

(a) movable or immovable property of great importance to the cultural heritage of every people, such as monuments of architecture, art or history, whether religious or secular; archaeological sites; groups of buildings which, as a whole, are of historical or artistic interest; works of art; manuscripts, books and other objects of artistic, historical or archaeological interest; as well as scientific collections and important collections of books or archives or of reproductions of the property defined above;

(b) buildings whose main and efective purpose is to preserve or exhibit the movable cultural property defined in sub-paragraph (a) such as museums, large libraries and depositories of archives, and refuges intended to shelter , in the event of armed conflict, the movable cultural property defined in subparagraph (a);

(c) centers containing a large amount of cultural property as defined in subparagraphs (a) and (b), to be known as "centers containing monuments".

The definition is broad enough to cover all the property which is considered to be of great importance to cultural heritage, whether religious or secular. Protection is also ofered by the Convention to temporary wartime shelters, to authorized means of emegency transport in times of hostilities, and to authorized specialist personnel.The concept is derived directly from the protection for civilian air -raid shelters, hospitals and ambulances in relation to humanitarian protection in the Geneva Conventions.

Protection

The 1954 Convention provides for two-tiers of cultural property protection: general and special protection. The scope of general protection is contained in Article 4 of the 1954 Convention. It provides that the High Contracting Parties agree to refrain from: (a) using cultural property , its immediate surroundings and appliances for purposes that are likely to expose it to damage in the event of armed conflict; (b) acts of hostility directed against cultural property; and (c) reprisals against cultural property , even if the enemy has unlawfully attacked cultural property . Article 4(3) further provides that parties are obliged to prevent theft, pillage, misappropriation and acts of vandalism against cultural property and shall refrain from requisitioning movable cultural property situated in the territory of another High Contracting Party . In addition, the protection afforded to cultural property may only be waived in the event where 'military necessity imperatively requires such waiver'.

Distinctive Emblem

The Convention also makes provision for a cultural property to bear a distinctive emblem so as to facilitate its recognitionThe distinctive emblem is to take the form of a single blue and white triangular shield and may be used alone or repeated three times to indicate the type of cultural property under protection. This emblem is to be prominently displayed on the exterior of the structure or within the perimeter of sites containing cultural property (Articles 6 and 16).

Military Measures

Chapter I of the Convention concludes with important provisions contained in Article 7, requiring the peacetime training of the armed forces:

1. The High Contracting Parties undertake to introduce in time of peace into their military regulations or instructions such provisions as may ensure observance of the present Convention, and to foster in the members of their armed forces a spirit of respect for the culture and cultural property of all peoples.
2. The High Contracting Parties undertake to plan or establish in peace-time, within their armed forces, services or specialist personnel whose purpose will be to secure respect for cultural property and to co-operate with the civilian authorities responsible for safeguarding it.

Special Protection

Article 8 of the 1954 Convention introduces a special protection regime for cultural property. It provides:

> There may be placed under special protection, a limited number of refuges intended to shelter movable cultural property in the event of armed conflict, of centres containing monuments and other immovable cultural property of very great importance, provided that they:
>
> (a) are situated at an adequate distance from any lage industrial centre or from any important military objective constituting a vulnerable point such as, for example, an aerodrome, broadcasting station, establishment engaged upon work of national defence, a port or railway station of relative importance or a main line of communication;
>
> (b) are not used for military purposes.

If the cultural property in question is situated in the vicinity of an important military objective, it may continue to benefit from special protection in accordance withArticle 8(5), provided that the Party concerned undertakes to make no use of the military objective.The special protection is accessible only to a 'limited number' of objects of 'very great importance'.

It is granted to cultural property by its entry into the 'International Register for Cultural Property Protection' made in accordance with the provisions and conditions of the Convention. Special protection may also be granted to transports exclusively engaged in the transfer of cultural property provided that the triple emblem along with a signed and dated authorization by the contracting party is displayed on the exterior of the mode of transport.

Enforcement and Regulations for Execution of the Convention

The execution of the Convention rests on six pillars: The system of Protecting Powers, international assistance, dissemination, reporting, a specific institutional framework and the criminal prosecution of persons violating the Convention. The High Contracting Parties are obliged to disseminate the contents of the Convention widely within their countries, certainly among the military , and if possible to the civilian population (Article 25). The concludingArticles of the Convention deals with a range of mainly technical legal issues, including a provision permitting the application of the Convention to colonies and other dependent territories, formalizing the relationship of the new Convention to existing general laws of war, and provisions relating to both individual denunciation by a High Contracting Party and for inter -governmental revision of the Convention and Regulations (Articles 28-40). The enforcement provisions contained in article 28 of the Convention provide: "The High Contracting Parties undertake to take, within the framework of their ordinary criminal jurisdiction, all steps necessary to prosecute and impose penal or disciplinary actions upon those persons, whatever nationality, who commit or order to be committed a breach of the present Convention".

UNESCO is assigned a special role, comparable to the ICRCŝ role in the Geneva Conventions, with regard to the co-ordination of ef forts and keeping records of specially protected cultural property . The 1954 Convention was amended by 'Regulations for the Execution of the Convention and Protocol I', which contains provisions to prevent exportation of cultural property from occupied territories and regulates the safeguard of cultural property in third States during armed conflict.

The Hague Regulations

The 1954 Hague Regulations, which form an integral part of the Convention, set out first the practical procedures to be followed in relation to the compiling by the Director-General of UNESCO of an international list of persons qualified to carry out the functions of Commissioners-General, and procedures to be followed in the event of armed conflict, including the arrangements for the appointment of cultural representatives, Commissioners-General and the responsibilities of the Protecting Powers (appointed in accordance with the Hague 1907 and Geneva 1949 principles).

The second part (Articles 1 1-16) of the Regulations deals with the practical arrangements and procedures for the granting and registration of 'Special Protection', including the notification of all proposals to every High Contracting Party and arrangements for the submitting of objections and for eventual arbitration on these if necessary, as well as provisions for the cancelling of 'Special Protection' where appropriate. Chapter III of the Regulations (Articles 17-19) sets out in some detail the procedures for the transport of movable cultural property to a place of safety for protection, with the approval of the neutral CommissionerGeneral overseeing cultural heritage matters during the conflict. The final part, Chapter IV, regulates the use of the Official Emblem and the identity cards and other identifying markers of persons duly authorized to undertake official duties in relation to the implementation of the Convention.

The 1954 Protocol

A separate legal instrument, concurrent to the Hague Convention was created known as the 1954 Protocol for the Protection of Cultural Property in the Event of Armed Conflict. The Protocol deals primarily with issues relating to the protection of movable cultural property from occupied territory and return of such exported property at the end of the conflict. The Protocol only applies to a limited class of objects those constituting the cultural or spiritual heritage of peoples.

In terms of Article 1 of the Protocol, Contracting Parties are to: (i) Prevent the exportation of cultural property from territories occupied by the party during armed conflict; (ii) Return any imported cultural property from any territory occupied by it; and (iii) Indemnify 'good faith' purchasers of cultural property when returning property to the previously occupied country." Article 5 of the protocol provides that when cultural property has been deposited for protection within the territory of another Contracting

Party, the objects are to be returned following the cessation of hostilities at the request of the competent authorities of the territory whence it came.

The objective of the Protocol is that it prohibits the looting and pillage of cultural property by belligerents during armed conflicts, thereby building on the foundation of the 1907 Hague Convention. A power in adverse occupation of another power's territory may not export from that territory any cultural objects which may be found within it. Under the Protocol, upon the cessation of hostilities, States are liable to return cultural property or pay compensation if such property was exported during their period of occupation of a territory and must pay an indemnity to anyone who has subsequently held the property in good faith. The Protocol also applies irrespective of whether such territory is a party to the Protocol.Where any party to the Protocol finds that cultural property has been improperly exported from the territory of a party to an armed conflict into its own territory, it must take control thereof with a view to return it immediately or on the request of the party from whose territory it came. S tates which adopt the First Protocol must enforce measures required for its implementation.

Shortcomings of 1954 Convention and Protocol

The definition of cultural property contained in Article 1 of the 1954 Convention differs from those contained in other IHL treaties. The Hague Regulations Respecting the Laws and Customs of War on Land 1907 as well as theAP I, both work on the basis of somewhat different categories of objects protected as "cultural property". In practice these differences need to be solved by determining in each particular situation of armed conflict which treaty is applicable and prevails over the other . Under the 1954 Convention the obligations to safeguarding and respect cultural property may be waived in cases where military necessity "imperatively" requires such a waiver. The Convention does not define what constitutes imperative military necessity. It is, therefore, up to each State Party to interpret these terms. This entails a high risk of ambiguity in State practice and a potential for misuse of this waiver.

The armed conflicts in Cambodia, former Yugoslavia, Iraq and Afghanistan have clearly revealed major problems in the implementation of the Convention. In particular, the Convention lacked full application, as most of the armed conflicts since 1954 have been of a non-international character. It also lacked proper execution as it is based on the functioning of 'Protecting Power ' and 'Commissioner General', which had been unworkable in practice. The Convention also lacked adequate provisions to cope with the extensive and systematic destruction of cultural property during recent armed conflicts, as it contains no mandatory criminal sanctions regime.

In particular the armed conflicts in Croatia and in Bosnia and Herzegovina, where the destruction of cultural property was part of the policy of so-called "ethnic cleansing" led to international efforts to revise the existing Convention with the goal of improving the protection of cultural property in the event of armed conflict. The weakness of the Convention stems largely from its reliance on national laws and ad hoc criminal tribunals to prosecute individuals. To date the Convention has only been invoked four times. In none of these instances did the Convention prevent the improper use or destruction of cultural property. Unfortunately, like most international agreements it appears that the lack of an effective international enforcement mechanism has rendered the Hague Convention impotent.

Currently, only 123 S tates are Parties to the 1954 Convention. The African, Asian or Latin-American S tates where armed conflicts recently took place such asAfghanistan, Algeria, Angola, Burundi, Congo, Ethiopia, Korea, Philippines, or Somalia are not Parties to the Convention. Only 100 States are Parties to the first Protocol to the Convention.

The 1999 Second Protocol to the Hague Convention

The 1954 Convention applied to various S tates Parties in a number of conflicts in the following forty-seven years. However , the destruction of cultural property in conflicts such as in Afghanistan following the Soviet invasion; in the Iran-Iraq war; in the First Gulf war particularly in Kuwait; and in the former Yugoslavia, highlighted a number of inadequacies in the Convention and required its revision, which took the form of a Protocol to the Convention in 1999. It has entered into force on 9 March 2004 and as on 31 December 2010 has been ratified by 53 countries. The Protocol has expanded the scope of protectionof cultural property during armed conflicts. It has established the 'Committee for the Protection of Cultural Property in the Event of Armed Conflict', consisting of twelve States Parties.

Article 5 of the Protocol provides that preparatory measures must be taken in time of peace for the safeguarding of cultural property against the foreseeable effects of an armed conflict.The provisions of Second Protocol could be put into practice by the S tate Parties by ensuring the following measures: (i) preparation of National Inventory of Cultural Property; (ii) preparing microfilms of documents or documentation of buildings; (iii) making viable disaster plans for each object; (iv) preparing evacuation plans indicating movable objects, their precise location and priority for evacuation; (v) constructing shelters for movable objects; and (vi) the training of civilian and military personnel.

Article 6, dealing with the respect for cultural property provide that with the aim of ensuring respect for cultural property (Article 4 of the Convention), a waiver on the basis of imperative military necessity may only be invoked to direct an act of hostility against cultural property as long as (i) cultural property has, by its function, been made into a military objective; and (ii) there is no feasible alternative available to obtain a similar military advantage to that offered by directing an act of hostility against that objective. The decision to invoke imperative military necessity shall only be taken by an officer commanding a battalion or larger force.

Article 7 dealing with precautions in attack provides that each part to conflict shall:

(a) do everything feasible to verify that the objectives to be attacked are not cultural property protected under Article 4 of the Convention;

(b) take all feasible precautions in the choice of means and methods of attack with a view to avoiding, and in any event to minimizing, incidental damage to cultural property protected underArticle 4 of the Convention;

(c) refrain from deciding to launch any attack which may be expected to cause incidental damage to cultural property protected under Article 4 of the Convention which would be excessive in relation to the concrete and direct military advantage anticipated; and

(d) cancel or suspend an attack if it becomes apparent: (i) that the objective is cultural property protected under Article 4 of the

Convention; (ii) that the attack may be expected to cause incidental damage to cultural property protected under Article 4 of the Convention which would be excessive in relation to the concrete and direct military advantage anticipated.

Under Article 8 of the Protocol, the Parties to the conflict must, to the extent feasible (i) remove movable cultural property from the vicinity of military objectives or provide for adequate in situ protection; and (ii) avoid locating military objectives near cultural property Article 9 of the Protocol provides that occupying nations "shall prohibit and prevent" the export, transfer of ownership or removal of cultural property illicit archaeological excavations, and the concealment or destruction of cultural or historical evidence.

Enhanced Protection: As the "special protection" regime of the 1954 Convention had turned out to be more or less inef fective in practice, the Second Protocol establishes a new (and third) category of cultural property—cultural property under "enhanced protection" (Chapter 3, Articles 10-14). In order to be eligible for enhanced protection, cultural property must fulfil the following three conditions:

- It must be a cultural heritage of the greatest importance for humanity
- It must be protected by adequate domestic legal and administrative measures recognizing its exceptional cultural and historic value and ensuring the highest level of protection, and
- It must not be used for military purposes or to shield military sites and a declaration must have been made by the Party which has control over the cultural property, confirming that it will not be so used.

The protection afforded to cultural property under enhanced protection differs from the level of protection of cultural property under "normal" protection pursuant to Chapter 2 of the Second Protocol and to Chapter I of the Convention. In exceptional cases, where a S tate Party requesting inclusion of cultural property in the list of cultural property under enhanced protection cannot fulfil the criteria of adequate domestic measures, enhanced protection may nevertheless be granted, provided that the requesting State submits a request for international assistance (Article 11 .8).

Article 15 establishes five new explicit crimes in relation to intentional breaches of the laws governing protection of cultural property: (i) making cultural property under enhanced protection the object of attack; (ii) using cultural property under enhanced protection or its immediate surroundings in support of a military action; (iii) extensive destruction or appropriation of cultural property protected under the 1954 Hague Convention and Second Protocol; (iv) making cultural property protected under the 1954 Hague Convention and Second Protocol the object of attack; and (v) theft, pillage or misappropriation of, or acts of vandalism directed against cultural property protected under the 1954 Hague Convention.

The first three of the aforementioned provisions are subject to universal jurisdiction and are extraditable offences. In addition, States are required to prosecute or extradite any person accused of committing offences against property under enhanced protection or of having caused extensive damage to cultural property. Provision is also made for general obligations with regard to mutual legal assistance, investigations, extraditions or the obtaining evidence.

Article 21 provides that parties to the Second Protocol must adopt the necessary legislative, administrative or disciplinary measures to terminate or to impose sanctions on other violations when they are committed intentionally. These include any use of cultural property in violation of the 1954 Hague Convention or the Second Protocol, and the intentional illicit export, other removal or transfer of cultural property.

Chapter 5 concentrates on non-international armed conflicts, such as civil wars and internal 'liberation' conflicts. It does not however apply to internal disturbances such as riots and isolated or sporadic acts of violence as specified by Article 22(2). The provisions of the 1999 Protocol may not be invoked as a justification for direct or indirect intervention by an external State in the territory in which the conflict occurs. Chapter 6 establishes a clear role for civil society. The International Committee of the Blue Shield (ICBS) and its constituent international professional non-governmental organizations, together with the ICRC, will have important standing advisery roles in relation to the to the Committee established under the Protocol.

The International Committee for the Protection of Cultural Property in the Event of Armed Conflict is assigned with the responsibility for maintaining a list of property under enhanced protection and to supervise the implementation of the Protocol (Article 24) States who wish to include their cultural property to the list, are to direct their proposals to the Committee who has the final decision for inclusion of property in the list. A fund is also established through which the Committee may provide financial and technical assistance to support preparatory measures in times of peace, emer gency measures during armed conflict and restoration measures after the cessation of hostilities.

Chapter 7 of the Protocol strengthens the 1954 Hague provisions in placing an obligation on States to ensure dissemination and training for the protection of cultural property. The Protocol obliges a State to take all the necessary steps under its domestic law to make such of fences punishable by appropriate penalties when they are committed intentionally and in direct violation of the 1954 Convention or the Protocol.

Protection under ICTY

The International Criminal Tribunal for the FormerYugoslavia (ICTY) has applied Article 3(d) of the 1993 ICTYStatute in a recent judgment in which Dario Kordic and Mario Cerkez, were found guilty of a crime against cultural property due to their deliberate armed attacks on ancient mosques in Bosnia and Herzegovina.[1]

Rome Statute

The 1998 Rome Statute of the International Criminal Court provides that "Intentionally directing attacks against buildings dedicated to religion, education, art, science or charitable purposes, historic monuments, hospitals and places where the sick and wounded are collected, provided they are not military objectives" are considered as "other serious violation of the laws and customs applicable in international armed conflict, within the established framework of international law" (Article 8).

UN Peacekeeping Forces

The UN Secretary General' s Bulletin of August 6, 1999 concerning the Observance by United Nations forces of IHLprohibits, the United Nations

---

1 *The Prosecutor v. Kordic and Cerkez,* case No.IT-95-14/2-T, Trial Chamber Judgment of 26 February 2001; and Appeals Chamber Judgment of 17 December 2004.

forces from "attacking monuments of art, architecture or history , archaeological sites, works of art, places of worship and museums and libraries which constitute the cultural or spiritual heritage of peoples." In particular, it prohibits, on the one hand, theft, pillage, misappropriation and any act of vandalism directed against cultural property , and on the other hand, engaging in reprisals against such property (Section 6.6).

Protection under Customary IHL

The basic principles concerning respect for cultural property enshrined in the 1954 Convention have become part of customary international law . According to the ICRC study on Customary IHL, a customary duty lies on States which have effective control over a territory, to respect, prevent and avoid systematic acts of destruction against cultural property. Rule 38, 40 and 41 of the Customary IHL provide:

> **Rule 38**: Each party to the conflict must respect cultural property:
>
> A. Special care must be taken in military operations to avoid damage to buildings dedicated to religion, art, science, education or charitable purposes and historic monuments unless they are military objectives.
>
> B. Property of great importance to the cultural heritage of every people must not be the object of attack unless imperatively required by military necessity.
>
> **Rule 40:** Each party to the conflict must protect cultural property:
>
> A. All seizure of or destruction or wilful damage done to institutions dedicated to religion, charity, education, the arts and sciences, historic monuments and works of art and science is prohibited.
>
> B. Any form of theft, pillage or misappropriation of, and any acts of vandalism directed against, property of great importance to the cultural heritage of every people is prohibited.
>
> **Rule 41:** The occupying power must prevent the illicit export of cultural property from occupied territory and must return illicitly exported property to the competent authorities of the occupied territory.

Protection under other Conventions

In 1966, the UN General Assembly adopted the International Covenant on Economic, Social and Cultural Rights. Although the Covenant does not explicitly mention cultural property , it recognizes "cultural rights" as intimately tied to human rights. The 1970 Convention on the Means of Prohibiting and Preventing the Illicit Import, Export, and Transfer of Ownership of Cultural Property stems the flow of stolen goods onto the international art and antiquities market. The Convention requires member states not only to identify and control the export of cultural property , but also to prevent the import of illegally obtained goodsThe 1972 Convention for the Protection of the World Cultural and Natural Heritage has created a new avenue for protection of immovable property during wartime and reaffirms the internationalist values of the 1954 Hague ConventionArticle 1 of the 1972 Convention defines cultural heritage as:

- **Monuments**: architectural works, works of monumental sculpture and painting, elements or structures of an archaeological nature, inscriptions, cave dwellings and combinations of features, which are of outstanding universal value from the point of view of history art or science;
- **Groups of buildings**: groups of separate or connected buildings which, because of their architecture, their homogeneity or their place in the landscape, are of outstanding universal value from the point of view of history, art or science;
- **Sites**: works of man or the combined works of nature and man, and areas including archaeological sites which are of outstanding universal value from the historical, aesthetic, ethnological or anthropological point of view.

Article 2 defines the natural heritage to include:

- Natural features consisting of physical and biological formations or groups of such formations, which are of outstanding universal value from the aesthetic or scientific point of view;
- Geological and physiographical formations and precisely delineated areas which constitute the habitat of threatened species of animals

and plants of outstanding universal value from the point of view of science or conservation;

- Natural sites or precisely delineated natural areas of outstanding universal value from the point of view of science, conservation or natural beauty.

Article 6 provides that the member -parties have an obligation to cooperate and must "give their help in the identification, protection, conservation, and presentation" of international cultural and natural heritage. The State Parties are prohibited from taking measures which might directly or indirectly damage or destroy listed sites.The World Heritage Convention provides for the protection of cultural property from direct military assault, as well as from the destabilizing conditions created by warfare. Because members are liable for the "indirect" effects of their actions, they may be accountable to occupied nations for cultural property losses.

Wars have long resulted in both the destruction of property and pillaging of property as war booty. Indeed, many wars have been based on these very aims. The earliest restraints on destruction of cultural property relate to the sparing of temples, churches and similarly sacred and hallowed places. This emerging concern for property that has a cultural value was cemented during the nineteenth century . Today, the rules governing the protection of cultural property in the event of armed conflict are well established in both treaty and customary IHL. The United Nations Educational, Scientific and Cultural Or ganization (UNESCO) plays important role in the protection of cultural property. It is the driving force behind the promotion and implementation of the international instruments governing the protection of cultural property in the event of armed conflict, of which it is the depositary . Measures to protect cultural property in the event of armed conflict need to be adopted in time of peace.The governments must draw up plans of action for the protection of cultural property, establish appropriate education and training programmes for armed forces, the emergency service members, the personnel of cultural institutions and the general public.

CHAPTER 12

Implementation of IHL

Introduction

The four Geneva Conventions of 1949 and their Additional Protocols of 1977 are the principal treaties governing aid to and protection of the victims of armed conflicts. In order to secure the guarantees provided by these instruments, it is essential that S tates implement their provisions to the fullest possible extent. The term implementation covers all measures that must be taken to ensure that the rules of IHL are fully respected. The measures—which must be taken in wartime as well as peacetime—are necessary to ensure that (i) both civilians and military personnel are familiar with the rules of humanitarian law; (ii) the structure, administrative arrangements and personnel required for compliance with the law are in place; and (iii) violations of humanitarian law are prevented and punished when they do occur. [1]

The four Geneva Conventions of 1949 in identical language stipulate[2] that the High Contracting Parties have an obligation to "undertake, in time of peace as in time of war, to disseminate the text of the present Convention as widely as possible in their respective countries, and, in particular , to include the study there of in their programmes of military and, if possible, civil instructions, so that the principles thereof may become known to the entire population, in particular to the armed fighting forces, medical personnel and the chaplains."

---

[1] ICRC advisory service on International Humanitarian Law: Implementing IHL: Form Law to Action, 2003.

[2] Article 47, 48, 127 and 144 of the respective four Geneva Conventions of 1949.

The 1954 Hague Convention for the Protection of Cultural Property and its Second Protocol of 1999, provide similarly that the High Contracting Parties undertake, to disseminate the text of the Convention and to include the study of the Convention in their programmes of military and, if possible, civilian training, so that its principles are made known to the whole population, especially the armed forces and personnel engaged in the protection of cultural property.

Obligations

Under IHL – that is, the four 1949 Geneva Conventions, their Additional Protocols , the 1954 Hague Convention on Cultural Property and its Second Protocol of 1999 – a range of measures must be taken by the High Contracting Parties. The main ones are:

a. To respect and to ensure respect for the Conventions and their Protocols in all circumstances;

b. To have the Conventions and Protocols translated into the national languages;

c. To train qualified personnel to facilitate the application of the IHL as widely as possible both within the armed forces and the general population;

d. To repress all violations listed as such in the above-mentioned instruments and, in particular , to adopt criminal legislation that punishes war crimes;

e. To ensure that persons, property and places protected by the law are properly identified, marked and protected;

f. To adopt measures to prevent the misuse of the Red Cross, the Red Crescent, the Red Crystal and other symbols and emblems provided for in the Conventions and Protocols;

g. To ensure that protected persons enjoy judicial and other fundamental guarantees during armed conflict;

h. To appoint and train persons qualified in IHL as legal advisers in the armed forces;

i. To provide for the establishment of (i) National Red Cross and Red Crescent Societies and other voluntary aid societies, (ii) civil defence organizations, and (iii) National Information Bureaux;

j. To take account of IHL when selecting military sites and in developing and adopting weapons and military tactics;

k. To provide for the establishment of hospital zones, neutralized zones, security zones and demilitarized zones;

l. To draw the services of the International Humanitarian Fact-Finding Commission (IHFFC) established under Article 90 of the AP I, which can assist in promoting respect for IHL through its fact-finding capacity and its good offices function.

Implementation Measures

The State Parties must take certain measures for the execution of their obligations under the four Geneva Conventions and the AP I. The preventive measures to be taken during peacetime include adoption of the treaties in national laws and the dissemination of their text through training and other measures. The State Parties must also adopt legislation to ensure the prevention of and punishment for the misuse of the protective emblems and distinctive signs. During the armed conflicts, the State Parties must ensure that the Conventions and Protocols are respected and violators of IHL are brought to justice.

National implementation measures are also required under various treaties banning certain types of weapons. For example, the 1972 Convention on the Prohibition of Bacteriological Weapons and their Destruction states that "each State Party must, in accordance with its constitutional processes, take any necessary measures to prohibit and prevent the development, production, stockpiling, acquisition, or retention of the agents, toxins, weapons, equipment and means of delivery within the territory of such State, under its jurisdiction or under its control anywhere".

National Committees for the Implementation of IHL

National implementation of humanitarian law is an on-going process requiring the cooperation of a range of government ministries and national organizations. The number of national committees on IHLhas continued to increase steadily and currently , there being more than 90 such bodies throughout all regions of the world at present. A number of S tates[3] have established national committees or working groups on IHL, bringing together national authorities, experts, and in some cases organizations such as the National Red Cross or Red Crescent SocietyThe role and composition of these committees vary from country to country, in some cases covering both human rights and humanitarian law While there is no legal obligation to establish such committees, they have been found to be a valuable means of promoting the national implementation of IHL.[4]

The organization and objectives of a national committee must be determined by the State at the time of the committee's formation. However, since its purpose is to further the implementation and promote awareness of IHL at the national level, the committee should have the following characteristics:

- It should be able to evaluate the existing national law in the light of the obligations created by the Conventions, Protocols, and other instruments of IHL.
- It should be in a position to monitor the implementation and to recommend improvements. This may involve proposing new legislation or amendments to existing law coordinating the adoption and implementation of administrative regulations and providing guidance on the interpretation and application of humanitarian rules.

---

[3] For example, the South Africa's National Committee on IHL was established in April 2006 by a decision of the executive management committee of the Department of Foreign Affairs. The Committee will be chaired by the Department of Foreign Affairs and composed of two representatives from relevant government entities (such as the ministries of Foreign Affairs, Justice, Defence, Police, Health and Education). The Committee may co-opt members from outside the government (e.g. the ICRC and academic circles). The Committee is assigned a broad mandate and should act as a focal point, providing leadership on all issues related to the domestic implementation and dissemination of IHL. In South Asia, only two countries, Nepal and Sri Lanka have constituted national committees for the implementation of IHL. Jha U.C., Implementation of the IHL in South Asian Countries, *ISIL Yearbook of International Humanitarian and Refugee Law*, Vol. IX, 2009, p. 151-173.

[4] The Intergovernmental Group of Experts for the Protection of War Victims recommended that States "be encouraged to create national committees, with the possible support of National Societies, to advise and assist governments in implementing and disseminating IHL" and "to facilitate cooperation between national committees and the ICRC".

- The committee should play an important role in promoting activities to spread knowledge of IHL. It should have the authority to conduct studies, propose activities, and assist in making IHL more widely known. The committee should therefore be involved in instructing the armed forces in this domain, teaching the principles of IHL at various levels of the public education system and promoting the basic principles of IHL among the general population.

Given its functions, a national humanitarian law committee requires a wide range of expertise.The committee must include representatives of all the government ministries concerned with implementing IHL. Precisely which ministries are relevant will depend on the committees mandate, but they are likely to include defence, foreign affairs, internal affairs, justice, finance, education and culture. It may also be useful to have representatives of legislative committees, members of the judiciary and personnel from the headquarters of the armed forces.

For example, Nepal's National Committee on the Implementation of IHL, constituted on 26 February 2007, has the minister for law justice and constituent assembly affairs as its chairperson and the joint secretary of international law division under the minister of law as its member secretary It has 11 members from various ministries, including the ministries of home, defence, foreign affairs, health and population, education, culture, and women, children and social welfare. The mandate of the Committee is to: (i) draft the necessary laws for the implementation of the conventions on IHL to which the government of Nepal is a party; (ii) review the existing laws in the light of the obligations created by the conventions; (iii) carry out all other activities for the implementation of the conventions on IHL including promotional activities, such as disseminating information to different levels/segments, and (iv) make recommendations to the government on whether Nepal is to become a party to other conventions on IHL. The Committee was successful in enacting the Geneva Convention Act, No. 4 of 2006 within a relatively short period of time. It maintained regular contact with the ICRC representatives in Colombo and New Delhi and invited comments from the ICRC on the draft Bill prior to its presentation in Parliament.

Dissemination

All four 1949 Geneva Conventions use virtually identical words to reaffirm the general obligation to disseminate the texts. [5] The third Geneva Convention adds that any military or other authorities who in time of war are responsible for POWs must possess the text of the Convention and be specially instructed as to its provisions (Article 127(2)). The of ficers in charge of POWs must ensure that these provisions are known to the camp staff and the guards and are held responsible for their application (Article 39). Furthermore, the Convention must be displayed at places where the POWs can read it (Article 41). The fourth Convention provides the same obligations with regard to any civilian, military, police or other authorities who assume responsibilities in respect of civilians, particularly in places of internment (Articles 99 and 144(2)). The obligation to disseminate the Conventions and the Protocols is reiterated in the 1977Additional Protocols (AP I, Article 83 and AP II, Article 19). Protocol I provides for specific measures with a view to strengthening the general obligation. Protocol II makes the obligation applicable to situations of non-international armed conflict.

The 1954 Hague Convention for the Protection of Cultural Property requires that its provisions be made known to the personnel engaged in the protection of cultural property (Article 25). The 1999 Second Protocol to the Convention requires that any military or civilian authorities who, in time of armed conflict, assume responsibilities with respect to its application be fully acquainted with the text. To that end, the States must incorporate guidelines and instructions on the protection of cultural property in their military regulations and must also develop and implement peacetime training and educational programmes in cooperation with UNESCO and relevant governmental and nongovernmental organizations (Article 30).

The 1954 Convention requires furthermore that services or specialist personnel be established for securing respect for cultural property (Article 7). If the programmes of military instruction are to be efective, guidelines

---

[5] The High Contracting Parties undertake, in time of peace as in time of war, to disseminate the text of the present Convention as widely as possible in their respective countries, and, in particular, to include the study thereof in their pro grammes of military and, if possible, civil instruction, so that the principles thereof may become known to all their armed forces and to the entire population. (GC I/II/III/IV, Articles 47/48/127/144).

should be adopted for teaching the law and IHL should be incorporated into military handbooks, and into the rules of engagement of the armed forces. States which provide troops for peacekeeping or peace enforcement operations conducted by the United Nations or under its auspices should ensure that the military personnel belonging to their contingent are instructed on the provisions of the law.

The 1980 Convention on Certain ConventionalWeapons also requires States to incorporate study of the text and of its Protocols in programmes of military instruction (Article 6). Its Second Amended Protocol specifies that each S tate must require its armed forces to issue relevant military instructions and operating procedures and to provide training for armed forces personnel that is commensurate with their respective duties and responsibilities (Article 14). Protocol IV stipulates that the S tates shall provide training for their armed forces (Article 2).

Every State party to the Convention on the Rights of the Child (Article 42) and to the Optional Protocol of 2000 on the involvement of children in armed conflict (Article 6) undertakes to make the principles and provisions of those instruments widely known by appropriate means, to adults and children alike.[6]

When a State transfer's weapons to or provides training to the military members of another State, it equips the recipient with the means and methods to engage in armed conflict – the conduct of which is regulated by IHL. Under common Article 1, the S tates have an obligation to "respect and ensure respect" for IHL. To ensure that violations of humanitarian law are not facilitated by unregulated access to arms and ammunition, arms transfer and training decisions should include a consideration of whether the recipient is likely to respect IHL and implement its provisions.

---

[6] Every State party to the Convention on the Rights of the Chi ld (CRC) and to the Optional Protocol of May 2000 on the involvement of children in armed conflict(OP to CRC) undertakes to make the principles and pr ovisions of those instruments widely known by appropriate means, to adults and childen alike. Article 42 of the CRC provides: "States Parties undertake to make the principles and provisions of the Convention widely known, by appropriate and active means, to adults and children alike." Similarly Article 6 of the OP to CRC provides: (1) Each State Party shall take all necessary legal, administrative and other measures to ensure the effective implementation and enforcement of the provisions of this Protocol within its jurisdiction. (2) State Parties undertake to make the principles and provisions of the present Protocol widely know and promoted by appropriate means to adults and children alike.

The obligation to disseminate, is a corollary to the commitment made by the States Parties to the instruments of IHLto respect and ensure respect for the provisions they contain. Educational and research institutions play a vital role in the dissemination of IHL. Dissemination must be carried out in peacetime, and stepped during armed conflicts. Dissemination promotes respect for the rules of the law , but it also helps inculcate principles of humanity that limit violence and preserve peace.

Training

Training in IHL is necessary to ensure compliance with it in times of armed conflict. Training and education must be undertaken in peacetime. This applies to the whole population, although special attention should be given to relevant groups such as armed forces personnel, personnel of national Red Cross societies, politicians, civil servants serving in the relevant government ministries, the academic community members of civil defence organizations, military cadets and the student community , medical professionals and journalists.

Members of the armed forces form the primary group for the application of the rules of IHL in any conflict. The States have a legal obligation to ensure that combatants learn and respect the rules of IHL and follow these in a conflict. Therefore IHL must form an integral part of the regular instructions and practical training of armed forces personnel. While civil servants have the primary responsibility for the S tate's IHL obligations, parliamentarians also have a critical role to play in enacting legislations that ensure that IHL is legally binding on the government, public officials and the civil society. Parliamnentarians can review executive ratifications or accessions to IHL treaties, support the development of new IHL instruments and allocate adequate resources for IHL training of the armed forces and other groups. Civil servants working in government ministries, in particular those directly involved in applying IHL, like the ministries of defence, foreign affairs, health and law, should be trained in IHL.

Academicians too need to be trained in IHL, as their expertise could be used in conducting research in IHL as well as imparting further training to students and military personnel. The fundamental principles of humanitarian law must be known to students as they represent the reservoir of potential recruits for each of society' s activities and because a lar ger percentage of the population can be reached by dissemination among students.

The Geneva Conventions and theirAdditional Protocols state the rights and duties of medical professional in times of conflict— whether international or non-international. The protection and immunity granted to medical personnel must be known to every medical professional.A lack of knowledge may create a dangerous situation during an armed conflict. Journalists have an essential role in shaping public opinion in favour of respect for IHL. They must have a basic understanding of the rules of IHL, so that they can report its violations correctly . The general public must have a basic understanding of the provisions of the Geneva Conventions to help reduce the violations and harm to civilians and their propertyespecially in a non-internal. It must be aware of the protective status of the Red Cross, the Red Crescent and the Red Crystal emblems and the prohibition of misuse.

Responsibility of Military Planner

Military planners must be aware of the relevant treaties to which the State is a party and the customary rules of IHL. In order to ensure that military doctrine reflects the relevant law , they must adopt a manual of IHL (the Law ofArmed Conflict) for use by the armed forcesThey must also ensure that the appropriate Rules of Engagement (ROE) cleared by appropriate political and legal authorities are in place. It is necessary for all military personnel trained on a regular basis in IHL and ROE to ensure they understand and comply with the humanitarian and legal obligations of the State. The commanders at appropriate levels should have the services of legal advisors for training and operations.

Responsibilities of Military Commanders

IHL, national laws, and military rules and regulations place responsibilities on military commanders at all levels. A commander may also be held criminally responsible, not only for his own acts but also for the acts of his subordinates. He is liable even if he does not order his subordinates to commit the unlawful act, but if he knew or ought to have known of them and failed to take steps to prevent them. Apart from being liable to be considered a party to war crimes committed by his subordinates, a commander is in any event under a general duty to maintain discipline and this includes a duty to take action in respect of war crimes committed or about to be committed by his subordinates or by other persons under his control. Commanders are to prevent and, where necessary , suppress and report to the competent authorities, the breaches of the Geneva Conventions and Protocols. They are to ensure that members of the armed forces under their command are aware of their obligations under the Conventions and Protocol (Article 87, paragraph 2, AP I).

IHL consists of a lage number of treaties, and the obligations imposed on combatants under these treaties are manifold. Every soldier and officer cannot be expected to know every article and every nuance of IHL. It would suffice if they understood the general principles of IHLand received training or instructions specifically related to their mission. Commanders can take the help of legal advisers in this regard.[7]

A commander must ensure that persons under his command are aware of the grave breaches and other serious violations of the four Geneva Conventions. The grave breaches are: (i)Wilful killing; torture or inhuman treatment, including biological experiments; wilfully causing great suffering or serious injury to body or health (Article 50/ 51/130/147 of GC I-IV respectively); (ii) Extensive destruction and appropriation of property, not justified by military necessity and carried out unlawfully and wantonly (Article 50/ 51/147 of GC I, II and IV respectively); (iii) Compelling a prisoner of war [or a protected person] to serve in the forces of the hostile Power (Articles 130 and 147 of GC III and GC IVrespectively); (iv)Wilfully depriving a POW or a protected person of the rights of fair and regular trial prescribed in the Convention (Articles 130 and 147 of GC III and GC IV respectively); (v) Unlawful deportation or transfer or unlawful confinement (Article 147, GC IV); and (vi) Taking of hostages (Article 147, GC IV).

In the conduct of an of fensive operation, a commander planning or deciding an attack must do everything feasible to verify that the target is a military objective. He must take all feasible precautions in the choice of weapons and tactics to avoid, or at least minimize death or injury to civilians or damage to civilian objects. He should cancel, suspend or re-plan the attack if its incidental ef fects are likely to be excessive in relation to the

---

[7] The role of the legal advisers is to advise military commanders at the appropriate level on the application of the Geneva Conventions and Additional Protocols (Article 82, AP I).

military advantage expected from the attack. He is also under an obligation to give effective advance warning of attacks which may affect the civilian population, unless circumstances do not permit this (Article 57, AP I).

Protection of Cultural Property: Commanders must respect cultural property situated within their own territory as well as within the territory of the opponent by refraining from any use of the property and its immediate surroundings for protection purposes which are likely to expose it to destruction or damage in the event of an armed conflict. Special care must be taken in military operations to avoid damage to buildings dedicated to religion, art, science, education or charitable purposes and historic monuments unless they are military objectives. Commanders must ensure that any property of great importance to the cultural heritage of people must not be the object of attack unless imperatively required by military necessity. The International Criminal Court under the 1998 Rome S tatute has jurisdiction over intentional attacks "against buildings dedicated to religion, education, art, science or charitable purposes, historic monuments, hospitals and places where the sick and wounded are collected, provided they are not military objectives", occurring both in international and non-international armed conflicts.

In conducting a military operation, a commander must do everything feasible to verify that the objectives to be attacked are not cultural property protected under the 1954 Convention. He should take all feasible precautions in deciding the means and methods of attack to avoid, and in any event to minimize, incidental damage to cultural property. He should refrain from launching any attack which may be expected to cause incidental damage to protected cultural property, and would be excessive in relation to concrete and direct military advantage. An attack must be suspended or cancelled if it becomes apparent that the objective is cultural property protected under Article 4 of the 1954 Convention or if the attack may cause incidental damage to the property. In order to protect a cultural property against the effects of hostilities, a commander must ensure that it is away from the vicinity of military objectives. He must at all time avoid locating military objectives near cultural property (Articles 7 and 8, Second Protocol to the Hague Convention of 1954).

Military commanders are responsible for respecting the protective nature of the emblems and may not use it for deceptive, perfidious, or direct military advantage. The use of the emblems on military vehicles or equipment commits that equipment to use for humanitarian reasons only . Commanders are responsible for ensuring that persons and places protected by the emblem are not attacked. Any violation of this constitutes a war crime.

If a commander is aware that persons under his command are going to commit or have committed breaches of the Conventions or Protocol, he must initiate such steps as are necessary to prevent those breaches and, where appropriate, initiate penal or disciplinary action against the violators (Article 87, AP I).

The Legal Adviser in the Armed Forces

Legal advisers have a dual role: they advise military commanders on the correct application of the Geneva Conventions and theAdditional Protocols, and they give guidance to commanders on how to teach these to the armed forces for which they are responsible. While these tasks are separate, they are also complementary, because training military personnel properly in times of peace will make the adviser 's advice more effective in times of war. The Additional Protocol I (Article 82) outlines the work of legal advisers, while leaving each S tate Party responsible for specifying their role and the conditions under which they fulfil it. Legal advisers must possess an adequate level of expertise on IHL if they are to advice military commanders effectively.

In a number of countries, of ficers of the Judge Advocate branch are expected to perform the dual functions of advising military commanders on IHL as well as on the application of military law during disciplinary proceedings. The judicial branches (judge advocates) of the armed forces need to be alienated from the military chain of command to withstand pressure from senior military commanders. The States must specify the role and position of the judge advocates in precise terms, so that they can carry out the tasks effectively and efficiently.

Military Manual

Incorporating the study of IHL into programmes of military instruction is the fundamental measure set forth in the treaties with a view to making the law known to the armed forces, who bear primary responsibility for its application. The AP I specifies that the military authorities must be fully acquainted with the text of the Protocol. This obligation is strengthened firstly by the fact that the States must ensure that legal advisers are trained to assist commanders in the application of the Geneva Conventions and the Protocol and to advice them on the appropriate instruction to be given to the armed forces on this subject, and, secondly by the fact that commanders must ensure that the military personnel under their command are aware of their obligations under these instruments.

At present, a number of States, particularly in the South Asian region, do not have any provision to deal with serious international crimes like war crimes, genocide and crimes against humanity, meaning that such crimes are not defined and codified in their domestic law in accordance with international standards. While there are some war crimes that can be prosecuted under military legal systems of these countries, there are many for which there is no jurisdiction in military criminal law. There is a need to include certain crimes pertaining to internal or international armed conflicts in military manuals. For example, (i) attacking civilians, (ii) attacking civilian objects, (iii) attacking personnel or objects involved in humanitarian assistance, (iv) employing prohibited means of warfare, (v) using protected persons as human shields, (vi) starvation as a method of warfare, and (vii) destroying or seizing the enemy's property. For the dissemination of IHL, it is necessary to publish a military manual on IHL and to distribute copies of it among military and paramilitary circles. Instructions on IHL need to be incorporated into the training of military and paramilitary forces in all the countries.[8]

Protection of Emblems

There are three distinct and equally important emblems for assisting victims during times of armed conflict: the Red Cross, the Red Crescent and the Red Crystal. These symbols are used by protected persons and places carrying out humanitarian functions in armed conflicts, such as military

---

[8] For instance, the Indian Army in 2004, has released its 'Doctrine' containing various aspects of military functioning. The 'Doctrine' focuses on operational and logistics training, professional progression and intellectual development at various levels. It states: " A dynamic, comprehensive and operationally-focused training philosophy is a mandatory requirement for producing combat-ready troops and units...Training must remain operationally-oriented, need-based, contemporary and structured towards practical applications." However, the Doctrine is silent upon the training in IHL.

hospitals, ambulances, and medical personnel. Military medical personnel are not considered combatants or legitimate military tagets and must provide care to sick and wounded persons impartially. In times of armed conflict, military authorities may extend the use of the emblem to protect non-combatants such as civilian hospitals, refugee camps, and designated humanitarian relief efforts such as POW transports.

The adoption of domestic measures to ensure respect for the emblems is a fundamental step in maintaining the impartiality associated with providing humanitarian assistance. Consequently, the care and protection of those receiving aid is enhanced. The failure of a S tate to take the appropriate measures can lead to the misuse of the emblems and lessen the respect and confidence which they enjoy In addition, the failure to suppress abuse during times of peace may contribute to abuse during armed conflict. This may erode the protective value of the emblems, endanger the lives of those legitimately entitled to employ them, and interfere with the care and protection of civilians and combatants alike. The responsibility for authorizing the use of the emblems rests with the State, which must regulate their use consistent with the terms of the Conventions and Protocols.

In a highly globalised environment, misuse of the emblems can impact on their legitimacy and undermine their ef fectiveness in providing humanitarian assistance to victims. The Geneva Conventions oblige States to stop the misuse of the emblems at all times, not just during armed conflict. In order to ef fectively control the utilization of the emblems, the States must adopt internal measures establishing the following: (i) the identification of the emblems that are recognized and protected; (ii) a national authority with the competence to regulate the use of the emblems; (iii) those entities with permission to employ the emblems; (iv) the uses for which permission is authorized. In addition, the States must enact national legislation prohibiting and punishing the unauthorized use of the emblems at all times. This legislation must apply to all forms of personal and commercial use and prohibit the use of imitations or designs capable of being mistaken for the Red Cross, the Red Crescent or the Red Crystal.[9]

---

[9] For further details of the emblem, please refer to Chapter 17 of the book.

Individual Responsibility

Certain serious violations of IHL are defined as war crimes. War crimes may occur in the same circumstances as genocide and crimes against humanity but the latter, unlike war crimes, are not linked to the existence of an armed conflict. Individuals bear personal responsibility for war crimes. States must, in accordance with their national law , ensure that alleged perpetrators are brought before their own domestic courts or handed over for trial by the courts of another State or by the ICC.

It is the duty of every S tate to exercise its criminal jurisdiction over those responsible for international crimes.The States which are not a party to the Rome Statute must ensure that serious crimes of international concern listed in the Rome Statute are incorporated into their domestic legislations. The States that do not strengthen their national criminal legislation may run a risk of being held 'unwilling or unable' to genuinely carry out proceedings. Most S tates would like to ensure that they can meet the complementarity test and retain the choice of prosecuting persons domestically, particularly where the person is a national or where the crime was committed on the territory of the S tate. It would be beneficial from a policy standpoint for the States to try violators of IHL as criminals under domestic law rather than as war criminals. Asserting that domestic jurisdiction exists to cover alleged violations of IHL may prevent jurisdiction from being asserted by another country or an international tribunal.

The International Fact-Finding Commission

Under Article 90 of theAdditional Protocol I an International Fact-Finding Commission competent to "enquire into any facts alleged to be a grave breach as defined in the Conventions and AP I or other serious violations thereof" and to "facilitate, through its good of fices, the restoration of an attitude of respect for the Conventions and this Protocol"The Commission is competent to investigate and not to decide on points of lawUnderArticle 90, paragraph 5, the Commission is required to submit a report to the Parties concerned on its findings of fact, with such recommendations as it deems appropriate. It is bound not to make its findings public, unless all the Parties to the conflict have requested it to do so. The Parties to the conflict are under an obligation to 'ensure respect for the law, and therefore must avail the services of the Commission in finding violations of IHL in an armed conflict.

Reparations

Article 91 of the Additional Protocol provides that a Party to the conflict which violates the provisions of the Geneva Conventions or AP I shall be liable to pay compensation. Further, it shall be responsible for all acts committed by persons forming part of its armed forces. The duty to make 'reparations' for violations of IHL is explicitly referred to in the Second Protocol to the Hague Convention for the Protection of Cultural Property (Article 38).

In March 2006, the UN General Assembly adopted the Basic Principles and Guidelines on the Right to a Remedy and Reparation for Victims of Gross Violations of International Human Rights Law and Serious Violations of IHL.[10] This UN document states that in cases of gross violations of international human rights law and serious violations of IHL constituting crimes under international law, States have the duty to investigate and prosecute the persons allegedly responsible for the violations. The term 'compensation' or 'reparation' must be understood in a broader sense and include a range of measures, including non-monetary means of restitution, satisfaction (apology) and rehabilitation (including medical or psychological claim, or legal and social rehabilitation), and guarantees of non-repetition.

There have been two cases decided by the International Court of Justice (ICJ), where reparations have been awarded to the victims, but have not been implemented yet. In *Nicaragua v. the United States of America*, the Court ruled that the United States was 'in breach of its obligation under the Treaty of Friendship with Nicaragua not to use force against Nicaragua' and ordered the United States to pay war reparations. In its final judgment in the *Congo case*, the Court held that the armed activities of Uganda in the Democratic Republic of Congo (DRC) between August 1998 and June 2003

---

[10] Adopted and proclaimed by General Assembly resolution 60/147 of 16 December 2005. Article 1 states that the States have an obligation under international law to ensure that their domestic law is consistent with their international legal obligations by: (a) Incorporating norms of international human rights law and international humanitarian law into their domestic law, or otherwise implementing them in their domestic legal system; (b) Adopting appropriate and effective legislative and administrative procedures and other appropriate measures that provide fair, effective and prompt access to justice; and (c) Making available adequate, effective, prompt and appropriate remedies, including reparation.

violated international human rights and IHL and ordered Uganda to pay reparations to the DRC. The system for award of individual reparations is yet to develop under IHL.

Role of the International Committee of the Red Cross

As guardian of IHL, the International Committee of the Red Cross(ICRC) performs an extensive role in the implementation of IHL and protection of the victims of a conflict. The ICRC has been given a mandate by the international community to assist in the promotion and development of IHL. This includes helping States to develop the study of IHL as a subject in academic institution and encouraging its study by the civiliansThe High Contracting Parties are under an obligation to grant the ICRC all facilities within their power so as to enable it to carry out the humanitarian functions assigned to it to ensure protection and assistance to the victims of conflicts. For further details on the functions and activities of the ICRC, please refer to Chapter 17 of the book.

IHL is intended to alleviate the efects of armed conflict by protecting those who are not, or are no longer taking part in conflict and by regulating the means and methods of warfare. S tates are obliged to comply with the rules of IHL to which they are bound by treaty or which form part of customary international law. The rules may also apply to non-State actors. Such compliance is a matter of international concern.Training in IHL to all the stake holders is necessary to ensure compliance with IHL in times of armed conflict. Training and education must also be undertaken in peacetime. This applies to the whole population, although special attention should be given to relevant groups such as law enforcement of ficials. Additional obligations apply to the training of military personnel. There is, therefore, a political, as well as a humanitarian interest, in the implementation of IHL and improving its compliance throughout the world.

CHAPTER 13

IHL and UN Peace Operations

Introduction

The Charter of the United Nations provides that the UN shall not intervene in the domestic jurisdiction of any state, except in enforcement measures taken under Chapter VII. The Security Council, while acting on behalf of the UN, has been conferred with the responsibility of maintaining of international peace and security. The parties to a dispute which is likely to endanger international peace and security are required to reach a solution by peaceful means. The Security Council may call upon the parties in this regard. Peacekeeping operations have traditionally been associated with Chapter VI of the UN Charter dealing with the 'Pacific Settlement of Disputes'. However, the Security Council need notrefer to a specific chapter of the Charter when passing a resolution authorizing the deployment of a peacekeeping operation and has never invoked ChapterVI. In recent years, the Security Council has adopted the practice of invoking Chapter VII of the Charter when authorizing the deployment of peacekeeping operations in volatile post-conflict settings where the State is unable to maintain security and public order.

The use of UN peacekeepers is a relatively recent development. Observers were first deployed in Palestine in 1948 and military forces were first used by the Security Council in 1956 during the Suez crisis. The UN does not have its own military force. It depends on contributions from member States. As of 28 February 201 1, 114 countries have contributed 99,117 military, police and civilian personnel to UN peacekeeping.[1] Most troops are provided by developing countries like Pakistan, Bangladesh,

---

[1] http://www.un.org/Depts/dpko/dpko/contributors/2011/feb11_1.pdf

India and Nigeria. In contrast, developed countries provide most of the funding (the USA tops the chart followed by Japan, Germany and the UK). Each country that has provided troops has its own military rules, the task of mission is always different and therefore, the Status of Forces Agreement (SOFA) may differ from mission to mission. UN peacekeeping operation is a separate entity and operates under different circumstances. Peacekeeping forces have a status, privileges and immunities which are granted under the UN Convention on Privileges and Immunities of 13 February , 1946, and the UN Convention on Safety of UN and its Personnel adopted by the General Assembly on 9 December, 1994. Peacekeeping personnel are to adhere to 'Ten Rules: For the code of personal conduct for blue-helmet.'[2]

Peacekeeping can be divided into two broad categories: (1) Military observer missions, composed of unarmed of ficers that range in strength from a few observers to several hundred, e.g. UN operations in Cyprus, the Golan Heights and Kashmir; and (2) Peacekeeping forces, composed primarily of armed military units ranging with strength from about a thousand to tens of thousands of troops. T oday, peacekeeping operations commonly support local authorities in: (i) the implementation of a peace agreement; (ii) the maintenance of stability through military and police interventions; (iii) the disarmament, demobilization and reintegration of former combatants; (iv) the supervision of cease-fires and troop withdrawals and manning buffer zones; (v) the return of refugees and internally displaced persons to their homes; (vi) the delivery of humanitarian services to those in need; (vii) the restructuring and reform of local armed forces and police; (viii) the maintenance of law and order; (ix) the strengthening of court and judicial systems and prison facilities; (x) the promotion and protection of human rights; (xi) the conduct and monitoring of elections (UN peace missions have supported elections in seven post-conflict countries – Afghanistan, Burundi, Haiti, Iraq, Liberia, the DRC and Timor); and (xii) the promotion of development and economic reconstruction.

---

[2] These rules, in brief, relate to dress, personal conduct and behaviour to be followed by UN peacekeepers. The rules also prohibit immor al acts of sexual, physical or psy chological abuse or exploitation of the local population, especially women and children. It requires the peacekeepers to show respect for and promote the environment, including the flora and fauna, of the host country. See footnote 7 for further details.

Accountability of Peacekeepers

The maintenance of the best possible relations with the civilian population by UN peacekeepers is a must. However, problems arise when individual members of the armed forces or a contingent commit serious crimes or violate IHL. The personnel serving in UN missions come from a variety of military cultures and training. Imposing a common code of conduct and discipline on such a heterogeneous force may pose a huge challenge. The problem has been highlighted by several cases of sexual abuse and misconduct by UN personnel in recent years. Issues relating to sexual misconduct, protection of cultural property and the use of prohibited weapons and methods of warfare in UN peace operations are discussed here.

Sexual Misconduct

Allegations of sexual misconduct by UN peacekeeping personnel goes back to 1992–93 in Cambodia. These allegations were mainly concerned with prostitution and were dismissed by the mission head with the often-cited observation that "boys will be boys". The UN mission in the former Yugoslavia also became embroiled in allegations that some of its military and civil police personnel were involved in human trafficking and prostitution rings fuelled by the presence of large numbers of UN and NATO peacekeepers in the region. Although a number of people were dismissed, a formal investigation again found insufficient evidence of widespread wrongdoing.

There were large-scale allegations of sexual misconduct by the UN peacekeepers deployed in the Democratic Republic of Congo (MONUC). The peacekeeping personnel stationed in the eastern town of Bunia and various other places were accused of rape, soliciting prostitution and exchanging money and food for sex with refugees — some as young as 12. The worst of the 150 or so allegations of misconduct—some of them captured on videotape—include pedophilia, rape, and prostitution. Since prostitution is legal in many troop-contributing countries, some peacekeepers tried to disguise rape as prostitution by giving the victims money or food. Complaints also emerged from Mozambique, West Africa, and Eretria. Sexual misconduct a grave breach of the Fourth Geneva Convention of 1949, however, despite detailed medical and circumstantial evidence, the allegations were dismissed by the UN for lack of evidence and the alleged of fenders returned to their home countries. The sexual exploitation and misconduct by peacekeepers made Ms. Jane Holl Lute, Assistant Secretary-General for peacekeeping comment: "The blue helmet has become black and blue through self-inflicted wounds. We will not sit still until the luster of that blue helmet is restored."

With 114 troop-contributing countries, each with widely differing laws and social mores and varying degrees of capacity in national criminal and military justice systems, it has been extremely difficult to reach a consensus on a uniform code of conduct. Obtaining the hard evidence needed for criminal prosecution has been another challenge. There has also been a tendency among many troop commanders to ignore some forms of sexual contact between soldiers and civilians, such as prostitution. Such liaisons have been accepted as an inevitable part of military life.

The UN Secretary-General appointed the Jordanian Ambassador to the UN, Prince Zeid Hussein, to develop proposals for a comprehensive reform of the disciplinary and training procedures related to peacekeeping personnel. A detailed report released in March 2005 concluded that sexual exploitation of women and girls by UN peacekeepers and civilian personnel in Congo was significant, widespread and ongoing. The report made recommendations in four general areas: (i) the creation of a common set of rules; (ii) the formation of a professional investigation capability; (iii) the introduction of measures to insure oganizational, managerial and command responsibility; and (iv) the establishment of procedures to ensure individual disciplinary, financial and criminal responsibility In April 2005, the Special Committee on Peacekeeping Operations held a review session to discuss the report and recommended that the General Assembly adopt the detailed rules in the Secretary General' s 2003 bulletin [3], 'Special measure for Protection from Sexual Exploitation and Sexual Abuse', as the uniform

[3] UN Secretary General's 2003 bulletin, Special Measure for Protection from Sexual Exploitation and Sexual Abuse. UN Doc. ST/SGB/2003/13 dated 9 October 2003. Para 3.2 and 3.3 of Bulletin provide: "In order to further protect the most vulnerable populations, especially women and children, the following specific standards which reiterate existing general obligations under the United Nations Staff Regulations and Rules, are promulgated: (a) Sexual exploitation and sexual abuse constitute acts of serious misconduct and are therefore grounds for disciplinary measures, including summary dismissal; (b) Sexual activity with children (persons under the age of 18) is prohibited regardless of the age of majority or age of consent locally. Mistaken belief in the age of a child is not a defence; (c) Exchange of

standard on sexual exploitation and abuse for every category of UN peacekeeping personnel.

Today there is a clear support for removing from service any UN employee who engages in sexual exploitation and abuse. The most severe administrative penalty that the UN is empowered to inflict is the termination of a civilian appointment and the immediate repatriation of a military member of a contingent who is found to have committed sexual exploitation and abuse by a UN investigation.This could be followed by sanctions for a contingent commander who does not enforce the standards.What is needed is a commitment from the troop contributing countries to prosecute their nationals who commit crimes within peacekeeping operations.

The conduct and discipline units in the Department of Peacekeeping Operations (DPKO) were established in November 2005 as part of a package of reforms to strengthen accountability and uphold the standards of conduct of the UN.The DPKO and Member States have put in place a comprehensive package of reforms to prevent misconduct by civilian and uniformed peacekeeping personnel and take swift action where breaches of UN standards occur. The headquarters of the 'conduct and discipline' team maintains global supervision of the state of discipline in all peacekeeping operations and provides overall direction for conduct and discipline issues in field missions. The units in peacekeeping operations act as principal advisers to heads of mission on all conduct and discipline issues involving all categories of peacekeeping personnel in the missions. The conduct and discipline units address all forms of misconduct by UN peacekeeping

---

money, employment, goods or services for sex, including sexual favours or other forms of humiliating, degrading or exploitative behaviour, is prohibited. This includes any exchange of assistance that is due to beneficiaries of assistance; (d) Sexual relationships between United Nations staff and beneficiaries of assistance, since they are based on inherently unequal power dynamics, undermine the credibility and integrity of the work of the United Nations and are strongly discouraged; (e) Where a United Nations staff member develops concerns or suspicions regarding sexual exploitation or sexual abuse by a fellow worker, whether in the same agency or not and whether or not within the United Nations system, he or she must report such concerns via established reporting mechanisms; (f) United Nations staff are obliged to create and maintain an environment that prevents sexual exploitation and sexual abuse. Managers at all levels have a particular responsibility to support and develop systems that maintain this environment.The standards set out above are not intended to be an exhaustive list. Other types of sexually exploitive or sexually abusive behaviour may be grounds for administrative action or disciplinary measures, including summary dismissal, pursuant to the United Nations Staff Regulations and Rules."

personnel, including acts of sexual exploitation and abuse.

Protection of Cultural Property

Cultural property may be damaged or demolished intentionally during an armed conflict or unintentionally as a result of collateral damage. In January 2008, peacekeepers of the UN Mission for the Referendum in Western Sahara vandalized a prehistoric site containing 6,000-years-old rock paintings. Since cultural property reflects and manifests the identity of conflicting identity groups, it may be subject to damage, pillage and looting by the conflicting parties. It has been observed that in majority of conflicts, cultural property having the identity of the opposing group is destroyed intentionally. The destruction of cultural property may also be used as a weapon of psychological warfare. During the conflicts in Bosnia and Kosovo, intentional devastation and burning of archeological sites was reported. The lack of financial resources and inadequate protection may also facilitate looting or theft by illegal traffickers in artefacts.

The protection of cultural property during peace operations under Chapters VI and VII of the UN Charter has been generally ignored. The model agreement between the UN and member States contributing personnel and equipment to peacekeeping operations was drafted in 1991. It includes a standard clause which states that the peacekeeping operations shall observe and respect the principles and spirit of general international conventions applicable to the conduct of military personnel. These international conventions include the four Geneva Conventions of 1949, the Additional Protocols of 1977 and the UNESCO Convention of 1954 on the protection of cultural property. In addition, Article 6.6 of the 1999 UN Secretary-General bulletin, which applies to UN peacekeepers, states:

> The United Nations force is prohibited from attacking monuments of art, architecture or history, archaeological sites, works of art, places of worship and museums and libraries which constitute the cultural or spiritual heritage of peoples. In its area of operation, the United Nations force shall not use such cultural property or their immediate surroundings for purposes which might expose them to destruction or damage. Theft, pillage, misappropriation and any act of vandalism directed against cultural property is strictly prohibited.

Article 4 of the Hague Convention (1954) provides that the High Contracting Parties must prohibit, prevent and, if necessary , put a stop to any form of theft, pillage or misappropriation of, and any acts of vandalism directed against, cultural property . They must also refrain from any act directed by way of reprisals against cultural property This provision of the Convention shows that the forces bound by IHL, like the UN peacekeepers, have an obligation to protect cultural property from destruction, theft, pillage or misappropriation. The UN peacekeepers, though not bound by the international treaties relating to IHL or the protection of cultural properties, remain subject to the principles and rules of the UN. Peacekeers must be legally responsible for the protection of cultural property and it should be defined in the Status of Force Agreements (SOFA).

Use of Prohibited Weapons and Methods

It has been reported that the UN forces have used riot-control agents (RCAs) on more than 40 separate occasions in 14 missions[4].The UN forces in Haiti relied heavily on RCAs to subdue victims of the January 2010 earthquake who turned aggressive while demanding food from relief workers. RCAs are temporary incapacitators and are banned chemical agents under the Chemical Weapon Convention (CWC), except when used in law-enforcement situations.[5]

RCAs are a class of less-lethal weapons that include tear gas, pepper spray, or other irritants which cause tears, coughing and sneezing. Each RCA has its own distinctive attributes. In healthy adults, RCAs can cause

---

[4] Fry James D, Gas Smells Awful: U.N. Forces, Riot-Control Agents, and the Chemical Weapons Convention, *Michigan Journal of International Law*, Vol.31,No.3, Spring 2010, p. 475-558.

[5] Tear-gas weapons and other RCAs were developed during late 18th Century. The term 'riot control agent' was coined after the use of such agent against rioters in Pittsburgh. Articles 22 and 23 of the 1907 Hague Gas Declaration provided that the "right of bell igerents to adopt means of injuring the enemy is not unlimited" and "i t is especially forbidden . . . to employ poison or poisoned weapons" or "to employ arms, projectiles, or material calculated to cause unnecessary suffering." Despite these broad prohibitions, gas weapons were used during the First World War. The subsequent 1925 Geneva Protocol for the Prohibition of the Use in War of Asphyxiating, Poisonous or Other Gases, and of Bacteriological Methods of Warfare (Geneva Gas Protocol) could not prohibit the use of approximately 8,000 tons of tear gas during the Second World War. One main reason for the failure of the Protocol was that it failed to spell out exactly which agents were prohibited, and the Protocol prohibited only first use. The US used lage amounts of tear gas in Vietnam in the 1970s, maintaining that tear gas was not covered by the Protocol because it did not kil the targets but merely incapacitated them while they were in contact with the agent.

bronchospams, chemical pneumonitis, pulmonary edema, heart failure, hepatocellular damage, gastroenteritis with perforation (if ingested), and serious dermatitis with erythema and blisters when a large dose is delivered in an area with high temperature and humidity—all of which can be fatal. Multiple exposure to RCAs can cause the formation of tumors, pulmonary disease, and reproductive problems. Chances of lethality increase when RCAs are used in lage doses, in confined spaces, and on weaker individuals such as the elderly , pregnant women, and children. RCAs are generally considered to be indiscriminate area weapons. They are so indiscriminate that even those who deploy them are not entirely safe from the effects.

The principle of discrimination requires that an attacker be able to differentiate between combatants and military objectives, on the one hand, and noncombatants and civilian objects, on the other . This principle essentially creates an obligation for combatants to exercise reasonable care to ensure that they cause no unnecessary suf fering to civilians. The IHL prohibition of indiscriminate attacks applies to all attacks, regardless of whether the weaponry is less lethal. This principle is contained in Article 48 of the Additional Protocol I to the Geneva Conventions:

> In order to ensure respect for and protection of the civilian population and civilian objects, the Parties to the conflict shall at all times distinguish between the civilian population and combatants and between civilian objects and military objectives and accordingly shall direct their operations only against military objectives.

The Chemical Weapons Convention (CWC) prohibits RCAs as a weapon or method of warfare.The stability of the CWC regime may sufer if the UN forces continue to use RCAs on a lar ge scale, not only because the CWC prohibits their use but also because the UN forces are meant to be exemplary forces.Though the UN and its forces do not have legal obligations directly under the CWC or customary rules of IHL relating to RCAs, there are numerous moral and strategic reasons for them to discontinue the use of RCAs. The Secretary-General must issue a directive through the UN Department of Peacekeeping Operations to all UN peacekeepers to refrain from carrying and using RCAs in any of their operations. The UN could also include a similar clause in the model SOF A. Instead, the UN forces could use non-toxic varieties of less-lethal weaponrysuch as slippery foams, and acoustic and heat rays which have the same ef fect as RCAs without violating the CWC regime.

IHL and Peace Operations

Initially there was some doubt about the applicability of IHL to UN forces. The UN had maintained that the international law of armed conflict does not apply the "blue helmet" UN peacekeepers because they are not combatants; they are not engaged in military ofensive operations and they are authorized to use force only in self-defence. It is now accepted that UN forces, whether performing duties of peacekeepingor enforcement are bound by IHL. While the armed forces of a State operate under national doctrine and guiding principles, when they serve as part of a UN peacekeeping operation, the following six basic international principles govern their actions.[6]

1. Impartiality

Impartiality and even-handedness always guide the actions of a military component of a UN peacekeeping operation. Impartiality is understood as an objective and consistent execution of the mandate, regardless of provocation or challenge. Impartiality does not mean inaction or overlooking violations. UN peacekeepers must be impartial in their dealings with the Parties to the conflict, but not neutral in the execution of their mandate, i.e., they must actively pursue the implementation of their mandate even if doing so goes against the interests of one or more of the Parties. If the peacekeeping force is perceived as being partial, people may lose confidence in the UN' s ability to act as a neutral Party, which can damage the credibility of the mission and threaten the peace process. At worst, a perception of UN partiality could lead Parties to the conflict to withdraw their consent to the presence of the mission and return to violence as a means of resolving the conflict.

2. Consent and cooperation

Peacekeeping and progress towards a just and sustainable peace rely on the consent and cooperation of the Parties to the conflict. In the

[6] Handbook on United Nations Multidimensional Peacekeeping Operations, Issued by Peacekeeping Best Practices Unit, Department of Peacekeeping Operations, United Nations, 2003.

absence of free consent, the military component and the peacekeeping operation as a whole may find it hard to implement its mandateThere is often very little trust between Parties in the immediate post-conflict phase and consent for a UN intervention may be uncertain. While political and military leaders may consent to a UN military presence, groups of combatants lower down the chain of command may disagree with their leaders and challenge the authority or mandate of the peacekeeping operation through violence or other acts of non-cooperation. Consent at all levels must be encouraged by building confidence among the parties and enhancing their stake in and ownership of the peace process. Impartiality is the best guarantee that a mission will gain and retain the consent of all parties.

3. Appropriate use of force

Since peacekeeping operations need the consent of the Parties to a conflict, military forces under UN command are not usually required to use force beyond that necessary for self-defence. Self-defence includes the right to protect oneself, other UN personnel, UN property and any other persons under UN protection. The use of force by the military component will depend on the mandate of the peacekeeping operation and the rules of engagement. The rules of engagement for the peacekeeping operation must clarify the different levels of force that can be used in various circumstances, how each level of force should be used and any authorizations that may need to be obtained from commanders.

4. Unity and International Character

To be effective, a peacekeeping operation must function as an integrated unit reflecting the will and presence of the international community as a whole. This is particularly true of a military component composed of several dif ferent national contingents. Military forces under UN command must always respect the international character of their duties and not serve any national or other interests. International forces may be vulnerable to attempts by Parties to a conflict to exploit differences between the contingents. Maintaining the integrated, strictly international character of the operation is the best safeguard against such attempts and enhances the legitimacy of the overall mission.

5. Respect for principles of IHL

The fundamental principles and rules of IHL are applicable to military forces under UN command. In case of violation of IHL, UN military personnel are subject to prosecution under their own national systems of military justice. Military forces under UN command must make a clear distinction between civilians and combatants and direct military operations only against combatants and military objectives. The right of a UN force to use means and methods of combat is also not unlimited. A UN force must respect the rules prohibiting or restricting the use of certain weapons and methods of combat under the relevant instruments of IHL. In the treatment of civilians, women and children require special protection from rape, enforced prostitution and any other form of indecent and criminal assault.

6. Respect for local laws and customs

All peacekeeping operation personnel must respect local laws and customs and maintain the highest standards of integrity in their personal conduct. When a peacekeeping operation includes a military component, especially formed military units of several thousand personnel, the presence of the peacekeeping operation is seen and felt throughout the mission area. Respect for the peacekeeping force is directly related to its success in maintaining high standards of professionalism, integrity, impartiality and in its general behaviour in interactions with the local population. This respect is required to sustain the cooperation and consent of the local population. Although a peacekeeping mission and its personnel enjoy certain privileges and immunities accorded to the UN to facilitate its effective operation, these do not change the obligation of all mission personnel to obey local laws and respect social, cultural and religious norms. In particularly in their personal behavior, military personnel must always maintain exemplary standards of conduct, in accordance with the Code of Conduct.[7] Those that breach the Code must be duly disciplined by

[7] Since 1998, uniformed personnel have been provided with pocket cards of the Ten Rules: Code of Personal Conduct for Blue Helmets. These are: 1. Dress, think, talk, act and behave in a manner befitting the dignity of a disciplined, caring, considerate, mature, respected and trusted soldier, displaying the highest integrity and impartiality. Have pride in your position as a peace-keeper and do not abuse or misuse your authority. 2. Respect the law of the land

their national authorities, including the imposition of legal sanctions, when appropriate.

Secretary-General's Bulletin on IHL

In 1995, the ICRC convened a group of experts tasked with identifying the core IHL provisions applicable in UN peacekeeping operations. The proposal of this group formed the "Secretary-General' s Bulletin on the Observance by United Nations Forces of International Humanitarian Law"[8]. The Bulletin (vide Section 10), entered into force on 12August 1999. The instructions contained in the Secretary-General's Bulletin are applicable to UN peacekeeping forces under UN command and control, when they are actively engaged as combatants in situations of armed conflict. They apply in Chapter VII operations or in Chapter VI operations in self-defence, to the extent and for the duration of their engagement.

The ten-section Bulletin includes the principles of distinction between civilians and combatants and between civilian objects and military objectives, means and methods of warfare, treatment of civilians and persons *hors de* combat, treatment of detainees, and protection of the wounded, the sick and medical and relief personnel.The fundamental principles and rules of IHL applicable to UN forces conducting operations under UN Command and Control are as follows.

---

of the host country , their local cultur e, traditions, customs and pr actices. 3. Treat the inhabitants of the host country with respect, courtesy and consideration. You are there as a guest to help them and in so doing wil l be welcomed with admiration. Neither soli cit nor accept any material re ward, honor or gift. 4. Do not indulge in immoral acts of sexual, physical or psychological abuse or exploitation of the local population or United Nations staff, especially women and children. 5. Respect and regard the human rights of all. Support and aid the infirm, sick and weak. Do not act in revenge or with malice, in particular when dealing with prisoners, detainees or people in your custody. 6. Properly care for and account for all United Nations money, vehicles, equipment and property assigned to you and do not trade or barter wi th them to seek personal benefits. 7 . Show mi litary courtesy and pa y appropriate compliments to al l members of the mission, including other Uni ted Nations contingents regardless of their creed, gender, rank or origin. 8. Show respect for and promote the environment, including the flora and f auna, of the host country. 9. Do not engage in excessive consumption of alcohol or any consumption or trafficking of drugs. 10. Exercise the utmost discretion in handling confidential information and matters of official business which can put lives into danger or soil the image of the United Nations.

[8] No. ST/SGB/1999/13 of 6 August 1999.

Section 1 - Field of Application

The fundamental principles and rules of IHL are applicable to UN forces when they are actively engaged as combatants in situations of armed conflict, to the extent and for the duration of their engagement: (i) Enforcement actions and (ii) Peacekeeping operations when the use of force is permitted in self-defence.

This does not affect the protected status of members of peacekeeping operations under the 1994 Convention on the Safety of United Nations and Associated Personnel or their status as non-combatants, as long as they are entitled to the protection given to civilians under the international law of armed conflict.

Section 2 - Application of National Law

It does not constitute an exhaustive list of principles and rules of IHL binding upon military personnel, and do not replace the national laws by which military personnel remain bound throughout the operation.

Section 3 - Status-of-forces Agreement (SOFA)

In the SOFA concluded between the UN and a S tate in whose territory a UN force is deployed, the UN undertakes to ensure that the force shall conduct its operations with full respect for the principles and rules of the general conventions applicable to the conduct of military personnel.

The UN also undertakes to ensure that members of the military personnel of the force are fully acquainted with the principles and rules of those international instruments.The obligation to respect the said principles and rules is applicable to UN forces even in the absence of a SOFA.

Section 4 - Violations of International Humanitarian Law

In case of violations of IHL, members of the military personnel of a UN force are subject to prosecution in their national courts.

Section 5 - Protection of the Civilian Population

1. The UN force shall make a clear distinction at all times between civilians and combatants and between civilian objects and military objectives. Military operations shall be directed only against

combatants and military objectives.Attacks on civilians or civilian objects are prohibited.

2. Civilians shall enjoy the protection aforded by this section, unless and for such time as they take a direct part in hostilities.

3. The UN force shall take all feasible precautions to avoid, and in any event to minimize, incidental loss of civilian life, injury to civilians or damage to civilian property.

4. In its area of operation, the UN force shall avoid, to the extent feasible, locating military objectives within or near densely populated areas, and take all necessary precautions to protect the civilian population, individual civilians and civilian objects against the dangers resulting from military operations. Military installations and equipment of peacekeeping operations, as such, shall not be considered military objectives.

5. The UN force is prohibited from launching operations of a nature likely to strike military objectives and civilians in an indiscriminate manner, as well as operations that may be expected to cause incidental loss of life among the civilian population or damage to civilian objects that would be excessive in relation to the concrete and direct military advantage anticipated.

6. The UN force shall not engage in reprisals against civilians or civilian objects.

Section 6 - Means and Methods of Combat

1. The right of the UN force to choose methods and means of combat is not unlimited.

2. The UN force shall respect the rules prohibiting or restricting the use of certain weapons and methods of combat under the relevant instruments of international humanitarian law . These include, in particular, the prohibition on the use of asphyxiating, poisonous or other gases and biological methods of warfare; bullets which explode, expand or flatten easily in the human body; and certain explosive projectiles. The use of certain conventional weapons, such as non-detectable fragments, anti-personnel mines, booby traps

and incendiary weapons, is prohibited.

3. The UN force is prohibited from employing methods of warfare which may cause superfluous injury or unnecessary suf fering, or which are intended, or may be expected to cause, widespread, long-term and severe damage to the natural environment.

4. The UN force is prohibited from using weapons or methods of combat of a nature to cause unnecessary suffering.

5. It is forbidden to order that there shall be no survivors.

6. The UN force is prohibited from attacking monuments of art, architecture or history, archaeological sites, works of art, places of worship and museums and libraries which constitute the cultural or spiritual heritage of peoples. In its area of operation, the UN force shall not use such cultural property or their immediate surroundings for purposes which might expose them to destruction or damage. Theft, pillage, misappropriation and any act of vandalism directed against cultural property is strictly prohibited.

7. The UN force is prohibited from attacking, destroying, removing or rendering useless objects indispensable to the survival of the civilian population, such as foodstuf, crops, livestock and drinking-water installations and supplies.

8. The UN force shall not make installations containing dangerous forces, namely dams, dikes and nuclear electrical generating stations, the object of military operations if such operations may cause the release of dangerous forces and consequent severe losses among the civilian population.

9. The UN force shall not engage in reprisals against objects and installations protected under this section.

Section 7 - Treatment of civilians and persons *hors de combat*

1. Persons not, or no longer , taking part in military operations, including civilians, members of armed forces who have laid down their weapons and persons placed *hors de combat* by reasons of sickness, wounds or detention, shall, in all circumstances, be treated

humanely and without any adverse distinction based on race, sex, religious convictions or any other ground. They shall be accorded full respect for their person, honour and religious and other convictions.

2. The following acts against any of the persons mentioned in section 7.1 are prohibited at any time and in any place: violence to life or physical integrity; murder as well as cruel treatment such as torture, mutilation or any form of corporal punishment; collective punishment; reprisals; the taking of hostages; rape; enforced prostitution; any form of sexual assault and humiliation and degrading treatment; enslavement; and pillage.

3. Women shall be especially protected against any attack, in particular against rape, enforced prostitution or any other form of indecent assault.

4. Children shall be the object of special respect and shall be protected against any form of indecent assault.

Section 8 - Treatment of detained persons

The UN force shall treat with humanity and respect for their dignity detained members of the armed forces and other persons who no longer take part in military operations by reason of detention. Without prejudice to their legal status, they shall be treated in accordance with the relevant provisions of the Third Geneva Convention of 1949, as may be applicable to them mutatis mutandis. In particular:

(a) Their capture and detention shall be notified without delay to the party on which they depend and to the Central Tracing Agency of the ICRC in particular in order to inform their families;

(b) They shall be held in secure and safe premises which provide all possible safeguards of hygiene and health, and shall not be detained in areas exposed to the dangers of the combat zone;

(c) They shall be entitled to receive food and clothing, hygiene and medical attention;

(d) They shall under no circumstances be subjected to any form of torture or ill-treatment;

(e) Women whose liberty has been restricted shall be held in quarters separate from men' s quarters, and shall be under the immediate supervision of women;

(f) In cases where children who have not attained the age of sixteen years take a direct part in hostilities and are arrested, detained or interned by the United Nations force, they shall continue to benefit from special protection. In particular, they shall be held in quarters separate from the quarters of adults, except when accommodated with their families;

(g) ICRC's right to visit prisoners and detained persons shall be respected and guaranteed.

Section 9 - Protection of the wounded, the sick, and medical and relief personnel

1. Members of the armed forces and other persons in the power of the UN force who are wounded or sick shall be respected and protected in all circumstances. They shall be treated humanely and receive the medical care and attention required by their condition, without adverse distinction. Only urgent medical reasons will authorize priority in the order of treatment to be administered.

2. Whenever circumstances permit, a suspension of fire shall be arranged, or other local arrangements made, to permit the search for and identification of the wounded, the sick and the dead left on the battlefield and allow for their collection, removal, exchange and transport.

3. The UN force shall not attack medical establishments or mobile medical units. These shall at all times be respected and protected, unless they are used, outside their humanitarian functions, to attack or otherwise commit harmful acts against the United Nations force.

4. The UN force shall in all circumstances respect and protect medical personnel exclusively engaged in the search for , transport or treatment of the wounded or sick, as well as religious personnel.

5. The UN force shall respect and protect transports of wounded and sick or medical equipment in the same way as mobile medical units.

6. The UN force shall not engage in reprisals against the wounded, the sick or the personnel, establishments and equipment protected under this section.

7. The UN force shall in all circumstances respect the Red Cross and Red Crescent emblems. These emblems may not be employed except to indicate or to protect medical units and medical establishments, personnel and material. Any misuse of the Red Cross or Red Crescent emblems is prohibited.

8. The UN force shall respect the right of the families to know about the fate of their sick, wounded and deceased relatives.To this end, the force shall facilitate the work of the ICRC Central T racing Agency.

9. The UN force shall facilitate the work of relief operations which are humanitarian and impartial in character and conducted without any adverse distinction, and shall respect personnel, vehicles and premises involved in such operations.

Peacekeepers as Legitimate Targets

It is well settled that UN military personnel who participate in peace enforcement operations that breach the threshold CommonArticle 2 of the Geneva Conventions are combatants. Accordingly, the 1994 Convention on the Safety of United Nations andAssociated Personnel clearly envisages that UN personnel engaging in a ChapterVII peace-enforcement action are combatants and may be lawfully targeted by the opposing force. Additionally, the 1999 Secretary General' s Bulletin regarding UN forces and IHL implies that UN forces, may at times be actively be engaged as combatants. The ICRC has maintained that IHL principles, recognized as part of customary international law are binding upon all States and upon all armed forces present in situations of armed conflict.

Command Responsibility in UN Peacekeeping Operations

UN peacekeeping operations are primarily military in nature; they are hierarchical and the majority of personnel are militaryThe UN instruments have accordingly tasked military superiors and commanders to prevent misconduct and take steps to ensure that offenders are punished. It is the contingent commanders' obligation to maintain the discipline and good order of the contingent. The criminal responsibility of commanders for war crimes committed by their subordinates, based on the commanders' failure to take measures to prevent or punish the commission of such crimes is a rule of customary international law. In a few instances where military commanders have failed to ensure discipline, they have been repatriated. Criminal jurisdiction over military personnel is exclusive to the sending state. The International Criminal Court (ICC) can exercise its jurisdiction when a state is unable or unwilling to investigate or prosecute a case.

A commander is held responsible if he knew or had reason to know that crimes were going to be, were being committed, or had been committed by his subordinate. The ICTY in *Prosecutor v. Delalic* (1998)[9] has held that knowledge could be actual knowledge, demonstrated by direct or circumstantial evidence, or constructive knowledge, which puts the commander/superior on notice that further investigation is necessary . In order to determine such knowledge, the ICTY suggested that the following factors be taken into consideration:

(a) The number of illegal acts;

(b) The type of illegal acts;

(c) The scope of illegal acts;

(d) The time during which the illegal acts occurred;

(e) The number and type of troops involved;

(f) The logistics involved, if any;

(g) The geographical location of the acts;

(h) The widespread occurrence of the acts;

(i) The tactical tempo of operations;

---

[9] Prosecutor v. Delalic (Judgment) Case No IT-96-21-T, Trial Chamber (16 November 1998) paras 141–6, 383, 393.

(j) The modus operandi of similar illegal acts;

(k) The officers and staff involved;

(l) The location of the commander at the time.[10]

The importance of command responsibility has been recognized by the UN, and the Model Memorandum of Understanding (MoU) now contains specific provisions obligating sending States to take action when a commander fails 'to cooperate with a UN investigation, fails to exercise effective command and control, or neglects to immediately report to the appropriate authorities or take action in respect of allegations of misconduct reported to the commander'. It is the commander's 'obligation to maintain the discipline and good order of the contingent'. Fulfilment of these obligations forms part of a commander's performance appraisal.[11]

The first requirement of command responsibility under Article 28(a) of the Rome Statue is that there exists a superior–subordinate relationship.[12] The most important aspect of this relationship is not the rank of the superior but the fact that the commander had command or authority over the subordinate. A military commander could be held criminally responsible for crimes committed by forces under his effective command and control as a result of his or her failure to exercise control properly over such forces. Thus, in the case where a subordinate peacekeeper commits a crime, in order to establish command responsibility , the person or persons who exercise effective command and control over that subordinate, needs to be determined. However, the command or authority and control must be effective.

A commander therefore has a duty to ensure that his forces are adequately trained in IHL and due regard is paid to IHL in operational decision making. He must ensure that an effective reporting system is established so that he is informed of incidents when violations of IHL might have occurred.

---

[10] Mettraux G., 2009. The Law of Command Responsibility, Oxford: OUP, p. 214–5.

[11] UN General Assembly, A/61/19 (Part III) dated 12 June 2007 , 'Revised draft model memorandum of understanding', available at: http://cdu.unlb.org /Portals/0/Documents/KeyDoc8.pdf, accessed 2 Feb 2011.

[12] For further details, please refer to Chapter 15 of the book on Command Responsibility.

Training in International Humanitarian Law

Training is the foundation of success in any military operation. Today, training of military, police and civilian personnel for UN peacekeeping is widely recognized as a necessary factor in the effectiveness of UN peacekeeping missions. In particular, the evolving complexity and multidimensional nature of peacekeeping in conjunction with the new challenges has prompted the need for changes in specialized training. The four major training areas are (i) subject training — to improve understanding of human rights, refugee law and IHL; (ii) language training — to improve communication among international forces; (iii) professional development and staff training — to improve the interoperability between different foreign contingents; and (iv) peace support operations training — to improve the understanding by military and civilian participants of multilateral peacekeeping and peacemaking operations. The aim of training in IHL is to influence the attitudes of the soldiers to comply with the law in the theatre of operation.

Although initially there was some doubt about the applicability of humanitarian law to UN forces, it is now well established that they are bound by IHL, while performing duties of a peacekeeping or enforcement nature.[13] The UN as an international organization is not in a position to become a party to the Geneva Conventions or Additional Protocols. However, the principles of humanitarian law recognized as part of customary international law are binding upon all States and all armed forces present in situations of armed conflict.The UN must issue guidelines on IHL which should be followed by the troop-contributing countries while imparting

[13] The UN Peacekeeping Operations Principles and Guidelnes (2008) provides, "IHL is designed to protect persons who do not participate, or are no longer participating, in the hostilities; and it maintains the fundamental rights of civilians, victims and non-combatants in an armed conflict. It is relevant to United Nations peacekeeping operations because these missions are often deployed into post-conflict environments where violence may be ongoing or conflict could reignite. Additionally, in post-conflict environments there are often large civilian populations that have been targeted by the warring parties, prisoners of war and other vulnerable groups to whom the Geneva Conventions or other humanitarian law would apply in the event of further hostilities. UN peacekeepers must have a clear understanding of the principles and rules of international humanitarian law and observe them in situations where they apply." UNDPKO, 'UN Peacekeeping Operations Principles and Guidelnes', p. 16, Peacekeeping Best Practices Section, Division of Policy, Evaluation and Training, Department of Peacekeeping Operations, United Nations, New York, January 2008. Available at:http://www.peacekeeping bestpractices. unlb.org/Pbps/Library/Capstone_Doctrine_ENG.pdf, accessed: 02 February 2011.

training to their armed forces, police and civilian personnel. Incidents of sexual abuse, prostitution and other serious misconduct have tarnished the reputation and effectiveness of UN peacekeeping operations. There is a need to adopt a zero-tolerance policy for crimes committed by the peacekeepers. The troop-contributing countries need to enforce the highest possible standard of conduct among military officials selected for peacekeeping missions.

CHAPTER 14

The Rome Statute of the International Criminal Court

Introduction

The Rome Statute of the International Criminal Court (ICC) was adopted on 17 July 1998. Prior to the Rome Statute, the only form of international criminal justice system were ad hoc tribunals, which were accused of delivering 'selective justice' or 'victor 's justice'. Some ad hoc tribunals established by the international community are those for Nurembug, Tokyo, the former Yugoslavia, Rwanda, East Timor, Cambodia, Sierra Leon, and Iraq.[1]

The preamble of the Rome Statute establishes the purpose of the ICC. It states: "Af firming that the most serious crimes of concern to the international community as a whole must not go unpunished and........to put an end to impunity for the perpetrators of these crimes........for the sake of present and future generations,.......to guarantee lasting respect for and the enforcement of international justice".The Rome Statute is unique in many ways. It has created a permanent tribunal, the ICC, to deal with all crimes of serious concern to the international community . The formation of the ICC is an example of States ceding their authority to international

---

[1] The most common criticisms of the post -World War II tribunals include: (1) The tribunals applied a body of law, which had not been clearly enumerated in treat y form, or were in treaties which were not fuly applicable to the events under scrutiny; (2) The tribunals wer one-sided, as possible war crimes committed by the Allies were neither fully considered at either tribunal nor dealt with elsewhere; and (3) Large numbers of guilty individuals were either not prosecuted at al, or were treated too leniently. At the same time the international community failed to react to crimes in East Pakistan (now Bangladesh), Uganda, Chile and those perpetrated on Turkish Armenians.

institutions. The ICC's jurisdiction and mandate are not limited to specific events in specific places, or to any specified time-frame. Its powers and functions include holding individuals accountable, and subjecting the accused to investigation, arrest, detention, prosecution and if found guilty, incarceration. The Rome Statute creates obligations on the part of the State parties to provide the means to enforce these powers. As of 15 March 2011, 114 countries are States Parties to the Rome Statute.

Structure of the ICC

The Court is composed of four organs. These are the Presidency, the Judicial Divisions, the Office of the Prosecutor and the Registry. The Presidency is responsible for the overall administration of the Court, with the exception of the Office of the Prosecutor, and for specific functions assigned to the Presidency in accordance with the Statute. It is composed of three judges of the Court, elected by their fellow judges for a term of three years.

The Judicial Division consists of 18 judges organized into the Pre-Trial Division, the Trial Division and the Appeals Division. The judges of each division sit in chambers which are responsible for conducting the proceedings of the Court at different stages. Judges are assigned to the divisions on the basis of the nature of the functions of each division and the qualifications and experience of the judges. This is done in a manner ensuring that each division benefits from an appropriate combination of expertise in criminal law and procedure and international law. The First Vice-President and six other judges sit in the Pre-Trial Chamber. The Second Vice-President and five other judges sit in the Trial Chamber. The President and four other judges sit in the Appeal Chamber.

The Office of the Prosecutor is in charge of examining information received on crimes committed within the jurisdiction of the ICC and examining referrals to the Court. It also conducts investigations that may lead to prosecutions before the Court. The Registry is responsible for the non-judicial aspects of the administration and servicing of the Court. It is headed by the Registrar, who is the principal administrative officer of the Court. The Registrar exercises his or her functions under the authority of the President of the Court.

The Court also includes a number of semi-autonomous offices such as the 'Office of Public Counsel forVictims' and the 'Office of Public Counsel for Defence'. These fall under the Registry for administrative purposes but otherwise function as wholly independent offices. The Assembly of States Parties has also established a Tust Fund for the benefit of victims of crimes within the jurisdiction of the Court and the families of these victims. The Court is funded by contributions from the States Parties and by voluntary contributions from governments, international organizations, individuals, corporations and other entities.

The ICC is an independent institution. It is not part of the United Nations, but it maintains a cooperative relationship with the UNThe Court is based in The Hague, the Netherlands, although it may also sit elsewhere.

Address: Maanweg 174, 2516AB, The Hague, Netherlands

Postal Address Po Box 19519,2500 CM, The Hague, Netherlands

Crimes under the Rome Statute

The ICC has jurisdiction only over crimes committed after 1 July 2002, when the Statute entered into force. It has a mandate to try individuals rather than States and to hold them accountable for the most serious crimes of concern to the international community - genocide, war crimes and crimes against humanity, and the crime of aggression. These crimes have been described as "the most serious crimes of concern to the international community as a whole", and as "unimaginable atrocities that deeply shock the conscience of humanity".Articles 6, 7 and 8 of the Rome Statute define the crimes of genocide, crimes against humanity , and war crimes. These definitions also contain a list of acts that can amount to the said crimes when the threshold test for each crime is met. These crimes are of recent origin and their recognition and subsequent development is closely associated with the human rights movements after the World War II.

A. Genocide

Article 6 of the Rome Statute reproduces the definition of genocide provided in Article II of the UN Convention on the Prevention and Punishment of the Crime of Genocide (1948). The Rome S tatute and the Genocide Convention identify five specific acts committed with the intent to destroy in whole or part, a national, ethical, racial or religious group.The five acts are: killing members of the group, causing serious bodily or mental harm to members of the group, imposing conditions on the group calculated to destroy it, preventing births within the group and forcibly transferring children of the group to another.

B. Crimes against Humanity

The definition of crimes against humanity contained in Article 7 of the Rome Statute is broader than that contained in the statutes of the Yugoslavia[2] and Rwanda[3] Tribunals. The list includes rape, sexual slavery, enforced prostitution, forced pregnancy, enforced sterilization, and any other form of sexual violence. It also includes the forced transfer of a population, enforced disappearance of persons and apartheid. Such acts, however, must be committed as part of a "widespread or systematic attack directed against any civilian population, with knowledge of the attack" and there must be "multiple commissions of [the specified act]... pursuant to or in furtherance of a State or organizational policy to commit such attack." These last requirements limit the scope of the ICC's jurisdiction over crimes against humanity, notwithstanding the comparatively broad list of offences.

C. War Crimes

War crimes do not have the heavy evidentiary requirements of crimes against humanity. The Rome Statute divides war crimes into four categories: (a) grave breaches of the Geneva Conventions of 12 August 1949;[4] (b) other serious violations of the laws and customs applicable in international armed conflict, within the established framework of international law; (c) in the case of a non-international armed conflict, serious violations of Article 3 common to the four Geneva Conventions; and (d) other serious violations of the laws and customs applicable to armed conflicts that are not of an international character, within the established framework of international law.

---

[2] 1993 Statute of International Criminal Tribunal for the former Yugoslavia.

[3] 1994 Statute of International Criminal Tribunal for Rwanda.

[4] The four Geneva Conventions of 12 August 1949: Convention (I) for the Ameloration of the Condition of the Wounded and Sick in Armed Forces in the Field, Convention (II) for the Amelioration of the Condition of Wounded, Sick and Shipwrecked Members of Armed Forces at Sea, Convention (III) Relative to the Treatment of Prisoners of War, Convention (IV) relative to the Protection of Civilian Persons in Time of War.

Article 8, paragraph 2 (a) lists eight acts as grave breaches of the Geneva Conventions of 1949, namely: (i) wilful killing; (ii) torture or inhuman treatment, including biological experiments; (iii) wilfully causing great suffering, or serious injury to body or health; (iv) extensive destruction and appropriation of property not justified by military necessity and carried out unlawfully and wantonly; (v) compelling a POW or other protected person to serve in the forces of a hostile Power; (vi) wilfully depriving a prisoner of war or other protected person of the rights of fair and regular trial; (vii) unlawful deportation or transfer or unlawful confinement; and (viii) taking of hostages. The crimes listed under Article 8 (2) (a) of the Rome Statute correspond exactly to the relevant provisions of the Geneva Convention and are subject to the same limitations, i.e. they shall be qualified as crimes only when committed in an international armed conflict, and against persons protected under the relevant Geneva Convention. Rape, sexual slavery, enforced prostitution, forced pregnancy and enforced sterilization occurring during international armed conflicts shall also be qualified as war crimes, provided they constitute a grave breach according to the Geneva Convention.

Article 8, Paragraph 2 (b) of the Rome Statute lists 26 serious violations of the laws and customs applicable in international armed conflict. Some of these violations are (i) intentionally directing attacks against the civilian population not taking direct part in hostilities; (ii) directing attacks against civilian objects; (iii) directing attacks against personnel, installations, material, units or vehicles involved in a humanitarian assistance or peacekeeping mission; (iv) launching an attack which may cause widespread, long-term and severe damage to the natural environment; (v) attacking or bombarding undefended towns, villages, dwellings or buildings; (vi) killing or wounding a combatant who has laid down his arms or has surrendered; (vii) making improper use of a flag of truce, flag or military insignia and uniform of the enemy or of the United Nations, as well as of the distinctive emblems of the Geneva Conventions; (viii) intentionally directing attacks against buildings dedicated to religion, education, art, science or charitable purposes, historic monuments or hospitals; (ix) declaring that no quarter will be given; (x) pillage; (xi) employing prohibited weapons of warfare; (xii) committing rape and outrages upon personal dignity, humiliating and degrading treatment; and (xiii) conscripting or enlisting children under the age of fifteen years into the national armed forces or using them to participate actively in hostilities.

Article 8, para 2 (c) and (d) apply to non-international conflict and relate to serious violations of Article 3 common to the four Geneva Conventions. The crimes included under this category are (i) violence to life and person, in particular murder of all kinds, mutilation, cruel treatment and torture; (ii) committing outrages upon personal dignity , in particular humiliating and degrading treatment; (iii) taking of hostages; and (iv) the passing of sentences and carrying out of executions without previous judgement pronounced by a regularly constituted court, affording all judicial guarantees which are generally recognized as indispensable; if committed against persons taking no active part in the hostilities. Article 8, para 2 (e) includes 12 other serious violations of the laws and customs applicable in armed conflicts not of an international character.

The Rome S tatute states that "the Court shall have jurisdiction in respect of war crimes, in particular when committed as part of a plan or policy or as part of a lar ge-scale commission of such crimes." While the ICC is guided to take cognizance of a suspected war crime only when it is a part of large-scale policy, the words "in particular" make it clear that this is not a requirement. The language does not preclude jurisdiction over a single act defined in Article 8, para 2, and says nothing about the rank or status of the person committing that single act.

D. Crime of Aggression

Aggression has been included as a crime within the Court' s jurisdiction. But the State Parties need to adopt an agreement setting out two things: a definition of aggression, which has so far proven difficult, and the conditions under which the Court could exercise its jurisdiction. Several proposals have been considered. Some countries feel that, in line with the UN Charter and the mandate it gives to the Security Council, only the Council has the authority to find that an act of aggression has occurred. If this is agreed upon then such a finding by the Council would be required before the Court could take any action. Other countries feel that such authority should not be limited to the Security Council.There are proposals under consideration that would give that role to the General Assembly or to the International Court of Justice, if an accusation of aggression were made and the Security

Council did not act within a certain time.

Since the drafting of the Rome Statute, the task of drafting a definition of aggression has become more and more problematic. In September 2002, the Assembly of State Parties to the Court established a Special W orking Group to elaborate proposals for a provision on the crime of aggression. The Working Group on the Crime of Aggression proposed a definition in 'Draft amendments to the Rome Statute of the International Criminal Court on the Crime ofAggression' at the Review Conference held in Kampala in May 2010.

On 11 June 2010, the Review Conference adopted by consensus a set of amendments to the Rome Statute which include a definition of the crime of aggression and a regime establishing how the Court will exercise its jurisdiction over such a crime. The conditions for entry into force decided upon in Kampala provide that the Court will not have jurisdiction over the crime until a decision is made to activate its entry into force bytState Parties after 1 January 2017.

The amendments set out a unique jurisdictional regime outlining when the ICC Prosecutor can initiate an investigation into a crime of aggression. Where a 'situation' is referred to the Prosecutor by the UN Security Council, the Court's jurisdiction is triggered in the same manner as with the other crimes in the S tatute, meaning the Prosecutor may proceed with an investigation into the crime of aggression. In contrast to Security Council referrals, the Prosecutor may only proceed with an own motion (*proprio motu*) investigation or an investigation based on a State referral of a situation into the crime of aggression after first ascertaining whether the Security Council has made a determination of the existence of an act of aggression and waiting for a period of six months; whether that situation concerns an act of aggression committed between State Parties; and after the Pre-Trial Division of the Court has authorized the commencement of the investigation.

The amendments also provide that S tate Parties may opt out of the Court's jurisdiction under the article by lodging a declaration of non-acceptance of jurisdiction with the Court's Registrar. Non-State Parties have been explicitly excluded from the Court' s jurisdiction into a crime of aggression under this article.

E. Offences against Administration of Justice

The ICC has jurisdiction over 'ofences against the administration of justice', where these relate to proceedings before the Court.[5] The Statute specifies that these must be committed intentionally . These are perjury or the presentation of evidence known to be false, or for ged; influencing or interfering with witnesses; corrupting or bribing officials of the Court or retaliating against them; an, in case of the officials of the Court, soliciting or accepting bribes. The Court can impose a term of imprisonment of up to five years or fine upon conviction.

In the wake of 11 September 2001, the Member States of the UN have undertaken the drafting of a comprehensive convention against terrorism. At a future review conference, if the S tate Parties so decide, the crime of terrorism could be added to the Court's jurisdiction.

Principle of Complementarity

An important element of the principles guiding the ICC is that the national criminal justice processes should be used if they are adequate to ensure the investigation, prosecution and punishment related to a crimeThis principle, called 'complementarity', is dealt with in the Preamble and in Articles 1 and 17 of the Rome Statute. For example, paragraph 4 of the Preamble affirms, "that the most serious crimes of concern to the international community as a whole must not go unpunished and that their ef fective prosecution must be ensured by taking measures at the national level and by enhancing international cooperation", and emphasizes, "that it is the duty of every State to exercise its criminal jurisdiction over those responsible for international crimes". Para 1 1 of the Preamble plainly states that the ICC shall be complementary to national criminal jurisdictions.

Article 17.1 of the Rome Statute states that according to the principle of complimentarity the Court shall determine that a case is inadmissible where:

(a) The case is being investigated or prosecuted by a State which has jurisdiction over it, unless the State is unwilling or unable genuinely to carry out the investigation or prosecution;

---

[5] Rome Statute, Article 70; Rules of Procedure and Evidence, Rules 162-169 and 172.

(b) The case has been investigated by a State which has jurisdiction over it and the State has decided not to prosecute the person concerned, unless the decision resulted from the unwillingness or inability of the State genuinely to prosecute.

The Statute is clear that national courts have the first right and duty to prosecute perpetrators of international crimes. However, the ICC is empowered to intervene not only where the existing national judicial machinery is not adequate to allow a successful prosecution, but also where national governments are unwilling or unable to fulfil their responsibility to prosecute. The Court shall determine unwillingness by whether one or more of the following situations exists: (i) the lack of substantive law or the existing legislation that does not meet the standards of the recognized international human rights; (ii) the national judicial proceedings are undertaken for the purpose of shielding the accused from criminal responsibility; (iii) the court proceedings have been unjustifiably delayed showing the State's lack of interest to impose justice; (iv) if the judicial proceedings are not being undertaken in an impartial and neutral manner. Thus, though the principle of complementarity preserves national criminal jurisdiction as primary, it allows the ICC to step in when States fail to act and allow a person accused of genocide, war crimes or crimes against humanity to escape justice altogether.

The complementarity principle is the fulcrum that prioritizes the authority of domestic forums to prosecute the crimes defined in Article 5 of the Rome Statute. It preserves the power of the ICC over irresponsible States that refuse to prosecute nationals who commit heinous international crimes, but balances that supranational power against the sovereign right of States to prosecute their own nationals without external interference. The basic descriptive meaning of complimetarity is that the ICC is not intended to replace national courts, but operates only when they do not. Article 18 in fact provides protection to the primacy of national jurisdiction.

Principles of International Criminal Law

The general principles of international criminal law are applied in the functioning of the ICC. These are listed in Articles 22 to 33 of the Rome Statute and are as follows: presence of mental element—intention and knowledge in the commission of the offence; no crime without law (*Nulla poena sine lege*); no punishment without law (*Non-retroactivity ratione personae*); non-retroactivity; no punishment to persons below 18 years; no immunity to government officials, including the head of the state; command responsibility—military as well as civilian superior; 'superior-order' not a defence; exclusion of criminal responsibility based on the lack of capacity to acknowledge the wrongfulness of the act—for example acting in self-defence or under the threat of imminent death. Article 66 of the Rome Statute relating to presumption of innocence states: "Everyone shall be presumed innocent until proved guilty before the Court in accordance with the applicable law ." Further, in order to convict the accused, the Court must be convinced of the guilt of the accused beyond reasonable doubt.

Command Responsibility

The responsibility of military leaders originates from the law of war and was codified in the Hague Convention IV of 1907 and its Regulations respecting the laws and customs of war on landThe commanders at various hierarchical levels are responsible for ensuring that while participating in an armed conflict, the forces under their command follow IHLThe doctrine of command responsibility has been codified in Article 28 of the Rome Statute. For further details on the subject please refer to Chapter 15 of the book.

The Right to Fair Trial

Under the Rome S tatute, the accused is protected to a great extent from arbitrary and summary trials, which is contrary to the view the world had during the trials of WW II criminals. The Rome Statute provides a detailed codification of procedural guarantees to an accused. Articles 66 and 67 of the ICC S tatute deal with the presumption of innocence and all other guarantees of a fair trial.Article 67 of the Rome Statute, entitled 'Rights of the Accused', is modelled on Article 14 (3) of the ICCPR.[6] The right to a

---

[6] Fundamental instruments as the Universal Declaration of Human Rights (UDHR) and the International Covenant on Civil and Political Rights (ICCPR), define basic minimum standards and include norms which must be respected by any judicial system aspiring to international legitimacy. Article 14 (3) of the ICCPR reads: In the determination of any criminal charge against him, everyone shall be entitled to the following minimum guarantees, in full equality: (a) To be informed promptly and in detail in a language which he understands of the nature and cause of the charge against him; (b) To have adequate time and facilities for the preparation of his defence and to communicate with counsel of his own choosing; (c) To be

fair trial is also enshrined in Articles 10 and 1 1 of the UDHR and in humanitarian law instruments.[7]

Article 67 of the Rome Statute states that in the determination of any charge, the accused shall be entitled to a public hearing conducted fairly and impartially. The accused shall have the following minimum guarantees:

(a) To be informed promptly of the cause and content of the chage, in a language which the accused fully understands and speaks;

(b) To have adequate time and facilities for the preparation of the defence and to communicate freely with a counsel of the accuseds' choosing in confidence;

(c) To be tried without undue delay;

(d) To be present at the trial, to conduct the defence in person or through legal assistance of the accused's choosing;

(e) To be informed, if the accused does not have legal assistance, of this right and to have legal assistance assigned by the Court in any case where the interests of justice so require, and without payment if the accused lacks sufficient means to pay for it;

(f) To examine the witnesses against him and to obtain the attendance and examination of witnesses on his behalf under the same conditions as witnesses against him. The accused shall also be entitled to raise defences and to present other evidence admissible

---

tried without undue delay; (d) To be tried in his presence, and to defend himself in person or through legal assistance of his own choosing; to be inf ormed, if he does not hav e legal assistance, of this right; and to have legal assistance assigned to him, in any case where the interests of justice so require, and without payment by him in any such case if he does not have sufficient means to pay for it; (e) To examine, or have examined, the witnesses against him and to obtain the attendance and examination of witnesses on his behal f under the same conditions as witnesses against him; (f) To have the free assistance of an interpreter if he cannot understand or speak the language used in court; (g) Not to be compelled to testify against himself or to confess guilt.

[7] Geneva Convention (III) Relative to the Treatment of Prisoners of war (1950), Articles 84-87 and 99-108; Geneva Convention (IV) Relative to the Potection of Civilians (1950), Article 5, and 64-76; Protocol Additional I (1977) to the 1949 Genev a Conventions and Relating to the Protection of the Victims of International Armed Conflicts, Article 75; Protocol Additional II (1977) and Relating to the Potection of the Victims of Non-International Armed Conficts, Article 6.

under this Statute;

(g) To have, free of any cost, the assistance of a competent interpreter and translations to meet the requirements of fairness;

(h) Not to be compelled to testify or to confess guilt and to remain silent, without such silence being a consideration in the determination of guilt or innocence;

(i) To make an unsworn oral or written statement in his defence; and

(j) Not to have imposed on him or her any reversal of the burden of proof or any onus of rebuttal.

Article 63 (2) of the Rome S tatute, however, provides that if the accused, being present before the Court, continues to disrupt the trial, the Trial Chamber may remove the accused and make provision for him or her to observe the trial and instruct the counsel from outside the courtroom, through the use of communications technology if required. Such measures are to be taken only in exceptional circumstances after other reasonable alternatives have proved inadequate, and only for such duration as are strictly required.

Penalty

According to the Rome Statute, the basic penalty to be imposed by the Court is one of imprisonment, up to and including life imprisonment in extreme cases. Article 77 of the Rome Statute declares that the Court may impose imprisonment for a specified number of years, which may not exceed 30 years.[8] Article 77 further states the Court may impose "a term of life imprisonment when justified by the extreme gravity of the crime and the individual circumstances of the convicted person." In addition to imprisonment, the Court may order fine and forfeiture of proceeds, property

[8] Rome Statute Article 77: Applicable Penalties

1. Subject to article 110, the Court may impose one of the f ollowing penalties on a person convicted of a crime referred to in article 5 of this Statute: (a) Imprisonment for a specified number of y ears, which may not exceed a maximum of 30 y ears; or (b) A term of l ife imprisonment when justi fied b y the extr eme gr avity of the crime and the individual circumstances of the con victed person. 2. In addition to imprisonment, the Court ma y order: (a) A fine under the criteria provided for in the Rules of Procedure and Evidence; (b)A forf eiture of proceeds, property and assets deriv ed directly or indir ectly from that crime, without prejudice to the rights of bona fide third parties.

and assets derived directly or indirectly from that crime, without prejudice to the rights of bona fide third parties. In imposing a sentence of imprisonment, the Court is to deduct the time previously spent in detention in accordance with an order of the Court. The Court may also deduct the period spent in detention during the trial.[9]

Compensations to Victim

The Statutes of the ICTY and ICTR clearly deny victims any right to reparation. The ICTY statute, for example , states that "the penalty imposed by the Trial Chamber shall be limited to imprisonment....in addition to imprisonment, the Trial Chamber may order the return of any property and proceeds acquired during criminal conduct, including by means of duress, to their rightful owners". On the other hand, the Rome Statute of the ICC explicitly allows for civil damages to be awarded in international cases, and states in Article 75:

> **Reparations to victims**
>
> 1. The Court shall establish principles relating to reparations to, or in respect of, victims, including restitution, compensation and rehabilitation. On this basis, in its decision the Court mayeither upon request or on its own motion in exceptional circumstances, determine the scope and extent of any damage, loss and injury to, or in respect of, victims and will state the principles on which it is acting.
>
> 2. The Court may make an order directly against a convicted person specifying appropriate reparations to, or in respect of, victims, including restitution, compensation and rehabilitation. Where appropriate, the Court may order that the award for reparations be made through the Trust Fund provided for in article 79.

---

[9] Rome Statute Article 78: Determination of the sentence. 1.In determining the sentence, the Court shall, in accordance with the Rules of Procedue and Evidence, take into account such factors as the gravity of the crime and the individual circumstances of the convicted person. 2. In imposing a sentence of imprisonment, the Court shalldeduct the time, if any, previously spent in detention in accordance with an order of the Court. The Court may deduct any time otherwise spent in detention in connection with conduct underlying the crime. 3. When a person has been convicted of more than one crime, the Court shall pronounce a sentence for each crime and a joint sentence specifying the total period of imprisonment. This period shall be no less than the highest individual sentence pronounced and shall not exceed 30 years imprisonment.

3. Before making an order under this article, the Court may invite and shall take account of representations from or on behalf of the convicted person, victims, other interested persons or interested States.

6. Nothing in this article shall be interpreted as prejudicing the rights of victims under national or international law.

With this, the international community has for the first time recognized the legal right of a victim to seek reparations. Such reparations include restitution, compensation and rehabilitation.The reparations are channeled through a victim trust fund (Article 79), which was established by the Assembly of State parties in 2002 and became operational in 2007.[10]

Appeal and Revision

The judgments of the Trial Chamber are subject to appeal. The prosecutor may appeal on grounds of procedural error , error of fact or error of law . The defendant may appeal against a conviction on grounds of procedural error, error of fact, error of law or any ground that af fects the fairness or reliability of the proceedings or decision. The prosecutor is also entitled to appeal against a conviction on behalf of the defendant. [11] The prosecutor and the convicted person may appeal against a sentence on grounds of disproportion between the crime and the sentence. If, during an appeal against a sentence, the Court considers that there are grounds to set aside a conviction, it may intervene to quash the judgment. The Court may also intervene on sentence during an appeal against only the conviction.

Where the Appeals Chamber grants appeal on a point of law or fact that materially influenced the decision, or because of unfairness at the trial proceedings affecting the reliability of the decision or sentence, it may

[10] The ICC has been haled as the first international criminal tribunal to give serious considerations to the role of victims. The Rome Statute has set up a complex victim compensation system involving the Court itself but also a more intriguing body, the Trust Fund for Victims (TFV). The TFV has a very crucial autonomous role that is largely independent fom the operation of the ICC. This role is characterized by a different source of monies, diferent beneficiaries, and a di fferent logic of dispensation. The TFV r eceives v oluntary contributions f rom governments, international organizations, individuals and corporations which are stored in a separate account from that of Court directed reparation orders which can be awarded at the Fund's discretions. Megret Frederic, 'Justifying Compensation by the ICC's Victim Trust Fund: Lessons from Domestic Compensation Schemes', *Brooklyn Journal of International Law*, (2010), Vol. 36, No. 1, p 123.

[11] Rome Statute, Article 81.

reverse or amend the decision or sentence, or order a new trial before a different Trial Chamber. It may vary a sentence if it finds it disproportionate to the crime. In a defence appeal, the Appeal Chamber cannot modify a decision to the detriment of the convicted person, for example, by increasing a sentence beyond that imposed at trial or by adding convictions under additional counts. In order to determine an issue, theAppeal Chamber can also call evidence. An appeal is decided by a majority of the judges.

On the discovery of new evidence, it is possible to seek revision of a conviction or sentence. Revision involves intervention at the appellate level that does not call into question the findings of the T rial Chamber. The discovered piece of evidence may relate to false evidence or a for ged or falsified document on which the conviction was based or to a serious misconduct or breach of duty on the part of a judge of theTrial Chamber.[12] While granting the review, the Trial Chamber may reconvene the original Trial Chamber, constitute a new Trial Chamber or dispose of the matter itself. In the event of discovery of a miscarriage of justice as a result of new facts where a person has already sufered punishment, that person is entitled to compensation, unless he was responsible for the non-disclosure of the fact in question.[13]

Cases and Situations

Pursuant to the Rome Statute, the Prosecutor can initiate an investigation on the basis of a referralfrom any State Party or from the Security Council. In addition, the Prosecutor can initiate investigations *proprio motu* (by its own motion) on the basis of 'communication', or information on crimes within the jurisdiction of the Court received from individuals or organizations. The Court may then exercise its jurisdiction over the matter if either the State in whose territory the crime was committed (territorial jurisdiction), or the State of the nationality of the accused, is a party to the Statute (active nationality jurisdiction). Non-State Parties may accept the Court's jurisdiction on an ad hoc basis. When a matter is referred by the Security Council, the Court has jurisdiction regardless of whether the State concerned is a party to the ICC treaty.

---

12 Rome Statute, Article 84.

13 Rome Statute, Article 85. The applicable procedure for compensation in such circumstances is provided in rules of Procedure and Evidence, rules 173-175.

To date, three S tate Parties to the Rome Statute – Uganda, the Democratic Republic of the Congo and the Central African Republic – have referred situations occurring on their territories to the Court. In addition, the Security Council has referred the situation in Darfur , Sudan – a non State Party. After a thorough analysis of the available information, the Prosecutor has opened and is conducting investigations in all of the above-mentioned situations. On 31 March 2010,the Pre-Trial Chamber II granted the Prosecution authorization to open an investigation *proprio motu* in the situation of Kenya. In addition to the ongoing issues, the Prosecutor's office is analyzing a number of other situations in dif ferent countries, including Afghanistan, Chad, Colombia, Cote d'Ivoire, Geogia, Guinea and Palestine. The Prosecutor has also received communications in relation to several other countries, including Iraq and Venezuela. A brief discussion on the five ongoing situations follows.

1. Uganda

In December 2003, the President of Uganda took the decision to refer the situation concerning the Lord's Resistance Army to the Prosecutor of the ICC. The Chief Prosecutor determined that there was a reasonable basis to open an investigation into the situation concerning Northern Uganda, following the referral by Uganda. The decision to open an investigation was taken in 2004, after a thorough analysis of the available information in order to ensure that the requirements of the Rome S tatute were satisfied. The Prosecutor also notified the State Parties to the ICC and other concerned States of his intention to start an investigation, in accordance with Article 18 of the Rome Statute.

Pertaining to the situation in Uganda, the case *The Prosecutor v. Joseph Kony, Vincent Otti, Okot Odhiambo and Dominic Ongwen* is currently being heard before the Pre-Trial Chamber II. In this case, five warrants of arrest were issued against the five top members of the Lords' Resistance Army. However, following the confirmation of the death of Mr Lukwiya, the proceedings against him have been terminated.The four remaining suspects are still at large.

2. The Democratic Republic of Congo

In June 2004, the Chief Prosecutor of the ICC announced his decision to open the first investigation in the cases of grave crimes allegedly committed on the territory of the Democratic Republic of Congo (DRC) since 1 July 2002. The decision to open an investigation was taken after a thorough consideration of the jurisdiction and admissibility requirements of the Rome Statute. The Prosecutor concluded that an investigation of the grave crimes in the DRC would be in the interest of justice and of the victims.

Millions of civilians have died as a result of the conflict in the DRC since the 1990s.The Court's jurisdiction extends to crimes committed after 1 July 2002, when the Rome S tatute of the ICC came into force. S tates, international or ganizations and non-governmental or ganizations have reported thousands of deaths by mass murder and summary execution in the DRC since 2002. The reports widespread rape, torture, forced displacement and the illegal use of child soldiers.

The cases related to the situation in the DRC, are being heard before the relevant Chambers: *The Prosecutor v. Thomas Lubanga Dyilo* ; *The Prosecutor v. Bosco Ntaganda*; *The Prosecutor v. Germain Katanga and Mathieu Ngudjolo Chui* and *The Prosecutor v. Callixte Mbarushimana* . Two of the cases are at the pre-trial stage, while the proceedings against Thomas Lubanga Dyiloare at the trial stage.The accused Thomas Lubanga Dyilo, Germain Katanga and Mathieu Ngudjolo Chui are currently in the custody of the ICC. The suspect Bosco Ntaganda remains at lage. Lubanga is allegedly responsible, as co-perpetrator, of war crimes consisting of:

- Enlisting and conscripting children under the age of 15 years into the Patriotic Forces for the Liberation of Congo (FPLC) and using them to participate actively in hostilities in an international armed conflict from early September 2002 to 2 June 2003 (punishable under Article 8(2)(b)(xxvi) of the Rome Statute);
- Enlisting and conscripting children under the age of 15 years into the FPLC and using them to participate actively in hostilities in a non-international armed conflict from 2 June 2003 to 13 August 2003 (punishable under Article 8(2)(e)(vii) of the Rome Statute).

Germain Katanga and Mathieu Ngudjolo Chui allegedly jointly committed through other persons, within the meaning of article 25(3)(a) of the Statute:

A. War Crimes:

a. using children under the age of fifteen to take active part in the hostilities, punishable under article 8(2)(b)(xxvi) of the Statute;

b. directing an attack against a civilian population as such or against individual civilians not taking direct part in hostilities punishable under article 8(2)(b)(i) of the Statute;

c. wilful killings punishable under article 8(2)(a)(i) of the Statute;

d. destruction of property punishable under article 8(2)(b)(xiii) of the Statute;

e. pillaging punishable under article 8(2)(b)(xvi) of the Statute;

f. sexual slavery punishable under article 8(2)(b)(xxii) of the Statute;

g. rape punishable under article 8(2)(b)(xxii) of the Statute.

B. Crimes against Humanity:

a. murder punishable under article 7(1)(a) of the Statute;

b. rape punishable under article 7(1)(g) of the Statute;

c. sexual slavery punishable under article 7(1)(g) of the Statute.

C. Darfur, Sudan

Following the referral from the UN Security Council on 31 March 2005, the Prosecutor received the documents of the International Commission of Inquiry on Darfur . In addition, the Of fice of the Prosecutor requested information from a variety of sources, leading to the collection of thousands of documents. The Office also interviewed over 50 independent experts. After a thorough analysis, the Prosecutor concluded that the statutory requirements for initiating an investigation were satisfied. In May 2005, The Chief Prosecutor decided to open an investigation into the situation in Darfur, Sudan.

In connection with the situation in Darfur Sudan, three cases are being heard before Pre-Trial Chamber I: *The Prosecutor v. Ahmad Harun and Ali Kushayb*; *The Prosecutor v. Omar Hassan Ahmad Bashir*; *The Prosecutor v. Bahar Idriss Abu Garda* and *The Prosecutor v. Abdallah Banda Nourain and Saleh Mohammed Jerbo Jamus*. The suspect Bahr Idriss Abu Garda appeared voluntarily for the first time before the Pre-Trial Chamber I in May 2009. He is not in custody. The three other suspects remain at large.

A. *The Prosecutor v. Abdallah Banda Nourain and Saleh Mohammed Jerbo Jamus*: The Pre-Trial Chamber I considered that there were reasonable grounds to believe that Abdallah Banda Abakaer Nourain and Saleh Mohammed Jerbo Jamus were criminally responsible as co-perpetrators or as indirect co-perpetrators for three war crimes under article 25(3)(a) of the Rome Statute:

- violence to life in the form of murder, whether committed or attempted, within the meaning of article 8(2)(c)(i) of the Statute;
- intentionally directing attacks against personnel, installations, material, units or vehicles involved in a peacekeeping mission within the meaning of article 8(2)(e)(iii) of the Statute; and
- pillaging within the meaning of article 8(2)(e)(v) of the Statute.

B. *The Prosecutor v. Bahar Idriss Abu Garda*: The Pre-Trial Chamber I was of the opinion that there were reasonable grounds to believe that Abu Garda was criminally responsible as a co-perpetrator or as an indirect co-perpetrator for three war crimes under article 25(3)(a) of the Rome Statute:

- violence to life in the form of murder, whether committed or attempted, within the meaning of article 8(2)(c)(i) of the Statute;
- intentionally directing attacks against personnel, installations, material, units or vehicles involved in a peacekeeping mission within the meaning of article 8(2)(e)(iii) of the Statute; and
- pillaging within the meaning of article 8(2)(e)(v) of the Statute.

On 8 February 2010, the Pre-Trial Chamber I refused to confirm the charges against Abu Garda. On 23 April 2010, the Pre-Trial Chamber I issued a decision rejecting the Prosecutor's application to appeal against the decision declining to confirm the charges. The decision does not preclude the Prosecution from subsequently requesting confirmation of the charges if such a request is supported by additional evidence.

The Case against the Sudanese President

On March 4, 2009, ICC judges issued a warrant for the arrest of Sudanese President Omar Hassan al-Bashir . The warrant held that there are "reasonable grounds" to believe that Bashir was criminally responsible for five counts of crimes against humanity and two counts of war crimes. In his application for an arrest warrant, filed in July 2008, the ICC Prosecutor affirmed that while Bashir did not "physically or directly" carry out abuses, "he committed these crimes through members of the state apparatus, the army, and the militia" as president and commander-in-chief of the Sudanese armed forces. The arrest warrant was not an indictment; under ICC procedures, charges must be confirmed at a pre-trial hearing.The ICC urged "all States, whether party or not to the Rome Statute, as well as international and regional organizations," to "cooperate fully" with the warrant. However, Sudanese government officials have rejected the ICC's jurisdiction.

D. Central African Republic

Grave crimes falling within the jurisdiction of the ICC were committed in the Central African Republic during 2002 and 2003 in an armed conflict between the government and rebel forces. Civilians were killed and raped; and homes and stores were looted. The Government of the Central African Republic referred the situation to the Prosecutor . The Cour de Cassation, the country's highest judicial body, subsequently confirmed that the national justice system was unable to carry out the complex proceedings necessary to investigate and prosecute the alleged crimes.The ruling was an important factor because under the Rome Statute, the ICC is a Court of last resort and intervenes in situations only when national judicial authorities are unable or unwilling to conduct genuine proceedings.

After a careful review of information from a range of sources, the ICC Prosecutor announced the decision to open an investigation in the Central African Republic in May 2007. He believed that grave crimes falling within the jurisdiction of the Court had been committed in the Central African Republic. This was the first time the Prosecutor opened an investigation in which allegations of sexual crimes far outnumber alleged killings. Hundreds of rape victims came forward to tell their stories, recounting crimes acted out with particular cruelty. Victims described being raped in public; being attacked by multiple perpetrators; being raped in the presence of family members; and being abused in other ways if they resisted their attackers. Many of the victims were subsequently shunned by their families and communities. To reach the decision to open an investigation, the Office of the Prosecutor reviewed information provided by the government in its referral, NGOs, international organizations and other highly knowledgeable sources.

In this connection , the case *The Prosecutor v. Jean-Pierre Bemba Gombo* is at the pre-trial stage of proceedings and is currently being heard before the Pre-Trial Chamber II. Jean-Pierre Bemba was allegedly responsible, as military commander, of:

- Two counts of crimes against humanity: murder (article 7(1)(a) of the Statute) and rape (article 7(1)(g) of the Statute);
- Three counts of war crime: murder (article 8(2)(c)(i) of the Statute); rape (article 8(2)(e)(vi) of the Statute); and pillaging (article 8(2)(e)(v) of the Statute).

E. The Republic of Kenya

On 6 November, 2009, the Presidency of the ICC issued a decision assigning the situation in the Republic of Kenya to the Pre-Trial Chamber II. On 31 March 2010, the Pre-Trial Chamber II granted the Prosecutor, authorization to open an investigation on the situation in Kenya.

Accusations of Bias

There have been allegations of bias against the functioning of the ICC. The ICC's investigations in Africa have raised concerns over African sovereignty and of foreign intervention on the continent. Some commentators allege that the Prosecutor has limited investigations to Africa because of geopolitical pressures, either out of a desire to avoid confrontation with major powers or as a tool of Western foreign policy. The attempt to prosecute Sudanese President Bashir has been particularly controversial, drawing rebuke from African governments and regional organizations. However, the Office of the Prosecutor maintains that its choice of cases is based on the relative gravity of abuses, and that crimes committed in Sub-Saharan

Africa are among the world's most serious.

The Role of NGOs in ICC Investigations

The human rights NGOs are often the first to reach the scene of massive violations of human rights and humanitarian laws. These NGOs therefore have a vital role in relation to ICC investigations. They may have direct knowledge of violations and contacts with victims and witness communities. They may be able to document violations after they occur and compile information regarding patterns of violations.

Article 42.1 of the Rome S tatute provides: "The Of fice of the Prosecutor shall act independently as a separate organ of the Court. It shall be responsible for receiving referrals and any substantiated information on crimes within the jurisdiction of the Court, for examining them and for conducting investigations and prosecutions before the Court".

According to Article 15 of the Rome Statute and Rule 104 of the ICC Rules of Procedure and Evidence, the Prosecutor may receive and seek reliable information from S tates, or gans of the United Nations, intergovernmental and non-governmental or ganizations, or other sources that he deems appropriate. NGOs are therefore capable of providing valuable assistance to the ICC Prosecutor . The following are some of the ways in which human rights NGOs could potentially work in relation to ICC investigations:

- Mapping or documenting patters of violence
- Conducting medical and forensic examinations
- Publishing reports and other information on violations
- Providing research assistance to ICC
- Explaining the role of the Office of the Prosecutor to the affected individuals or communities
- Advising the ICC on witness protection
- Providing assistance to victims or witnesses
- Organizing victims for the purpose of participation and reparations

- Providing training to lawyers who might represent victims
- Acting as *amicus curiae* in court proceedings

The 2010 Rome Statute Review Conference

The first Review Conference on the Rome Statute of the ICC took place in Kampala, Uganda from 31 May to 1 June 2010. ICC State Parties, observer States, international organizations, NGOs, and other participants discussed the proposed amendments to the Rome Statute. More than 600 coalition members played a central role in enhancing the dialogue on the Rome system and ensured that the voices of civil society were truly heard through a number of debates, roundtables and other events. Debates focused on the impact of the Rome Statute on victims and affected communities, complementarity, cooperation, and peace and justice, issues truly central to the system's fair, effective, and independent functioning.

Pledges and the Kampala Declaration

During the Review Conference, 112 pledges with the purpose of strengthening the Rome Statute system were made by 37 State Parties, as well as the United States and the European Union. In addition, the Conference adopted the Kampala Declaration, reaffirming the States' commitment to the Rome Statute and its full implementation, as well as its universality and integrity. The Review Conference further adopted a resolution on strengthening the enforcement of sentences. In parallel, the ICC signed three agreements with Belgium, Denmark, and Finland, on the enforcement of sentences. The Coalition and its global membership are committed to work to maintain the momentum with States, the UN, other regional bodies and the Court to ensure that the commitments made in Kampala result in concrete actions.

Amendments

Article 124: Article 124 of the Rome Statute permits State Parties to refuse ICC jurisdiction over war crimes committed on their territory or by their own nationals for a period of up to seven years Article 124, also known as the 'opt–out provision', was criticized by human rights advocates, and was to be reviewed at the Review Conference. States Parties have agreed not to delete Article 124 of the Rome Statute but to review it in five years.

Article 8: Belgium submitted three proposals for amendments to Article 8 of the Rome Statute regarding the criminalization of certain weapons as war crimes in non-international armed conflicts. It was decided that only the first of the proposals put forward by Belgium would be submitted to the Review Conference. This proposal extends the criminalization of the use of (i) poison or poisoned weapons; (ii) asphyxiating, poisonous or other gases and analogous liquids, materials or devices; and (iii) bullets that expand or flatten in the body to armed conflicts not of an international character. The use of the weapons listed in this draft amendment is already incriminated by Article 8, paragraph 2, (b), (xvii) to (xix) of the Statute in case of an international armed conflict.

The adoption of the weapons amendment would initiate a sound movement towards greater protection for civilians as well as combatants in non-international armed conflict and would bring Article 8 of the Statute more in line with the content of customary international humanitarian law

The proposed amendments[14] to the Rome Statute of the International Criminal Court on the Crime of Aggression

1. Article 5, paragraph 2, of the Statute is deleted.

2. The following text is inserted after Article 8 of the Statute:

Article 8 *bis*: Crime of aggression

1. For the purpose of this Statute, "crime of aggression" means the planning, preparation, initiation or execution, by a person in a position effectively to exercise control over or to direct the political or military action of a State, of an act of aggression which, by its character, gravity and scale, constitutes a manifest violation of the Charter of the United Nations.

2. For the purpose of paragraph 1, "act of aggression" means the use of armed force by a State against the sovereignty, territorial integrity or political independence of another State, or in any other manner inconsistent with the Charter of the United Nations. Any of the

[14] The amendments to Rome Statute will be in accordance with the procedure laid down in Article 121 of the Statute.

following acts, regardless of a declaration of war, shall, in accordance with United Nations GeneralAssembly resolution 3314 (XXIX) of 14 December 1974, qualify as an act of aggression:

(a) The invasion or attack by the armed forces of a State of the territory of another State, or any military occupation, however temporary, resulting from such invasion or attack, or any annexation by the use of force of the territory of another State or part thereof;

(b) Bombardment by the armed forces of a State against the territory of another State or the use of any weapons by a State against the territory of another State;

(c) The blockade of the ports or coasts of a State by the armed forces of another State;

(d) An attack by the armed forces of a State on the land, sea or air forces, or marine and air fleets of another State;

(e) The use of armed forces of one State which are within the territory of another State with the agreement of the receiving State, in contravention of the conditions provided for in the agreement or any extension of their presence in such territory beyond the termination of the agreement;

(f) The action of a State in allowing its territory which it has placed at the disposal of another State, to be used by that other State for perpetrating an act of aggression against a third State;

(g) The sending by or on behalf of a State of armed bands, groups, irregulars or mercenaries, which carry out acts of armed force against another State of such gravity as to amount to the acts listed above, or its substantial involvement therein.

3. The following text is inserted after Article 15 of the Statute:

Article 15 *bis*: Exercise of jurisdiction over the crime of aggression (State referral, *proprio motu*)

1. The Court may exercise jurisdiction over the crime of aggression in accordance with article 13, paragraphs (a) and

(c), subject to the provisions of this article.

2. The Court may exercise jurisdiction only with respect to crimes of aggression committed one year after the ratification or acceptance of the amendments by thirty States Parties.

3. The Court shall exercise jurisdiction over the crime of aggression in accordance with this article, subject to a decision to be taken after 1 January 2017 by the same majority of the State Parties as is required for the adoption of an amendment to the Statute.

4. The Court may , in accordance with article 12, exercise jurisdiction over a crime of aggression, arising from an act of aggression committed by a State Party, unless that State Party has previously declared that it does not accept such jurisdiction by lodging a declaration with the Registrar . The withdrawal of such a declaration may be effected at any time and shall be considered by the State Party within three years.

5. In respect of a State that is not a party to this Statute; the Court shall not exercise its jurisdiction over the crime of aggression when committed by that State's nationals or on its territory.

6. Where the Prosecutor concludes that there is a reasonable basis to proceed with an investigation in respect of a crime of aggression, he or she shall first ascertain whether the Security Council has made a determination of an act of aggression committed by the State concerned. The Prosecutor shall notify the Secretary-General of the United Nations of the situation before the Court, including any relevant information and documents.

7. Where the Security Council has made such a determination, the Prosecutor may proceed with the investigation in respect of a crime of aggression.

8. Where no such determination is made within six months after the date of notification, the Prosecutor may proceed with the investigation in respect of a crime of aggression, provided that

the Pre-Trial Division has authorized the commencement of the investigation in respect of a crime of aggression in accordance with the procedure contained in article 15, and the Security Council has not decided otherwise in accordance with article 16.

9. A determination of an act of aggression by an organ outside the Court shall be without prejudice to the Court's own findings under this Statute.

10. This article is without prejudice to the provisions relating to the exercise of jurisdiction with respect to other crimes referred to in article 5.

4. The following text is inserted after Article 15 of the Statute:

Article 15 *ter*: Exercise of jurisdiction over the crime of aggression (Security Council referral)

1. The Court may exercise jurisdiction over the crime of aggression in accordance with article 13, paragraph (b), subject to the provisions of this article.

2. The Court may exercise jurisdiction only with respect to crimes of aggression committed one year after the ratification or acceptance of the amendments by thirty States Parties.

3. The Court shall exercise jurisdiction over the crime of aggression in accordance with this article, subject to a decision to be taken after 1 January 2017 by the same majority of the State Parties as is required for the adoption of an amendment to the Statute.

4. A determination of an act of aggression by an or gan outside the Court shall be without prejudice to the Court's own findings under this Statute.

5. This article is without prejudice to the provisions relating to the exercise of jurisdiction with respect to other crimes referred to in article 5.

5. The following text is inserted after Article 25, paragraph 3 of the Statute:

3. In respect of the crime of aggression, the provisions of this article shall apply only to persons in a position effectively to exercise control over or to direct the political or military action of a State.

6. The first sentence of Article 9, paragraph 1 of the Statute is replaced by the following sentence:

1. Elements of Crimes shall assist the Court in the interpretation and application of articles 6, 7, 8 and 8 *bis*.

7. The *chapeau* of Article 20, paragraph 3, of the Statute is replaced by the following paragraph; the rest of the paragraph remains unchanged:

3. No person who has been tried by another court for conduct also proscribed under article 6, 7, 8 or 8 *bis* shall be tried by the Court with respect to the same conduct unless the proceedings in the other court.

The ICC is an independent, permanent court that tries persons accused of the most serious crimes of international concern, namely genocide, crimes against humanity and war crimes. It is a court of last resort. It will not act if a case is investigated or prosecuted by a national judicial system unless the national proceedings are not genuine, for example if formal proceedings were undertaken solely to shield a person from criminal responsibility. In addition, the ICC only tries those accused of the gravest crimes. In all of its activities, the ICC observes the highest standards of fairness and due process. Article 67 of the Rome Statute guarantees the highest standards of protection for the rights of the accused in all trials before the ICC. The right to a fair trial and the other due process protections in the Rome Statute were derived principally from the ICCPR and partly from the UDHR. These rights need to be guaranteed by all the countries in every trial conducted at the national level, including trials of international crimes.

CHAPTER 15

Command Responsibility in Armed Conflict

Introduction

Holding a military commander responsible for the conduct of his subordinates in an armed conflict is not new . Around 500 BC, Sun Tzu wrote in 'The Art of War' that it is the duty of commanders to ensure that their subordinates conduct themselves with a certain level of civility in armed conflict. In 1439, Charles VII of France issued the Ordinance of Orleans, which imposed a blanket responsibility on commanders for all unlawful acts of their subordinates without requiring any standard of knowledge. About 200 years later , the Swedish King Adolphus ordered that: "No Colonell or Capitaine shall command his soldiers to doe any unlawful thing: which who so does, shall be punished according to the discretion of the Judges."

The armed forces have certain peculiar characteristics. They have centralized command and a definite hierarchy and their principle objective is to fight and win wars. The centralized command structure ensures that a continuous chain of command links the lowest soldier with the supreme commander. The forces are arranged in a pyramid of authority , in which each echelon owes explicit and peremptory obedience to its superior. The military legal systems of almost all countries provide that disobedience of a lawful command of a superior of ficer is a serious military crime. The commanders at various hierarchical levels are responsible for ensuring that while participating in an armed conflict, the forces under their command follow the laws of war.

What is Command Responsibility?

The modern doctrine of command responsibility can be defined as the responsibility of commanders for war crimes committed by subordinate members of their armed forces or other persons subject to their control. This responsibility includes the failure to prevent or punish subordinates for unlawful actions. The concept of command responsibility embraces two issues. In the first place, it concerns the responsibility of a commander who has given an order to a subordinate to commit an act which is in breach of the law of armed conflict or whose conduct implies that he is not averse to such a breach being committed. It also covers the plea of the subordinate that he is not responsible for any breach because he was acting in accordance with the orders of or what he presumed to be the wishes of his commander a plea that is more commonly described as that of 'compliance with superior orders'. A subordinate putting forward such a plea contends that the superior alone is responsible.

Development of Law of Command responsibility

Article 1 (1) of the Regulations annexed to the 1899 Hague Convention on the Laws and Customs of W ar on Land states that the laws, rights, and duties of war apply not only to armies, but also to militia and volunteer corps, under the conditions, among others, that those paramilitary personnel are "commanded by a person responsible for his subordinates". This provision has been reproduced verbatim in theAnnex to the Fourth Hague Convention of 1907 respecting the Laws and Customs of War on Land. Article 3 of the Hague Convention (IV) provides that if there is a violation of the articles or regulations, the belligerent State so violating them would be responsible for the acts committed by its military and would be liable to pay compensation for the same.

In 1919, after WW I, the Commission on the Responsibility of the Authors of the W ar and on the Enforcement of Penalties recommended action against some 895 alleged war criminals. However, for political reasons, only 12 German officers were brought to trial before the German Supreme Court and the longest sentence was four years of imprisonment. The German Court accepted the defence of superior orders, which is the logical adjunct to the concept of command responsibility. The doctrine of command responsibility as established by the Hague Convention IV was applied for the first time by the German Supreme Court in the Trial of Emil Miiller. He was sentenced for failing to prevent the commission of crimes and to punish the perpetrators thereof.

Until World War II, it had been common wisdom that criminal liability under international law could only be incurred where an individual had been personally involved in the commission of a crime. In the case of a military commander or civilian leader, this meant that to be liable he had to have taken a personal part in the commission of a crime as, for instance, by ordering that crime or by aiding and abetting it. One of the most significant advances of the post-war era was the development of a doctrine that attributes criminal responsibility to military and civilian leaders, not only where they have taken a personal or direct part in the commission of a crime, but also where they have failed to prevent or punish crimes of subordinates. The new term 'command responsibility' was coined to provide the enforcement of a minimum standard of responsibility for leaders and commanders with respect to the conduct of their subordinates. The fact that military commanders and civilian leaders could be held accountable under international law for failing in their duties of supervision was a significant leap in international criminal law.

Trial of General Yamashita

General Yamashita was the commander of the 14th Army Group between 9 Oct 44 and 2 Sep 45 and also Military Governor of the Philippines. During this period, his troops committed widespread and brutal atrocities on the civilian population resulting in the death of over 25,000 people including women and children. The trial of General Yamashita is perhaps the most frequently cited WW II command responsibility case. It was the first international trial to find a military commander criminally liable for the crimes committed by his subordinates.

The case against General Yamashita was that, between 9 October 1944 and 2 September 1945, in the Philippine Islands, "while commanding the armed forces of Japan at war with the United States of America and its allies, he unlawfully disregarded and failed to discharge his duty as commander to control the operations of the members of his command, permitting them to commit brutal atrocities and other high crimes against the people of the United States and of its allies and dependencies, particularly the Philippines; and he...... thereby violated the laws of war". The US Military Commission charged with trying him found that a military commander could in some cases be held criminally responsible when there is no effective attempt on his part to discover and control the criminal acts of his subordinates. It did not lay down in any detail the conditions under which such consequences could ensue for a commander.

The law of 'command responsibility', as the Commission viewed it, was much removed from the fundamental requirements of personal fault and culpable mindset which criminal law generally requires for a criminal conviction. The standard of liability set out by the Commission amounted to a form of objective liability pursuant to which a commander could be held criminally responsible for crimes committed by his troops where he failed to discover and control the criminal acts of his subordinates despite the absence of proof of knowledge on his part that such crimes had been committed.

In appeal, the US Supreme Court ruled that: "The law of war presupposes that its violation is to be avoided through the control of the operations of war by commanders who are to some extent responsible for their subordinates". The Court cited The Hague Convention of 1907, and Article 26 of the Geneva Convention of 1929 to support its position that commanders have affirmative duties and responsibilities for their subordinates under international law. It also held that commanders had an affirmative duty to take such measures as were within their power to protect POWs and the civilian population. The standard applied by the court was that the atrocities were so widespread that Yamashita "must have known" of them despite no evidence of knowledge or direct connection to the accused. The Yamashita has come to be accepted as a precedent, not for the position that the Military Commission or the Supreme Court took in relation to the elements of the doctrine of superior responsibilitybut for the statement of the principle that a commander could be held criminally responsible in relation to crimes committed by his men under international law.

The *Yamashita* trial was the first international war crimes trial to find a military commander criminally liable without any direct evidence linking him affirmatively to the crimes committed by his subordinates, i.e., it established the principle of negative criminality, or liability for a failure to act. There are views that GeneralYamashita was probably morally culpable as a military commander , his conviction was not based on a principled approach to criminal justice and that the Tribunal's judgment was an example of judicially-sanctioned vengeance, rather than justifiable retribution. As such, the doctrine of command responsibility began as an instrument of victor 's justice, rather than as a well-considered theory of criminality.[1]

Geneva Conventions of 1949

The Geneva Convention of 1949 lays down that each belligerent Party bears responsibility under international law for the conduct of all members of its armed forces, and that the State is obliged to maintain discipline, law and order at all times.All members of armed forces are subject to the military and criminal code of the States they serve, and in case of infraction they are liable to be prosecuted before military or civil courts of that State. The third Geneva Convention (Article 129) states: "The High Contracting Parties undertake to enact any legislation necessary to provide effective penal sanctions for persons committing, or ordering to be committed, any of the 'grave breaches' of the present Convention".The 'grave breaches' to which Article 129 relates are listed in Article 130 as (i) wilful killing, (ii) torture or inhuman treatment, including biological experiments, (iii) causing great suffering or serious injury to body or health, and (iv) compelling a POW to serve in the forces of the hostile Power, or depriving a POW of the rights of fair and regular trial.

Article 3 of the Geneva Conventions of 1949 (CA 3) states that in cases of armed conflict not of an international character occurring in the territory of one of the High Contracting Parties, each Party to the conflict shall be bound to apply as a minimum the provisions related to protected persons i.e., those not taking active part in hostilities; members of armed forces who have laid down their arms; members of the armed forces who are *horse de cambat* by sickness, wounds, detention etc.The acts prohibited against such persons are: (1) violence to life and person, in particular murder of all kinds, mutilation, cruel treatment and torture; (2) taking of hostages; (3) outrages upon personal dignity, in particular, humiliating and degrading treatment; and (4) the passing of sentences and the carrying out of executions without previous judgment pronounced by a regularly constituted court

[1] O'Reilly Arthur Thomas, Command Responsiblity: A Call to Realign Doctrine with Principles, *American University International Law Review*, Vol. 20 (1), (2004), p. 78.

affording all the judicial guarantees which are recognized as indispensable by civilized peoples.

Its status as customary law was confirmed with its inclusion in Article 7(3) of the Statute of the International Criminal Tribunal for the former Yugoslavia (ICTY) and article 6(3) of the Statute of the International Criminal Tribunal for Rwanda (ICTR), as well as Article 28 of the Rome Statute for an International Criminal Court (ICC). It should be noted that international law recognizes the principle of command responsibility both in international and in internal armed conflict. Thus, the ICTR Statute explicitly provides for command responsibility including for grave breaches of common Article 3 of the Geneva Conventions, in the context of the conflict in Rwanda, which is by definition application of superior liability in a non-international conflict.

Additional Protocol I

The Additional Protocol I to the Geneva Conventions, adopted in 1977, was the first international treaty to codify the doctrine of command responsibility. The provisions relating to command responsibility are contained in Articles 86 and 87 of the Protocol.

Article 86 - Failure to act

1. The High Contracting Parties and the Parties to the conflict shall repress grave breaches, and take measures necessary to suppress all other breaches, of the Conventions or of this Protocol which result from a failure to act when under a duty to do so.

2. The fact that a breach of the Conventions or of this Protocol was committed by a subordinate does not absolve his superiors from penal or disciplinary responsibility, as the case may be, if they knew or had information which should have enabled them to conclude in the circumstances at the time, that he was committing or was going to commit such a breach and if they did not take all feasible measures within their power to prevent or repress the breach.

Article 87 - Duty of commanders

1. The High Contracting Parties and the Parties to the conflict shall require military commanders, with respect to members of the armed

forces under their command and other persons under their control, to prevent and, where necessary, to suppress and to report to competent authorities breaches of the Conventions and of this Protocol.

2. In order to prevent and suppress breaches, High Contracting Parties and Parties to the conflict shall require that, commensurate with their level of responsibility, commanders ensure that members of the armed forces under their command are aware of their obligations under the Conventions and this Protocol.

3. The High Contracting Parties and Parties to the conflict shall require any commander who is aware that subordinates or other persons under his control are going to commit or have committed a breach of the Conventions or of this Protocol, to initiate such steps as are necessary to prevent such violations of the Conventions or this Protocol, and, where appropriate, to initiate disciplinary or penal action against violators thereof.

A commander is liable for grave breaches committed by a subordinate "if he knew, or had information which should have enabled him" to conclude in the circumstances at the time, that his subordinate was committing or was going to commit such a breach and did not take all feasible measures within his power to prevent or repress the breach. Apart from being liable to be considered a party to war crimes committed by his subordinates, a commander has a general duty to maintain discipline and this includes a duty to take action in respect of war crimes committed, or about to be committed by his subordinates or by other persons under his control. Protocol I places the responsibility on the High Contracting Parties to ensure that commanders prevent breaches, train their subordinates and take action against offenders.

The commanders are to prevent and, where necessary , suppress and report to the competent authorities about the breaches of the Geneva Conventions and Protocol I. This applies in relation to members of the armed forces and other persons under their command. The commanders are also responsible for making members of the armed forces and other persons under their command aware of their obligations under the Conventions and Protocol.

International Criminal Tribunal for former Yugoslavia and Rwanda

In the wake of the human rights violations committed in the former Yugoslavia, the UN Security Council, relying on Chapter VII of the United Nations Charter as authority, created the International Criminal Tribunal for the Former Yugoslavia (ICTY). The Security Council felt that there was a link between the maintenance of peace in the former Yugoslavia and the restoration of justice. A statute was drafted giving the court both substantive and personal jurisdiction over certain individuals and particular types of criminal activity. The intent of the Security Council was to create an international criminal tribunal that would apply the standards of customary international law including command responsibility.

Though the strife in Rwanda was internal, the UN Security Council viewed the genocide and massive human rights violations as a threat to international peace and security. After receiving a request from the Rwandan government, it established an International Criminal Tribunal for Rwanda (ICTR) for the prosecution of persons responsible for "genocide and other serious violations of international humanitarian law committed in the territory of Rwanda". The Rwandan court was authorized by the UN Security Council to hold individuals liable on a theory of command responsibility. The *Yamashita* rules were applied in both tribunals—ICTY and ICTR; even though the Security Council apparently viewed the conflict in former Yugoslavia as being of an international character and the armed conflict in Rwanda as being purely internal in nature.

The ICTY has jurisdiction over four types of crime committed in the territory of former Yugoslavia: (i) grave breaches of the 1949 Geneva Conventions, (ii) violations of the laws or customs of war, (iii) genocide, and (iv) crime against humanity. It can try only individuals, not organizations or governments. It is the first international criminal court to enforce the existing body of international humanitarian law and in particular, judicially determine aspects of its customary law.

Article 7 of the ICTY includes a provision for holding commanders criminally responsible for the acts of their subordinates. It reads:

Individual criminal responsibility

1. A person who planned, instigated, ordered, committed or otherwise aided and abetted in the planning, preparation or execution of a crime referred to in articles 2 to 5 of the present Statute, shall be individually responsible for the crime.

2. The official position of any accused person, whether as Head of State or Government or as a responsible Government of ficial, shall not relieve such person of criminal responsibility nor mitigate punishment.

3. The fact that any of the acts referred to in Articles 2 to 5 of the present Statute was committed by a subordinate does not relieve his superior of criminal responsibility if he knew or had reason to know that the subordinate was about to commit such acts or had done so and the superior failed to take the necessary and reasonable measures to prevent such acts or to punish the perpetrators thereof.

4. The fact that an accused person acted pursuant to an order of a Government or of a superior shall not relieve him of criminal responsibility, but may be considered in mitigation of punishment if the International Tribunal determines that justice so requires.

There are two standards of knowledge are included in Article 7(3): 'knew' and 'had reason to know'. 'Knew' refers to actual knowledge, which can be established either directly or through circumstantial evidence. The meaning of 'had reason to know' had been the most contentious aspect of command responsibility before the ICTY. The ICTY Appeal Chamber had held that the ordinary meaning of Article 86 of the Additional Protocol I required the commander to some information available to him, to put him on notice of the commission of unlawful acts by his subordinates.

The ICTY set a large number of legal and institutional precedents: (i) it applied the modern doctrine of criminal responsibility of superiors; (ii) it removed uncertainty about the level of knowledge to be expected from a superior whose subordinates were about to commit crimes or had actually committed them; and (iii) it expanded the legal elements of the crime of grave breaches of the Geneva Conventions of 1949 by further defining the test of overall control. In the *Celebici* (2001) case, the ICTY elaborated a threefold requirement for the existence of command responsibility: (i) the existence of a superior-subordinate relationship; (ii) that the superior knew or had reason to know that the criminal act was about to be or had been committed; and (iii) that the superior failed to take the reasonable measures to prevent the criminal act or to punish the perpetrator thereof.

Depending on the origin of the command structure, the requirement of a superior-subordinate relationship may be met in two independent ways: *de jure* and *de facto.* A *de jure* command may be both civilian and military as established by the ICTR in the *Akayesu* (1998) case. It has been accepted that what matters is not rank as such, but subordination. There are four structures of hierarchy for the purpose of establishing *de jure* command responsibility: (i) policy command: heads of state, defence minister or defence secretary; (ii) strategic command: chief of defence staff, chief the army staff; (iii) operational command: military leadership; and (iv) tactical command: direct command over troops on the ground.There are two special cases of *de jure* commanders: (i) POW Camp Commander: the ICTY established in the *Aleskovski* (1999) case that POW camp commanders are entrusted with the welfare of all prisoners, and subordination in this case is irrelevant; and (ii) Executive Commanders—supreme governing authority in the occupied territory: their responsibility is the welfare of the population in the territory under their control, as established in the *High Command* and *Hostages* cases after World War II.

Evidence of *de facto* control requires proof of superior -subordinate relationship, i.e. a chain of command (except in the case of POW Camp Commanders). It could be established by the following three indicators: (i) capacity to issue orders; (ii) the power of influence; and (iii) evidence stemming from distribution of tasks.The ICTY has established in the *Nikolic* (2003) case that superior status could be deduced from the analysis of distribution of tasks within the unit, and it applies both to operational and POW camp commanders.

As regards applicable standards of knowledge, the ICTY in the *Celebici* (2001) case ruled that actual knowledge may be established by either direct or indirect evidence. Article 7(3) of the ICTY statute provides that absence of knowledge is not a defence where the accused didn't take reasonable steps to acquire such knowledge. In the *Blaskic* (2000) case, the ICTY defined the obligation to prevent or punish, stating that this standard doesn't provide the commander with two alternative paths to pursue: where the superior knew or had reasons to know the criminal acts were to be committed and failed to prevent their commission, he cannot merely punish the perpetrators and escape from criminal responsibility.

The treatment of command responsibility is virtually identical in both the ICTY Statute and the ICTR Statute, which suggests that the customary international law standard for holding commanders liable in internal armed conflicts is now the same as that for international armed conflicts. Both statutes were created by the UN Security Council and both tribunals, the only international tribunals since World War II and the only currently sitting international criminal tribunals, codify the *Yamashita* standard.

The Rome Statute of the International Criminal Court

The Rome Statute has created a permanent tribunal, the ICC, to deal with all crimes of serious concern to the international community. The jurisdiction and mandate of the ICC are not limited to specific events in specific places or to any specified time-frame. The Rome Statute provides that the ICC, unlike the other permanent international tribunals, such as the International Court of Justice shall exercise jurisdiction over individuals, The ICC's powers and functions include holding individuals accountable, and subjecting the accused to investigation, arrest, detention, prosecution and if found guilty, incarceration. The Rome Statute creates obligations on the part of State parties to provide the means to enforce these powers.

The doctrine of command responsibility has been codified in Article 28 of the Rome Statute:

> 1. A military commander or person effectively acting as a military commander shall be criminally responsible for crimes within the jurisdiction of the Court committed by forces under his or her effective command and control, or effective authority and control as the case may be, as a result of his or her failure to exercise control properly over such forces, where:
>
> (a) That military commander or person either knew or, owing to the circumstances at the time, should have known that the forces were committing or about to commit such crimes; and

(b) That military commander or person failed to take all necessary and reasonable measures within his or her power to prevent or repress their commission or to submit the matter to the competent authorities for investigation and prosecution.

2. With respect to superior and subordinate relationships not described in paragraph 1, a superior shall be criminally responsible for crimes within the jurisdiction of the Court committed by subordinates under his or her effective authority and control, as a result of his or her failure to exercise control properly over such subordinates, where:

(a) The superior either knew, or consciously disregarded information which clearly indicated, that the subordinates were committing or about to commit such crimes;

(b) The crimes concerned activities that were within the ef fective responsibility and control of the superior; and

(c) The superior failed to take all necessary and reasonable measures within his or her power to prevent or repress their commission or to submit the matter to the competent authorities for investigation and prosecution.

Article 28 imposes individual responsibility on military commanders for crimes committed by forces under their effective command and control if they 'either knew or, owing to the circumstances at the time, should have known that the forces were committing or about to commit such crimes'. Interpreted literally, Article 28 adopts the stricter "should have known" standard. It is felt that this provision will serve as a deterrent, giving incentive to a commander to be aware of what his subordinates are doing. The offences dealt with under the Rome Statute are genocide, war crimes and crimes against humanity. The definition of superior responsibility incorporated in the ICC S tatute is an advancement when compared with other statutory provisions like the ICTY or ICTR. The ICC Statute defines the doctrine of superior or command responsibility in positive terms, as a separate form of liability.

The statute for the first time expressly acknowledges that the doctrine applies not only to a military commander, but also to a non-military superior or civilian. However, it lays down different form of liability for the military commander and the non-military superior The standard provided for a non-military superior [Article 28 (b)] is consistent with customary international law, whereas the standard of liability [Article 28 (a)] for a military superior a person effectively acting as a military commander includes the 'should have known' level of *mens rea*. Under the ICC Statute, a superior has three obligations: (i) to prevent, (ii) to repress, or (iii) to submit the matter to the competent authorities for investigation and prosecution. The principles of IHL demand that a superior should ensure that the forces under his command are properly organized, disciplined and are capable of complying with humanitarian standards. His obligations to prevent or punish crimes of subordinates, in certain circumstances, would be satisfied by reporting the matter to the superior authority.

The ICC is complementary to national jurisdictions and will intervene only where S tates are unable or unwilling to act. In order to meet its international obligations, the UK has passed the International Criminal Court Act, 2001. The military manuals of the USA, Canada and Australia have also been amended to incorporate provisions relating to command responsibility. The Australian and the British provisions relating to command responsibility are as follows.

Australia: International Criminal Court Act, 2002

268.115 Responsibility of commanders and other superiors

(1) The criminal responsibility imposed by this section is in addition to other grounds of criminal responsibility under the law in force in Australia for acts or omissions that are offences under this Division.

(2) A military commander or person effectively acting as a military commander is criminally responsible for offences under this Division committed by forces under his or her effective command and control, or effective authority and control, as the case may be, as a result of his or her failure to exercise control properly over those forces, where:

(a) the military commander or person either knew or , owing to the circumstances at the time, was reckless as to whether the forces were committing or about to commit such offences; and

(b) the military commander or person failed to take all necessary and reasonable measures within his or her power to prevent or repress their commission or to submit the matter to the competent authorities for investigation and prosecution.

(3) With respect to superior and subordinate relationships not described in subsection (2), a superior is criminally responsible for of fences against this Division committed by subordinates under his or her effective authority and control, as a result of his or her failure to exercise control properly over those subordinates, where:

(a) the superior either knew, or consciously disregarded information that clearly indicated, that the subordinates were committing or about to commit such offences; and

(b) the offences concerned activities that were within the effective responsibility and control of the superior; and

(c) the superior failed to take all necessary and reasonable measures within his or her power to prevent or repress their commission or to submit the matter to the competent authorities for investigation and prosecution.

UK: International Court Act, 2001

Section 65: Responsibility of commanders and other superiors

(1) This section applies in relation to:

(a) offences under this Part, and

(b) offences ancillary to such offences.

(2) A military commander, or a person effectively acting as a military commander, is responsible for offences committed by forces under his effective command and control, or (as the case may be) his ef fective authority and control, as a result of his failure to exercise control properly over such forces where:

(a) he either knew, or owing to the circumstances at the time, should have known that the forces were committing or about to commit such offences, and

(b) he failed to take all necessary and reasonable measures within his power to prevent or repress their commission or to submit the matter to the competent authorities for investigation and prosecution.

(3) With respect to superior and subordinate relationships not described in subsection (2), a superior is responsible for offences committed by subordinates under his effective authority and control, as a result of his failure to exercise control properly over such subordinates where—

(a) he either knew, or consciously disregarded information which clearly indicated, that the subordinates were committing or about to commit such offences,

(b) the offences concerned activities that were within his efective responsibility and control, and

(c) he failed to take all necessary and reasonable measures within his power to prevent or repress their commission or to submit the matter to the competent authorities for investigation and prosecution.

(4) A person responsible under this section for an offence is regarded as aiding, abetting, counselling or procuring the commission of the offence.

(5) In interpreting and applying the provisions of this section (which corresponds to article 28) the court shall take into account any relevant judgment or decision of the ICC. Account may also be taken of any other relevant international jurisprudence.

(6) Nothing in this section shall be read as restricting or excluding—

(a) any liability of the commander or superior apart from this section, or

(b) the liability of persons other than the commander or superior.

UN Convention for the Protection of All Persons from Enforced Disappearance, 2006

The principal of command responsibility is well-established in the recently adopted UN Convention for the Protection of All Persons from Enforced

Disappearance. Article 6 of the Convention provides that the State Parties are to take the necessary measures to hold criminally responsible an individual or superior , who commits, orders, solicits or induces the commission of, or participates in an enforced disappearance. No order or instruction from any public authority , civilian, military or other , may be invoked to justify an offence of enforced disappearance. Paragraph 1.1 (b) of Article 6 places responsibility on a superior who:

(i) Knew , or consciously disregarded information which clearly indicated, that subordinates under his or her effective authority and control were committing or about to commit a crime of enforced disappearance;

(ii) Exercised effective responsibility for and control over activities which were concerned with the crime of enforced disappearance; and

(iii) Failed to take all necessary and reasonable measures within his or her power to prevent or repress the commission of an enforced disappearance or to submit the matter to the competent authorities for investigation and prosecution.

The Convention against Forced Disappearance has come into force since 23 December 2010[2] The UN Committee against Torture, in its general comment on the obligations of the Convention against Torture, has affirmed that "those exercising superior authority, including public officials cannot

[2] The crime of enforced disappearance is one of the most serious human rights violations and can constitute a crime against humanity if committed as part of a widespread or systematic attack against civilians. The legal significance of the Convention is marked, since it not only provides a legal definition of the crime of enforced disappearance, but also establishes a set of obligations of States to prevent and prosecute this crime through concrete measures at the national level. The Convention recognises in particular the right to information, the right to know the truth, the right to justice and the right to reparation. On 23 November 2010, the Republic of Iraq deposited the 20th instrument of ratification for the International Convention for the Protection of All Persons from Enforced Disappearances to the Secretary General of the Unted Nations. Iraq becomes the 20th State to ratify this treaty. The Convention entered into force on 23 December 2010, 30 days after the 20th accession or ratification. The Convention, as of 31 December 2010, has been signed by 87 countries and ratified by 21. The Convention puts an obligation on State parties to take measures to prosecute the perpetrators of this crime when they are present on their territories, under the principle of universal jurisdiction, irrespective of the nationalty of the victims and the alleged perpetrators, as well the country where the crime was committed.

avoid accountability or escape criminal responsibility for torture or ill-treatment committed by subordinates where they knew or should have know that such impermissible conduct was occurring, or was likely to occur, and they failed to take reasonable and necessary preventive measures. The Committee considered it essential that the responsibility of any superior officials, whether for direct instigation or encouragement of torture or ill-treatment or for consent or acquiescence therein, be fully investigated through competent, independent and impartial prosecutorial authorities."

The Law Member of the War Crimes Tribunal, Tokyo (1949) had stated: "When some of the participants in war, whether in high or low place, violate those principles of decency, honour, fair play, and humanity which we have come to know as 'civilized', they must be punished. The machinery is new, but the principles are ageless." The doctrine of command responsibility , developed primarily after the conclusion of WWII, holds that a commander may be criminally liable for violations of the law of war committed by the forces under his command. Over the years, the doctrine has obtained the status of customary international law and has been codified in various statutes. This doctrine is based on the unique position that the commander holds in a military organization. It recognizes that for military discipline it is the commander's responsibility to maintain command and control over his subordinate forces. The doctrine of command responsibility whether direct or indirect, applies equally to military and civilian superiors.

CHAPTER 16

Mercenaries and Private Military Companies

Introduction

The Oxford English Dictionary defines the term 'mercenary' as 'a professional soldier serving a foreign power'. A mercenary is a professional soldier who is willing to serve in any army solely for the motive of personal gain. The phenomenon of mercenarism is deeply rooted in the history of warfare and can be traced back to ancient Egypt and Mesopotamia, where their services were essential aspects of imperial control. When the Roman Empire ceased to rely upon its citizen armies, it turned instead to mercenaries that led to its eventual disintegration. For centuries, mercenary armies were used extensively as nation-states were yet to emerge and, therefore, regular armies were virtually non-existent. The mercenary bands commonly employed in the sixteenth and seventeenth centuries often turned into a menace both to their former employers and to the country in which they would operate as freebooters once the money paid to them had run out.

In the nineteenth century, regular soldiers often took leave from their own armies and joined service under foreign powers. France created the France Foreign Legion, one of the famous mercenary bands, to provide a force to fight in the long war of conquest in Algeria. Mercenaries could also meet a part of the military requirement of wealthy imperial powers which could afford to hire them. The US's Central Intelligence Agency and France's intelligence service were directly involved in the recruitment of mercenaries to fight against the Marxist regime in Angola. By the second half of 1976, a number of European mercenaries were captured, tried and executed in Angola, Lebanon and Rhodesia. This raised the issue of legality of recruiting and employment of mercenaries in armed conflict zones.

The private military and security companies (PMSCs) constitute a new form of mercenarism. The PMSCs are just a less pejorative category of mercenaries, the only diference being that these 'mercenaries'are legally enlisted by corporations rather than surreptitiously hired by rough States.[1] With the advent of the new war on terror led by the United States and United Kingdom, in Iraq andAfghanistan, the recruitment of former military personnel and ex-policemen by PMSCs has been an ongoing practice.The PMSCs today perform various activities under governmental contracts and sometimes under international inter governmental agreements in conflict zones. However, they do not fall, in most cases, under the "traditional" legal definition of a mercenary.[2] It has become a debatable issue whether PMSCs operate in a legal vacuum.[3]

Mercenaries

Traditionally, a mercenary was a person who fought for personal gain rather than loyalty, and was often not a subject of the ruler employing the warrior The issue of financial gain has been an essential factor in determining a mercenary. Mercenaries were useful partly because of the economics of war. About three centuries ago, most rulers did not have lar ge standing armies, so they employed mercenaries during contingencies. Thus, rulers were spared the expense of paying soldiers to sit around undeemployed in barracks for most of their careers. They hired mercenaries when the need arose and discharged them when the job was done. The term 'mercenary' in that era did not have the negative connotations that it now has. Like the

---

[1] For instance, Saracen International, a PMSC, is based in South Africa, with corporate offshoots in Uganda and other countries. The company was formed with the remnants of Executive Outcomes, a priv ate mer cenary firm composed largely of f ormer South African special operations troops who worked throughout Africa in 1990s. Mark Mazzetti and Eric Schmitt, Private security firms playing a role in global war, *THE HINDU*, 24 January 2011.

[2] UN General Assembly Document: A/63/225 dated 25 August 2008; Use of mercenaries as a means of violating human rights and impeding the execise of the right of peoples to self determination, paragraph 44.

[3] Since the in vasion of Iraq in 2003, the US has outsour ced a number duties to PMSCs estimated to have a strength of about 20,000 to 50,000 personnel (the exact number has not been publicly disclosed) to carry out duties such as tactical combat opetions, strategic planning, intelligence gathering and analysis, operational support, troop training, prisoners security and interrogations, and military technical assistance, all of which has traditionally been allocated to the mil itary and the intell igence community. Though ther e is specif ic reference to mercenaries in IHL, there is no such reference to PMSCs either in IHL treaties nor are they specifically regulated in customary international law.

word 'mercy', it had a Latin root derived from 'reward'. Governments were not strong or well oganized and so mercenaries provided a valuable service. In a number of situations, the campaigns fought by mercenaries dragged on for a long time because the longer they fought the greater was the amount of money they stood to receive.Also, because mercenaries had no home to go back to, they made the most of war.

At end of theThirty Years War in Europe (in the late 1640s), the nation state system began with the rise of strong central governments. National anthems, languages and identities were invented to build up a national spirit of devotion and service to the countryThese national governments recruited their own citizens to fight for patriotic reasons rather than financial ones. Soldiers were recruited through the system of national patriotism.The role of mercenaries, therefore, declined and became somewhat discredited

However, the market for mercenaries did not totally disappear. In the twentieth century the practice of mercenarism evolved and reappeared in a different form. Mercenarism intensified within the context of decolonization in the 1960s and the recognition of the right to self-determination. These independent mercenaries referred to as 'soldiers of fortune', or 'wild geese', surfaced in post-colonial Africa and were used to destabilize newly independent governments. They were employed in African conflicts, such as Congo, Nigeria, Mozambique and Angola. The majority of those mercenaries have been soldiers of the former imperial powers. The first British company of modern mercenaries (under the guise of private security) was created in Britain in 1967 by World War II veteran and founder of the Special Air Service (SAS) Colonel David S tirling. His company, Watch Guard International, employed former SAS personnel to train the military for Middle Eastern rulers. The high level of professionalism created an international benchmark.

Mercenaries and IHL

The international legal framework to prohibit mercenaries has been envisaged through norms regulating the general use of force between States. Article 4 of the 1907 Hague Convention Respecting the Rights and Duties of Neutral Powers and Persons in Case of W ar on Land (Convention V), stipulated that "corps of combatants cannot be formed nor recruiting agencies opened on the territory of a neutral Power to assist the belligerents".

States that have chosen to remain neutral during an armed conflict are obliged under Article 4 to prevent the formation of mercenary groups on their territory. However, IHL made no formal distinction between mercenaries and other combatants prior to the adoption of the 1977 Additional Protocol I.

Africa has been on the receiving end of mercenary activities since World War II, such as the Congo in 1964 and Angola in 1975. In fact, mercenarism has contributed to undermining of the continent's peace and security. Mercenaries have featured in African coups which have violated a plethora of human rights guaranteed under the African Charter on Human and Peoples' Rights. The first international attempt to outlaw mercenaries was initiated by the Organization of African Unity (OAU). In 1977, the OAU adopted the Convention for the Elimination of Mercenarism in Africa which came into force in 1985. Article 1 of the Convention defines the crime of mercenary as "anyone who, not a national of the State against which his actions are directed, is employed, enrolls or links himself willingly to a person, group or organization whose aim is to overthrow a government of an OAU member state, to undermine its independence, or territorial integrity, or to block the activities of any liberation movement recognized by the OAU". This definition was unusual because there was no mention of monetary gain in it.

The OAU Convention is significant because it created a specific offence of mercenarism and contained a series of corresponding obligations, including the adoption of measures to eradicate mercenary activities, and the prosecution or extradition of those committing an offence under the Convention. Additionally, State representatives may be punished if a State accused of involvement in mercenary activities is brought before any competent OAU or international tribunal and is found to have breached the Convention. However, the OAU Convention is regional in scope and applicable to those States in the African region, who have ratified it.

In the early 1970s, updating the four 1949 Geneva Conventions started with the aim of making them applicable to the new kind of warfare, such as the use of guerrilla warfare. African countries also used the Geneva Diplomatic Conference as an opportunity to restrict the use of mercenaries which led to the inclusion of Article 47 of AP I and the drafting of the 1989 Mercenary Convention.

Additional Protocol I

The AP I contains only one provision,Article 47, which specifically address the issue of mercenaries. It defines a mercenary as one who:

(a) is specifically recruited locally or abroad in order to fight in an armed conflict;

(b) does, in fact, take direct part in the hostilities;

(c) is motivated to take part in the hostilities essentially by the desire for private gain and, in fact, is promised, by or on behalf of a party to the conflict, material compensation substantially in excess of that promised or paid to combatants of similar ranks and functions in the armed forces of that party;

(d) is neither a national of a party to the conflict nor a resident of territory controlled by a party to the conflict;

(e) is not a member of the armed forces of a party to the conflict; and

(f) has not been sent by a state which is not a party to the conflict on official duty as a member of the armed forces.

The above definition of mercenary is cumulative, i.e., a mercenary is defined as someone to whom all the six conditions apply .[4] It states that mercenaries are denied the privileged status of a combatant or a POW and that they can, therefore, be held responsible by the opposing State for having taken part in an international armed conflict.The four Geneva Conventions have stripped mercenaries of any combatant or POW status.[5]

Efforts by the UN

In principle, the UN is opposed to the recruitment and the use of mercenaries. In 1970, the General Assembly, by its resolution 2625 (XXV) adopted the

---

[4] The aim of the article was to sanction the criminal prosecution of persons identified as mercenaries. The definition does not apply to persons acting as advisors, technicians or trainers and to the persons acting for ideological reasons. It applies only to those who are not members of the armed forces of a party to the conflict and this could be avoided by signing enlistment papers or taking up special appointment. However, the definition of mercenary contained in the OAU Convention and the UN Convention are more extensive than applied in Article 47 of AP I.

[5] Article 4 of the third Geneva Conventions of 1949.

Declaration on Principles of International Law concerning Friendly Relations and Cooperation among States in accordance with the Charter of the United Nations. The first principle of the declaration deals with the ban on the use of force and falls under international customary law . The declaration makes it a duty of the State not to use "mercenaries, irregular forces or armed bands" against the territorial integrity or independence of another State. The declaration does not, however, define what is meant by irregular forces or armed bands.

In 1980 the General Assembly established Ad Hoc Committee for the drafting of an International Convention against the Recruitment, Use, Financing and Training of Mercenaries. The committee submitted a draft convention for final negotiation and adoption. The Convention was originally opened for signature until 31 December 1990.

UN Convention against the Recruitment, Use, Financing and Training of Mercenaries, 1989: The treaty, also referred to as the UN Mercenary Convention, entered into force in 2001 after more than a decade of negotiations in response to increasing concern over the accountability of private military companies providing services traditionally performed by State agencies. The treaty has been signed and ratified by 32 countries. Under the Convention, the State Parties must prohibit and criminalize the recruitment, financing, training and use of mercenaries.

The term 'mercenary' has been defined in Article 1 of the Convention. In its definition of 'mercenary', the Convention takes into consideration not only situations of armed conflict but also of violence organized to bring about the collapse of a government, to undermine constitutionality or to act against the territorial integrity of a State. The Convention criminalizes the recruitment, financing, training and use of mercenaries. Article 1 of the Convention provides:

1. A mercenary is any person who:

(a) is specially recruited locally or abroad in order to fight in an armed conflict;

(b) is motivated to take part in the hostilities essentially by the desire for private gain and, in fact, is promised, by or on behalf of a party to the conflict, material compensation substantially in excess of that promised or paid to combatants of similar rank and functions in the armed forces of that party;

(c) is neither a national of a party to the conflict nor a resident of territory controlled by a party to the conflict;

(d) is not a member of the armed forces of a party to the conflict; and

(e) has not been sent by a State which is not a party to the conflict on official duty as a member of its armed forces.

2. A mercenary is also any person who, in any other situation:

(a) is specially recruited locally or abroad for the purpose of participating in a concerted act of violence aimed at: (i) overthrowing a Government or otherwise undermining the constitutional order of a S tate; or (ii) undermining the territorial integrity of a State;

(b) is motivated to take part therein essentially by the desire for significant private gain and is prompted by the promise or payment of material compensation;

(c) is neither a national nor a resident of the State against which such an act is directed;

(d) has not been sent by a State on official duty; and

(e) is not a member of the armed forces of the State on whose territory the act is undertaken.

The scope of the Convention is similar to that of Additional Protocol I, but the Convention expands the definition of mercenary to cover situations other than armed conflict. It includes situations in which individuals are recruited to participate in a concerted act of violence for the purpose of overthrowing a government or undermining the constitutional order , or infringing on the territorial integrity of a State. A mercenary, who participates directly in hostilities or in a concerted act of violence, commits an offence under the Convention. The States Parties to the Convention are not to recruit, use, finance or train mercenaries for the purpose of opposing the legitimate exercise of the inalienable right of peoples to self-determination, as recognized by international law. They are to take the appropriate measures to prevent the recruitment, use, financing or training of mercenaries for that purpose. The State Parties are also obliged to ensure that the offences contained in the Mercenary Convention are made punishable through the national legislations.

The Convention obliges S tates to extradite or prosecute any mercenaries found in their territory , regardless of where the offence was committed. The S tate prosecuting the mercenary is to notify the UN Secretary General of the result of prosecution and transmit the information to the other concerned S tates. A person who has been tried as mercenary shall be authorized to communicate with the nearest appropriate representative of the State of which he is a national or which is otherwise entitled to protect his rights or, if he is a stateless person, the State in whose territory he resides (Article 10 and 14).The States Parties are to assist each other in connection with criminal proceedings imitated under the Mercenary Convention (Article 13). Although the Convention is a binding instrument of international law, it lacks widespread ratification.

According to the UN Special Rapporteur on mercenary activity , the rule against mercenarism has become customary international law because the activity infringes on individual rights and freedoms, and is inconsistent with political aspirations of the international community. In his report on the question of the use of mercenaries as means of violating human rights and impeding the exercise of the rights of peoples to self-determination, the rapporteur stated: " The aim of customary international and treaty law is to condemn a mercenary act as the buying and selling of criminal services in order to interfere with the enjoyment of human rights, sovereignty , or the self-determination of people; and there is international jurisprudence condemning interference by one state, not to speak of individual organizations, in the internal affairs of another state and in the lives of its peoples".[6]

However, mercenaries are entitled to certain protection under Article 75 of AP I, which af fords 'fundamental guarantees' and the 'right to be treated humanely' to an individual. They have the right to be protected against murder, torture, mutilation, corporal punishment and outrage upon personal dignity. It also guarantees the right to a fair trial and due process

[6] UN Doc. E/CN.4/1997/24 (1997).

in respect of penal offences.

Model Law

In 2005, 12 States members of the Commonwealth of Independent States adopted a model law on counteracting mercenarism, in which a modern multidimensional definition of mercenary activities was agreed upon. The model law postulates a possibility of mercenarism based on motivation of non-material gains including ideological and religious motivations. The law strengthens the rights of States to prevent the operation of foreign mercenaries and recruiting organizations (companies) on their territories, and to punish parties for spreading propaganda about mercenary-related activities or the financing of such activities. It attempts to bridge the gap between regulation of mercenaries and the regulation of private military and security companies. At the national level, countries those have passed laws on mercenarism include: Belgium, Italy, South Africa, New Zealand, France and Zimbabwe.

The top countries with PMSCs, including the US, the UK, and South Africa, are not parties to the Mercenary Convention and thus are not legally bound by its provisions. The Convention's critics highlight the inadequate definition of the term "mercenary", the lack of monitoring mechanisms, and the lackluster support for it by the majority of the world's countries.

Private Military and Security Companies (PMSCs)

In the post–cold war period mercenary activities have increased and diversified in both theory and practice. It is no longer predominantly confined to the African continent. The modern mercenary activities are now thriving under a new name: Private Military and Security Companies (PMSCs). In the 1990s PMSCs specializing in military services supplemented the use of traditional mercenaries. Groups of professionals have partially replaced the relatively small number of individuals that dominated the mercenary scene between the 1960s and 1980. Instead of asking coalition soldiers to clear the landmines and the cluster bombs after the First Gulf War in 1991, the Kuwait Government employed PMSCs. A British company, Royal Ordnance was awarded $90 million contract to clear the explosives from Kuwait's oil and gas fields.

The PMSCs are companies that specialize in providing security and protection of personnel and property including humanitarian and industrial assets. They specialize in military skills, including combat operations, strategic planning, intelligence collection, operational support, logistics, training, procurement and maintenance of arms and equipment.While most PMSCs serve governments and the armed forces, some have helped democratize foreign security forces, and have worked for the UN, NGOs, and even environmental groups. Others have worked for dictators, regimes of failing states, organized crime, drug cartels, and terrorist-linked groups.

In recent conflicts in Iraq and Afghanistan, PMSCs employed more than 50,000 private persons to perform a range of tasks, which were traditionally performed by the military. These included training of military personnel, maintenance of weapons, building military installations, supplying food and weapons to military at the front, transportation, guarding civilian installations or military establishments, escorting military convoys, controlling prisons, care and interrogation of prisoners, de-mining and destruction of explosives; and numerous other functions.The transnational PMSCs, mainly from the US and the UK, and also from Australia, Canada, Israel are presently exporting their services to over 50 countries, in particular where low intensity armed conflicts are ongoing, including Afghanistan, Iraq, the Democratic Republic of the Congo, Somalia and the Sudan. The industry is estimated to earn between $100 and $120 billion annually. The PMSCs also contract third country nationals from all regions of the world in order to cut costs and increase profits.

Whether the personnel of PMSCs should be regarded as civilians or combatants? There is a view that guarding civilian or military installation is merely a 'policing function' and is not a direct participation in hostilities. The employees of PMSCs are not members of the armed forces, and therefore, are not combatants. A contrast view is that guarding a military installation, or military personnel against enemy attack per se constitutes direct participation in hostilities. According to another view, the crucial test is whether a civilian's activities are an essential and indispensable ingredient of the military action.

IHL and Human Rights Violations by PMSCs

The personnel employed by the PMSCs, can and do violate IHL and human rights laws like a soldier. Under common Article 1 of the four Geneva

Conventions of 1949, the S tates that have hired PMSCs have the responsibility to ensure respect for the Convention in all the circumstances. They have the responsibility to ensure that that the personnel of PMSCs hired by them do not violate the provisions of IHL. Regarding POWs, under Article 12 of the GC III, the hiring S tate would be responsible for any violation of IHL by its private contractor Similarly allowing the PMSCs to operate POW camps and interrogate prisoners would be a violation of IHL as the detaining power is responsible for the treatment given to the prisoners. The PMSCs violating the rights of civilians could be held liable as Article 27 of the GC IV provides that the protected persons shall at all times be humanely treated, and shall be protected against all acts of violence.

The civilian population is often the victim of the activities of PMSCs, which put their employees in direct contact with the public. For instance, employees of Blackwater allegedly opened fire and killed 17 and injured more than 20 civilians, including children and women in Baghdad on 16 September 2007. Under an order issued by the Administrator of the Coalition Provisional Authority on 27 June 2004, foreign private contractors were immune from prosecution. Similarly, in 2005, armed security guards of a North Carolina based security company Zapata, opened fire on unarmed Iraqi civilians and on a Marine outpost tower in Fallujah. The Marines arrested and jailed the 19 men of company but they were eventually released. Other PMSCs have been reported to be involved in a number of incidents of human rights violations, in particular: the torture of prison inmates, illegal use of forces, extra-judicial killings, accidental deaths, sexual abuses, injury to property and unethical labour practices in various parts of Iraq and Afghanistan.

The failure to regulate and hold PMSCs and their personnel accountable led to a belief that the industry and its clients not only fail to respect and protect human rights and IHL but also fail adequately to remedy their violation. This, in turn, resulted in a perception that the industry does not contribute to public security but creates public insecurity and PMSCs have no respect for law.

IHL and PMSCs

There is no reference to PMSCs either in IHL treaties or customary international law. IHL makes a fundamental distinction between members of the armed forces and civilians. The members of the armed forces may not be tried for activities normally associated with the conflict — namely killing, inflicting grievous bodily harm, carrying firearms, and so on.They may not be subjected to prosecution by the capturing state for taking part in the conflict. If captured, they are entitled to a POW status. The third Geneva Convention also includes extra categories of civilians, who are entitled to POW status. These persons are associated with the army in one form or another but are not actual combatants. A main purpose of the distinction between the armed forces and civilians was to limit civilian casualties. For this purpose, it was traditionally understood that, with minor exceptions, members of the armed forces are 'combatants' and they are entitled to take part in hostilities and may also be directly targeted by the adversary. Other persons, i.e., the civilians may not be tar geted by the adversary, unless they 'take a direct part in hostilities'.

Under Article 4 of the third Geneva Convention, persons belonging to three categories of groups are entitled to POW status:

(a) members of the armed forces of a Party to the conflict as well as members of militias or volunteer corps forming part of such armed forces;

(b) inhabitants of a non-occupied territory , who on the approach of the enemy spontaneously take up arms to resist the invading forces; and

(c) members of other militias and members of other volunteer corps, including those of organized resistance movements, belonging to a Party to the conflict and operating in or outside their own territory even if this territory is occupied, provided that such militias or volunteer corps, including such organized resistance movements, fulfil the following conditions:

(i) that of being commanded by a person responsible for his subordinates;

(ii) that of having a fixed distinctive sign recognizable at a distance;

(iii) that of carrying arms openly; and

(iv) that of conducting their operations in accordance with the laws

> and customs of war.

The ICRC commentary to the meaning of the words 'belonging to a party to the conflict' states that it is essential that there should be a *de facto* relationship between the resistance oganization and the party to the conflict. Most of the PMSCs fail to meet the above requirements, and therefore, would not be entitled to POW status under Article 4 of the third Geneva Convention.

Article 44 of Additional Protocol I specifies that any combatant, as defined in Article 43, who falls into the power of an adverse party shall be a POW. Article 43 states:

> 1. The armed forces of a Party to the conflict consist of all organized armed forces, groups and units which are under a command responsible to that Party for the conduct of its subordinates, even if that Party is represented by a government or an authority not recognized by an adverse Party. Such armed forces shall be subject to an internal disciplinary system which, *inter alia*, shall enforce compliance with the rules of international law applicable in armed conflict.
>
> 2. Members of the armed forces of a Party to the conflict (other than medical personnel and chaplains) are combatants, that is to say, they have the right to participate directly in hostilities.
>
> 3. Whenever a Party to the conflict incorporates a paramilitary or armed law enforcement agency into its armed forces it shall so notify the other Parties to the conflict.

The main change in the AP I definition of combatant from the 1949 Geneva Convention is that there is no longer a difference, for the purposes of combatant status, between the regular armed forces and other armed groups. The combatants are, however, required to distinguish themselves from the civilians with some sort of external sign; where this is not possible, combatants must carry their arms openly during the preparation and commission of each military engagement. If they fail to do so, they will not be entitles to POW status. Since PMSCs do not belong to a Party to the conflict and its personnel are also not under the chain of command [responsible to a Party to the conflict], they are not entitled to POW status under the AP I.

The environment in which PMSCs currently operate has been called a "legal vacuum". The reason is that IHL does not directly provide for the use of force by non-state actors, including PMSCs. They carry out diverse array of functions in and around the conflict area which includes transportation, weapons training, equipment maintenance, intelligence gathering, and interrogation of prisoners. The breadth of these activities makes it increasingly difficult to distinguish PMSCs from ordinary soldiers, especially when battle lines are fluid and there are no clear 'front' separating warring parties.

Like ordinary soldiers, personnel of PMSCs bear arms and are associated, directly or indirectly, with a party to a conflict, and may find themselves on the battlefield alongside the army. The members of PMSCs are generally former soldiers who have either retired from a national force or have left it voluntarily to work for the private sector . Their military background and training make it easy for them to integrate with the soldiers they are hired to support, though soldier and contractors typically remain subject to distinct chains of command.

IHL provides that in international armed conflict, civilians accompanying the armed forces are entitled to POW status, if captured by the enemy. In an international armed conflict or occupation, only members of regular armed forces and paramilitary groups that come under military command and meet certain criteria (carry their weapons openlydistinguish themselves from civilians, and generally obey the laws of war) qualify as combatants. However, the status of armed PMSC personnel in such circumstances falls into a grey area. PMSC personnel would not be entitled to POW status as they remain outside the military chain of command.

In case of a non-international armed conflict within the meaning of common Article 3 (CA3), customary international law does not distinguish between 'unlawful' and 'lawful' combatants. Its protections extend to all persons who are not or are no longer participating in combatThe personnel of PMSCs captured by enemy forces who had participated in hostilities would be entitled to the minimum set of standards contained in CA3, but their right to engage in hostilities in the first place would be determined in accordance with the local law. CA 3 does not provide for POW status.

Accountability of PMSCs

There has been a lack of clear lines of accountability with PMSCs. As compared to PMSCs, the national armies are accountable domestically through the political process. Soldiers who commit war crimes together with their military commanders and political superiors who bear responsibility can be prosecuted in national courts or the International Criminal Court. It is doubtful that this liability under IHL would also be applicable to employees of PMSCs.A weak government which is dependent for its security on a PMSC may not be in a position to take such action. In practice, the extent of accountability of PMSCs may depend on who is employing them.

States bear the primary responsibility for ensuring that IHLis respected, and for punishing individuals who commit war crimes. In addition PMSCs operating in armed conflicts may attract legal liability if they are involved in wilful killing, torture or inhuman treatment and wilfully causing serious injury. States may exercise universal jurisdiction over such offenders under common Article 49(2)/50(2)/129(2)/146(2) of the four Geneva Conventions of 1949.

Moreover, IHL provides that commanders are to be held responsible not only for war crimes committed pursuant to their orders but also where they failed to prevent or punish their subordinates when they had reason to know that the same were about to commit or committed war crimes. This responsibility is applicable to both military and civilian superiors (Articles 86 and 87, theAP I; Article 28, the Rome Statute). Therefore, in the case of PMSCs forming part of the armed forces of a S tate party to the conflict, responsibility for violating IHL committed by PMSC employees can be attributed to his immediate superior as well as further up the chain of command.

Difference: Mercenary and PMSCs

Singer (2003) has distinguish mercenaries from PMSCs: (i)A mercenary is not a citizen of the state in which he or she is fighting; (ii)A mercenary is not integrated into any national force, and is bound only by contractual ties of a limited employee; (iii) A mercenary fights for individual short-term economic reward, not for political or religious goals; (iv) A mercenary is brought in by circuitous ways in order to avoid legal prosecution; (v) A mercenary usually functions in 'temporary and ad hoc ' groups, perhaps due to the black market nature of the business; and (vi) A mercenary's focus is only on 'combat service for single clients'[7]. The PMSCs, therefore, differ from mercenaries in that the or ganization of PMSCs is a prior corporate structure and their motives are driven by business profit rather than individual profit. The PMSCs are legal, public entities active in the open market and their services have a wider range and their clientele are varied. The recruitment of PMSCs is specialized and public and in terms of links, they have ties to corporate holdings and financial markets. PMSCs could be treated as unlawful combatants or unprivileged belligerents, even though their employment is not prohibited by international law . They do not qualify for POW treatment under the third Geneva Convention or the AP I. Because mercenaries are not entitled to combat immunity, they may be tried and if found guilty and punished for their hostile actions. However, in international conflicts, they would be entitled to 'fundamental guarantees' under Article 75 of the AP I.

The Montreux Document

In September 2008, one year after employees of Blackwater, a PMSC, killed 17 innocent civilians in Baghdad, seventeen states signed the "Montreux Document on Pertinent International Legal Obligations and Good Practices for States related to Operations of Private Military and Security Companies during Armed Conflict". The Document was the outcome of two years of consultations, initiated and led by the Swiss Government and the ICRC in response to the growing role of PMSCs in international conflicts. This document was developed with the participation of governmental experts from Afghanistan, Angola, Australia, Austria, Canada, China, France, Germany, Iraq, Poland, Sierra Leone, South Africa, Sweden, Switzerland, the UK, Ukraine, and the United States of America.

The Preface to the Montreux Document makes clear that it is 'not a legally binding instrument and does not afect existing obligations of states under customary international law'or treaty law, including the UNCharter. It clarifies that the Document 'should not be interpreted as limiting,

---

[7] Singer, P. W. 2003. *Corporate warriors: the rise of the priv atized military industry,* Ithaca: Cornell University Press.

prejudicing, or enhancing in any manner existing obligations under international law, or as creating or developing new obligations under international law'. The Document highlights the responsibilities of the contracting states (countries that hire PMSCs), territorial states (countries on whose territory PMSCs operate) and home states (countries in which PMSCs are based).

The Montreux Document states that "'PMSCs' are private business entities that provide military and/or security services, irrespective of how they describe themselves. Military and security services include, in particular, armed guarding and protection of persons and objects, such as convoys, buildings and other places; maintenance and operation of weapons systems; prisoner detention; and advice to or training of local forces and security personnel." It provides standards in the form of 73 'good practices', which provide practical regulation of PMSCs through contracts, codes of conduct, national legislation, regional instruments and international standards. These good practices address issues as diverse as regulation of PMSCs' use of force, direct participation in hostilities, vetting and training of their personnel, accountability obligations and immunities from foreign jurisdiction. Some of the good practices (GP) listed in the Document for Contracting States are:

- To establish a transparent procedure for the selection and contracting of PMSCs and ensure that it is properly supervised [GP 2 and 4].
- To adopt quality control for the selection of PMSCs that are relevant to ensuring respect for IHL and human rights law [GP 5].
- To select PMSCs based on past conduct; possession of required authorizations; personnel and property records; adequate training in IHL and human rights law; lawful acquisition and use of equipment (including weapons) [GP 6-12].
- To include in the contract an obligation to comply with the selection criteria and specifically require respect for IHL also by subcontractors [GP 14, 15]. The terms of the contract should also oblige contracted PMSCs to ensure that PMSC personnel are personally identifiable when carrying out their activities [GP 16].

Paragraph 22 of the Document states the obligation of PMSCs and their personnel to comply with national law , including IHL and human rights obligations incorporated into national law Paragraph 23 affirms that the personnel of PMSCs are obliged to respect the law of both the territorial state and, as far as applicable, the state of their nationality . Paragraph 26 clarifies certain additional matters for PMSC personnel.They are (a) directly obligated by the rules of IHL; (b) protected as civilians under IHL, unless they lose that protection as provided for by IHL; (c) in certain circumstances entitled to prisoner of war status; (d) obliged to comply with states' IHL obligations, if they exercise governmental authority; and (e) subject to prosecution for the commission of crimes under national or international law. Paragraph 27 addresses superior responsibility . It states that the superiors of PMSC personnel can be prosecuted for the most serious crimes (war crimes, torture etc. under international law) not only if they commit these themselves, but also if, as superiors, they fail to prevent or put an end to crimes committed by their subordinates. This provision sidesteps the question of the nature of the knowledge and intent a superior must possess in order for his her responsibility to be triggered, by stating that superior responsibility arises 'in accordance with the rules of international law'.

The Montreux Document also contains an affirmation that the human rights which the PMSCs and States must protect, extends to the human rights of workers in the industry as protected by labour laws.The Document has been considered useful because it enhances the protection afforded to people affected by armed conflicts. A number of States including the US, UK,[8] China, Iraq, Afghanistan, and others, have endorsed the Montreux Document. However, it is felt that the Document may provide States with a

---

[8] Up to 80 per cent of all PMSCs worldwide are said to be registered in the UK and the US. Though the first British PMSCs were registered in 1967, the UK developed a private defence industry mainly in the mid-1980s. The UK Government does not have any register for the PMSCs. However, there are about 40 UK-based large PMSCs which operate internationally. Of them, 21 companies are permanent or provisional members of the British Association for Private Security Companies and only 4 or 5 companies are regularly contracted by the UK Government. Others are contracted by foreign government agencies (the US, the UAE, Saudi Arabia, Algeria, Nigeria, and other countries), and sometimes by international organizations (including the United Nations), as well as by non-governmental contractors in the business sector. At present, there is no special registration system for private military security companies in the United Kingdom. The registration of PMSCs follows the same rules as the registration of any British company. The United Kingdom Government is yet to follow the guiding principles contained in the Montreux Document. Nikitin Alexander, Chairperson-

fig-leaf to hide the absence of more rigorous efforts to regulate this industry improve its standards, and ensure accountability for human rights and IHL.

PMSCs and UN Peacekeeping

There are views that the use of PMSCs may offer a solution for the UN peacekeeping operations. The UN has been plagued by delay or inaction in responding to crises with properly trained and disciplined military forces as governments have been reluctant or unable to contribute their forces for controversial commitments. Misconduct by some UN peacekeeping forces, including rape, child prostitution and human rights abuses has also been reported. It is felt that well-trained and disciplined PMSCs might be deployed faster and for substantially less cost than military forces provided by governments.

The PMSCs have been used extensively in a variety of peacekeeping operations to provide logistical and support services. The US and the British governments, reserve the right to use PMSCs in its Memorandum of Understanding with the UN Department of Peacekeeping Operations to provide some logistical functions. The British company, Defence Systems (DSL) has provided local guards to UN peacekeepers in Angola in the past. The protection of humanitarian relief operations is considered part of peacekeeping responsibilities and is an area in which PMSCs are involved in large and growing numbers, mainly to perform security and policing functions.

In the cases of emergencies in a State, the international community can provide humanitarian assistance. If the host government is unable to provide a safe passage for the delivery of aid and the international community is reluctant to intervene militarily, the onus is on humanitarian agencies to be responsible for their security arrangements. The PMSCs may play an important role in providing safe passage for the delivery of aid material.

There is a possibility that in the near future the UN may have to rely on lean, non-hierarchical, and cost-effective organizations that are capable

Rapporteur: Report of the Working Group on the use of mercenaries as a means of violating human rights and impeding the exercise of the right of peoples to self-determination; Mission to the United Kingdom of Great Britain and Northern Ireland (26-30 May 2008); Human Rights Council Tenth session Agenda item 3. A/HRC/10/14/Add.2 dated 19 February 2009.

of executing quick, agile and flexible field operations. These operations may range from security services, logistical support, humanitarian assistance, counter drug operations, counterinsugency and limited combat actions. Further, they may also include military training and assistance, intelligence gathering, threat analysis and counter cyber warfare operations. The PMSCs can meet these demands.They could be an attractive alternative to provide a more cost-ef fective way of providing the same number of personnel because of their lean organizational structure and their limited overhead costs compared to State's armed forces.

Even if it became feasible to use PMSCs in a given instance, it is highly unlikely that the UN Department of Peacekeeping Operations would recommend their use to S tates. One of the reasons is that the PMSC personnel are involved in foreign conflicts for essentially financial gain and are considered mercenaries in the traditional sense. The UN has repeatedly condemned the use of mercenaries and there is an International Convention against the Recruitment, Use, Financing and Training of Mercenaries.

According to IHL, mercenaries are civilians taking part in hostilities without being members of the armed forces of parties to the conflict. The Rome Statute of the ICC does not include the crime of mercenarism within its jurisdiction. A mercenary could be penalized by a S tate Party to the Mercenary Convention for taking part in hostilities as a civilian. Some authors have called PMSCs modernized mercenaries and are of the view that PMSCs operate in a legal vacuum. In particular, a former UN Special Rapporteur of the UN Commission on Human Rights on the Effects of the Use of Mercenaries has ar gued that there is no fundamental difference between PMSCs and mercenaries. The growth of the PMSC sector has been accompanied by rising concern about the role of private economic interest in military affairs. In contrast with mercenaries who operate in hiding, PMSCs have established offices and some of them follow internal good practices to abide by international law . The Montreux Document addresses substantive legal concerns, such as the status of PMSC personnel under the 1949 Geneva Conventions, individual accountability for misconduct in different jurisdictions, and the authorities' duty to oversee and screen the actions of firms for potential misconduct.The Document is useful because it enhances the protection af forded to people af fected by armed conflicts. It does so by clarifying and reaffirming international law, by encouraging the adoption of national regulations on PMSCs designed to strengthen respect for international law, and by offering guidance on how and in what light this should be done, based on lessons learnt.

CHAPTER 17

International Committee of the Red Cross

Introduction

Henry Dunant, in his book *A Memory of Sulferino,* has vividly described the suffering of victims of war witnessed by him in 1859. [1] The battle between the Austrian army and the French and allied forces was fought by more than 200,000 soldiers. It resulted in more than 6000 soldiers being killed, over 20,000 wounded and 5000 captured or missingThis experience changed Dunant's life and his business activities became secondary . His concerted efforts led to the adoption of a 10-article Geneva Convention in 1864, [2] the progenitor of modern IHL. Today, almost 150 years later, IHL has developed considerably , and the or ganization started by him—the International Committee of the Red Cross (ICRC)—enormouslyThe ICRC has grown into a universal movement and is present in over 80 countries through delegations, offices and missions, duly supported by millions of volunteers.

The International Red Cross and Red Crescent Movement

Today, the International Red Cross and Red Crescent Movement is the largest humanitarian network in the world. The components of the

---

1 Henry Dunant in his book, "A Memory of Solferino" made two solemn appeals: (i) for relief societies to be formed in peace-time, wth zealous, devoted and thoroughly qualified volunteers who would be ready to carefor the wounded in war time; and (ii) for these volunteers, who would be called upon to assist the army medical services, to be recognized and protected through an international agreement.

2 The text of the 1864 Genea Convention please refer to Chapter 1 of the book. It was on the ICRC's initiative that the States adopted the Genev a Convention of 1864. Since then, the ICRC, with the support of the Red Cross and Red Crescent Movement, has constantly urged governments to respect IHL to changing circumstances, so as to pro vide more effective protection and assistance to the victims of armed conflict.

Movement are:

- The International Committee of the Red Cross (ICRC), founded in 1863 in Geneva.
- The International Federation of Red Cross and Red Crescent Societies (IFRC), founded in 1919, having its secretariat at Geneva. It coordinates activities between the National Red Cross and Red Crescent Societies.
- National Red Cross and Red Crescent Societies formed in nearly every country in the world. Presently there are nearly 186 National Societies recognized by the ICRC and admitted as full members of the Federation.

The three institutions together constitute a worldwide humanitarian movement. Its mission is to prevent and alleviate human suffering wherever it may be found; to protect life and health and ensure respect for the human being, in particular in times of armed conflict and other emer gencies; to work for the prevention of disease and for the promotion of health and social welfare; to encourage voluntary service and a constant readiness to give help by the members of the Movement, and a universal sense of solidarity towards all those in need of its protection and assistance.[3]

Fundamental Principles of the Movement

Although each of the Red Cross and Red Crescent Movements' components engages in different activities, they are all united by the same fundamental principles. These principles are fixed in the Preamble of the Statute of the Red Cross and Red Crescent Movement and reaffirm that, in pursuing its mission, the Movement shall be guided by the following fundamental principles: [4]

---

[3] Preamble to the Statutes of the International Red Cross and Red Crescent Movement, adopted by the 25th International Confe rence of the Red Cross at Genev a in October 1986 and amended by the 26th International Conference of the Red Cross and Red Crescent at Geneva in December 1995 and by the 29th International Confe rence of the Red Cr oss and Red Crescent at Geneva in June 2006.

[4] Available at: http://www .icrc.org/eng/resources/documents/misc/fundamental-principles-commentary-010179.htm.

Humanity: The International Red Cross and Red Crescent Movement, born of a desire to bring assistance without discrimination to the wounded on the battlefield, endeavors, in its international and national capacity, to prevent and alleviate human sufering wherever it may be found. Its purpose is to protect life and health and to ensure respect for the human being. It promotes mutual understanding, friendship, cooperation and lasting peace amongst all peoples.

Impartiality: It makes no discrimination as to nationality , race, religious beliefs, class or political opinions. It endeavours to relieve the suffering of individuals, being guided solely by their needs, and to give priority to the most urgent cases of distress.

Neutrality: In order to continue to enjoy the confidence of all, the Movement may not take sides in hostilities or engage at any time in controversies of a political, racial, religious or ideological nature.

Independence: The Movement is independent.The National Societies, while auxiliaries in the humanitarian services of their governments and subject to the laws of their respective countries, must always maintain their autonomy so that they may be able at all times to act in accordance with the principles of the Movement.

Voluntary Service: It is a voluntary relief movement not prompted in any manner by desire for gain.

Unity: There can be only one Red Cross or one Red Crescent Society in any one country . It must be open to all. It must carry on its humanitarian work throughout its territory.

Universality: The International Red Cross and Red Crescent Movement, in which all Societies have equal status and share equal responsibilities and duties in helping each other, is worldwide.

The first principle 'humanity' is the greatest principle and the motivating force and ideal of the Red Cross MovementAll other principles represent the means of achieving this aim. The principles of voluntary service, unity and universality are relevant mainly for the internal functioning of the Red Cross Movement, the other principles – humanity, impartiality, neutrality and independence provide the basis for discussion of the ethical framework of humanitarian action in general.

International Committee of the Red Cross (ICRC)

The ICRC is an independent and neutral organization. Its work is based on the Geneva Conventions of 1949, their Additional Protocols, its Statutes – and those of the International Red Cross and Red Crescent Movement – and the resolutions of the International Conferences of the Red Cross and Red Crescent. The ICRC is governed by an Assembly, an Assembly Council and a Directorate, which functions as the executive body The Assembly is the supreme governing body of the ICRC. It oversees all the ICRC's activities. The members of the ICRC Directorate are appointed by the Assembly for four-year terms.

As the founding institution of the Movement, the ICRC has certain statutory responsibilities towards the other components. In particular, it is responsible for ensuring respect for and promoting knowledge of the Fundamental Principles; recognizing new National Red Cross or Red Crescent Societies that meet the conditions for recognition; and discharging the mandates entrusted to it by the International Conference of the Red Cross and Red Crescent. The ICRC is actively involved in the International Conference of the Red Cross and Red Crescent. National Societies in their own country and the ICRC both have the mandate to assist the victims of armed conflicts. National Societies are the main operational partners of the ICRC, particularly in the fields of medical and relief assistance and restoring family links.

Mission and Role

The mission of the ICRC is defined in the following term:[5]

- The ICRC is an impartial, neutral and independent organization whose exclusively humanitarian mission is to protect the lives and dignity of victims of armed conflict and other situations of violence and to provide them with assistance.
- The ICRC also endeavours to prevent suffering by promoting and strengthening humanitarian law and universal humanitarian

[5] The International Committee of the Red Cross: Its Mission and Work, *International Review of the Red Cross*, Vol. 91, No. 874, p. 400.

principles.

- Established in 1863, the ICRC is at the origin of the Geneva Conventions and the International Red Cross and Red Crescent Movement. It directs and coordinates the international activities conducted by the Movement in armed conflicts and other situations of violence.

The role of the ICRC, in accordance with its Statute is as follows:[6]

(a) to maintain and disseminate the Fundamental Principles of the Movement, namely humanity , impartiality , neutrality , independence, voluntary service, unity and universality;

(b) to recognize any newly established or reconstituted National Society, which fulfils the conditions for recognition set out in Article 4, and to notify other National Societies of such recognition;

(c) to undertake the tasks incumbent upon it under the Geneva Conventions, to work for the faithful application of international humanitarian law applicable in armed conflicts and to take cognizance of any complaints based on alleged breaches of that law;

(d) to endeavour at all times – as a neutral institution whose humanitarian work is carried out particularly in time of international and other armed conflicts or internal strife – to ensure the protection of and assistance to military and civilian victims of such events and of their direct results;

(e) to ensure the operation of the Central Tracing Agency as provided in the Geneva Conventions;

(f) to contribute, in anticipation of armed conflicts, to the training of medical personnel and the preparation of medical equipment, in cooperation with the National Societies, the military and civilian medical services and other competent authorities;

(g) to work for the understanding and dissemination of knowledge of

[6] Article 4, Statute of the International Committee of the Red Cross.

international humanitarian law applicable in armed conflicts and to prepare any development thereof;

(h) to carry out mandates entrusted to it by the International Conference.

The ICRC may take any humanitarian initiative which comes within its role as a specifically neutral and independent institution and intermediary and may consider any question requiring examination by such an institution.

The Legal Basis of the ICRC's Actions

The main legal basis for the ICRC's work is to be found in IHL. The four Geneva Conventions of 1949 andAdditional Protocol I confer on the ICRC a specific mandate to act in the event of international armed conflict.[7] The ICRC has the right to visit prisoners of war and civilian internees. In non-international armed conflicts, the ICRC enjoys a right of humanitarian initiative recognized by the international community and enshrined inArticle 3 common to the four Geneva Conventions. In the event of internal disturbances and tensions, the ICRC also has a right of initiative, which is recognized in the Statute of the International Red Cross and Red Crescent Movement. Therefore, in situations where IHL does not apply, the ICRC may offer its services to governments without interfering in the internal affairs of the State concerned.

Activities of the ICRC

The main activity of the ICRC is to provide general protection to persons in situations of armed conflict. It therefore seeks to: minimize dangers to which people are exposed; prevent and put an end to violations of the law to which persons are subjected; draw attention to their rights and make their voices heard; and bring them assistance. Some of the activities of the ICRC are as follows.

---

[7] All of the world's 194 States are party to the four Geneva Conventions of 1949; 168 and 164 States are parties to 1977 Additional Protocol I and II respectively In addition, 41 countries have ratified or acceded to Additional Protocol III. 71 States are party to Article 90 of Additional Protocol I which provides for the establishment of an International Fact-Finding Commission to enquire into allegations of serious violations of humanitarian law. Information as of 10 May 2010. Harland Christopher 2010. *Basic Documents on International Humanitarian Law: South Asia Collection*, New Delhi: ICRC, p. 1123-1128.

A. Protection

The ICRC has adopted a protection approach to ensure preservation of life, security, dignity and physical and mental well-being of people affected by armed conflict. It also tries to prevent the possible violations of IHL. The person likely to benefit from the programme are (i) the people deprived of their freedom, (ii) resident and displaced civilians, (iii) people separated from their relatives because of conflict or natural disasters, and (iv) missing people and their families.

The objective of the ICRC in respect of persons deprived of their freedom is to ensure that their physical and mental integrity is fully respected and that the conditions of detention are in accordance with international standards. The ICRC strives to prevent forced disappearances or extrajudicial executions, ill-treatment and failure to respect fundamental judicial guarantees, and, whenever necessary , takes action to improve conditions of detention. The visits to places of detention are carried out by the ICRC in accordance with the following conditions: (i) delegates must be provided with full and unimpeded access to all detainees falling within the ICRC's mandate, (ii) visit must be allowed to all places of detention, (iii) delegates must be able to hold private interviews with the detainees of their choice, (iv) delegates must be able to repeat their visits, and (v) detainees falling within the ICRC's mandate must be notified by name to the ICRC, and it must be able to draw up lists of their names.

Protection for the civilians is intended to ensure that individuals no longer taking a direct part in hostilities are fully respected and protected. The ICRC may engage in dialogue with the relevant parties to conflict to discuss humanitarian issues and to remind them of their legal obligations. In order to restore family links or maintain contact between members of families, including people deprived of their freedom, the ICRC may use radio broadcasts, the telephone and the Internet via the worldwide Red Cross and Red Crescent network. It may also issue travel documents to people who, owing to a conflict, do not have identity papers and are about to be repatriated or resettled in a third country.

B. Assistance

The aim of assistance is to preserve life and restore the dignity of individuals or communities adversely affected by an armed conflict or other situation of violence. Assistance activities enable them to maintain an adequate standard of living in their respective social and cultural context until their basic needs are met by the authorities or through their own means. The assistance programmes include providing people in need with the goods and services essential for their survival, provision of drinking water,health related services, curative and preventative health interventions, and physical rehabilitation of persons with disabilities to ensure their full participation and inclusion in society. The ICRC's physical rehabilitation projects aim to allow the disabled to participate fully in society , both during and after the period of assistance.

Finally, the ICRC acts as lead coordinating agency the international relief operations conducted by the Red Cross and Red Crescent in situations of armed conflict, internal strife and disasters. Some of the protection and assistance activities undertaken by the ICRC in 2009 are as follows.[8]

- The ICRC delegates visited nearly 480,000 detainees, held in 1,890 places of detention in 74 countries. Of this 28,170 detainees (2,425 women; 1,486 minors) were registered and visited for the first time in 2009. With support provided by the ICRC, nearly 28,100 detainees benefited from family visits.
- Nearly 933,000 peoplecontacted ICRC offices in 2009 for services or advice related to protection and family linksThe ICRC collected about 254,000 and distributed nearly 255,000 Red Cross messages, to members of families separated as a result of armed conflict, disturbances or tensions to exchange news in the year 2009.
- The ICRC registered about 3,000 unaccompanied/separated children, including 656 demobilized children during 2009. Once their families had been located and with the agreement of the children and their relatives, it organized the reunification of 1,025 children with their families. By the end of the 2009, the cases of about 1,700 unaccompanied or separated children were still being handled, which involved tracing their relatives, maintaining contacts between the children and their families, or ganizing family

[8] ICRC Annual Report: 2009, Geneva: International Committee of the Red Cross.

reunification and/or identifying another long-term solution for the children concerned.

- The ICRC has undertaken assistance programmes in 47 countries, specifically in Afghanistan, Chad, Cote d'Ivoire, the Democratic Republic of the Congo, Geor gia, Iraq, Israel and the occupied Palestinian territory, Pakistan, the Philippines, the Russian Federation, Sri Lanka, Somalia, Sudan, Uganda and Zimbabwe.
- The assistance programme included the supply of items like food, seed, essential household goods, medical and physical rehabilitation material, and water . More than 4,068,000 internally displaced persons (IDPs), returnees, and people living in rural/difficult areas received aid in the form of food and essential household and hygiene items.
- Besides providing necessary help to 268 hospitals and 373 other healthcare facilities, the ICRC also supported various first-aid posts located near combat zones, providing emergency treatment for weapon-wounded patients. The ICRC's physical rehabilitation technicians provided support in 23 countries, enabling about 183,000 patients to receive services and care.
- The ICRC's forensic services supported field operations in more than 40 countries to help prevent and resolve cases of missing persons, including in emergencies. Activities consisted mainly of promoting and supporting the implementation of forensic best practice for the proper and dignified recovery , management and identification of human remains in armed conflict, other situations of violence and natural disaster.

C. Prevention

The aim of prevention is to foster an environment that is conducive to respect for the life and dignity of those af fected by an armed conflict or other situation of violence.The prevention activities have medium- to long-term effect and relate to communicating, developing, clarifying and promoting implementation of IHL and acceptance of the ICRC's work.

Implementation activities aim to promote the universal ratification of IHL treaties and to foster compliance with IHL during armed conflicts. It also ensures that the national authorities, the armed forces and other bearers of weapons correctly understand the law. This involves (i) promoting IHL treaties among the authorities by making representations to governments, (ii) drafting technical documents and guidelines to further national implementation, (iii) providing technical advice and support for translating texts and materials of IHLinto different national languages, (iv) encouraging and helping authorities to integrate IHL into the military doctrine, (vi) education and training of national armed, police and security forces, (v) providing training in IHL to non-governmental sector , and (vi) devising training and education programmes for future leaders and opinion-makers in universities and schools.

The ICRC furthers the development of customary IHL by assessing State practice. This involves (i) monitoring new developments, carrying out studies, organizing meetings of experts and drafting proposals, and (ii) in taking part in meetings of experts and diplomatic conferences held to develop new treaties or other legal instruments, and formulating bilateral and multilateral initiatives to promote their acceptance by governments and relevant organizations. The ICRC maintains links with academic circles to consolidate a network of IHL experts and develops partnerships with institutes and research centres specializing in IHL. It also produces print, audio-visual and web-based communication materials to support and communicate the ICRC's activities.The ICRC promotes measures to restrict or prohibit the use of weapons that have indiscriminate ef fects or cause superfluous injury or unnecessary suf fering. This includes faithful implementation of treaties such as the Mine Ban Convention and the Convention on Certain Conventional Weapons.

D. Other Responsibilities

As the founding institution of the Movement, the ICRC has statutory responsibilities towards the other components. It is responsible for ensuring respect for and promoting knowledge of the fundamental principles; recognizing new national Red Cross or Red Crescent societies and discharging the mandates entrusted to it by the International Conference of the Red Cross and Red Crescent. National societies in their country and the ICRC both have the mandate to assist the victims of armed conflicts, particularly in providing medical and relief assistance and restoring family links.

The ICRC contributes to the development of National Red Cross and Red Crescent Societies in the following areas: dissemination, promotion and implementation of IHL; in the event of armed conflict and other situations of violence, evacuation and care of the wounded; relief assistance; restoring family links; mine action including risk reduction and victim assistance; technical and legal assistance in establishing and reconstituting national societies; revision of national society statutes; and supporting national societies in their efforts to adhere to the Fundamental Principles.

In 2009, the ICRC published 'Interpretive Guidance on the Notion of Direct Participation in Hostilities under International Humanitarian Law'. The Guidance sets out the ICRC' s recommendations as to how existing IHL relating to civilian participation in hostilities should be interpreted in contemporary armed conflicts. Its primary purpose is to enhance the civilian population's protection against erroneous or arbitrary targeting. It does so by clarifying the generic distinction between civilians and combatants, as well as between civilians who are and those who are not "directly participating in hostilities".

E. Confidentiality in Functioning

The ICRC maintains confidentiality in its functioning. It enables the ICRC to build trust and help people af fected by insecurity, violence and armed conflict. In situations where ICRC delegates observe cases of abuse or neglect; they take up the matter directly with the concerns authorities or other parties to the conflict. However, the ICRC reserves the right to publish its findings in exceptional cases. For example, if an authority issues excerpts from one of its confidential reports without consent, the ICRC reserve the right to publish the entire report in order to prevent any inaccurate or incomplete interpretations of its observations and recommendations.

Action in the Event ofViolation of IHL: In order to dischage its mandate 'to promote the application of IHL and to protect and assist civilian and military victims of armed conflict', the ICRC adopted guidelines in 1981. The guidelines have been reviewed recently and the ICRC takes following action in the event of violation of IHL.[9]

---

[9] Action by the International Committee of the Red Cross in the event of violations of international humanitarian law or of other fundamental rules protecting persons in situations of violence, *International Review of the Red Cross*, Vol. 87, No. 858, June 2005, p.393-400.

(a) General rule: The ICRC shall take appropriate steps to put an end to violations of IHL or of other fundamental rules protecting the persons in situations of violence, or to prevent the occurrence of such violations. These steps are taken at various levels and through various modes of action, according to the nature and the extent of the violations.

(b) Principle mode of action-bilateral and confidential representations: The ICRC will confidentially approach the representatives of the parties concerned directly responsible for the violation. Confidentiality brings in an atmosphere of trust to finding solutions and avoids the risk of politicization of the debate.

(c) Subsidiary modes of action: In case the ICRC is unable to improve the situation in humanitarian terms and bring greater respect for the law through bilateral confidential representations, it reserves the right to have recourse to other modes of action.

(i) Humanitarian Mobilization: The ICRC may share its concerns about violations of IHL with governments of third countries, with international or regional or ganizations, or with persons that are in a position to support its representations to influence the behaviour of parties to a conflict. Howeverthe ICRC takes such steps only when it has every reason to believe that the third parties approached will respect the confidential nature of its representations to them.Common Article 1 of the four Geneva Conventions and Article 1 of the AP I requires States that are not party to an armed conflict to strive to ensure respect for the law by taking every possible measure to put an end to violations of the law by a party to a conflict.

(ii) Public declaration: The ICRC may publicly express its concern about the quality of its bilateral confidential dialogue with a party to a conflict, or about the quality of the response given to its recommendations regarding a specific humanitarian problem. This mode of action, i.e., public declaration, is aimed at strengthening the impact of the ICRC's bilateral and confidential dialogue with a party to a conflict when that dialogue is not having the desired results on the issues raised in the ICRC's representations.

(iii) Public condemnation: The ICRC reserves the right to issue a public condemnation of specific violations of IHL providing the following conditions are met: (*i*) the violations are major and repeated or likely to be repeated; (*ii*) delegates have witnessed the violations with their own eyes, or the existence and extent of those violations have been established on the basis of reliable and verifiable sources; (*iii*) bilateral confidential representations and humanitarian mobilization efforts have failed to put an end to the violations; and (*iv*) such publicity is in the interest of the persons or populations affected or threatened. The ICRC takes recourse to this measure only when it has exhausted every other reasonable means. However such exceptional measures may be taken only when all of the four above-mentioned conditions have been met.

The ICRC does not provide testimony or confidential documents in connection with investigations or legal proceedings relating to specific violations. The ICRC does not act as a commission of inquiry and does not take part in an inquiry procedure. However , if solicited by one or more parties to a conflict, the ICRC may encourage them to appeal to the International Fact-Finding Commission or may offer its good offices to set up a commission of inquiry and may propose non-ICRC persons who are qualified to be part of such a commission.

ICRC Staff Security

In the present day conflict, particularly the non-international, there is a blurring of lines between political, military and humanitarian action. This casts doubt on the neutrality of humanitarian work and increases the risk to its workers. At times the politically motivated violence is more specifically targeted against the aid workers. These acts of violence demonstrate the unwillingness of a party to conflict to accept a humanitarian organization. The number of ICRC staf working in the field and the volume of operations conducted by the or ganization has constantly increased in recent years. Presently the ICRC maintains a permanent presence in over 60 countries and conducts operations in 80 with nearly 12,500 employees, 1550 expatriates and 11,000 national staff.[10]

The staff of the ICRC has also been subjected to threat and violence. For instance, in January 2009, three ICRC staff members, though later released, were taken hostage in the Philippines. The incident has prompted the ICRC to focus even more on the safety and security of its personnel and field activities. The ICRC's security management model is based on decentralized initiative, decision-making and responsibility for field security: the head of delegation decides on and implements the measures required by the general environment and the context in which the delegation works. The security and stress unit plays an advisory role. The field staffs exercise this extensive autonomy within a clearly defined institutional framework that has three components: the ICRC's mandate, its principles and its security concept.

In the field, each delegation assesses its security environment in light of the current situation and on the basis of the or ganization's frame of reference, the seven 'pillars of security'. These are:

- Acceptance: To be able to operate, the ICRC must first ensure that it is accepted by the parties to a conflict. They will accept ICRC's its presence and working procedures, as its role is exclusively humanitarian, it works as an independent and impartial organization.
- Identification: Once its special role has been accepted, the ICRC must be uniquely identifiable. Identification is based on the use of the Red Cross, Red Crescent or Red Crystal emblemTo distinguish itself from other humanitarian agencies, the ICRC uses a logo consisting of a red cross surrounded by two concentric black circles between which appear the words "COMITE INTERNA TIONAL GENEVE". The ICRC vehicles and buildings are marked with a protective sign or logo of appropriate size; flags are used in sensitive situation to attract special attention.
- Information: Information is a fundamental element of security . Internal information is monitored by the head of delegation or by the person designated by him.The head of delegation is responsible for circulating general information and organizing exchanges of

---

[10] Brugger Patrick, ICRC operational security: staff safety in armed conflct and internal violence, *International Review of the Red Cross*, Vol. 91, No. 874, June 2009), p. 431-445.

information both within the delegation and among locally hired staff, National Society personnel participating in an operation and seconded staff. All security incidents are analyzed so as to establish to what extent, if any , the delegates' conduct was a contributory factor.

- Security regulations: The security regulations for expatriate staf f are drawn up under the authority of the head of delegation and are specific to each country . Based on the analysis of the situation, they lay down appropriate rules and procedures designed to take account of the dangers and risks. These are reviewed on a regular basis. The head of delegation is responsible for ensuring compliance with the regulations; violations are penalized and, if serious, can result in the staff member's return to headquarters or dismissal.

- Personality: The quality of a staf f member is determined by the person's character and level of resilience. Staff members must be professionally competent and believe in the oganization's mission. They must also display certain fundamental traits, in particular a sense of responsibility and solidarity . The safety of the ICRC' s field activities depends on the personal attributes of each staf f member. In dangerous or threatening situations, the security of several individuals may depend on one person's reactions, attitude and ability to gauge a situation, in particular when that person is a hierarchical superior.

- Communication: Effective telecommunication equipment and networks are a key component of security in the field. The ICRC staff can choose from a wide range of technological telecommunication aids: HF and VHF radio systems, fixed and mobile telephones, satellites and computer networks.

- Protective measures: Additional protective measures in the form of alarm, security guard, physical barriers, reinforced building, etc., can be used to strengthen the other pillars of security . Armed protection must be avoided.

The ICRC's expatriate and locally hired staff is employed on the basis of their expressed willingness to accept an inevitable degree of risk. Security training is intended for expatriate and delegation employees taking into account the specific risks each person faces, and is adapted to their actual tasks and duties.Training takes place at headquarters and in the delegations and involves self-learning. The ultimate goal is to improve security arrangements, while drawing each participant' s attention to the limits of the ICRC's mandate, so as to prevent staf f from taking risks that would overstep those Limits.

The Emblem

There are three distinctive emblems: the Red Cross, Red Crescent and Red Crystal. The Red Cross emblem was oficially approved in Geneva in 1863, the same year ICRC was founded. The emblem is based on the Swiss flag with colors reversed.[11]

During the Russo-Turkish War of 1876-1878, the Ottoman Empire,[12] declared that while respecting the red cross sign protecting the ambulances of enemy armies, it would thenceforth use the red crescent on a white ground to mark its own ambulances,.The unilateral declaration generated exchange of correspondence between the Ottoman Empire, Switzerland, and the other States Parties. Ultimately , the Red Crescent sign was accepted only temporarily, for the duration of the conflict under way . During the 1899 and 1907 Hague Peace Conferences and the 1906 Geneva Revision Conference, the delegations of the Ottoman Empire, Persia and Siam requested recognition of particular signs for identification of their ambulances and hospital ships: the Red Crescent for the Ottoman Empire, the red lion and sun for Persia, and the red flame for Siam. In order to emphasize that the protective emblem (Red Cross) had no religious

---

[11] The sign of Red Cross on a white background originated in the International Conference in Geneva in 1863, and laid the f oundations of the Red Cr oss Movement. The Diplomatic Conference in 1864, which drew up the FirstGeneva Convention, officially adopted the Red Cross on white backgr ound as a single distinctiv e emblem for all armed f orces medical personnel, and for military hospitals and ambulances. It was adopted to facilitate access of relief workers to the wounded and sick soldiers who were horse de combat, and other victims of war so that humanitarian re lief and assistance could reach them. The 1906 Conference, which revised the Convention, stated that the emblem was adopted as a tribute to Switzerland, and was formed by reversing the Swiss Federal Flag colors. The four Geneva Conventions of 1949 which now form the basis of IHL retained this emblem as the distinctive sign of the Medical Services of the Armed Forces. F or details see: Articles 38-44, GC I; Articles 41-45 GC II, Article 18, GC IV Articles 18 and 38, AP I, Article 12, AP II and AP III.

[12] It had acceded to the Geneva Convention of 1864 without any reservation.

significance, the 1906 Conference adopted new resolution stating that the emblem had been devised by reversing the Swiss federal colours.

In 1929, when the Geneva Convention came for revision in order to incorporate the lessons of the First World War, the Turkish, Persian and Egyptian delegates insisted that the emblems of the Red Crescent and the Red Lion and Sun be recognized, emphasizing that those emblems had been used in practice without giving rise to any objection. The resolution acceded to the request and Article 19 of the Geneva Convention of 27 July 1929, incorporated the Red Crescent and the Red Lion and Sun on a white ground as a distinctive sign, while proclaiming that no similar requests would be accepted in the future.[13]

In the Diplomatic Conference convened in 1949 to revise the Geneva Conventions in the aftermath of the Second World War, the Israel proposed for the recognition of a new emblem, the Red Shield of David, which was used as the distinctive sign of the Israeli armed forces medical services. The Israeli delegate explained about the historical, cultural and symbolic significance of the Red Shield of David. He pointed out that this sign had been used for almost 20 years by the Israeli relief society the Magen David Adom (Red Shield of David), and had been used as the distinctive sign of the Israeli armed forces medical services during the recent Palestine conflict. The Israeli proposal was eventually rejected by a single vote. During the Diplomatic Conference on the Reaffirmation and Development of IHL (1974-1977), Israel made another unsuccessful attempt for recognition of the sign of the Red Shield of David.

In 1992, Mr Sommaruga, President of ICRC advocated for the adoption of an additional emblem, devoid of any national, religious or political connotation, which would be available to States and national societies unable to adopt either of the existing emblems. In the ICRC's opinion, the adoption of an additional distinctive sign and its recognition alongside the Red Cross

---

13 In 1980, the Islamic Republic of Iran declared that it was waiving its right to use of the red lion and sun and would thenceforth use the red crescent as the distinctive sign of its armed forces medical services, while reserving the right to return to the red lion and sun should new emblems be recognized. More than a quarter of a century has now elapsed since the sign of the red lion and sun was last used. The Statutes of the Movement as revised in 1986 mention neither the emblem nor the name of the red lion and sun.

and Red Crescent was the most realistic way of settling the question of the emblem and of satisfying the aspirations of countries and national societies that could accept neither the Red Cross nor the Red Crescent.[14]

On 8 December 2005, partly in response to growing pressure to accommodate Magen David Adom as a full member of the Red Cross and Red Crescent movement, a new emblem, the Red Crystal, was adopted by Third Protocol Additional to the Geneva Conventions of 12 August 1949. The new emblem was designed to be easily recognizable. No country or national society is obliged to change their emblems, and none are obliged to use the new one; but all are required to respect it in the same manner as the other emblems. On 22 June 2006, along with its recognition of the Palestine Red Crescent Society (PRCS) and Magen DavidAdom, the ICRC announced the formal adoption in its statutes of the Red Crystal as a third official symbol. In the further discussions, the use of term 'emblem' or 'Red Cross' denotes all the three recognized emblems.

Under IHL (the four Geneva Conventions of 1949 and their three Additional Protocols of 1977 and 2005, Ottawa Convention on Anti-personnel Landmines, UN Convention on Certain Conventional Weapons etc), the 'distinctive emblem' signifies the protected status of the armed forces medical services, when they are engaged in neutral and impartial humanitarian activities in situations of armed conflicts. The emblems are also used by national societies of the Red Cross and Red Crescent Movement for identification purposes. The Geneva Conventions and theirAdditional Protocols contain several articles on the emblems about the use, size, purpose and placing of the emblems, the persons and property they protect, who can use them, what respect for the emblems entails and the penalties for misuse. The Geneva Conventions and theirAdditional Protocols also require the State parties to enact legislation defining the use and preventing the misuse of the emblems on the national level.

Use of Emblem

There are two main uses of the emblems: the "protective use" and the "indicative use".[15] In protective use the emblems are used as visible sign in armed conflict to provide the protection to the medical services, equipment

[14] Bugnion Francois. 2007. *Red Cross, Red Crescent, Red Crystal*, Geneva: ICRC, p. 38.

and buildings of the armed forces under international law. That protection also extends to certain humanitarian or ganizations working alongside the military to relieve the suf fering of the wounded, prisoners and civilians caught up in the conflict. In indicative use, the National Red Cross and Red Crescent Societies around the world are allowed to use the emblems to identify themselves as part of a global network known as the International Red Cross and Red Crescent Movement.

Article 39 of the GC I, provides that under the direction of the competent military authority, the emblem shall be displayed on the flags, armlets and on all equipment employed in the Medical Service. The following personnel are to wear distinctive emblem afixed to the left arm; on a water-resistant armlet issued and stamped by the military authority:[16]

(i) Medical personnel exclusively engaged in the search, collection, transport or treatment of the wounded or sick (Article 24, GC I);

(ii) The staff of National Red Cross Societies and other Voluntary Aid Societies, duly recognized and authorized by their Governments, who may be employed on the same duties as the personnel under Article 24 (Article 26, GC I);

(iii) The members of a recognized society of a neutral country lending the assistance of its medical personnel and units to a Party to the conflict with the previous consent of its own Government and the authorization of the Party to the conflict concerned (Article 27, GC I).

The above mentioned personnel, in addition to wearing the identity disc (Article 16, GC I), shall also carry a special identity card bearing the distinctive emblem. These personnel cannot be deprived of insignia/identity cards or of the right to wear the armlet. In armed conflicts, the protective emblem must be in red on a white background with no additions. It must be clearly displayed in a lage format on protected buildings, such as hospitals,

---

[15] Article 44 of the First Geneva Convention makes the distinction between the protective use and the indicative use of the distinctive emblems. The emblem may be used for protective purposes during armed conflict only to identiy a limited number of persons and objects. The indicative use is primarily a peacetime use.

[16] Article 40, GC I.

and vehicles. Emblems on armbands and vests for protected personnel must also be clear and stand alone.A deliberate attack on a person, equipment or a building carrying a protective emblem is a war crime under international law.[17]

Protective use of the emblem is not restricted to medical and religious services of armed forces. The Fourth Geneva Convention (Article 18, para 3) mentions that, under certain strictly defined conditions, civilian hospitals and persons regularly and solely engaged in the operation and administration of these hospitals may also use the distinctive emblems.Additional Protocol I extends this list of civilian entities permitted to bear the emblem by granting the right to civilian medical and religious personnel, medical units and medical transportation.[18]

The authorized users of the emblem, thus, are: (i) The armed forces medical services, their personnel, units, installations and means of transport; (ii) ICRC; (iii) IFRC (International Federation of Red Cross & Red Crescent Societies); and (iv) National Red Cross Societies; and (v) First Aid Centers that offer totally free medical assistance and are authorized by the National Red Cross/Red Crescent Society. When the components of the Red Cross Movement use this emblem, it signifies the seven Fundamental Principles which underlie their humanitarian and relief activities in situations of armed conflicts and natural disasters.

In the indicative use, the national societies may in peacetime make use of the name and emblem for their activities other than assistance to the medical service of the armed forces. The indicative use is primarily a peacetime use. As an exceptional measure, in conformity with national legislation and with the express permission of one of the National Red Cross Societies, the emblem may be employed in time of peace to identify vehicles used as ambulances and to mark the position of aid stations exclusively assigned to the purpose of giving free treatment to the wounded or sick.[19]

---

[17] Article 8(2)(b)(vii) of the Rome Statute of the International Criminal Court.

[18] Article 18, para 3 and 4, AP I. Article 18(3) authorizes the identification of civilian medical and religious personnel by means of the emblem only "in occupied terri tory and in areas where fighting is taking place or is likely to take place".

Double Emblem: The use of double emblem by a State, i.e., the use of two recognized emblems –a combination of a Red Cross, Red Crescent, or Red Crystal – side by side is inadmissible, as this would amount to using an altered form of the emblem, which is not permitted by the 1949 Geneva Conventions or their Additional Protocols. The Commentary on the First Geneva Convention states that 'The protective sign, consisting of a Red Cross on a white ground, as prescribed by the Geneva Convention, should always be displayed in its original form, without alteration or addition'. The use of two emblems side by side would also reduce visual effectiveness. The use would transform what is usually instantly recognizable into something more complicated for the eye to distinguish. States working under a coalition have another option under AP III to avoid any risk of being perceived as using a double emblem. Article 2(4) of Protocol III provides: "The medical services and religious personnel of armed forces of High Contracting Parties may, without prejudice to their current emblems, make temporary use of any distinctive emblem referred to in paragraph 1 of this Article where this may enhance protection." Display of the emblem with the international organization's sign (for example United Nations) in proximity could also cause the Movement to be wrongly associated with other organizations and thereby affect the perception of its independence and neutrality.[20]

Protection of Emblem

The use of the emblem by those who are not authorized by the law; improper use of the emblem by those who are authorized to use it; imitation of the Red Cross emblem by using a symbol similar to it; and perfidious use of the emblem to betray the confidence of the adversary in a military action is considered as misuse of the emblem. Under certain conditions, the perfidious use of the emblem may even constitute a war crime. Article 85(3)(f) of AP I states that perfidious use of the red cross, red crescent and red lion and sun, in violation of Article 37, qualifies as a grave breach when the act is committed wilfully and results in death or serious injury to body or health.

---

[19] Article 44, GC I.

[20] For further details see: Rolle Baptiste and Edith Lafontaine, The emblem that cried wolf: ICRC study on the use of the emblems, *International Review of the Red Cross*, Vol. 91, No. 876, (December 2009) p. 759-778.

Article 6(1) of AP III explicitly mentions two particular kinds of misuse to be prevented or repressed. The first is perfidy, where, for the purpose of killing, injuring or capturing, an appeal is made to the good faith of the adversary with the intention of deceiving him/her through the use of a distinctive emblem in order to feign protected statusThe second is imitation, or using a sign that because of its form and/or colour is likely to be mistaken for a distinctive emblem.

It has been observed that in the SouthAsian countries, the members of medical, dental, and nursing professions; private pharmaceutical companies; private clinics, medical colleges, hospitals and nursing homes, ambulances, NGOs working in health sector, the government agencies/offices like the health departments and blood banks misuse the emblem. Even the use of the Red Cross emblem by a member , staff, doctor of the Red Cross Movement on their personal vehicles/buildings or belongings would constitutes a misuse. However, they can wear a small size Red Cross badge to indicate that he/she is linked with the Red Cross Movement.

The emblem has existed for nearly 150 years as the visible sign of the protection afforded under IHL to certain categories of persons affected by armed conflicts and to those providing them with humanitarian aid. It also symbolizes the neutrality, independence, and impartiality of the International Red Cross and Red Crescent Movement. Today the Red Cross/Crescent/ Crystal emblem has become a universally known and legally sanctified neutral sign to identify the people with protected status in situations of armed conflict, i.e. the armed forces medical units, the chaplains and relief committees. They are in the battlefield exclusively for the amelioration of the wounded and sick soldiers and other victims of war, and are protected from all kinds of hostile military action under IHLThe distinctive emblems as a matter of principle to be solely perceived as symbols of aid and must not have any religious, ethnic, racial, regional or political significance. The State Parties must adopt adequate national laws to prevent improper use of the distinctive emblems and to deter and punish perpetrators.

The International Red Cross and Red Crescent Movement is the largest humanitarian network in the world today. The ICRC acts as a guardian and promoter of IHL. The ICRC's operational framework is characterized by a range of activities at the three complimentary levels: first preventing or alleviating the immediate effect of an emer ging or established pattern or abuse; second, restoring dignified living conditions through rehabilitation and reparations; and third; fostering a social, cultural, institutional and legal environment conducive to full respect for IHL. The four Geneva Conventions and theirAdditional Protocols deal with the use and the abuse of the recognized emblems. States must strengthen the national legislations to increase awareness and eliminate abuses of the emblem.

CHAPTER 18

IHL: New Challenges

Introduction

International humanitarian law, as contained inthe four Geneva Conventions of 1949 and the three Additional Protocols, is a monumental work of over 600 articles. It is based on the idea that certain categories of individuals must be spared the effects of violence, regardless of the side to which they belong and regardless of the justification given for armed conflict. The Geneva Conventions, together with the 1899 and 1907 Hague Regulations, represent a carefully thought out balance between the principles of military necessity and humanity. What is necessary today is that the existing law must be understood, assimilated and respected.

In spite of the fact that the four Geneva Conventions have nearly universal ratification, violations of IHL continue to occur with impunity. Air and missile attacks during the recent conflicts in Israel, Afghanistan, Iraq and Libya have resulted in a large number of civilian casualties and damage to civilian property. Military planners and commanders had apparently disregarded the risk to civilians in ordering attacks on suspected enemy combatants. In a few instances, weapons violating the fundamental principles of IHL have been used. States have also failed to take criminal actions against those responsible for grave breaches of IHL, thus failing to respect and ensure respect to the four Geneva Conventions and their Protocols. This last chapter covers certain challenging issues related to IHL.

Cyber Warfare

Cyber warfare deals with the management and use of information in all its forms and at all levels to achieve a decisive military advantage. It has been defined as "an electronic conflict in which information is a strategic asset worthy of conquest or destruction", where computers and other communication and information systems become attractive first-strike targets.[1] Cyber warfare, information warfare, knowledge war or net-warfare, are a few terms which are being used interchangeably to describe the ability to destroy or disrupt the computer networks. Cyber technologies and expertise are easy and cheap to acquire, which allows weaker S tates and even non-state actors to cause considerable damage to countries with superior military power. Some of the activities of cyber warfare could be stealing sensitive information from computers, cyber espionage, incapacitate a computer or computer network, physical destruction, the corruption of hardware or software, and flooding it with information to cause its collapse.

Cyber Weapons and Attacks: Cyber weapon has become a major security challenge as individuals, terrorists, or foreign countries capable of penetrating these information systems could wreak havoc with a country's defence or civilian infrastructures. Cyber weapons are very different from conventional weapons in the sense that they are very easy to replicate without spending much money.[2] In fact total expenditure is only in creation of the first or original weapon. Cyber weapons in the form of Trojan horses, logic bombs, viruses and worms can be installed in a computer through chipping, hacking, or e-mailing them. [3] The attack (whether in of fence or defence) can be directed against an individual computer, specific computer s within

---

[1] Winn Schwartau. 1994. *Information Warfare: Chaos on the Electonic Superhighway*, Thunder's Mouth Press, p. 13.

[2] Cyber warf are may inv olve new wa ys of fighting, for example, hacker activities, viruses, Trojan horses and worms. Attacks could be conducted from a distance, through radio waves or international communications networks, without physical intrusion beyond enemy borders and without immediate traditional physical damage. The consequences of warfare may be devastating if certain system malfunctions are caused. For example a virus may be used to attack a nuclear power plant computer system causing the r elease of dangerous f orces. Dormann Knut, Computer Network Attack and IHL, Cambridge R eview of International Affairs. A vailable at: <ht tp://www.icrc.org/eng/resources/documents/misc/5p2alj.htm> accessed 2 March 2011.

[3] The tools for cyber warfare include virus, worm, Trojan Horses, logic bomb, and trap doors. The simplest type of at tack is a virus, which is a code fr agment that attaches i tself to a program and only operates when its host pro gram begins to run. While dif ficult to direct, viruses can cause significant damage. For example, the "I Love You" virus, released in the spring 2000, caused an estimated $6. 7 bil lion in damage. A worm is an independent program that copies itself onto other computers but usually does not change other programs. Worms can cause damage merely by eating up network resources or destroying data and

a network, or an entire computer network.Through the application of these weapons, one can adversely afect individuals, organizations and countries—both singly and combined.

The cyber attack has capability to paralyse the critical infrastructure of the country. The damage of such an attack could range from a simple shut down of a computer system to complex paralysis of significant portion of critical infrastructure. The attacks could aim at national security set up and a country involved in cyber espionage need not cross international borders. A cyber attack could disable power plants; cut of f the military command and control network; cause warplanes to crash, nuclear reactors to meltdown and weapons to malfunction.[4]

In cyber warfare, the enemy' s main goal is to penetrate the rival' s computer network, exploit its communication net work and manipulate its digital information. Malicious computer programmes could also be embedded into enemy's computer system to steal information without user knowledge. The software is so designed that it remains undetected and sensitive information stored in computers can be siphoned off from across the world during peace as well as war In cyber warfare the adversary is not only invisible but also can attack with a high degree of unpredictability on defence and civil assets. Stealth and anonymity are the other advantages of well-planned cyber warfare.[5]

Cyber Warfare Systems: The cyber warfare systems are currently being developed and used by at least 120 countries. More advanced 'cyber weapons' have been introduced in the digital battlefield and few states, like the US have created national cyber command authorities.The UK and

---

are particularly effective over networks. Trojan Horses are code fragments that disguise worms or viruses and allow attackers to gain access to systems. If deployed correctly, they do not leave a trace. A logic bomb is a particular type of Trojan horse that activates only when a certain condition is met. It can lie dormant in a system f or long periods of time bef ore activating. Trap doors are mechanisms that allow a programmer to access software at any time without the owner's knowledge. Analogous totrap doors, chipping involves embedding hidden functions in the hardware itself to allow the designer access to or control over the chip at a later point, for example, by blacking out radar systems during an attack.

4 Roscini Marco, World Wide Warfare – *Jus ad bellum* and the use of Cyber Force, *Max Planck Yearbook of United Nations Law*, Vol. 14, 2010, p. 87-88.

5 The New Warrior: The Cyber Warfare poses a big challenger to India, *Geopolitics*, Vol. I, Issue IX, January 2011, p. 38-44.

Australia have established cyber security centers to monitor the internet for threats, and China has formed cyberspace battalions and regiments. During the Kosovo conflict, some US officials were reportedly worried about the legal implications of launching the world' s first cyber war, for which they found no clear basis in law. A booklet issued in May 1999, by the US Government containing guidelines for waging cyber war warned commanders to be cautious of tar geting institutions that are essentially civilians.[6] The Russian Federation used cyber warfare in the second Chechen war against the insurgents' websites in order to prevent them from spreading anti-Russian propaganda. Cyber attacks also tar geted several Israeli government websites during 2008-2009 operation in Gaza strip. Peacetime cyber attacks have hit the US, the UK, India, Taiwan, South Korea, Lithuania, Kyrgyzstan, Switzerland and Montenegro. India has been the target of several attacks, allegedly originating from Pakistan and China.[7]

There is a possibility that cyber attack could be carried out by specialized personnel, who may not necessarily be combatants.They might or might not be incorporated in the armed forces of a party to a conflict. In case such personnel are incorporated into the armed forces, they would have all the rights and liabilities of combatants; and could be attacked and entitled to POW status. However, if they are captured in the adversary' s territory without uniform, they would be treated as spies and not be entitled to POW status.

Cyber Warfare and International Law: Cyber warfare challenges international law in several ways. First, communication signals from one country can easily transit international borders and thus af fect other telecommunication systems in distant countries. Such an intrusion could be regarded as violation of territorial sovereignty , a universally accepted international legal principle. Second: the damage that an information operation attack may cause is essentially diferent from the physical damage using conventional weapons. The devastation caused by conventional weapons is easier to comprehend; in contrast, the destruction of an information network could produce intangible damage to a civilian or

---

[6] Kassimeris George and John Buckley. 2010. *Modern Warfare*, USA: Ashgate, p. 123-144.

[7] The New W arrior: The Cyber W arfare poses a big challenger to India, *Geopolitics*, Vol. I, Issue IX, January 2011, p. 38-44.

government agency. Third: it is difficult to pinpoint whether an information operations attack is "an act of war", as it would be difficult to define the targets as legitimate military targets, or prohibited civilian targets.[8]

Currently, there is no provision in IHLor customary international law that explicitly outlaws cyber warfare carried out independently or during war. However, the existing IHL principles should be used to analyze the legality of cyber attacks. [9] IHL applies during the international armed conflict. It is applicable to all parties to the conflict in exactly the same manner, no matter who may have started the conflictThe general principles of IHL that could af fect information operations are distinction, proportionality and necessity.

The principle of distinction as defined in Article 48 of API states: "In order to ensure respect for and protection of the civilian population and civilian objects, the parties to a conflict are required at all times to distinguish between the civilian population and combatants and between civilian objects and military objectives and accordingly must direct their operations only against military objectives. The rules of IHLthat emerge from this principle are (i) the obligation to direct attacks only against 'military objectives'; (ii) the prohibition of indiscriminate attacks; (iii) the need to minimize collateral civilian damage and to abstain from attacks if such damage is likely to be disproportionate to the value of the military objective to be attacked; and

---

[8] The cyber attack against a military computer could be the work of a curious child, the work of terrorists, or the work of belligerent armed forces around the world. It will be difficult to trace the sour ce of attack. Even if the source could be tr aced, it may lead only to an anonymous remailer. If an ICBM were launched fom China, it would be a clear signal of the start of an armed conflict. However, even if an information attack could be traced to China, it would be difficult to confirm whether the child, the terrorist, or the government is behind the attack. Aldrich, Richard W., The International Legal Implications of Information Warfare, INSS Occasional Paper 9, Information Warfare Series, (April 1996), USAF Institute for National Security Studies US Air Force Academy, Colorado. Available at: http://www.iwar.org.uk/law/resources/iwlaw/aldrich.htm. Accessed 03 March 2011.

[9] The Martens Clause, a well-accepted principle of humanitarian law, provides that whenever a situation is not covered by an international agreement, "civilians and combatants remain under the pr otection and authori ty of the principles of international la w derived from established custom, f rom the principles of humani ty, and f rom the dictates of publ ic conscience." By this norm, all occurrences during armed conflict are subject to application of humanitarian law principles; there is no lawless void. Schmitt, Michael N., Wired Warfare: Computer network attack and *jus in bello, International Review of the Red Cross,* Vol. 84, No. 846, p. 365-399.

(iv) the need to take the necessary precautions to ensure that the above three rules are respected.

The principle of proportionality limits the amount of force that can be used against a military taget so that it does not cause unnecessary collateral damage to civilian property or unnecessary suf fering to the civilians. Proportionality closely relates to the concept of indiscriminate attacks. Article 51(5)(b) describes an indiscriminate attack as one that "may be expected to cause incidental loss of civilian life, injury to civilians, damage to civilian objects, or a combination thereof, which would be excessive in relation to the concrete and direct military advantage anticipated." These principles are important to cyber warfare because they require that the attacker refrain from attacks that may be expected to cause excessive collateral damage. Cyber attack that would not have a reasonably predictable scope of destructive application would be prohibited by the principle of proportionality. Cyber attack that disrupts civilian telecommunications network could subsequently affect even various life-sustaining health care processes. Therefore cyber attack would not be permissible under the proportionality principle.

The principle of military necessity entails the cumulative impact of attacks against particular tar gets. The principle poses no problem to information operation strategies as long as the systems under attack are purely military targets. A cyber attack against systems that have a dual-use capability among a state's military forces and its civilian population could be problematic. The conventional military targets like electrical power grids and other telecommunications networks would be unlawful tagets because of their interconnection and interdependence with systems serving the civilian population. In addition the principle of humanity prohibits the employment of any kind or degree of force not necessary for the purposes of war that is for the partial or complete submission of the enemy with the least possible expenditure of life, time and physical resources. Cyber attacks directed at non-military cyber structure must be considered as violations of IHL.

Article 36 of AP I deals with review of new weapons. The intent of Article 36 is to determine the lawfulness of new weapons before they are developed, acquired, or incorporated into a military's arsenal. Legal experts are of the view that the legality, means, and methods of new warfare is so basic that it applies to all nations, even those not a party to theAP I. Thus, the states attacking computer network in a conflict must ensure that 'new innovations' do not run against international obligationsArticle 36 ofAP I states: "In the study development, acquisition or adoption of a new weapon, means or method of warfare, a High Contracting Party is under an obligation to determine whether its employment would, in some or all circumstances, be prohibited by this Protocol or by any other rule of international law applicable to the High Contracting Party". The computer programmes relating to a virus, worm etc., need to be considered as new weapons by the international community. They could be many more times harmful and destructive when compared to a conventional weapon.

The United Nations: The UN Charter, Article 2, paragraph 4 provides that all members of the UN shall refrain from in their international relations from the threat or use of force against the territorial integrity or political independence of any state, or in any manner inconsistent with the purposes of the United Nations. This provision reflects customary international law and prohibits threat and the use of force.A number of states have included cyber technology in their military doctrine and have set up military units' expert in cyber warfare. The cyber weapons consisting of T rojan horses, viruses and worms are means of warfare, and could be equated with other weapon systems.A cyber attack that shut down an enemy air defence system or destroys an enemy aircraft must be considered as a use of 'force'. Thus cyber threat or warfare amounts to the use of 'force' and therefore unlawful.

Cyber security has become a general concern of the international community. The UN General assembly has adopted a number of resolutions relating to dissemination and the use of information technologies; means affecting the interest of the international community; and criminal misuse of information technology.[10]

[10] The General Assembly it its Resolution A/RES/64/25, adopted on 14 January 2010 has called upon the Member States to pomote further at multilateral levels the consideration of existing and potential theats in the field of inbrmation security, as wel as possible measues to limit the threats emeging in this field, consistent wth the need to peserve the free flow of information. Other Geneal Assembly Resolution on the subject are: 53/70 of 4 December 1998, 54/49 of 1 December 1999, 55/28 of 20 Nov ember 2000, 56/19 of 29 No vember 2001, 57/53 of 22 Nov ember 2002, 58/32 of 8 December 2003, 59/61 of 3 December 2004, 60/45 of 8 December 2005, 61/54 of 6 December 2006, 62/17 of 5 December 2007 and 63/37 of 2 December 2008.

Computer technology has advanced to the point where military forces have the capability to inflict injury, death, and destruction via cyberspace. The doubt however exists whether IHL in the existing form would be applicable to this new form of technology . The Geneva and Hague Conventions deal with the issues of laws of war on land or at sea. Information warfare takes place in cyberspace, an ethereal place that does not neatly fit into the land, sea, air and space dichotomy . Information warfare involves conduct and ef fects that transcend national boundaries and render such distinctions superfluous.

There are views that the current IHL framework can be applied to cyber warfare by analogy . At the same time there are opinions that the existing framework of IHL is not suited to cope with cyber warfare's new paradigm. Cyber warfare requires greater international legal and diplomatic initiatives—both bilateral and multilateral. Nations have a mutual interest in limiting any resort to cyber warfare. There is a need for modern international law to define the criteria to distinguish which state actions are permissible as normal computer-generated trans-border data flow from those cyber-activities that might qualify as an act of cyber warfare. It is felt that this can only be achieved only through a new international convention.[11]

Targeted Killing

In recent years, a few States have adopted policies that permit the use of targeted killings, including in the territories of other States. The states have tried to justify such policies as a necessary and legitimate response to "terrorism" and "asymmetric warfare".A targeted killing is the intentional, premeditated and deliberate use of lethal force, by states, their agents, or by an organized armed group in armed conflict, against a specific individual who is not in the physical custody of the perpetrator. In a targeted killing, the aim is to use lethal force. The use of lethal force is intentional and deliberate, with a degree of pre-meditation, against an individual or individuals identified in advance by the perpetrator . Israel has used the targeted killing against Palestinian fighters and political leaders since 2000, while the United States has used drones and airstrikes for targeted killings

[11] Brown David, A Proposal for an International Convention To Regulate the Use of Information Systems in Armed Conflict, *Harvard International Law Journal*, Vol. 47, No. 1, (Winter 2006), p. 179-220.

in Afghanistan, Pakistan and Iraq.[12]

The means and methods of targeted killing vary , and include sniper fire, shooting at close range, missiles from helicopters, gunships, drones, the use of car bombs, and poison. New technologies like drones have made it easier to kill targets, with no risks to the targeting State. In the struggle against terrorism, States have tried to justify many criminal acts by bringing them within the framework of IHL.There has been blurring and expansion of the boundaries of the applicable legal frameworks of IHL and the human rights laws.

Under IHL, targeted killing is only lawful when the target is a "combatant" In the case of a civilian, he can be attacked only for such time when the person "directly participates in hostilities (DPH)."[13] In addition, the killing must be military necessity the use of force must be proportionate

---

[12] Israel officially adopted a targeted killing policy after the beginning of the Second Intifada (the Palestinian uprising) in 2000. Since then, at least 386 Palestinians have been killed as the result of this policy; among them are 154 innocent civilians. Israel's targeted killing have taken place by shooting missiles from helicopters, explosive loads, sniper fire, short-range shooting, and artillery shooting. Bader Majd, The Israeli Policy: Targeted Killing for Preventive Self-Defense or Extra-Judicial Executions? December 2008. Available at:http://works.bepress.com/cgi/viewcontent.cgi?article=1000&context=maged_bader. Accessed 4 March 2011.According to Lotrionte (2006).... in a world with more dangerous weapons and in the hands of actors wilng to use them, killing regime leaders...may be an appropriate policy option....and policy makers may consider following criteria: (i) **The Target**: the killing itself should be limited to the greatest extent possible to the persons within the regime that are responsible for the threats; (ii) **A Level of Certainty**: access to accurate and reliable intelligence information that provides a high level of certainty of the identity of the individual responsible for the threat; (iii) **A Likelihood of Success**: founded on a strong likelihood that the attempt to eliminate the leader will be successful and the leaders' elimination will remedy the problem and do no less harm to civilian population than another form of action would; (iii) **A Necessary Action**: there is no other feasible, reasonable, less extreme way of stopping the regime leaders action; (v) **A Proportionate Action**: the killing of the regime leader is proportionate to the threat posed by that leader and the consequences of killing of the regime leader is less destructive than the use of conventional warfare to resolve the threat; and (vi) **A Discriminate Action**: targeting the responsible individuals will avoid the deaths of innocent victims. Lotrionte Catherine. 2006. 'Targeting Regime Leaders During Armed Hostilities: A Effective Way to Achieve Regime Change', in Hensel Howard M (ed.), *The Law of Armed Conflict: Constraints on the Contemporary Use of Military Force*, USA: Ashgate, p.33.

[13] In 2009, the ICRC issued its Interpretive Guidance on Direct Participation in Hostilities (DPH). Under the ICRC's Guidance, each specific act by the civilian must meet three cumulative requirements to constitute DPH: (i) There must be a "threshold of harm" that is objectively likely to result from the act, either by adversely impacting the military operations or capacity of the opposing party, or by causing the loss of life or property of protected civilian persons or objects; and (ii) The act must cause the expected harm directly, in one step, for example, as an integral part of a specific and coordinated combat operation (as opposed to harm

so that any anticipated military advantage is considered in light of the expected harm to civilians in the vicinity, and everything feasible must be done to prevent mistakes and minimize harm to civilians. These humanitarian principles apply regardless of whether the conflict is international or non-international. Reprisal or punitive attacks on civilians are prohibited. The legality of a killing outside the context of IHL is governed by human rights standards. Killing is legal only if it is required to protect life and there are no other means, such as capture or incapacitation. At the same time there remains an obligation to minimize the level of force used, regardless of the amount that would be proportionate, through the use of warnings, restraint and capture. Therefore under human rights law, a targeted killing in the sense of an intentional, premeditated and deliberate killing by law enforcement officials can never be legal. In case a targeted killing violates IHL, then regardless of who conducts it – intelligence personnel or State armed forces – the author, as well as those who authorized it, can be prosecuted for war crimes.

In November 2000, the Israeli Government confirmed the existence of a policy pursuant to which it justified targeted killings in self-defence and under IHL because the Palestinian authority was failing to investigate and prosecute terrorism, and prevent suicide attacks directed at Israel. The Israeli Supreme Court in December 2006 [14] judgment did not prohibit or permit targeted killings by Israeli armed forces. However, it held that the lawfulness of each killing must be determined individually and customary IHL was applicable in such situations. It rejected the Government's contention that terrorists were "unlawful combatants" subject to attack at all times. Instead, it held that the applicable law permitted the targeted killing of civilians for such time as they "directly participated in hostilities"

---

caused in unspecified future operations); and (iii) The act must have a "belligerent nexus" – i.e., it must be specifically designed to support the military operations of one party to the detriment of another.

[14] Israel High Court of Justice, *The Public Committee Against Torture v. The Government of Israel*; HCJ 769/02, Judgment of 14 December 2006. The court referred to Article 1 of Chapter 1 of The Hague Convention (IV), Respecting the Laws and Customs of War on Land, (18 October 1907): The laws, rights, and duties of war apply not only to armies, but also to militia and volunteer corps fulfilling the following conditions: 1. To be commanded by a person responsible for his subordinates; 2. To have a fixed distinctive emblem recognizable at a distance; 3. To carry arms openly; and 4. To conduct their operations in accordance with the laws and customs of war.

as long as four cumulative conditions were met: (i)Targeting forces carried the burden of verifying the identity of the taget as well as the factual basis for meeting the "direct participation" standard; (ii) Even if the tar get was legally and factually identified by the Government as legitimate, State forces could not kill the person if less harmful means were available; (iii) After each tar geted killing, there must be a retroactive and independent investigation of the "identification of the tar get and the circumstances of the attack"; and (iv) Any collateral harm to civilians must meet the requirement of proportionality under IHL.

Nuclear Weapons

Though the international law as such does not ban the use of nuclear weapon, there is no doubt that the nuclear weapons are instruments of terror by definition because of their indiscriminate violence on an extreme scale. In 1945, during the final stages of WW II, the US dropped two atom bombs over the cities of Hiroshima and Nagasaki in Japan, the first on August 6, 1945 and the second onAugust 9, 1945.The radiation covered a wider area affecting public health, agriculture, natural resources and infrastructure for years to come.These two events are the only active deployments of nuclear weapons in war to date.

Dr Marcel Junod, an ICRC delegate, was the first foreign doctor in Hiroshima to assess the effects of the atomic bombing and to assist its victims. His testimony[15] is about the havoc caused by the nuclear weapon: "We....witnessed a sight totally unlike anything we had ever seen before. The centre of the city was a sort of white patch, flattened and smooth like the palm of a hand. Nothing remained.The slightest trace of houses seemed to have disappeared.The white patch was about two kilometers in diameter Around its edge was a red belt, marking the area where houses had burned, extending quite a long way further...covering almost all the rest of the city". In a few seconds after the blast "thousands of human beings in the streets and gardens in the town centre, struck by a wave of intense heat, died like flies. Others lay writhing like worms, atrociously burned. All

---

[15] Extracts from the book "The Hiroshima disaster – a doctor's account" written by Dr. Marcel Junod. Dr. Junod, the new head of the ICRC' s delegation in Japan, arriv ed in Tokyo on 9 August 1945, the day the US dropped second atomic bomb on Nagasaki. Accessed 4 March 2011, available at: http://www .icrc.org/eng/resources/documents/misc/hiroshima-junod-120905.htm.

private houses, warehouses, etc., disappeared as if swept away by a supernatural power. Trams were picked up and hurled yards away, as if they were weightless; trains were flung off the rails.....Every living thing was petrified in an attitude of acute pain".

Limitations of the Use of Nuclear Weapon: There is a large body of conventional international law pertaining to various limitations on nuclear weapons, such as possession, testing, deployment, use or threat of use. There are regional constraints on nuclear weapons in Antarctica, Latin America, the South Pacific, South-East Asia and among members of the Organization of African Unity (OAU).[16] The testing, deployment or use of nuclear weapons is prohibited in earth orbit, outer space, on the moon and other celestial bodies.[17] Deployment of nuclear weapons is also prohibited on the seabed, on the ocean floor and subsoil thereof beyond the twelve-mile limit of national territorial seas. There are certain limitations on the deployment and proliferation of nuclear weapons in the peace treaties following the Second World War signed by Bulgaria, Finland, Hungary, Italy and Romania in 1947.

The five nuclear weapon states (NWS) have signed the Treaty on the Non-Proliferation of Nuclear Weapons (NPT) in 1968. The NWS are

---

[16] The Antarctic Treaty of 1959 provides that Antarctica shall be used only for peaceful purposes. Army measures of a military nature and the testing of any type of weapons are prohibited. The Treaty also prohibits nuclear explosions and the disposal of radioactive waste in Antarctica.There are five existing regional nuclear weapon free zones established by treaty. The provisions of each zone vary with the language of each respective treaty; however each treaty prohibits the manufacture, production, possession, testing, acquisition, and receipt of nuclear weapons. The Treaty for the Prohibition of Nuclear Weapons in Latin America and the Caribbean (Treaty of Tlatelolco) was opened for signature in 1967 and brought into force in 1968.

Cuba, which has signed the treaty, remains the only country left to ratify. South Pacific Nuclear Free Zone Treaty (Treaty of Rarotonga) opened for signature 1985, entered into force 1986. The treaty has been signed and ratified by all but three countries in the region. The United States, though it has signed the two additional protocols, remains the only country that has not ratified the protocols. The Rarotonga Treaty differs from Tlatelolco in that it includes an unequivocal ban on nuclear explosions and explosive devises for peaceful purposes, and prohibits its members from dumping nuclear waste into the zone's waters. The South East Asian Nuclear-Weapon-Free- Zone Treaty (Treaty of Bangkok) opened for signature in 1995 and came into force in 1996. The African Nuclear Weapon Free Zone Treaty (Treaty of Pelindaba) opened for signature in 1996, and has still not come into force.

[17] Treaty on Principles Governing the Activities of States in the Exploration and Use of Outer Space, including the Moon and Other Celestial Bodies (Outer Space Treaty) 1967, Agreement Governing the Activities of States on the Moon and Other Celestial Bodies 1979.

committed to nuclear disarmament. The treaty proclaims that NWS will not use a nuclear weapon against NPT signatories of nonnuclear weapon states (NNWS).[18]. The Comprehensive Nuclear-Test-Ban Treaty (CTBT) prohibits every kind of nuclear weapon test explosion or any other nuclear explosion. The test ban constrains development and qualitative improvement of current types of nuclear weapons, or development of new types of nuclear weapons.

There are a number of general principles of a customary law that need to be considered with regard to the legality of nuclear weapons.These are:

- The right to adopt means of injuring the enemy is not unlimited
- It is prohibited to use means and methods of warfare that cause unnecessary aggravated devastation and suffering.
- It is prohibited to use indiscriminate methods and means of warfare that do not distinguish between combatants and civilians
- It is prohibited to use asphyxiating, poisonous or other gases and all analogous materials
- The means and methods of warfare should not cause widespread, long-term or severe damage to the environment
- It is prohibited to ef fect reprisals that are disproportionate to legitimate military objectives.

Similarly, there are a number of IHL treaties which need to be considered in the context of the legality of nuclear weapons.

- The St Petersburg Declaration 1868: the right to injure the enemy is not unlimited and that means of warfare that cause unnecessary suffering are prohibited.
- The Hague Conventions of 1899 and 1907: the belligerents' choice

[18] The UN Securi ty Council in 1995 adopted Resolution [UNSC Res. 984 (1995)] on both negative and positive security assurances. The resolution took note of the statements made by the United States, the United Kingdom, Fance and the Russian Federation in which they gave security assurances against the use of nuclear weapons to NNWS that are Parties to the NPT. They reaffirmed that nuclear weapons shall not be used against NNWS Parties to the NPT, except in the case of invasion or any other attack on their territories, armed forces or other troops, their allies or a State to which they have given a security commitment.

of means and methods of combat with the enemy is not unlimited, and that the prohibition of any weapons and methods of combat that may cause unnecessary suffering.

- The four Geneva Conventions of 1949 confirm the distinction between combatants and non-combatants and the prohibition of unnecessary and aggravated suffering.
- The Hague Cultural Property Convention of 1954 protects cultural property during armed conflict.
- The Convention on the Prohibition of Military or Any Other Hostile Use of Environmental Modification Techniques (ENMOD) prohibits the hostile use of environmental modification techniques having widespread, long-lasting or severe effects.
- Additional Protocol I of 1977 reconfirm the basic principles of limitations to choose methods of warfare that should not cause unnecessary suffering or superfluous injury . It also prohibits methods or means of warfare that are intended or may be expected to cause widespread, long-term and severe effects to the environment. Indiscriminate attacks are prohibited and cultural objects and places of worship are protected from military attack.
- The 1981 Convention on Certain Conventional Weapons, in particular its third Protocol on Prohibition or Restrictions on the Use of Incendiary Weapons prohibits the use of incendiary weapons against the non-combatants.
- The 1998 Rome Statute of the International Criminal Court protects the environment during armed conflict, because it establishes individual criminally responsibility for excessive damage to the environment.

The UN General Assembly Declaration on the Prohibition of the Use of Nuclear and Thermonuclear Weapons,[19] states that the use of nuclear weapons is a 'direct violation of the UN Charter ', 'contrary to the rule of international law and to the laws of humanity' and 'a crime against mankind and civilization'. The Security Council at its 6191st meeting (24 September

[19] UNGA Res 1653 (XVI) (24 November 1961).

2009) confirmed its commitment to the goal of a world free of nuclear weapons and established a broad framework for reducing global nuclear dangers. The Security Council reaffirmed that proliferation of weapons of mass destruction, and their means of delivery , constitutes a threat to international peace and security. The opening paragraph of the resolution 1887 (2009) resolves to seek a safer world for all and to create the conditions for a world without nuclear weapons, ….in a way that promotes international stability, and based on the principle of undiminished security for all.[20]

Nuclear-Earth Penetrating Weapons (EPW): There are reports that the US is planning to develop nuclear-earth penetrating weapons (EPW) as its potential adversaries have number of hard and deeply buried targets (HDBTs).[21] HDBTs are difficult to characterize, as satellite imagery can reveal their existence, but not necessarily their function. These potential targets offer a tremendous challenge as their depth and reinforced cover are, by design, difficult to destroy . If these HDBT are attacked with a conventional warhead there would be the problem of damage assessment. Satellite or aerial imagery may provide confirmation that the weapon has successfully exploded on the target; however, the facility may still be intact deep underground.[22] In addition, the military or political leadership may have to provide proof to the world that a military response against a particular HDBT was justified. At the same time, attacked adversary may claim that a non-military facility like pharmaceutical research laboratory or similar benign facility was destroyed.

The scientists developing nuclear-EPW argue that a nuclear attack on HTBTs would have less collateral damage because the thermal effects of a nuclear explosion would vaporize the potential chemical or biological hazard. A nuclear weapon would certainly increase the probability of HTBT destruction, there are a myriad of issues associated with its use.

[20] S/RES/1887 (2009) of 24 September 2009.

[21] Such facilities may serve as military or political leadership shelters; command, control, and communications (C3) centers; weapons production, assembly , storage and deployment facilities, especially for weapons of mass destruction (WMD); missile operations tunnels and garrisons; and point or integrated area defence system facilities.

[22] During the Gulf War the Guided Bomb Unit-28 (GBU-28) was developed in an effort to penetrate hardened Iraqi command centers. This 5,000-pound laser-guided system used a modified 203-milimeter artillery tube as its penetrating casing. After an extremely quick acquisition and testing process this weapon was delivered to theater and used against Iraqi command and control sites.

Though IHL or international law does not prohibit the use of nuclear weapons in armed conflict, it is necessary to consider the concepts of "proportionality and necessity" with respect to determining the acceptability of using a nuclear-EPW. The principle of proportionality places a duty on leaders to choose a form of attack that avoids or minimizes damage to civilians. In particular, the attacker should refrain from launching an attack if the expected civilian casualties would outweigh the importance of the military objective. Article 23 of the Hague Regulations prohibits the use of weapons and means of warfare likely to cause unnecessary suf fering. Military necessity does not allow military measures to be taken that violate IHL or that do not have a military purpose, i.e., that are not intended to defeat the enemy, or that would excessively harm civilians. Considerations of military necessity cannot, therefore, justify departing from the rules of humanitarian law in armed conflict to seek a military advantage using forbidden means.[23]

The position of the ICRC on nuclear weapons, as a humanitarian organization goes beyond a pure legal analysis. In the opinion of the ICRC, nuclear weapons are unique in their destructive power and they pose serious threat to the environment and humanity . The ICRC welcomed the International Court of Justice' s (ICJ) reaf firmation of the principles and rules of IHL as applied to the use of nuclear weapons.[24] The ICRC refined its own position in the light of the Court's opinion. The position reaffirms that "the principles of distinction and proportionality and the prohibition on causing superfluous injury or unnecessary suffering, apply to the use of nuclear weapons". In view of the unique characteristics of nuclear weapons the ICRC further called on all States not to use nuclear weapons, irrespective of whether they considered them legal or not, to take measures to limit the risk of proliferation and to pursue negotiations on a complete ban on nuclear weapons and their elimination.[25]

---

[23] Fleck Dieter. 2009. *The Handbook of I nternational Humanitarian Law*, Oxford: Oxford University Press, p.38.

[24] The advisory opinion of the International Court of Justice in "Legalty of the Threat or Use of Nuclear Weapons, Advisory Opinion (1996).

[25] <http://www.icrc.org/eng/war-and-law/weapons/nuclear-weapons/overview-nuclear-weapons.htm> Accessed 1 March 2011.

Today, the nuclear weapons are the only weapons of mass destruction which are not specifically prohibited by a treaty; however , as discussed above, there are international conventions, customary rules, and state practices that limit the use of nuclear weapons.The ICJ in "Legality of the Threat or Use of Nuclear Weapons, Advisory Opinion (1996)" has opined that 'a threat or use of force by means of nuclear weapons which is contrary to Article 2, paragraph 4, of the UN Charter and that fails to meet all the requirements of Article 51, is unlawful'. If we consider Martens Clause earnestly, which "makes usages (or practices) among civilized peoples, the laws of humanity and the dictates of public conscience obligatory, even in the absence of a treaty", we would come to conclusion that just because a nuclear weapon is not officially banned does not mean that it is allowed. There is a need to negotiate nuclear weapon convention [26] for achieving global nuclear disarmament.[27]

Depleted Uranium Weapons

Since the last two-decades the weapons containing depleted uranium (DU) are being used in international armed conflict. It has been alleged that since 1991, the US has staged four wars using DU weaponry illegal under all international treaties, conventions and agreements as well as under the US military law.[28] DU weapons have the following advantages:

---

[26] In April 1997, Lawyers' Committee on Nuclear Policy/International Association of Lawyers Against Nuclear Arms, International Physicians for the Prevention of Nuclear War, and International Network of Engineers and Scientists Against Proliferation released a Model Nuclear Weapons Convention (MNWC). It was drafted by an international consortium of lawyers, scientists, disarmament experts, physicians and activists. The Model NWC prohibits the use, threat of use, possession, development, testing, deployment and transfer of nuclear weapons and provides a phased program for their elimination under effective international control. It provides for the verified elimination of nuclear weapons in much the same way comparable treaties have banned landmines and chemical and weapons. An updated version of model "Convention on the Prohibition of the Development, Testing, Production, Stockpiling, Transfer, Use and Threat of Use of NuclearWeapons and on Their Elimination" of April 2007 is annexed to the UN General Assembly document A/62/650 of 18 January 2008.

[27] The UN General Assembly in its Resolution A/RES/65/72 adopted on 13 January 2011 has urged the nuclear-weapon states to accomplish the total elmination of their nuclear arsenals, leading to nuclear disarmament

[28] Ammunition containing DU was used in recent conflicts in Iraq and Kuwait (Gulf War); Bosnia–Herzegovina; and Afghanistan. The 30-mm DU rounds, which were used by the US air force in the Gulf War and in Kosovo, can pierce steel armor up to a thickness of 9 cm. DU weapons were first given by the US to Israel for use under US supervision in the 1973 Sinai war against Arabs. Since then the US has tested, manufactured, and sold DU weaponry

- Because of its very heavy density (1.7 times of lead, 2.5 times of iron) and hardness, when used to tip bullets, DU increases the penetration power of the bullets, and displays tremendous capacity to open holes in thick iron plates and concrete.
- Even when there are no explosives inside the bombshell, it explodes upon impact, and the capacity to kill and injure the enemy is high because of the extreme temperature it causes while burning.
- It is very cheap because its raw materials are radioactive wastes.

When the penetrator hits a hard object, e.g., an armored vehicle, the penetrator pierces the metal sheet, generally leaving the jacket behind.The DU dust which may be formed during impact can be dispersed and contaminate the environment. The exposure to DU is critically dependent on whether it is external or internal. External exposure to DU mainly occurs during combat activities when DU aerosols are generated, or when DU fragments are picked up. The affected organ is the skin. Internal exposure to DU can occur through three pathways: ingestion (food and water); Inhalation (aerosol); and embedded fragments or contaminated wounds. Direct ingestion of uranium in particular for children, through hand contamination is possible. Direct ingestion of contaminated soil by cattle and sheep as a pathway to humans has also to be considered. DU can also enter the body in the form of uranium metal from fragments and as uranium oxides from oxidized DU formed after impact on hard targets.[29] Uranium is absorbed into the blood, carried and retained in body tissues and organs. Once inside the body system uranium can cause various disorders like abnormal births and birth defects, acute auto-immune symptoms, acute respiratory failure, bone tumours and cancer , chronic kidney and liver

---

systems to 29 countries. However, they were used for the first time on the battlefield of Iraq and Kuwait. Moret Leuren, Depleted Uranium: The Trojan Horse of Nuclear War, *World Affairs*, April-June 2004, Vol. 8, No. 2. p. 110-135.

[29] The clinical effects of DU exposure in Gulf War veterans having embedded DU shrapnel in their body were compared with non exposed Gulf War veterans. DU-exposed Gulf War veterans were found to excrete elevated levels of urinary uranium even 7 years after their first exposure. Bleise, A., Danesi, P.R., and Burkart, W., Properties, use and heath effects of depleted uranium (DU): a general overview, *Journal of Environmental Radioactivity*, Vol. 64 (2003), p. 107.

disorder, genetic alterations, etc.[30] Several birth defects have been reported in babies born to contaminated civilians in Iraq, [31] Yugoslavia and Afghanistan and the incidents and severity of defects are increasing day by day.

DU weapons are presently regarded as conventional weapons. The military use of DU, however, violates IHL, including principle that there is no unlimited right to choose the means and methods of warfare (Article 22 of the Hague Convention IV and Article 35 of the AP I), the ban on causing unnecessary suffering and superfluous injuries (Article 23 Hague Convention IV, Article 35 AP I), indiscriminate attack (Article 51, paragraph 4C and 5B, AP I) as well as the use of poison and poisonous weapons under the customary IHL.

White Phosphorous Weapons

The US armed forces have recently used white phosphorous (WP) based weapons to flush out suspected insurgents in Fallujah in 2005. A Pentagon spokesman later claimed, "it is not a chemical weapon. They are not outlawed or illegal." The Israeli Government has admitted that it used controversial WP weapons in its attacks against targets in open ground during its month-long war in Lebanon in 2006. It has been claimed that the Israeli army uses phosphorus weapons according to the rules of international law. However, there have been numerous reports that Israeli phosphorus munitions have injured and killed many civilians in Lebanon. The British and American armed forces have extensively used WP based weapons during WW II. However, its use is on increases in 21st century warfare.

---

30 Moret Leuren, Depleted Uranium: The Trojan Horse of Nuclear War, *World Affairs*, April-June 2004, Vol. 8, No. 2. p. 118.

31 "The UK forces have used about 1.9 metric tons of DU ammunition in the Iraq war in 2003", UK Defense Secretary Liam Fox said in a written reply to the House of Commons. The announcement came after a joint study by the environment, health and science ministries in Iraq said there were communities near the cities of Najaf, Basra and Fallujah with increased rates of cancer and birth defects over the past five years. It has been reported that the US and British forces have used up to 2,000 tons of DU ammunitions during the Iraq war. More than 40 sites across Iraq are contaminated with high levels of radiation and dioxins. The long- term effect of DU is a virtual death sentence. Iraq is a toxic wasteland. Anyone who is there stands a good chance of coming down with cancer and leukemia. In Iraq, the birth rate of mutations is totally out of control. http://www.tehrantimes.com/index_View.asp?code=223505.

White phosphorus is a flare/smoke producing incendiary weapon, or smoke-screening agent, made from a common allotrope of the chemical element phosphorus. It is used in bombs, artillery shells, mortar shells, and hand grenade which burst into burning flakes of phosphorus upon impact. The armed forces have legitimate requirement for substance that can illuminate a battlefield or to provide cover during day light to mark a target or to set fire to material targets such as ammunition of fuel stores. WP weapon is suitable for many of these tasks because it ignites easily when exposed to oxygen and produces dense white smoke. It is ideal for laying quick smoke screen or as a component of incendiary weapon. WP bombs and shells are essentially incendiary devices, but can also be used as an offensive anti-personnel flame compound capable of causing serious burns or death.[32]

WP weapons are controversial today because of its potential use against humans, for whom one-tenth of a gram is a deadly dose. WP is toxic and can cause blistering of the skin and mucous membranes. Burning WP is difficult to extinguish and tends to reignite unless fully smothered. [33] WP can cause injuries and death in three ways: by burning deep into soft tissue, by being inhaled as a smoke and by being ingested. Extensive exposure in any way can be fatal. It also releases phosphorous pentoxide, which can cause chemical burns, and on contact with water phosphoric acid, which is corrosive. Smoke inhalation can cause temporary discomfort, however effect could be serious in case of length and severity of exposure.

The use of incendiary weapon is not prohibited under IHL treaties. [34] However, if we consider its incendiary , poisonous and chemical ef fects,

---

[32] MacLeod I.J., and Rogers A.P.V., White Phosphorous and the Law of War, in McCormack Timothy L.H. (ed.), *Yearbook of International Humanitarian Law*, Vol. 10, 2007, TMC Asser Press, p. 76-97.

[33] Incandescent particles of WP cast off by a WP weapon' s initial explosion can produce extensive, deep (second and third degree), painful burns. Phosphorus burns carry a greater risk of mortality than other forms of burns due to the absorption of phosphorus into the body through the burned area, resulting in liver, heart and kidney damage, and in some cases multi-organ failure. These weapons are particularly dangerous to exposed people because white phosphorus continues to burn unless deprived of oxygen or until it is completely consumed, in some cases burning right down to the bone.

[34] The Protocol III to the Convention on Certain Conventional Weapon of 1980, dealing with incendiary weapons prohibits to make any military objective located within a concentration of civilians the object of attack by air delivered incendiary weapons. Incendiary weapons

the WP weapon needs to be banned under customary IHL.[35] The principle of 'unnecessary suffering' prohibits the use of WP weapon as means or method of warfare. The 'indiscriminate' principle requires that attacks to be directed against military objectives without disproportionate incidental damage to civilian and civilian property. Besides, Article 23 of the Hague Regulations 1907 prohibits employment of 'poison or poisonous weapons' and the Geneva Gas Protocol of 1925 prohibits the use of asphyxiating, poisonous or other gases and of all analogous liquid materials or devices in war. The US officials are of the view that white phosphorus burns people, rather than poisoning them, and are covered only by the CWC Protocol II on incendiary weapons, which the US has not signed. However, WP is both incendiary and toxic and violates principle of IHL.

Incapacitating Chemical Agents

Since the last decade there has been a keen interest in chemicals that act on the central nervous system to 'incapacitate' a person or to alter a person's mood, emotion, cognition or perception.These chemicals are different from chemical agents or riot-control agents. The NATO defines incapacitating agent as: "a chemicals which produce temporary disabling conditions which (unlike those caused by riot control agents) can be physical or mental and persist for hours or days after exposure to the agent has ceased. Medical treatment, while not usually required, facilitates a more rapid recovery".[36]

---

must not be used against civilians or civilian objects. However, it does not prohibit the use of incendiary weapon such as WP against the combatants. Under the Chemical Weapon Convention, the state parties are not to use riot control agent as methods of warfare under any circumstances; and the ban on use of chemical weapons is total. The CWC defines a "toxic chemical" as a chemical which though its chemical action on life processes can cause death, temporary incapacitation or permanent harm to humans or animals (Article II). An annex lists chemicals that fall under this definition, but WP is not listed, possibly because its primary function was not seen to be chemical. However, there is potential for white phosphorus to fall under the classification of a chemical weapon.

35 While the use of WP as a smoke signal or flare is uncontroversial, direct use against enemy soldiers is problematic. This is a result of blurred boundaries: "burning"a chemical reaction with oxygen, is the hallmark of incendiary weapons, while those due to "chemical effects" signify a chemical weapon. Due to this blurred boundary many armies do not use WP in its anti-personnel role against areas which may have civilians. If WP is used as a weapon based on its toxic properties it may constitute a violation of several conventions, in spirit if not in letter.

36 'Chemical agent' is defined as "a chemical substance which is intended for use in military operations to kil, seriously injure, or incapacitate personnel through its physiological effects. The term excludes riot control agents, herbicides and substances generating smoke and

With major advances in modern drug development, many experts see a role for "incapacitating chemical agents (ICA)" in counterterrorismThere are views that ICA can be used as a 'non-lethal' class of weapon by the armed forces.[37] At the same time there are arguments that such "agents", even if described as "non-lethal", are in fact lethal. The rapid advances in science have made it possible to develop an ICA that can be used in a consistently non-lethal manner. Their fatality or lethality will be a function of the physiology of the victim, the actual dose of the drug, the proximity of appropriate medical care and the availability of the necessary antidote.

There are many factors that could affect the lethality of ICA. These include: (i) the risk of overdose depending on the proximity of an individual to the source of and the duration of exposure to the agent; (ii) the risk of airway obstruction; (iii) the risk of inhaling vomit; (iv) the heterogeneity of the target group's physiology and health (e.g. pre-existing medical complaints; pregnancy; the age of group members); and (v) the risk of secondary injuries when someone has been incapacitated (e.g. falling from a height; falling onto a hard surface; falling onto a sharp object).[38]

In armed conflicts, the potential use of ICA poses challenge from the perspective of the principle of distinction between combatants and civilians, particularly in situations where combatants intermingle with civilians or are in close proximity to civilians.[39]

---

flame. Similarly the term 'riot control agent' has been defined as "a substance which produces temporary irritating or disabling physical effects that disappear within minutes of removal from exposure. There is no significant risk of permanent injury and medical treatment is rarely required. The NATO Glossary of Terms and Definitions of 7 August 2000. The Chemical Weapons Convention contains the following relevant definitions: Riot control agent —Any chemical not listed in a Schedule, which can produce rapidly in humans sensory irritation or disabling physical effects which disappear within a short time following termination of exposure. Toxic chemical—Any chemical which through its chemical action on life processes can cause death, temporary incapacitation or permanent harm to humans or animals. This includes all such chemicals, regardless of their origin or of their method of production, and regardless of whether they are produced in facilities, in munitions or elsewhere. In August 1963 the UK defined an incapacitating agent as, "a substance which can render hostile persons incapable of either aggression or resistance for a limited time without permanently injuring them."

[37] For further details See: Davison, N.2009. *Non-Lethal Weapons*, Palgrave Macmillan.

[38] The ICRC had convened an expert meeting entitled "Incapacitating Chemical Agents: Implications for International Law" from 24 to 26 March 2010 in Montreux, Switzerland. Summary Points of the Expert Meeting prepared by the ICRC at p. 71 of the Minutes.

[39] Articles 51.1, 51.2, 51.4, 51.5 and 57.2 of Additional Protocol I, 1977.

The question arises whether ICA can be used in a consistently non-lethal manner during law-enforcement and security operations? Few States maintain that ICA could be used by the UN peacekeepers for "law enforcement" purposes and are permitted by Article II of the Chemical Weapon Convention (CWC). There is a possibility that these agents would inevitably find their way into armed conflict and can be used for prohibited purposes. While it may be argued that crowd control is a justification for equipping peacekeeping troops with such incapacitating agents, the same peacekeeping troops might deploy those agents in a situation that might develop into combat, thus resulting in the use of a chemical weapon in an armed conflict. Also once a weapon system has been produced and deployed, it becomes widely available.

Countries, especially non-parties to the CWC, may use ICA for urban or guerilla warfare, rescue missions, pacifying hostile POWs, covert operations, or use against mixed populations of combatants and non-combatants. There is a possibility that such weapon system would fall into the hands of insurgent, terrorist or criminal organizations, who will use it to commit unlawful acts. Use of ICA for hostile purposes would be a breach of the CWC. In addition, any use of ICA might be identified by the targeted person or persons as an attack with a classical chemical weapon and that might result in retaliation with a classical chemical weapon.

The customary IHL prohibits the use of chemical weapons, poison and poisoned weapons and the biological weapons. The term chemical weapon is now understood in light of the CWC definition, i.e., any chemical which through its chemical action on life processes can cause death, temporary incapacitation or permanent harm to humans or animals. In addition Rules 11 and 12 of the ICRC study on Customary IHL prohibit the use of indiscriminate weapons. Any toxic chemical that has an incapacitating effect is subject to the provisions of the CWC and is, therefore, banned in warfare. There is a need to examine the issue of likely use of ICA, engaging a broad range of experts including policy makers, law-enforcement professionals, security and military personnel, health professionals, scientists and lawyers with IHL, human rights and disarmament expertise.

Drone

Drone or Unmanned Aircraft System (UAS)[40] is a powered, aerial vehicle that does not carry a human operator, uses aerodynamic forces to provide vehicle lift, can fly autonomously or be piloted remotely, can be expendable or recoverable, and carries a lethal or nonlethal payload.[41] The drones play an important role on the battlefield and are also used extensively for surveillance purposes. They spare the lives of pilots, since the unmanned aerial vehicle is flown from a site far from the attack zone. Drones can fly low and target more precisely. If a drone is shot down, there is no loss of human life. The US drones are capable of carrying several Hellfire missiles and multiple 500-pound laser-guided bombs, and have struck targets in Afghanistan and Pakistan since 2001.

In April 2009 issue of *The News*, published from Pakistan, it was reported that from January 14, 2006 to April 8, 2009, the US drone bombings killed 687 civilians and 14 al-Qaeda operatives, amounting to a ratio of nearly 50 civilians killed for every al-Qaeda operative, or a 94% civilian death rate. The report stated that out of 60 total strikes, only 10 hit al-Qaeda targets. The sources attributed the failed drone attacks to "faulty intelligence information" which resulted in the "killing of hundreds of innocent civilians, including women and children." [42] While few analysts doubt over the large number of civilian casualties reported, one cannot ignore the fact that property and homes have been destroyed and innocent civilians have been killed or injured in drone attacks in Afghanistan and Pakistan.

A significant number of States now possess drone-technology. These drones have explosive weapons which can be fired from such vehicles by remote control.[43] This development presents a number of concerns relating

---

[40] The United States uses the term Unmanned Aircraft System (UAS) for drone. The US first used drones as weapon during the combat in Afghanistan that began on October 7, 2001.

[41] Ballistic or semi ballstic vehicles, cruise missles, and artillery projectiles are not considered unmanned aerial vehicles.

[42] Kantar Max, International Law: The First Casualty of the Drone War; A comprehensive legal analysis of US drone strikes in Pakistan. <http://www.ipdop.org/International_Law_Drones_Max_Kantar.pdf> Accessed 27 February 2011.

[43] A number of countries like Belarus, Canada, China, India, Israel, Pakistan, Russia, the UK and the USA have incorporated drones in their military systems.

to compliance with IHL.Although there is nothing inherently illegal about the use of drones in armed conflict, it is unclear whether all the persons targeted by drones were combatants or were directly participating in hostilities, thus raising questions about compliance with the principle of distinction. Drone attacks causing hundreds of civilian casualties have raised questions about compliance with the principle of proportionality . Additionally, accountability for failure to comply with international law is difficult to ensure when drone attacks are conducted outside the military chain of command and beyond transparent mechanisms of civilian or military control.[44]

The distinction between civilians and combatants in drone strikes is an undisputed requirement of IHL.The civilians can be tageted in an armed conflict only when they 'directly participate in hostilities'. According to the ICRC,[45] criminal activity, political support, financial assistance, or other general and indirect war supporting activities is not considered conduct that would constitute 'direct participation in hostilities' or qualify as a 'continuous combat function'. The individual engaging in such activity must not be tar geted. The international human rights law prohibits "extrajudicial executions".[46] Anyone accused of an ofence, however serious, has the right to be presumed innocent until proven guilty and to have their guilt or innocence established in a regular court of law in a fair trial. The States having drone in their military arsenal must respect the principles of necessity, proportionality and humanity in carrying out drone attacks. A clearer understanding of the legal issues raised by drone strikes is necessary to ensure the long-term implications of such a practice in future armed conflicts.

---

[44] Report of the Secretary -General to the Securit y Council on the protection of civil ians in armed conflict, S/2010/579, dated 11 November 2010, para 17.

[45] International Committee of the Red Cross, Interpretative Guidance on the Notion of Direct Participation in Hostilities under International Humanitarian Law, May 2009.

[46] On 3 Nov ember 2002, the CIA used a drone to fir e laser-guided Hell fire missiles at a passenger vehicle traveling in a thinly populated region of Yemen. At that time, the US Air Force controlled the entire drone fleet, but raised concerns about the legalty of attacking in a place where there was no armed confl ict. CIA agents based in Djibouti carried out the killing. All six passengers in the vehicle were kil led. The Bush administration justi fied the strike under the law of armed confl ict in the "Global War on Terror." In January 2003, the United Nations Commission on Human Rights received a report on the Yemen strike from its special rapporteur on extrajudicial, summary, or arbitrary killing. The rapporteur concluded that the strike constituted "a clear case of extrajudicial kil ling." UN Doc. E/CN.4/003/3, paras. 37 – 39.

Respect for IHL

Today in spite of near universal ratification of the four Geneva Conventions, the respect for the rules of IHL during armed conflict remains a perpetual problem. It is the result of both, lack of political will and practical ability of parties to an armed conflict to comply with their legal obligations. The States as well as the armed groups, particularly those involved in non-international armed conflicts, are to be blamed for this.

In 2008, the ICRC has released the document "Increasing Respect for International Humanitarian Law in Non-International Armed Conflicts".[47] This publication is based on ICRC experience in non-international armed conflicts. It summarizes some of the considerable challenges the ICRC has faced and the lessons it has learnt in its efforts to increase respect for IHL. Some of the challenges relating to lack of implementation of IHL in non-international armed conflict are:

- Lack of political will to implement IHL
- Denial of applicability of IHL by a State party
- Non-State groups deny the applicability of IHL by refusing to recognize a body of law created by States, or claim that they cannot be bound by obligations ratified by the government against whom they are fighting
- Non-international armed conflicts differ enormously and range from those that resemble conventional warfare to those that are unstructured
- The parties to conflict vary widely in character: their motives for taking part in armed conflict, chain of command, communication capabilities, and the extent of territorial control has direct impact on the compliance with IHL
- Bearers of arms involved in fighting do not have any understanding or training in IHL

---

[47] The publication also includes an overview of the dissemination activities, the legal tools, and the methods of persuasion that the ICRC has used for improving compliance with IHL. Document available at: http://www.icrc.org/eng/resources/documents/publication/p0923.htm.

Under Article 1 common to the four Geneva Conventions, states undertake to “respect and ensure respect” for these conventions in all circumstances.[48] Article 1 also confers a negative legal obligation to neither encourage a party to an armed conflict to violate IHL nor take action that would assist in such violations. For example, there is prohibition for a State to undertake the transfer of arms or sale of weapons to a State or other party to an armed conflict who is known to use such arms or weapons to commit violations of IHL. Third states also have an implicit responsibility under common Article 1, to take appropriate steps against parties to a conflict that is violating IHL. They can intervene with States or armed groups over which they might have influence to stop the violations. The third States could also exert diplomatic pressure or undertake coercive measures against violating states.

States parties to non-international armed conflict are bound to “respect and ensure respect” for IHL by their own armed forces. One of the methods by which a State party to a non-international armed conflict could address the challenge to “respect and ensure respect” would be to enter into a special agreement with the armed opposition group, as provided in common Article 3 the four Geneva Conventions. Through such agreements the parties to a non-international armed conflict may make commitment to comply with rules of IHL. The language of common Article 3 indicates that a special agreement does not affect the legal status of the parties. In cases where a special agreement is not possible, a unilateral declaration by an armed group of its commitment to comply with IHL could be made. The obligation ‘to respect and to ensure respect…in all circumstances’, is a generic reminder of an obligation to abide by the Geneva Conventions and of the fact that all contracting States are expected to see to it that all others abide by the Conventions and ensure respect for the rules of IHL.

---

[48] The same provision is contained in Article 1 of AP I. Acording to the International Court of Justice, the obligation to respect and ensure respect for IHL also applies in respect of obligations provided for in common Article 3 to the four Geneva Conventions of 1949. The Nicaragua case, Military and Paramilitary Activities in and against Nicaragua (*Nicaragua v. United States of America*), ICJ Reports, 1986, p. 14.

BIBLIOGRAPHY

1. *A Guide to the Legal Review of New Weapons, Means and Methods of Warfare: Measures to Implement Article 36 of Additional Protocol I of 1977*. 2006. Geneva: ICRC.

2. Action by the International Committee of the Red Cross in the event of violations of IHL or of other fundamental rules protecting persons in situations of violence, *International Review of the Red Cross*, Vol. 87, No. 858, June 2005, p. 393-400.

3. Adam Roberts, Lives and statistics: are 90% of war victims civilians?, *Survival*, Vol. 25, No. 3, June–July 2010, p. 115–135.

4. *Air Force Operations and the Law* (2009), published by the USA 's Judge Advocate General (Air) School and available at: http://www.afjag.af.mil/library/.

5. Aldrich, Richard W., *The International Legal Implications of Information Warfare*, INSS Occasional Paper 9, InformationWarfare Series, (April 1996), USAF Institute for National Security Studies US Air Force Academy, Colorado. Available at: http://www.iwar.org.uk/law/resources/iwlaw/aldrich.htm. Accessed 03 March 2011.

6. Alley Roderic. 2004. *Internal Conflict and the International Community: Wars Without Ends?* Dartmouth: Ashgate.

7. Anastassov Anguel, Are Nuclear Weapons Illegal? The Role of Public International Law and the International Court of Justice, *Journal of Conflict & Security Law,* (2010), Vol. 15, No. 1, p. 65–87.

8. Antonio Pablo and Fernandex Sanchez (ed.). 2005. *The New Challenges of International Humanitarian Law in Conflicts,* Leiden: Martinus Nijhoff Publishers.

9. Arkin, William, Damian Durrant, and Marianne Cherni. 1991. *On Impact: Modern Warfare and the Envir onment. A Case Study of the Gulf War*, London: Greenpeace.

10. Arnold Guy. 1999. *Mercenaries: The Scour ge of the Thir d World*, UK: Macmillan Press Ltd.

11. Auwera Sigrid Van Der, Peace Operations and the Protection of Cultural Property during and after Armed Conflict, *International Peacekeeping*, Vol. 17, No. 1, February 2010, p. 3-16.

12. Avant, DD. 2005. *The market for force: the consequences of private security*. New York: Cambridge University Press.

13. Austin J.E. and Carl E. Bruch. 2000*The Environmental Consequences of War*, Cambridge: Cambridge University Press.

14. Bailke Major Joseph P., United Nations Peace Operations:Applicable Norms and the Application of the Law of Armed Conflict, *The Air Force Law Review*, (2001), Vol. 50, No.1, p. 1-63.

15. Balguy-Gallois Alexandre, The protection of journalists and news media personnel in armed conflict, *International Review of the Red Cross*, Vol. 86, No. 853, March 2004, p. 37-67.

16. Barkham Jayson, Information Warfare and International Law on the Use of Force, *International Law and Politics*, Vol. 34 (2001), p. 57-113.

17. Barrow Amy, UN Security Council Resolutions 1325 and 1820: constructing gender in armed conflict and International humanitarian law, *International Review of the Red Cross*, Vol. 92, No. 877, March 2010, p. 221-234.

18. Boothby William H. 2009. *Weapons and the Law of Armed Conflict*, Oxford: Oxford University Press.

19. Breen, Claire. 2007. When Is a Child Not a Child? Child Soldiers in International Law, *Human Rights Review*, Vol. 8(2), p. 71-103.

20. Brett Rachel and Eve Lester, Refugee law and IHL: parallels, lessons and looking ahead: A non-governmental organization' s view,

International Review of the Red Cross, Vol. 83, No. 843, September 2001, p. 713-726.

21. Broomhall Bruce. 2004. *International justice and the International Criminal Court: Between Sovereignty and the Rule of Law*, Oxford: OUP.

22. Brown David, A Proposal for an International Convention To Regulate the Use of Information Systems in Armed Conflict, *Harvard International Law Journal,* Vol. 47, No. 1, Winter 2006, p. 179-220.

23. Brugger Patrick, ICRC operational security: staf f safety in armed conflict and internal violence, *International Review of the Red Cross*, Vol. 91, No. 874, June 2009, p. 431-445.

24. Bugnion Francois. 2007. *Red Cross, Red Crescent, Red Crystal*, Geneva: ICRC.

25. Carvin, Stephanie, In times of war the law is not so silent, *International Journal of Human Rights*, Vol. 12, No. 3, 2008, p. 471–478.

26. Charlotte Lindsey. 2001. *Women Facing W ar: ICRC S tudy on the Impact of Armed Conflict on Women*, ICRC, Geneva.

27. Chesterman Simon & Chia Lehnardt (ed.). 2007. *From Mercenaries to Market: The Rise and the Regulation of Private Military Companies*, Oxford: OUP.

28. Children in the Ranks: The Maoists' use of Child Soldiers in Nepal. 2007. *Human Rights Watch*, Volume 19, No. 2(C). Available at: http://hrw.org/reports/2007/nepal0207/nepal0207web.pdf.

29. Christian J.Tams, The Use of Force Against Terrorists, Vol. 20, *European Journal of International Law*, 2009, p. 359-83.

30. Clapham, A.2006. *Human Rights of Non-stateActors.* Oxford: Oxford University Press.

31. Cockayne James. 2009. *Beyond Market Forces: Regulating the Global Security Industry*, New York: International Peace Institute.

32. Cryer Robert.2005. *Prosecuting International Crimes* , Cambridge: Cambridge University Press.

33. Cullen Anthony. 2010. *The Concept of Non-International Armed Conflict in International Humanitarian Law*, Cambridge: Cambridge University Press.

34. Damgaard Ciara. 2008. *Individual Criminal Responsibility for Core International Crimes*, Berlin: Springer.

35. Detter Ingrid. 2000. *The Law of W ar*, Cambridge: Cambridge University Press.

36. Dormann Knut, Computer Network Attack and IHL, *Cambridge Review of International Affairs*, Accessed 3 March 201 1. http://www.icrc.org/eng/resources/documents/misc/5p2alj.htm.

37. Draper G.I.A.D., Humanitarian Law and Internal Armed Conflicts, *Georgian Journal of International and Comparative Law* , Vol. 13, 1983, p. 257.

38. Droege Cordula, ElectiveAffinities? Human Rights and Humanitarian Law, *International Review of the Red Cr oss*, Vol. 90, No. 871, September 2008, p. 501-548.

39. Duarte Sergio, Nuclear Weapons and International Law: A Nuclear Non-Proliferation Regime for the 21 st Century; Speech: Nuclear Weapon and the Rule of Law , *Fordham International Law Journal*, Vol. 33, 2010, p. 573-584.

40. Durham Helen and O'Byrne Katies, The Dialogue of Dif ference: Gender Perspective on International Humanitarian Law *International Review of the Red Cross*, Vol. 92, No. 877, March 2010, p. 31-52.

41. *Enhancing Protection: For Civilians in Armed Conflict and Other Situations of Violence*. 2008. Geneva: ICRC.

42. *European Union Guidelines on Human Rights and International Humanitarian Law*, March 2009, Germany: European Communities.

43. Fleck Dieter (ed.). 2008.*The Handbook of International Humanitarian Law*, Oxford: Oxford University Press.

44. Focarelli Carlo, CommonArticle 1 of the 1949 Geneva Conventions: A Soap Bubble? *The European Journal of International Law*, Vol. 21, No. 1 (2010), p. 125–171.

45. Fonseka, Bhavani. 2001. The Protection of Child Soldiers in International Law, *Asia-Pacific Journal on Human Rights & the Law* Vol. 2 (2), p. 69-89.

46. Forrest, Craig. 2010.*International Law and the Protection of Cultural Heritage*. London and New York: Routledge.

47. Francis, David J. 2007. 'Paper Protection' Mechanisms: Child Soldiers and the International Protection of Children in Africa's Conflict Zones, *Journal of Modern African Studies*, Vol. 45(2), p. 207-231.

48. Fry James D., Gas Smells Awful: U.N. Forces, Riot-Control Agents, and the Chemical Weapons Convention, *Michigan Journal of International Law*, Vol. 3, p. 475-558.

49. Gardam Judith and Micjelle J. Jarvis. 2001.*Women, Armed Conflicts and International Law*, The Hague: Kluwer Law International.

50. Gardam Judith, A feminist analysis of certain aspects of international humanitarian law, *Australian Yearbook of International Law*, Vol. 12 (1992), p. 265.

51. Gasser Hans-Peter. 1993. *International Humanitarian Law: An Introduction*, (Separate Print from Hans Haug, Humanity for All), New Delhi: International Committee of the Red Cross.

52. Gasser Hans-Peter, International Humanitarian Law and Human Rights Law in Non-international Armed Conflict: Joint Venture of Mutual Exclusion? Vol. 45, *German Yearbook of International Law*, 2002, p. 149.

53. G. Robin, Name, rank, date of birth, serial number and the right to remain silent, *International Review of the Red Cr oss,* Vol. 87, No. 860, December 2005, p 721-735.

54. Gillard, E-C, Business goes to war: private military/security companies and international humanitarian law, *International Review of the Red Cross*, Vol. 88, No. 863, September 2006, p. 525-572.

55. Glasius Marlies. 2006. *The International Criminal Court: A Global Society Achievement*, New York: Routledge.

56. Glen Plant (ed.). 1992.*Environmental Protection and the Law of War*, London: Behaven Press.

57. Graham David E., The Treatment and Interrogation of Prisoners of War and Detainees, *Georgetown Journal of International Law* , Vol. 37, No.1, Fall 2005, p. 61-93.

58. Gumedze, Sabelo. 2008. *Elimination of Mer cenarism in Africa: A Need for a New Continental Appr oach*, ISS Monograph Series, No. 147.

59. Hampson Francoise J,The Relationship Between International Human Rights Law and Humanitarian Law from the Perspective of a Human Right Treaty Body, *International Review of the Red Cr oss*, Vol. 90, No. 871, September 2008, p. 549-572.

60. *Handbook on United Nations Multidimensional Peacekeeping Operations*, Issued by Peacekeeping Best Practices Unit, Department of Peacekeeping Operations, United Nations, 2003.

61. Harland Christopher (ed.). 2010. *Basic Documents on International Humanitarian Law-South Asia Collection: Treaties, National Legislations, Case-Law and other Documents*. New Delhi: ICRC.

62. Haye Eve La. 2008. *War Crimes in Internal Armed Conflicts* , Cambridge: Cambridge University Press.

63. Henckaerts Jean-Marie, S tudy on customary international humanitarian law: A contribution to the understanding and respect for the rule of law in armed conflict,*International Review of the Red Cross*, Vol. 87, No. 857, March 2005, p. 175-212.

64. Hensel Howard M (ed.). 2008.*The Legitimate Use of Military Force: Just War Tradition and the Customary Law of Armed Conflict*, USA: Ashgate Publishing Company.

65. Holt Victoria and Taylor Glyn. 2009. *Protecting Civilians in the Context of UN Peacekeeping Operations: Successes, Setbacks and Remaining Challenges*, New York: United Nations.

66. Holtzendorff Leonie von and Claus Kreb,The Kampala Compromise on the Crime ofAggression, *Journal of International Criminal Justice*, Vol. 8 (2010), p. 1179-1217.

67. Humphrey, D.R., Belligerent Interdiction of Neutral Shipping in International Armed Conflict, available at: <jcsl.oxfordjournals.org> accessed 07 February 2011.

68. ICRC advisory service on International Humanitarian Law , *Implementing IHL: Form Law to Action*. 2002. Geneva: ICRC.

69. *ICRC Annual Report: 2009*, Geneva: International Committee of the Red Cross.

70. International humanitarian law and the challenges of contemporary armed conflicts Document prepared by the International Committee of the Red Cross for the 30th International Conference of the Red Cross and Red Crescent, Geneva, Switzerland, 26–30 November 2007, *International Review of the Red Cross*, Vol. 89, No. 867, September 2007, p. 719-757.

71. *International Humanitarian Law and International Human Rights Law: Similarities and differ ences*, (01/ 2003), Advisory Service on IHL, Geneva ICRC.

72. Jan Hladik, The 1954 Hague Convention for the Protection of Cultural Property in the Event of Armed Conflict and the Notion of Military Necessity, *International Review of the Red Cross*, Vol. 835, 1999, p. 621-635.

73. Jaquemet Stephane, The cross-fertilization of international humanitarian law and international refugee law *International Review of the Red Cross*, Vol. 83, No. 843, September 2001, p. 651-674.

74. Jenks Chris, Law forAbove: UnmannedAerial Systems, Use of Force, and the Law of Armed Conflict, *North Dakota Law Review*, Vol. 85 (2009), p. 649-671.

75. Jensen Eric Talbot, The International Law of EnvironmentalWarfare: Active and Passive Damages During Armed Conflicts, Vol. 38 (1), *Vanderbilt Journal of International Law*, 2005, p. 146-186.

76. Jinks Derek, The Declining Significance of POW S tatus, *Harvard International Law Journal*, Vol. *45,* No. 2, Summer 2004, p. 367-442.

77. Kelsey, Jeffrey T.G., Hacking into International Humanitarian Law, *Michigan Law Review,* Vol. 106 (May 2008), p. 1427- 1451.

78. Kerekes, A., Capote-Cuellar, A., Koteles, G.J., Did NATO attacks in Yugoslavia cause a detectable environmental efect in Hungary?*Health Physics*, Vol. 80, (2001), p. 177–178.

79. Kinsey Chris. 2010. 'T urning War into Business: Private Security Companies and Commercial Opportunism', in Kassimeris Geoge and John Buckley (ed.),*Modern Warfare*, UK:Ashgate Publishing Limited, p. 183-199.

80. Kondoch Boris (ed.). 2007 . *International Peacekeeping,* USA: Ashgate.

81. Koppe Erik. 2008. *The Use of Nuclear Weapons and the Protection of the Environment during International Armed Conflict*, Oxford and Portland, Oregon.

82. Kraska Commander James, Grasping "The Influence of Law on Sea Power", *Naval War College Review*, Vol. 62, No. 3, Summer 2009, p. 113-135.

83. Kuper Jenny. 2005.*Military Training and Children in Armed Conflict: Law, Policy and Practice*, Leiden: Martinus Nijhoff Publishers.

84. Kwaka, E, The current status of mercenaries in the law of armed conflict, *Hastings International and Comparative Law Review* , Vo. 14 (1990), p. 67-92.

85. Lehnardt Chia, Individual Liability of Private Military Personnel under International Criminal Law, *The European Journal of International Law*, Vol. 19, No. 5 (2008), p.1015-1034.

86. Liu, Hin-Yan. Leashing the corporate dogs of war: the legal implications of the modern private military company , *Journal of Conflict and Security Law*, Vol. 15, No. 1, 2010, p. 141–168.

87. Lotrionte Catherine. 2006. 'Targeting Regime Leaders DuringArmed Hostilities: A Effective Way to Achieve Regime Change', in Hensel Howard M (ed.), *The Law of Armed Conflict: Constraints on the Contemporary Use of Military Force*, USA: Ashgate.

88. Low Luan and David Hodgkinson, 1995. Compensation forWartime Environmental Damage: Challenges to International Law after the Gulf War, Vol. 35 (2), *Virginia Journal of International Law*, p. 405-483.

89. Machel, Graca. 2001. *The Impact of W ar on Childr en*, New York: Palgrave.

90. Mahnoush H. Arsanjani, The Rome S tatute for an International Criminal Court, Vol. 93 (1993), *AJIL*, p. 22-25.

91. Marks Stephen and Nicholas Cooper, The Responsibility to Protect: Watershed or Old Wine in a New Bottle, V ol. 2, *Jindal Global Law Review*, No. 1, September 2010, p. 87-131.

92. May Larry, Killing Naked Soldiers: Distinguishing between Combatants and Noncombatants,*Ethics and InternationalAffairs*, Vol. 19 (3), 2005, p.39-53.

93. Maybee Larry and Benarji Chakka (ed.). 2006. *Customs as a Source of International Humanitarian Law* , New Delhi: International Committee of the Red Cross.

94. Maybee Larry and Sowmya K.C. 2008*30 Years of the 1977Additional Protocols to Geneva Conventions of 1949*, New Delhi: ICRC.

95. McClean Emma, The Responsibility to Protect: The Role of International Human Rights Law, *Journal of Conflict & Security Law* Vol. 13, No. 1, 2008, p. 123–152.

96. McCormac Timothy L.H. and Simpson Gerry J. 1997. *The Law of War Crimes: National and International Approaches*, The Hague: Kluwer Law International.

97. McCoubrey Hilaire and Nigel D White. 1996. *The Blue Helmets: Legal Regulations of UN Military Operations*, USA: Dartmouth.

98. Megret Frederic, Justifying Compensation by the ICC's Victim Trust Fund: Lessons from Domestic Compensation Schemes, *Brooklyn Journal of International Law*, (2010), Vol. 36, No. 1, p 123.

99. Mettraux Guenael. 2009. *The Law of Command Responsibility* , Oxford: Oxford University Press.

100. Michael Walzer. 2000. *Just and Unjust Wars*, New York: Basic Books.

101. Moir Lindsay. 2002. *The Law of InternalArmed Conflict*, Cambridge: Cambridge University Press.

102. Moloto, Judge Bakone Justice, Command Responsibility in International Criminal Tribunals, *Berkeley Journal of International Law*, Vol. 3 (2009), p. 12-25.

103. Moore Major W., Twenty-First Century Embedded Journalists: Lawful Targets? *The Army Lawyer*, July 2009, p.1-32.

104. Mullerson Rein, International Humanitarian Law in Internal Conflicts, *Journal of Conflict and Security Law*, Vol. 2 (2), 1997, p. 109-133.

105. Murphy Ray. 2007. *UN peacekeeping in Lebanon, Somalia and Kosovo: Operational and Legal issues in Practice* , Cambridge: Cambridge University Press.

106. Newton, Lt Col. MichaleA., Comparative Complementarity: Domestic Jurisdiction Consistent with the Rome Statute of the ICC, 167*Military Law Review*, (March 2001), p. 20-73.

107. Nils Melzer, Keeping the Balance Between Military Necessity and Humanity: A Response to Four Critiques of the ICRC' s Interpretive Guidance on the Notion of Direct Participation in Hostilities,Vol. 42, *NYU Journal of International Law and Politics*, (2010), p. 829- 858.

108. Nsongurua J. Udombana, War is Not Child's Play! International Law and the Prohibition of Children' s Involvement in Armed Conflicts, Vol. 20, *Temp Intl & Comp L.J.*, (Spring 2006), p. 57-64.

109. Odello Marco, Tackling Criminal Acts in Peacekeeping Operations: The Accountability of Peacekeepers, *Journal of Conflict & Security Law* (2010), Vol. 15 No. 2, 347–391.

110. Orakhelashvili, Alexander, Overlap and Convergence: The Interaction between *Jus ad Bellum* and *Jus in Bello*, Vol. 12, *Journal of Conflict and Security Law*, (2007) p. 157.

111. O'Reilly Arthur Thomas, Command Responsibility: A Call to Realign Doctrine with Principles, Vol. 20 (1), *American University International Law Review*, (2004), p. 71-107.

112. Orna Ben-Naftali and Keren Michaeli, We Must Not Make a Scarecrow of the Law: A Legal Analysis of the Israeli Policy of Targeted Killings, Vol. 36, *Cornell Int'l L.J.* (2003-2004), p. 233-234.

113. Patty Gerstenblith, From Bamiyan to Baghdad: warfare and the Preservation of Cultural heritage at the Beginning of the 21st Century, *Georgetown Journal of International Law*, Winter 2006, p. 245-352.

114. Perrigo, Sarah and Whitman, Jim (ed.). 2010. *The Geneva Conventions Under Assault*. London and New York: Pluto.

115. Perrin Benjamin, 'Promoting Compliance of PMSCs with IHL, *International Review of the Red Cross*, Vol. 88, No. 863, September 2006, p. 613-636.

116. Pfanner Toni, Various mechanisms and approaches for implementing international humanitarian law and protecting and assisting war victims, *International Review of the Red Cr oss*, Vol. 91, No. 874, June 2009, p. 279-328.

117. Pictet Jean S. 1958. Commentary on the Geneva Conventions of 12 August 1949, Relative to the Protection of Civilian Persons in Time of war, Geneva: ICRC.

118. Provost Rene. 2002. *International Human Rights and Humanitarian Law*, Cambridge: Cambridge University Press.

119. Ratner, M. and Ray, E. 2004. *Guantanamo: What the World Should Know*, Vermont: Chelsea Green Publishing.

120. Roach J Ashley, Legal Aspects of Modern Submarine Warfare, in J. A. Frowein and R. Wolfrum (ed.), *Max Planck Yearbook of United Nations Law*, Vol. 6, 2002, p. 367-385.

121. Roberts Adam and Richard Guelff. 2000. *Documents on the Laws of War*, Oxford: Oxford University Press.

122. Roger O'Keefe. 2006. *The Pr otection of Cultural Pr operty*, Cambridge: Cambridge University Press.

123. Rogrers Major General (Retd) A.P.V., Command responsibility Under the Law of War, available at: http://www .lcil.cam.ac.uk/lectures/lecture_papers.php

124. Rolle Baptiste and Edith Lafontaine, The emblem that cried wolf: ICRC study on the use of the emblems, *International Review of the Red Cross*, Vol. 91, No. 876, December 2009, p. 759-778.

125. Robert D. Sloane, The Cost of Conflation: Preserving the Dualism of Jus ad Bellum and Jus in Bello in the Contemporary Law of War, Vol. 34, *Yale Journal of International Law*, (2010), p. 82.

126. Roscini Marco, World Wide Warfare – *Jus ad bellum* and the use of Cyber Force, *Max Planck Yearbook of United Nations Law*, Vol. 14, 2010, p. 85-130.

127. Rosen, David M. Child Soldiers, International Humanitarian Law , and the Globalization of Childhood, *American Anthropologist,* 109 (2), 2007, p. 296-306.

128. Roy S. Lee (ed.). 1999. *The International Criminal Court. The Making of the Rome S tatute: Issues, Negotiations, Results,* Boston: Kluwer Law International.

129. *San Remo Manual on International Law Applicable in Armed Conflict at Sea.* 1995. Cambridge University Press.

130. Sassoli Marco, Antoine A. Bouvier and Anne Quintin. 2011. *How Does Law Protect in War?* Geneva: ICRC.

131. Sassoli Marco. 2007.' *Ius ad bellum* and *Ius in Bello* ', in Schmitt Michael N., and Jelena Pejic (ed.), *International Law and Armed Conflict: Exploring the Faultlines* , Boston: Martinus Nijhof f Publishers.

132. Sassoli Marco, The Implementation of IHL: Current and Inherent Challenges, *Yearbook of International Humanitarian Law* , Vol. 10, 2007, p.45-73.

133. Schabas William. 2004.*An Introduction to the International Criminal Court*, UK: Cambridge University Press.

134. Schabas W. 2006. *The UN International Criminal T ribunals: The Former Yugoslavia, Rwanda and Sierra Leone*, Cambridge: Cambridge University Press.

135. Schmitt, Michael N., Investigating Violations of International Law in Armed Conflict, *Harvard National Security Journal*, Vol. 2(1), 2011, p. 31-84.

136. Schmitt, Michael N., Wired Warfare: Computer network attack and *jus in bello, International Review of the Red Cross,* Vol. 84, No. 846, p. 365-399.

137. Schmitt Michael and Jelena Pejic (ed.). 2007*International Law and Armed Conflict: Exploring the Faultline* , Leiden: Martinus Nijhoff Publishers.

138.Segall Anna.2001. *Punishing Violations of International Humanitarian Law at the National Level* , Geneva: International Committee of the Red Cross.

139. Sepinwall Amy J. Failures to Punish: Command responsibility in Domestic and International Law, *Michigan Journal of International Law,* Vol. 30, 2009, p. 251-302.

140. Shraga Daphna, UN Peacekeeping Operations: Applicability of INH and Responsibility for Operation-Related Damage,*American Journal of International Law*, Vol. 94, 2000, p. 406-123.

141. Singer, P W. 2003. *Corporate war riors: the rise of the privatized military industry,* Ithaca: Cornell University Press.

142. Sloane, Robert D., The Cost of Conflation: Preserving the Dualism of *Jus ad Bellum* and *Jus in Bello* in the Contemporary Law of War, Vol. 34, *The Yale Journal of International Law* , (2008), p. 47-1 12.

Available at:<http://papers.ssrn.com/sol3/papers.cfm?abstract_id =1117918>

143. Smidt, Major Michael L.Yamashita, Medina and Beyond: Command Responsibility in Contemporary Military Operations, Vol. 164, *Military Law Review*, 2000, p. 155-234.

144. Smith Thomas W., The New Law of War: Legitimizing Hi-Tech and Infrastructural Violence, *International Studies Quarterly* , Vol. 46, (2002), p. 355-374.

145. Solis Gary D. 2010. *The Law of Armed Conflict: International Humanitarian Law in War*, Cambridge University Press.

146. Solis Gary, Targeted Killing and the Law of Armed Conflict, *Naval War College Review*, Spring 2007, Vol. 60, No. 2, p.127-146.

147. Swanson Lesley, The Era of Cyber Warfare: Applying IHL to the 2008 Russian-Georgian Cyber Conflict, Loy. L. A. Int'l & Comp. L. Rev, Vol.32, P.303-333.

148. *The domestic implementation of international humanitarian law: a manual.* 2010. Geneva: ICRC.

149. The International Committee of the Red Cross (ICRC): Its mission and work (Adopted by the Assembly of the ICRC on 19 June 2008), *International Review of the Red Cross*, Vol. 91, No.874, June 2009, p. 399-413.

150. The HPCR *Manual on International Law Applicable to Air and Missile Warfare* (2010).

151. *The Manual of the Law of Armed Conflic.* 2004. UK Ministry of Defence, Oxford: OUP.

152. *The Montreux Document: On pertinent international legal obligations and good practices for States related to operations of private military and security companies during armed conflict* ICRC, Geneva, August 2009.

153. Tiefenbrun Susan, Child Soldiers, Slavery and the Trafficking of Children, *Fordham International Law Journal*, Vol. 31, No. 2, January 2008, p. 415-485.

154. Tomuschat Christian, Human Rights and International Humanitarian Law, *The Eur opean Journal of International Law* , Vol. 21, No. 1 (2010), p. 15-23.

155. *United Nations Peacekeeping Operations: Principles and Guidelines*, United Nations Department of Peacekeeping Operations, Department of Field Support, United Nations, 2008.

156. Van Bueren, Geraldine. 1994. The International Legal Protection of Children in Armed Conflicts, *The International and Comparative Law Quarterly*, Vol. 43(4): 809-826.

157. Watts Sean, Combatant Status and Computer NetworkAttack, *Virginia Journal of International Law*, Vol. 50 (2010), p. 392-447.

158. Weill Sharon, The Targeted Killing of Salah Shehadeh: From Gaza to Madrid, *Journal of International Criminal Justice,* Vol. 7 (2009), p. 617-631.

159. While Nigel D. The UN Charter and Peacekeeping Forces: Constitutional Issues, (1996), *International Peacekeeping,* Vol. 3, p. 43-63.

160. WHO 2001. *Depleted Uranium, Sources, Exposure and Health Effects* WHO, Geneva.

161. Williams Paul D., *Enhancing Civilian Protection in Peace Operations: Insights from Africa*, September 2010, Africa Center for Strategic Studies Research Paper No. 1, Washington DC: National Defence University Press.

162. Williamson Jamie Allan, Some considerations on command responsibility and criminal liability, *International Review of the Red Cross*, Vol. 90, No. 870, June 2008, p. 303-317.

163. Wing Lieutenant Colonel Ian. 2010. *Private Military Companies and Military Operations*, Working Paper No. 138, Australia: Land Warfare Studies Centre.

164. Wortel Eva, Humanitarians and their moral stance in war: the underlying values, *International Review of the Red Cr oss*, Vol. 91, No.876, December 2009, p. 779-802.

165.Zanghi Claudio. 2005. The Protection of Journalists in Armed Conflicts, in Fernandez-Sanchez Pablo Antonio (ed.), *The New Challenges of Humanitarian Law inArmed Conflicts*, Martinus Nijhoff Publishers, p. 145-162.

INDEX

E

H

I

O

P

R

S

T

U

W

www.ingramcontent.com/pod-product-compliance
Lightning Source LLC
Chambersburg PA
CBHW051542260926
51849CB00011B/504/J
9789380177755